The Will To Win

IVAN MAUGER

The Will To Win

THE AUTOBIOGRAPHY
WITH **MARTIN ROGERS**

Golden Key Limited

IVAN MAUGER
The Will To Win
THE AUTOBIOGRAPHY

with Martin Rogers

First published in 2010 by Golden Key Limited in association with Pinegen Ltd

© Copyright Ivan Mauger and Martin Rogers 2010

Ivan Mauger and Martin Rogers assert their rights under the Copyright, Designs and Patent Act of 1988 to be identified as the authors of this work.

Design and production by Bob Johnson
Cover design by Terry Mulligan

All rights reserved. This book is sold subject to the condition that it shall not, by way of trade or otherwise, be lent, resold, hired out or otherwise circulated without the publisher's prior consent in any form of binding or cover other than that in which it is published and without a similar condition including this condition being imposed on the subsequent purchaser. No part of this book may be reproduced or transmitted in any form or by any means, electronic or mechanical, including photocopying, recording or by any information storage and retrieval system, without prior permission in writing from the publisher.

Distributed in the United Kingdom by Pinegen Ltd, 9 Coppergate Mews, Brighton Road, Surbiton, Surrey KT6 5NE www.pinegen.co.uk

A CIP catalogue record of this book is available from the British Library.

ISBN 978-0-9552376-9-0

IVAN MAUGER OBE MBE

The most decorated speedway rider in the history of the sport, born in New Zealand, his skills and reputation honed in England and around the world, Ivan and his wife Raye moved to Australia's Gold Coast in 1987. He has written and/or collaborated with Peter Oakes on nine books: *Triple Crown Plus* (1971), *Ivan Mauger's Speedway Book* (1972), *Ivan Mauger's World Speedway Book* (1973), *Ivan Mauger's Speedway Spectacular* (1975), *Ivan Mauger's Speedway Extravaganza No.1* (1975) *No.2* (1976) and *No.3* (1977), *Speedway Quiz Book No.1* (1976) and *Who's Who of World Speedway* (1976).

MARTIN ROGERS

A prominent administrator, journalist and historian intimately involved in British speedway for 30 years, Martin and his wife Lin were promoters at Leicester, King's Lynn and Peterborough before moving to Australia in 1988. Among the 20 sporting titles he has written and/or edited, *The Illustrated History of Speedway* is one of the top-selling speedway books of all time. Ivan Mauger is the fourth world champion with whom he has collaborated, the others being Barry Briggs, Bruce Penhall and Jason Crump.

Dedication

January 1955

To Raye, the love of my life who has never stopped believing in me. Thank you for your never-ending support and being my best friend for 55 years.

And to our children and grandchildren who remain a constant source of love and inspiration

January 2010

ACKNOWLEDGEMENTS

Ivan Mauger on co-author Martin Rogers: This book probably would not have happened but for Martin's efforts. Fortunately he has the knowledge, ability and professionalism to work with words so everything ends up exactly as I would have written them if I had been a writer rather than speedway rider!

Martin on Ivan: All the ingredients which made Ivan the champion of all time were on show at different stages of this book. I have worked with many sportsmen but never one more prepared to devote time, effort and commitment to such a project. Hopefully that much will be evident from the following pages.

ATTENTION TO DETAIL is a key element in producing a life story, just as it is in creating the achievements which define a sporting legend.

In offering *Ivan Mauger – The Will To Win* for the critical attention of followers of speedway and long track racing, every effort has been made to ensure accuracy and to properly salute the contributions others have made.

Ivan was not just any motorcycle champion, he was by popular acclaim 'the man of the millennium', an accolade which did not happen by accident.

Indeed, not much in his gold-encrusted years in the saddle came about by chance. His world titles, six individual, three team, two pairs and three long track, were as a result of his relentless pursuit of excellence.

Ivan and co-author Martin Rogers wish to acknowledge the support and assistance of the many helpers from around the world without whom this project would not have happened.

First to the respective wives, Raye Mauger and Lin Rogers, and family members whose encouragement at all stages has been outstanding.

Bob Johnson, whose experience and expertise made light of the pre-press operation, Ivan's longtime secretary Janice Forbes and pictorial wizard Terry Mulligan all played a big role.

Equally appreciated is the participation of the following and anybody else whose contribution may have been inadvertently omitted:

Jim Airey, Allan Batt, Simon Biagi, Kym Bonython, John Chaplin, Jason Crump, Wilfried Drygala, Evžen Erban, Graeme Frost, Dave Gifford, Jimmy Hone, Mike Hunter, Howard Jones, Jan Křivka, Tony Lethbridge, Tony Loxley, Chris Macdonald, Tony McDonald, Jan Mauger, Trevor Mauger, Bill Meyer, Phil Muskett, Peter Oakes, Harry Oxley, Mike Patrick, Debbie Pritchard, Phil Rising, Ashley Scott, Andrew Skeels, John Skinner, John Somerville Collection, Gordon and Margaret Stobbs, Chris Sweetman, Ian Thomas, David Thomson, Alf Weedon.

CONTENTS

WORTH HIS WEIGHT IN GOLD by Jason Crump xii

THE GREATEST by Peter Oakes xiv

Heat 1 – DARE TO DREAM 1

Heat 2 – THROUGH THE EYES OF A CHILD 21

Heat 3 – VOYAGE OF DISCOVERY 47

Heat 4 – BACK TO THE FUTURE 63

Heat 5 – ROUGH DIAMOND 83

Heat 6 – DOWN WEMBLEY WAY 103

Heat 7 – THE MAKING OF A CHAMPION 119

Heat 8 – ACES HIGH 137

Heat 9 – GOLDEN RUN 151

Heat 10 – THE WORLD IS MY OYSTER 167

Heat 11 – FROM FEAST TO FAMINE 189

Heat 12 – FLYING WEST 207

Interval – IVAN'S GOLD ALBUM 222

Heat 13 – FIVE IS NOT ENOUGH 241

Heat 14 – TAKING CARE OF BUSINESS 261

Heat 15 – ONE MORE TIME 281

Heat 16 – ROAD TO THE COLISEUM 299

Heat 17 – SIX AND OUT 323

Heat 18 – ON GOLDEN POND 347

Heat 19 – THE WAY WE WERE 375

Heat 20 – THE LAST WORD by Raye Mauger 405

Appendix I – MAUGER RESULTS 429

Appendix II – MAUGER ACHIEVEMENTS 430

Worth his weight in gold

by Jason Crump

WHEN IVAN CALLED me up and asked if I would write a foreword for his book it was one of those moments in life where you have to pinch yourself.

I may not have had the privilege to be part of the generation who saw him racing, but here is unquestionably the greatest speedway rider ever asking humble Jason Crump to kick-start his book.

Of course I am honoured to have this opportunity to introduce it on his behalf, a from-the-heart account from the current world champion to a multiple champion.

Throughout my life, speedway racing has been everything to me. Through my grandfather Bill (Neil) Street and dad Phil's involvement in the sport all I have ever wanted to do was get on a bike and race.

But then there is the special ingredient ... not only racing but having that single-mindedness to want to win every time you head towards the starting gate.

I don't profess to know Ivan well enough to know what motivated him when he was at his peak, but you have to have that same single-mindedness to win a world championship more than once.

To win it is an incredible feeling, to get back up there and do it again (and again) I think you have to be made of something stronger. Winning the world championship a second time and then a third, it gets better and better.

Ivan was the standard-bearer in this, the rider who stuck the flag pole in the ground and told the sport: 'Love me or hate me, you're never gonna forget me.'

Heaven only knows how many world individual titles he would have won had there been a Grand Prix system in place as there is in our sport today. There wouldn't have been any Szczakiels to stop him, that's for sure.

Where I know Ivan and I are very alike is the need to have our families around us. Never a world championship went by without Ivan having his wife, Raye, and his children, Julie, Kym and Debbie there with him.

I am the same. My wife and children are always there. They all have to be part of my life as a speedway rider. Racing becomes about more than just yourself and what happens on the race track.

Dynamics change and a family means a different build-up but never would Ivan or I have been without them. When you're winning it's great, but whatever happens they are always there to share the experience through the good and bad.

When the show's over I know my wife and children are my escape, giving me the wonderful trusting support we all need from those closest to us to keep things in perspective.

Anyone privileged enough to know the Mauger family will give testimony that 30 years on you still won't find a closer-knit family than the Ivan clan and their experiences and emotions shared together as a family have only consolidated this.

I'll give you another example of where we are similar.

At the end of the 2006 season I got a call from the great man asking if I would come to a Gold Coast awards dinner Mayor Ron Clarke MBE had asked for me to attend.

I told Ivan to get them to send me an invite and I would be there. A few days later the invite arrived: Mr and Mrs J Crump are cordially invited, etc etc.

I called Ivan straight away and told him I wouldn't be able to make it because there was no invite for my two children.

His reaction was exactly what I thought it would be. He said to me 'Jason, you are absolutely right. Throughout my career, there were numerous occasions when my children were not included and I insisted they be. Leave it with me.'

With that, within 24 hours, another invite turned up. The Crump family attended. It was a great honour to meet Mayor Clarke – a sporting icon – and we all had a wonderful evening.

I'll close the way I started.

Ivan has never been what I would call a 'mentor' to me during my career, but what he has been is that understanding voice on the other end of a telephone throughout my racing life.

> **❛Ivan taught me the skills to focus on my mental preparation and these techniques are world-beaters ❜**

He's been that bit of reassurance with a knowing word or two.

He's always been a man of few words, because what he says is enough for you to listen and learn.

That's why the words that follow in this book are just like his special bike … worth their weight in gold.

He's got to the top because he's a stubborn old bastard and I love that about him.

● *JASON CRUMP is a superstar of the modern era and winner of speedway's world championship in 2004, 2006 and 2009. His Australian base is on the Gold Coast and the Crump and Mauger families have been close for almost 40 years.*

The Greatest

Peter Oakes thinks so

HISTORY HAS AN uncanny habit of debunking myths.

Sometimes the passage of time merely enhances reputations; often it can destroy them.

But when it comes to sport there's a tendency to overrate the here-and-now.

Today's heroes are always bigger, better, fitter and faster than their predecessors, usually because our High Definition world adds a far shinier gloss to any image than the black-and-white, grainy days of yore.

So where does Ivan Gerald Mauger stand in the pantheon of speedway stars?

It would be hard for anyone to put forward a convincing case against him being classed as the Greatest of All Time.

His record more than speaks for itself. Six world titles (a tally equalled only by Sweden's Tony Rickardsson and bettered by no one). Three successive World Final victories, something nobody else has achieved.

And a collection of glittering trophies from all around the world that would fill practically every room of his waterside family home on Australia's Gold Coast.

Of course, I might be biased in my verdict. I've known Ivan and his family for nearly half a century, since early 1963 when he returned to Britain as a re-born racer.

He'd already spent a couple of unproductive seasons as a stand-by member of the great Wimbledon team of the fifties and a relatively successful competitor in the Southern Area League with Rye House and, later, Eastbourne.

But when he left the UK at the end of 1958 he was a disillusioned teenager and few fans around the country took any notice.

Most had written him off as a much-ballyhooed flop, another of tomorrow's 'world champions' who would never make the grade.

Ivan had other ideas – and he had the steely determination and astonishing mental toughness to rebuild his career in his native New Zealand and Australia before he was enticed over by multi-track promoter Mike Parker to join his Newcastle side.

Mauger had turned down previous approaches to return to

Europe, principally because no other track boss was willing to fork out for the fares for himself, his wife Raye and, by then, their three children, Julie, Kym and Debbie.

Their birth certificates happily told much of their parents' peripatetic sporting existence. Julie had been born in England, Kym in New Zealand and Debbie in Australia.

At the time of Ivan's second coming, I was a young journalist working as a news and sports reporter at the North West freelance agency.

I supplemented my weekly income by writing for *Speedway Star* and some press work for Parker who had his home and office in the Manchester area.

He also owned several houses, most of which were in one of the less salubrious areas of the city.

One of those Victorian dwellings in Upper Chorlton Road was the Maugers' adopted home and for anyone who believes Ivan and his family were born with a silver spoon I just wish they had been around in those days and visited them there, as I often did.

I have probably written more words about Ivan than any other journalist – we collaborated on columns for a variety of different magazines and newspapers, we worked together on several books – and, for many years, we were partners in a business.

In more recent times we spent many, many hours discussing the current book but eventually decided that it would be an impractical partnership given our across-the-world bases.

I was, though, delighted when Martin Rogers agreed to take on my former role. Ivan could not have brought in a more worthy tactical substitute!

Believe me while it is Ivan who has basked in the glory of a magnificent career the rock on which his whole life was built came in the family unit.

And one of his greatest personality traits is his immense loyalty to his friends.

There must be 20, 30, maybe 50 people who have been part of the extended Mauger family for decades.

I can still recall those Sunday lunchtime curries Raye would cook for us all; the days at the Commonwealth Games; the special meal at London's Veccia Riccioni restaurant where we all celebrated his MBE.

I also have so many sporting memories (not least that great day in Poland when he became the first and only rider to win three successive World Finals).

But more important than any of those glorious nights, I'm proud to say I still have his friendship.

● *PETER OAKES is the most published and highly respected speedway journalist in Great Britain. A longtime friend, confidant and collaborator with Ivan, with a distinguished administrative and managerial pedigree, he is Peterborough Panthers Director of Speedway.*

Winning isn't everything but the will to win is everything

– Vince Lombardi (1913–1970)
Legendary American football coach

Heat 1

DARE TO DREAM

Let nothing hold you back from
exploring your wildest fantasies,
wishes, and aspirations.
Don't be afraid to dream big
and to follow your dreams
wherever they may lead you.
Open your eyes to their beauty;
open your mind to their magic;
open your heart to their
possibilities.

Whether they are in colour
or in black and white,
Whether they are big or small,
easily attainable
or almost impossible,
look to your dreams,
and make them become reality.
Wishes and hopes are nothing
until you take the first step
towards making them something!

Because only by dreaming
will you ever discover
who you are, what you want,
and what you can do.
Don't be afraid to take risks,
to become involved,
to make a commitment.
Do whatever it takes to make
your dreams come true.
Always believe in miracles,
and always believe in you!

(Julie Anne Ford)

IT all starts with a dream. As an impressionable youngster, I sustained my ambition with dreams and sentiments like those above.

If I had been a poet rather than a motorcycle racer I would have been only too happy to express my thoughts just as Australian writer Julie Anne Ford does.

She very neatly summarises the inspiration needed to fuel my dream of becoming world champion. This was before the age of super coaches and

YOU BEAUTY – after winning the World Final for a record sixth time, Katowice, 1979

2 – Ivan Mauger

scientific analysts and puts into words the ready-made philosophy which comforted me when things were tough at the beginning. At no time did I think it was impossible.

In a largely individual sport, you need to be your own best judge, critic and motivator, anyway. I had big dreams, took the risk to go to England, made the commitment, turned it into reality and always believed in myself to make it happen.

World and Olympic champions in a variety of sports also had a dream and were able to imagine themselves standing in the winner's position on the podium. Whether attending Sportsman of the Year presentations, TV personality shows or similar functions around the world, I came across many greats, male and female, who had the same philosophy of mind power and visualisation.

Organisers would put a lot of effort into table plans but when the time came for everyone to be seated no one could care less. I got into a routine of arriving early to see who was supposed to be where and then move myself to sit next to someone sure to be really interesting company.

I have often wondered if Edmund Hillary, Roger Bannister, Sebastian Coe, Daley Thompson and a few others figured it was more than a coincidence that we were seated next to each other on several occasions.

Achieving the correct mindset to succeed in speedway is not so different from what sprint runners and swimmers have to do. Their preparation for the starts is similar to what I had to do, especially at international and world championship events.

Approaching the start line with almost 100,000 spectators and millions of TV viewers watching and a world title just around the corner can be a very lonely place.

I learned that in any sport or field of human endeavour all the great achievers had a dream and the ability to identify where they where going and what they wanted to be.

These are not the dreams everyone has at night when asleep – they are the dreams you have in an alpha state of consciousness.

That is when you have the ability to slow down your mind and concentrate on mind power and to be able to visualise what you want to do next year, in six months, next month, next week or tomorrow.

Sometimes the process can be a lengthy one. It took me from the age of 15 to almost 29 before the dream of becoming world speedway champion came to fruition.

When we came to England for a second time it was with the express intention of making up for five lost years. I was 18 when I went back to New

The Will To Win – 3

HISTORY ON MY MIND – deep concentration before Heat 17 at the 1979 World Final in Katowice

Zealand after two seasons at Wimbledon where I hardly got a ride, and 23 when I returned to ride for Newcastle.

Many images coursed through my mind but the picture of standing on top of the dais listening to the New Zealand national anthem was a recurring one.

As my career and my life unfolded, other more specific plans would be months rather than years in the making, like my sixth and last speedway title.

The 1978 World Final at Wembley was my worst. I finished eighth after never having been placed lower than fourth in all my others. My night went pear-shaped after my engine seized going into the pit turn in my first race when I was in tight company with Ole Olsen and Gordon Kennett and I had to lay it down.

While I was lying on the track I told myself it would be a different story next year and I had my visualisation working from that second until the 1979 final in Katowice. It took me a year of getting my head around it, plus determination and mind power to succeed in Poland and erase that race and the 1978 final from my mind.

I learned a tremendous amount about mind power from fellow guests at those celebrity functions by asking them certain questions and knowing the answers I would give if asked those same questions. Almost without exception they gave me familiar answers which were all positive. That told me we had very similar ideas when it came to goal setting and using the power of the mind to anticipate different scenarios.

There have been many stories written about me in relation to my mind power, concentration levels, and visualisation techniques and so on – mostly by people who do not possess any of these attributes to any significant degree and consequently have little or no understanding of what I was about.

A lot of observers reckoned much of my success was as a result of my ability to get out of the start. I did it so often and so consistently there were plenty who questioned the legality of my methods but that is a price you pay for regularly succeeding where others are found lacking.

No doubt a lot of people found the preamble and the delays frustrating. But in an era when tapes offences often went unpunished – unlike recent times when an infringement at the start can result in immediate disqualification – you needed to be mentally sharp.

With the old starting system there were loads of riders who were not clever starters at all. They were simply what I called 'chancers' who just dropped the clutch when they thought the tapes were going up.

To succeed under that starting system you needed to be dialled in, have massive concentration levels and also have a very clear perception of the mental strength of the guy who was going to press the button – the referee!

I used my thought transference powers many times on officials. When they used to give the riders a briefing in the dressing room before a meeting they regularly gave their 'starting system' speech to tell everyone they would disqualify us for such and such an offence.

My mental powers and visualisation gave me the ability to read if they had stronger mental powers than me and over time I was able to assess if they would make decisions that were unpopular with the crowd. I figured most would not. One look often confirmed most would not do what they had just told us.

The rule whereby a rider is excluded for touching the tapes is the single best rule introduced into speedway. It was in most European countries domestically for 10 years before the British League and FIM thought of it.

A lot of riders would regularly push the tapes in British speedway and FIM meetings and make a big percentage of their starts. OK, I was one of them but mostly that was part of the strategy so any 'chancer' would not do it.

The system of the day more or less made it a necessity to push the tapes, and hold up proceedings long enough to force the referee into not allowing the chancers to go. But you had to know when the official would break them

The Will To Win – 5

on your front wheel – that's when it was vital to know if you had stronger mind power than the referee.

The fact is I made a bigger proportion of my starts in Europe on Sundays on a speedway bike, a long track bike or a grass track bike when we all had to sit still. When I was confident no one else would move I was better able to concentrate on the terrain, surface, grip, the amount of throttle required and it didn't matter what type of discipline it was or what type of bike.

In my 30 years as a racer there were a dozen or more starting systems tried in the various branches of the sport. It's an old refrain that good starters are good starters no matter what the system. The same guys get to the corner first every time.

No riders pushed the tapes as much as Erik Gundersen or Hans Nielsen and with that system they made plenty of their starts. But as soon as the tape touching rule came in both instantly made a bigger percentage of their starts. They were better starters than their rivals so the no-touching rule worked in their favour, too.

ON HIS WAY – Ivan Mauger leads Heat 3 of the 1970 World Final from Gennadi Kurilenko, Jan Mucha and Barry Briggs

6 – Ivan Mauger

Success can be a great stimulant and aid to further achievement. If you have been there and done that, you will know and understand the process involved in obtaining the desired outcome.

But disappointment and failure is an equally powerful motivational tool if applied effectively. My early career had its fair share of frustrations and the trick is to learn from every experience and emerge stronger and wiser. That's the lesson to be taken from adversity.

A pivotal moment for me was standing on the Tilbury dockside in 1958, watching my wife Raye and our baby daughter Julie sail off to New Zealand – just a year after the two of us, newly married and with little more than a pocketful of dreams between us, had arrived in England with high hopes and expectations.

That first season was so far removed from the dream that we found our faith and ambition put to the most severe test.

The second, when we were separated by 12,000 miles, I promised myself 100 times over that when I came back next time it would be different. I was determined to never again find myself in that position.

Happily, we got through it, and grew in confidence and accomplishment as we built a life which ultimately enabled us to live out the 'wildest fantasies, wishes, and aspirations' mentioned by Julie Anne Ford.

One recurring theme for me was the absolute determination not to be in such a dark place as when we were apart, near-penniless teenagers clinging on to our hopes and plans by a fingernail.

Any and all future speedway contracts had first to include provision to enable us to be together as a family unit, one which grew to include three children by the time we were just into our twenties.

We all – Raye, Julie, Kym and Debbie – trooped around the world on the smell of an oily rag until my second attempt at a British career paved the way to new and greater successes and excitements. The prospect of better times and whatever went with starting to win races and then bigger and more significant events was the prize which sustained us.

It sharpened my resolve as I never forgot the tough times. That experience moulded me and made me the person I am. And as things started to improve, it was possible to envisage the rewards and potential satisfaction which lay in wait. There was evidence of possible pitfalls, too.

Ronnie Moore, the man who was my first and greatest inspiration, and Jack Young, my most helpful mentor, both won a couple of world titles without achieving the type of security and lifestyle their exceptional talents and achievements warranted. My grand plan included a firm commitment to build a better life for my family and myself.

Yet it was never like going to work. I am so lucky to have had a hobby job all my life and it is something I can still indulge with my schools and academies around the world.

The would-be riders of today and stars of tomorrow come in all shapes and sizes. The will to win, to do whatever it takes to learn from a difficult apprenticeship and put the lessons learned to good effect is what will separate the men from the boys.

So many young kids go to England nowadays and ask 'Do I get a van? Do I get a house? Who pays for my petrol?'

This attitude does not sit well with me. It is easy to lose patience with youngsters who do not allow for or handle disappointment. Too many of them expect everything instantly and often I have found myself questioning how they would have handled the sort of trials which littered my early career.

In spite of my circumstances I grew up expecting to be a winner. I don't know how or why it first happened but in the weeks before the school running championship in Christchurch and later at cross country races I always could 'see myself winning'. I did not know the word 'visualisation' at that stage but that is precisely the art I had at a very young age.

Conditioning the mind as well as the body provides a foundation for subsequent achievement. I have had very strong legs since I was 11 or 12 from playing rugby, hockey, running, riding on cycle speedway and training. Running up the steep incline at the Rapaki track a few times a week gave me a stamina which proved invaluable later on.

When the ambition of making it big in England was put on temporary hold, the long-term goals remained intact. In the meantime, riding in Australia for four southern summers sharpened my focus and in 1962 I won the Australian five mile long track title after spending a couple of years convinced I could and would do so.

The championship, five laps round the Port Pirie track in South Australia, was as big as anything up to that point in my career. I led the race at Easter 1960 until the last corner when my Jap seized up. Fred Jolly loaned me the first ESO that came into Australia and a year later I led again until almost the same point on the final turn and the clutch came off.

Over the next 12 months I mentally rehearsed and planned how to win the event and not over rev the engine, conserve the chains and look after the rear tyre.

I did make it third time lucky, in possibly the slowest five laps I ever did at the track. Still I did not know the word 'visualisation' but that was exactly what I was doing from Easter 1961 to Easter 1962.

People often come to different stages of their life wishing that they had known at 18 or 21 what they later learned as a result of experience and finding out what worked for them. What worked for me does not necessarily have the same effect on someone else but there are certain truths in which I have complete faith.

VISUALISATION

Time seems to slow down and you find you have plenty of time to do what others find incredible.

Everything is easier to achieve if you have already been there in your mind.

Your opponents are in awe of your ability to perform when required.

The art is to have 'self time', 10 minutes every day and for one hour before competition.

BENEFITS OF MENTAL REHEARSAL

Your mind and body co-ordination is improved.

Your peak performance is more readily achieved.

You can consistently perform at a higher level.

You are disciplined in your attention to every detail.

MENTAL TOUGHNESS.

Unshakeable self-belief makes you better than the rest.

Even if you are not the best, then pretend to be the best.

Have an insatiable desire to succeed.

Thrive on pressure – accept that anxiety is inevitable.

Do not be affected by performance of your rivals.

GOAL SETTING

Goals are dreams with a deadline.

This gives a specific urgency to an ambition.

As an example, whatever dream you have of success you should put a date on it:

I want to win xyz by the time I am 21

or

I need to lose xyz kg in two months.

From the time we went back to England, every season revolved around the desire to be a champion. You have to want something to achieve it, and to achieve it you have to be prepared to cultivate mental strength and strategies to deal with whatever obstacles there may be along the way.

Most people make and quickly break their New Year resolutions. When I was racing, January 1 was the opening of a whole new page, a starting point, a renewal and affirmation of what I was doing and what I wanted to achieve in the months to come. My training routine and eating and sleeping pattern was all designed around a schedule which, particularly after I became world champion, might involve 150 meetings in a year.

The Will To Win – 9

FLYING HIGH – receiving the bumps after winning the World Final run-off with Bernie Persson, 1972

The world championship was at the centrepiece of everything. I knew most of the tracks where World Finals and the various rounds were staged and pre-planned the engine settings, compression ratios, ignitions, tyre pressures and even the type of tyre best suited for each of those places.

The dates and venues were pretty much known at this stage, including the British Final and all the other big ones, although not which qualifying

ACCLAIM – New Zealand Sportsman of the Year 1977, with Olympic and world champion runner John Walker in the background. Another such award came Ivan's way two years later

rounds we had to do. These were allocated about a month in advance and Australian and New Zealand riders were included in the UK rounds until the mid 1970s.

Advocates of the Grand Prix system reckon it is a much tougher road than it was in the days of the old one-off World Final. What they overlook is that after a series of qualifiers, semi-finals, a British Final, maybe a British-Nordic Final (depending where the final was) there would be an Inter Continental or European Final to negotiate.

This all added up to a procession of hard qualifying meetings which as often as not required a place in the top handful to qualify for the next round. As the later stages were all knockout affairs, there could be a slim margin for error, especially if there was a mishap or the bike stopped. There were no second chances.

To ensure nothing was missed in the preparation, I placed a high priority on my 'self time' and would go to a quiet place. If we were in England at the start of the year I regularly went to the moors near Buxton and sat down to think and plan what I was going to do during the year.

When we were in Australia I set off to try to find a wooded area or maybe a secluded spot in the sand dunes. Back on familiar territory in Christchurch I would go half way up the Rapaki track and sit and think.

The Will To Win – 11

If people were looking for me Raye would just say I had gone away for a while and would be back later in the day. Sometimes it took me only an hour or so to crystallise all my thoughts and other times it took me several hours.

The preparation allowed for the unexpected, too. For more than 10 years I was racing for around 46 weeks of the year and calculated in ten and a half months there could be at least a dozen crashes and a percentage of them would probably hurt.

When I had accidents and ended up with a bad knee, hip, ribs, or shoulder I was able to overcome the bangs and bruises much quicker than rivals who used to come into the dressing rooms and complain about a sore knee or a sore shoulder. If the injuries were serious, I tried to find a way to minimise the effect and not give in to the discomfort.

Ordinarily, I expected to maintain a high standard of fitness, because I made sure I worked harder at it than anybody else. Training with the Manchester City footballers, as I did for several years, helped me achieve a level few if any of my rivals could approach.

The one constant was to ensure that whether I was healthy or hurting, my mind was on the job. As a rider, I courted success, not popularity. As an entertainer, I figured there is nothing more entertaining than winning. The supporters who are with you ask for little more than that you can go out and win races, especially when it counted for the team.

Of course there will always be fans who have their own particular favourite and their special treat is to see their man beating the star opponent. That is how it is and always will be. Listening to a crowd giving me the bird more often than not meant I was doing my job well.

At least I was guaranteed a good reception at home. We usually had kids and animals around our house and I was always popular with them. I might get in from a meeting at two o'clock in the morning and the dog was there wagging its tail and glad to see me. The kids would get up at eight o'clock and everyone loved me. It really didn't matter if several thousand people had been shouting abuse at me the night before.

I didn't set out to be unpopular. I had a job to do, wanted to do it my way and accepted that in every walk of life, getting to the top involves upsetting people. Criticism was one of the spurs that made me try harder because I always liked to prove everyone wrong.

I stepped on plenty of toes, and probably took some of my routines and obsessions to extremes. I was a bad loser but not, I think, a bad sportsman as plenty of people chose to believe. Sure, there were the mind games, the tactics which can reinforce personal belief and create doubt and uncertainty in the mind of rivals. But from the year dot, gamesmanship has been a part of every game.

My mission simply was to do whatever it took to establish a presumption of superiority over opponents. I made a point of looking straight into the eyes of the other competitors before a meeting, and with many of them that was all it took to know I was stronger than they were.

Of course you still had to do the job but it was a huge advantage to see their character, and the strength or weaknesses in their eyes. Because I hardly spoke to anybody before the racing some people saddled me with a reputation of being big-headed. I never was but I let all my rivals believe I was.

There is a saying 'it is not my business what you think of me' and I let them think what they liked, I had my mind power under control and what they thought and said only undermined their confidence and made me much harder to beat.

I often tell young riders Muhammad Ali never crept into a boxing ring and asked the referee 'Please sir, where can I sit?'

He climbed into the boxing ring like he owned the whole stadium. I used to enter the pits in a similar manner. No wonder a lot of fans didn't like me. But it made me stronger, to go to away tracks and have people booing me. Even if there were 90,000 at Wembley or 130,000 at Katowice, I never gave the fans the satisfaction of affecting my focus. I was mentally and psychologically stronger than them.

They didn't know what I was doing, or where I was coming from – but I did. They were there to see their hero win and didn't properly appreciate why I was there. I wanted what I came for more than them. Following years of disappointment, I was there with an agenda and a will to succeed far greater than any thoughts they had about wanting me to fail.

An hour before a World Final, I would never say much, but I would be thinking if I was stronger than those thousands in the crowd I would definitely be stronger than the other 15 sitting on their tool boxes.

Spectators who complained I was 'boring' because I won a lot of races by virtue of my gating ability obviously never had to try to dodge a faceful of flying shale while trying to pass an Ole Olsen or a Peter Collins at a million miles an hour.

Riders who are very physical and all over their bike tend to look very spectacular. I'm like everybody else and appreciate watching the dazzling racers such as a Kelly Moran and Mark Loram but sometimes economy is a better option. It certainly was for me.

As a consequence most people found my style less eye-catching than some others. I also had to put up with accusations I was grumpy, arrogant, uncommunicative, and lacking in charm, or social graces.

At least some of those labels were a way from the truth but I'll plead no contest to the suggestion I was very often wrapped up in my own thoughts to the exclusion of all else and all others.

Many's the time family members or close friends might pass me in the pits area and I blanked them, so oblivious was I to anything but the business of racing and whatever exclusive focus that required.

If you want to walk a different road to the rest, which I did, then my best way of ensuring my performance was at the desired level was to perfect the whole process and let the outcome take care of itself.

Having the sense of well-being physical fitness brings was another important element. It is as important nowadays as ever it was. Riders may be required to be in a stadium from early in the morning for machine examination and other commitments. Much of the time they are on their feet and when the most important race of the day comes round that might have stretched out to several hours.

If you had ambitions of winning you could not afford to be tired in any respect because as soon as you are physically tired you become mentally tired. When you are lining up for a heat which might decide a world championship you need to be sharp.

MAGIC MOMENT – Ivan's support crew rush to salute the 1977 world champion moments after his title-clinching Heat 18 win in the wet

14 – Ivan Mauger

Getting my mental toughness into gear was the password to unlocking the right solution to whatever situation presented itself. Riders, officials or press people who saw me with my eyes closed in the dressing rooms assumed I was sleeping.

I vaguely heard them in the background but took none of it on board – I was not asleep but going over every start in all my races and working out plan A and then plan B (there was never time for a plan C from the start).

I had a plan if I was leading out of the first corner and another plan if I was second or third. Each of my rivals had their own preference to use different parts of the track so they were all creatures of habit and therefore quite predictable. That made it easy to choose what part of the track to pass them if they made a mistake

There were instances at media conferences after major meetings when an interviewer would comment on a great move I had made in such and such a race at high speed. I often had to think what that move was because I had visualised every possible scenario. With that resource upon which to call, everything people thought was great and very fast was playing out in slow motion for me.

When the stakes were at their highest – a World Final for example – there was no end to the attention to detail. Officials complained if I moved from my allocated pit space but there were many reasons why I often did not conform.

At some stadiums the spectators were a nuisance on certain sides, but for the most part foreign organisers only had thoughts for their own riders. Visitors were allocated the hot and sunny positions for afternoon meetings, or cramped and poorly-lit areas for night events.

My race crew always knew where we wanted to be, so they commandeered the positions which suited us best, regularly inviting protests from riders, team managers, referees or the clerk of the course. Almost invariably, we stayed where we wanted to be.

Conquering the psychological high ground was never more important than at finals abroad. For many years sporting officialdom in Eastern European countries in the old Communist bloc made a great play on their own methods of preparation. That is why winning the 1970 title in Wrocław meant so much to me, even more than my first, which was so special, or my last, which surpassed every dream and original expectation.

My first taste of Polish kidology and psychology was on a Great Britain tour there in 1966. There was a mess-up at Heathrow and I had to go the day after everyone else because there wasn't a ticket for me.

By the time I arrived everyone had paired up to go into rooms and I shared with the PZM official and team manager Zbigniew Puzio – known

EARLY INFLUENCES – Ronnie Moore and Jack Young, pictured tangling in a Golden Helmet match race, inspired a future world champion

to one and all as Charlie – and the Polish team bus driver. The three of us ended up rooming together all tour.

For most of that trip, Charlie was with me and we often would talk late into the night. I asked why the federation had us driving all over the country when we could get to a stadium in a couple of hours – the truth is they were doing it to unsettle us before the meetings.

He would never reply and countered with the question: 'who is your trainer?'

I told him I was my own trainer, and had learned a lot from Ronnie Moore and from Jack Young. I talked about the top riders I respected and those from whom I learned a great deal. Still Charlie repeatedly asked me who my trainer was.

He had a diploma of speedway and was a university-qualified trainer, as were many of the PZM officials. He used to wake up in the morning and start his psychology. He would say 'our new boys are now having training'. That was at six or seven o'clock.

Then Charlie would do press-ups to impress me. If he did 20 or 50, I did more. Whatever he had done I would do 10 extra. It didn't hurt that he packed a lot more weight, but I just wanted to beat him at his mental game.

VICTORIOUS – in Wrocław, 1970

Charlie was very serious about his methods. I used to make jokes and one night after a hiding we went back to the hotel at two o'clock in the morning – we always seemed to have a reception after the meetings – and he would be asking me what I thought about such and such a rider. He would always be talking about a rider who had beaten me by half a lap.

I didn't want to give any ground and told him that rider was stupid because he was still full throttle when he came into the pits until the trainer would tell him it was all right to shut off the throttle. Those trainers demanded blind faith, and controlled everything. My point was they allowed no room for individuality or initiative.

In one respect, it might have been good but I couldn't imagine how a rider can have respect for someone with a degree in training who had not ridden a speedway bike.

Most of the British and Commonwealth riders hated going to Eastern Europe because most of them got sucked in by the mind games. But I was determined to find a way past all that. Winning the European Final in Leningrad in 1970 demonstrated what was possible.

Trying to win in Wrocław that year was the biggest test. Nobody had won three world titles in a row. Everybody knew the Poles would be fired up big time. We had been there for four days and it was extremely hot. No surprise then to find my position was in the hottest part of the pits.

It took an almighty row with a gang of Polish officials but we moved out to the back of the pits, shaded by a huge concrete pillar, and stayed where we were. We were quite a bit away from the gates which led on to the track but in the cool and relaxed.

Eventually most of the officials melted away as they were meant to be on duty on the centre green. That was not the end of it, though. The clerk of the course and the pit marshal kept getting the western riders on to the track and sitting on their bikes in the heat. Meanwhile the Polish riders were being wrapped in damp towels and making the others wait.

The Will To Win – 17

I quickly realised that ploy was happening and had my guys stationed at various locations passing the word to each other until they reached Gordon Stobbs and me. My signals told me not to bother to start getting ready until the Polish riders were on the track and sitting in the heat.

It was a day on which everything had to be perfect; the build-up, the bikes, the mental and physical preparedness. One mistake could have ruined everything. But I didn't make one. Five races, four copybook laps each time. The Polish contingent didn't have an answer.

Scoring a flawless maximum blew the myth and discredited their methods once and for all. And I had a message for my old friend Charlie. Afterwards I couldn't resist saying: 'See, I think for myself'.

So there are no apologies for the attention to detail and the emphasis I placed on the world championship. But as a so-called self-absorbed and self-interested loner I also put a lot of effort and commitment into doing my best in domestic racing, which meant trying to help my club win the league.

At all the clubs I rode for, I did my bit to improve their fortunes and their image. We won the Provincial League in my second year at Newcastle, had three British League titles in succession at Belle Vue, won the title at Exeter and finished a desperately close second at Hull. They were all some way down in the lower orders of the League before I joined them.

From Belle Vue on, part of my contract was I had a say in which riders were in the team and who rode with whom at home and away. We had a clean-out of a lot of dead wood within and on the fringes of the various sides and I fell out with plenty of people but the results spoke for themselves.

Opposition promoters could guarantee a good show from a visiting team which came with the right attitude. Frequently it meant upsetting the locals but the bottom line is good teams mean good business for everybody.

The promoters with whom I was involved were all happy to have my input and I was fortunate to ride for a lot of very good team managers. There was Eddie Glennon at Newcastle, Dent Oliver at Belle Vue, Peter Oakes at Exeter and Ian Thomas at Hull. Our objective was to get the best out of each individual and we worked on the basis that if something was good for the team then it was the way to go.

My contribution was more than just scoring points. But it was a matter of professional pride to strive to be the best at that as well. In the later stages at Newcastle I was paid an overall guarantee and that was the case for every season with Belle Vue, Exeter and Hull.

There are promoters who don't like guarantees because they think it allows a rider to slip into a comfort level and take advantage. Racing has been good to me financially, and there's something in the old story about hungry fighters, but money will never win you a race. You have to love to race and love to win.

As I did not have to earn prize money it was a great source of satisfaction that from 1968 and for 11 of the next dozen years I was at or close to the top of the British League charts and averaged way over 11 points for much of that time.

To achieve that level does not just happen. It is important to know you have given yourself the best chance to win races. Dropped points are inevitable, maybe because an experiment goes wrong, sometimes when an opponent just is too good. The trick is to be good and ready for the big moments and the big meetings.

It's simple, really. There is no substitute for hard work and dedication. I tell young riders if they seriously want to be successful, they have to love what they are doing, eat and sleep speedway, train hard, be dedicated and gather good loyal people in their support team.

Whether at the start of a career or any later stage, application is all. Chart everything, analyse everything, and treat your favourite engine like a baby, record results, weather conditions, particular races, best gates, tyre pressures and gear ratios.

If all the ingredients are there, winning should become the fun part. Mind you, even a maximum is no good if you're not riding well. It isn't acceptable to win simply because others were worse. It's OK to lose if you have put in the mental and physical effort and important to respect the other guy if he just does it better on the day.

Some of the best advice I ever had was from Guy Allott, my engine tuner for many years. During the winter of 1964–65 we stayed in England to get ready for the challenge of the first season of British League and I spent days out at his place talking about motors and speedway in general.

Guy believed all young riders needed to do an apprenticeship and I had done that. He said: 'Winning is only a habit. You have been winning everything for a couple of years in England and a few years in Aussie and you will keep on winning no matter what your opposition is like.'

I have told the same thing to a lot of young guys in New Zealand, Australia and America who have wanted to go to England and ride in the top league. My recommendation is for them to do at least two seasons in the lower division, get into the habit of winning and they will be winners when the time comes to test themselves at a higher level.

That's what happened to Jason Crump, who won his third world championship last year. It's been a similar story with Tai Woffinden and Chris Holder, two new guys on the Grand Prix roster for 2010.

Darcy Ward did his apprenticeship on 125cc bikes from when he was about 10 and then 350s before he practised on 500s, He rode in a couple of the 80cc FIM Gold Cup meetings in 2007, and went to England for the Conference League for a while in 2008.

The Will To Win – 19

Last year he topped the Premier League averages, won the World Under-21 and was signed by Poole. He did the complete speedway apprenticeship and is now on his way up.

Not all have followed this path and thought they were above doing an apprenticeship. Just as it was when I first went to Wimbledon, it's still all too easy to score next to nothing in the big league. Too many decent prospects have become so disappointed with speedway and not gone on with it when they had much to offer the sport.

I refused to contemplate failure even though a lot of people described me as one when I was 17 and 18. The moral of my story is that the ones who make the grade do so because they use their brain as well as their throttle hand, although I'm not sure too many of today's youngsters think enough about the psychological side or the detailed preparation required to go all the way.

I hear too much of them talking endlessly about who is the best tuner – Brian Karger, Marcel Gerhard, Klaus Lauch, Hans Zierk, or whoever. Bikes are still 500cc single cylinder race machines just as they have been for more than 80 years. And it's who is on them that matters the most.

My greatest stroke of fortune was to be supported every step of the journey by Raye. She continued to believe in me even on those odd occasions when I may have been feeling sorry for myself and wondering if there might not be some other way of spending my time.

Fortunately I always managed to answer my own question. You can't put a price on that most basic human emotion – the will to win. Most top racers and athletes are similar in ability and on any given day, because they are human, can perform better, or worse, than their close rivals. Only the ones with the complete package consistently win the big occasions.

I thought I had seen everything, done everything and experienced everything but being voted 'Man of the Millennium' when readers of the *Speedway Star* and *Vintage Speedway* magazines were polled to rate the outstanding riders of the 20th century was something of a shock. I had been retired for 14 years at that point.

It was difficult to reconcile with those fans who had given me so much stick in previous years. If I didn't realise beforehand how people felt about me and how I dared to dream, this was the wake-up call. It was fantastic to realise that after all that time, people at last recognised what I had done, where I was coming from, and respected me enough to pay such a tribute.

In the end it is proof positive that if you have the right dream and mind power working when it really matters, you will be able to visualise and achieve the result when you believe it. Ultimately that was what defined and shaped my career.

That's me. This is who I am.

TIME FOR A SKID – on the sands at South Brighton with brother Trevor and Dad (top picture, in background) in the winter of 1955

Heat 2

THROUGH THE EYES OF A CHILD

IT WAS Saturday, January 29, 1949 when the speedway came to town. It also was my own personal D-Day, as in D for Destiny.

A lifetime associated with motorcycle sport has provided a million memories – many of them to be covered in this book – and none more vivid than the night the Aranui track in suburban Christchurch, on New Zealand's South Island, opened its doors.

As with many other nine-year-old kids brought along by their mums and dads among the 10,000 people who turned up, it was love at first sight.

Dad and Mum took brother Trevor, 12, half-sister Pat, 14, and me in their six-cylinder in-line Essex car which was quite something then. Trev was also watching speedway for the first time and so too were my mates. We were spellbound. What planet were these blokes from?

Speedway racing has had its ups and downs for longer than my lifetime but for thousands their first experience of the sight, sound and smells of speedway has been a life-altering experience. Everyone has their own particular recollection.

Not so many of those first hooked as a fan have the inclination or receive the opportunity to live out the dream on track, racing around the world and getting rewards and experiences to fill a book.

My wife Raye and our children Julie, Kym and Debbie have shared in some unforgettable occasions, some incredible highs and plenty of lows, too. As the Aussies say, I wouldn't have missed it for quids.

From that first evening at Aranui, I was captivated. It was raw, rough and ready and incredibly exciting. It had been the talk of the town for weeks. This was a confirmation that anticipation and expectation sometimes lives up to its advance billing.

Tracks were springing up around New Zealand in the years after the war and team racing was soon to become popular.

Solos had first been staged in Christchurch in 1929. Several circuits opened and closed over the next 20 years with Monica Park in Ferry Road, Woolston – just walking distance from my home – one the most successful, although it never quite recovered from the fatal accident which in 1935 claimed the life of one-time New Zealand champion Charlie Blacklock.

One of the first Kiwi riders to venture overseas, Charlie rode for Crystal Palace, then for Stamford Bridge and Nottingham. He won the New Zealand title in 1932–33. My parents were in the crowd on the night he crashed.

OLD TIMERS – Edwin Arthur Mauger (Ivan's father) shows off his 1906 belt-driven Triumph to brother-in-law Alfred Frederick Melrose

My father was a motorcycle enthusiast from way back, with family pictures showing him posing proudly alongside his new 500cc single cylinder belt-drive Triumph in 1906, and later taking his first wife Caroline for a ride in a rickshaw-type trailer hooked behind his bike.

My grandparents, Philip John and Margaret Matilda Mauger, were born in Jersey and arrived in New Zealand at Lyttleton, the port of Christchurch, on February 8, 1876, with their four-month-old son (also Philip John) along with Margaret's sister, her husband and son, and her mother .

The voyage from London on the three-masted barque *Otaki* had taken 101 days and their arrival brought to 17 the total of family members to make Christchurch their new home as part of the Vogel Immigration Scheme, assisted by the New Zealand Government.

British-born, Sir Julius Vogel was Prime Minister for two spells between 1873-76 and is credited with being hugely responsible for railway construction, communications and other infrastructure and public works, as well as being a prime mover to give women the vote – which New Zealand did before any other country.

Vogel House was the official residence of New Zealand Prime Ministers for most of the 20th century, and the Vogel Building in Wellington is now home to the Ministry of Justice.

THE HOUSE DAD BUILT – 50 Isis Street, Woolston, in suburban Christchurch, pictured in October 1915

One of the first places to benefit from the infrastructure programme and receive overseas workers was Christchurch, on the east coast of the South Island, a developing town which had been founded as recently as 1848 although there was settlement locally from around 1000 years ago.

Philip John and Margaret Matilda seem to have quickly adapted to their new surroundings, and at the last count there were around 230 Maugers or extended family members in or around Christchurch and elsewhere in New Zealand.

Several strands of the family stayed close to their roots – there are 34 Maugers listed in the Jersey telephone book. There even was a Stan Mauger who rode speedway for Coventry between 1929–31 but whether he was a Jersey man, a Kiwi, or even a relative, nobody knows.

The Mauger name goes back hundreds of years, and my nephew Harold's wife Jan has compiled a very detailed family tree which makes fascinating reading.

Philip John and Margaret Matilda settled in Ferry Road, Woolston and my father, Edwin Arthur Mauger, was the eighth of 11 children. Four died in infancy, whereas Dora Florence, last but one in the line, lived to within three months of what would have been her 95th birthday.

24 – Ivan Mauger

My father married Caroline Charlotte Mantell in 1911. Their house at 50 Isis Street, Woolston – where I grew up – was built in that year and Dad and his brothers were involved in the building of it.

A feature was a couple of windmills which pumped up the lovely artesian water which runs under Canterbury. Christchurch is one of the very few places in the world that can bottle its tap water and sell it, as the aquifers deep down fed by the mountains are so pure.

Dad and Caroline had five children but sadly in 1927 she died giving birth to Shirley Caroline, my only surviving half-sister whom I met for the first time in October last year.

In 1935, my father, who was then 52, married the 23-year-old Alice Rita Fuller Forscutt, who had come to work as his housekeeper at Isis Street.

Mum already had a two-year-old daughter, Patricia Mae – no one in the family knew who the father was, but my brother Trevor (born on September 23, 1936) and I are sure it was Eddie Payne who Mum married (and quickly divorced) a while after Dad died in 1959.

When I was born at Burwood Hospital on October 4, 1939, New Zealand as a nation was 89 years young, its population was 1.63 million, and like the mother country, had been at war with Hitler's Germany for just over a month.

While Christchurch is still a 'small town' now it was even smaller then. I did my growing up in Woolston, a small, quiet, light industrial and residential suburb. It is situated three kilometres south-east of the Christchurch city centre, close to two state highways.

The Heathcote River provided Woolston with water for industries like wool scouring, and in the city's early days wharves were used by small ships to service the area. The Lyttleton rail line continued to sustain Woolston as a prime location for industry.

Over the 20th century the area grew to become the centre of the New Zealand rubber industry. Other industries grew here and included a nugget factory and a gelatine and glue works.

My awareness of all this was pretty much as you would expect of a normal kid in those pre-television days. Home was home and most of what went on in the rest of the world was a wonderful mystery.

Even from an early age, though, I must have had streak of adventure – and rebellion.

One of my first memories is of going to kindergarten in Opawa Road, probably aged four. Mum used to take me in a seat on the back of her bicycle. One day I decided I'd had enough and walked home what must have been about three and a half miles.

THE THREE OF US – Ivan with brother Trevor and half-sister Pat in the 1940s

When I got home Pat and Trev were at school and Mum and Dad at work. I passed that fitness test but both my brother and I had the usual childhood illnesses. At one time I had to spend a few weeks in Glenelg Health Camp, a rehabilitation unit for sick children on Murray-Aynsley Hill behind Christchurch.

I can remember saving sweets for wartime kids in England. Trev and I put them into Golden Syrup tins and Dad had to solder the lids on, presumably to keep the sweets secure and fresh.

Trev and I shared a bedroom at home, and we have always been great friends apart from being brothers. When I started at Opawa School in Ford Road we would walk there together and as soon as we got bicycles we would ride our bikes.

Dad always had a car. Most New Zealanders had English models but he had a succession of American motors. The Essex was manufactured in Detroit.

I remember Dad going to work as a linesman for the post and telegraph department of Christchurch, but he retired when I was quite young. He was a heavy smoker and suffered with emphysema that caused a collapsed lung.

Not surprisingly I have been against smoking from that day to this and for some years I have done voluntary work for Smokefree, the anti-smoking agency in New Zealand.

Mum used to work for Charlie Lunney and his wife doing housework, washing and shopping for them. Charlie was the biggest building contractor in Christchurch and they lived in a huge house in Fendalton, absolutely the top district in town at that time.

Their house had a massive lawn that went down to the Avon River. When their four daughters got married Charlie built houses for them all in the grounds.

I remember going there with Mum during school holidays and it had a very long gravel drive with massive trees on either side. She used to ride her bicycle to Fendalton and back which is probably an hour each way.

Like a lot of ladies in that era she did not get a driver's licence until my dad had passed away.

There were family get-togethers and we had neighbours and acquaintances who years later turned out to be relatives. We always had Christmas dinner at Isis Street and then went to visit Dad's eldest son George in Caledonian Road, St Albans.

George had four sons, Edward, Philip, Ronnie and Harold. He died a few years ago.

Christchurch was not the centre of the universe but there always was something going on. I remember the Centenary celebrations (1850–1950) and rode my bicycle to Hagley Park in the middle of town for a big firework display.

Another memory is of the 1953 Coronation of Queen Elizabeth II. New Zealand is still very closely related to England. It was even closer then so the newspapers were full of it and whenever we went to the movies for about a year afterwards they played all the pictures of the Coronation.

CYCLE SPEEDWAY – the mighty Riley Stars, Graham Hanstock, Barry Meikle, Ivan, Kelly Brown and Paul Morton

Challenging that for screen time and newspaper space was coverage of Edmund Hillary, the first person to climb Mount Everest and the hero of every New Zealander.

Sport was what appealed to most youngsters and kept us healthy and active most of the time. By and large much of what was happening in the outside world completely passed us by. I was quite small, certainly shorter than all the other kids at school, but it never affected me much.

While the opening of Aranui was the most thrilling thing to have happened along, my mates and I of course were several years away from being old enough to race.

For the meantime, the neighbourhood kids had their own non-powered mini-version – cycle speedway. There was no need to persuade me to get involved because the sport quickly became very popular in just about every district of Christchurch and also the suburbs of any town in New Zealand that had a speedway track.

Woolston Cycle Speedway Club was my first team, on a section of waste ground close to home. When that site was sold for housing some of my mates and myself physically built another circuit on the other side of Woolston, including the track and pits with an outgate and an ingate.

Every cycle speedway track had two or three teams with seniors, intermediates and juniors. When I started riding at age 10 it was in the under 12 C grade division.

Des Brown was the captain of the senior (or A team) at Woolston and later became one of the first cycle speedway guys to ride on speedway. I soon decided I wanted to be like him on cycle speedway and then follow him into proper speedway.

Eventually that land was also sold and we built another track behind Riley Crescent, the street next to Isis Street. There was an earth mound almost all the way round and we cut the grass with our dads' lawnmowers so spectators could stand and watch.

We called ourselves the Riley Stars. There was intense rivalry between the various district and suburban organisations. Our season ran parallel with the speedway season, through the southern summer.

Riders included Graham Hanstock, Barry Meikle, and, later, Trev. The whole thing appealed enormously to me, whether it was being with mates, riding in competition, or working alone on building up a bike or doing some task at the track

It wasn't just a passing interest. This for a long time was the most important activity in my life. Cycle speedway definitely conflicted with my education. I couldn't wait for school to finish so I could go and practise at the track.

I always wanted to be winning things and I can't remember when that came about. I did win the Under-12 C Grade cycle speedway championship at the end of my first season and that was held at my home track in Christchurch. I got second in the South Island Championship at the Wainoni track.

Later when I got a delivery job with Paulson's Opawa Chemist in Opawa Road I used to practise after my work had finished. All the cycle speedway training, my delivery job with the chemist and running up the Rapaki track strengthened my legs.

Roller skating was another popular sport and we used to go to the main Christchurch rink in Kilmore Street. There was a sign up asking for nominations for a roller hockey team and of course I put my name down.

They put me in the B grade team and once a month there would be a match with other teams in town. Our team also went to several other centres in the South Island but I never could afford to go with them.

When I went to school, although it's not a great thing to admit, I saw it more as a focal point for sporting and social activity rather than a centre of learning. In the later years the headmaster used to say 'you are only here to play hockey and rugby and the inter-schools competition athletic championships'.

He was right, of course!

Rugby practice was after school on Mondays and Wednesdays and we played on Friday afternoons in the Christchurch inter-school competition. Hockey practice was Tuesday and Thursday after school and we played on Saturday mornings, also in the inter-schools comp. In the afternoon I played for the Woolston club.

I only had one pair of boots and two pairs of laces. There would be fresh whitened laces in my boots for Friday afternoon and when I got home after those matches I would wash the laces and they would be dry for Saturday morning.

I would polish my boots with black shoe polish and go off on my bike to play for the school on Saturday mornings. Mostly that was in Hagley Park, about a 40 minute ride from Woolston, so I usually didn't go home at lunchtime. Instead I had a bag that I used to attach to the front of my bike to put the school colours in and I also had shoe polish.

Between Saturday morning and wherever I had to be on Saturday afternoon for the club – which could be anywhere in Christchurch – I polished my boots again and put the whitened laces in them.

That sort of attention to appearance stayed with me all my racing career. No matter what the weather I always wanted to be neat with clean leathers and a clean bike before the start of any meeting.

No doubt the Opawa teachers were great people and committed educators but most of it was lost on me. The two I remember are Miss Saunders, who told us how she went to England for two years, and Nelson Loney, who was the rugby master.

My best mates at school were Ronnie Kirby, Kerry Burke and Allan (Happy) Halliday. Ronnie later worked for the railways most of his life. Kerry (now Sir Kerry) became a Member of Parliament and Speaker of the House of Representatives in David Lange's time but Allan Halliday I lost touch with after our teenage years.

I started running there and soon wanted to be school champion so I trained for session after session and won it at my second attempt.

Allan Halliday and I were big rivals for the championship, held over one lap around a 600 yard grass track. I won it when I was only 13 and Allan was second.

That inspired me to join the Olympic Harriers, which was one of the most competitive clubs on the Canterbury scene, and for about three winters I did a lot of cross-country running races.

Lionel Fox, one of the founder members, and Jack Clarke represented New Zealand in the 1950 British Empire Games marathon, when Jack was the bronze medallist.

They were names to look up to but the single athletics achievement which really caught the imagination was when Roger Bannister broke the four-minute mile barrier in England in July 1954.

Years later I parked myself next to him at BBC Sports Personality of the Year functions and tried to pick his brains for any guidance as to how to develop the mindset which separates champions from the rest.

My bubble was pricked when Allan Halliday beat me in the next schools championship but a few weeks later came the very substantial consolation of selection for Canterbury in the public schools 'A' titles.

The running was in the summer time so I was continually either running or practising for rugby, practising for hockey, or doing something sporting.

RUN IVAN, RUN – Opawa School running champion 1953

Having the ability to run and the endurance to go with it was helpful to me in other sports. The teachers must have considered me something of a leader as I became captain of the rugby and hockey teams and enjoyed the responsibility and status which went with it.

That led to selection for Canterbury in rugby at schoolboy level in weights (schoolboy rugby was based on your weight and not your age). I also represented Canterbury and later South Island at hockey and twice won the Hatch Cup, the New Zealand Championship for schoolboys.

Before one rugby match Mr Loney said he wanted me to play on the left wing instead of the right, my normal position. That was a bit of a surprise.

'You are ambidextrous so you can play on either wing,' he said.

I didn't know what the word ambidextrous meant and at first feared it was a disease of some kind. It wasn't until I got home I asked my parents and they told me that it means you can use your left or right hand or left or right foot equally.

Mr Loney must have seen me in practice because I could pass to the left or the right and although I was a better kicker with my right foot the left was pretty useful.

Even if I had convinced myself from day one that I was going to be a speedway rider, like the rest of my mates at that age I also briefly dreamed of success as an All Black – despite my lack of size. Every Kiwi kid has that fantasy.

While speedway, and Christchurch in particular, has contributed to New Zealand sports history in a big way, there still is and probably never will be anything bigger than the national rugby union team.

It is a constant source of amazement to people that a country so small should continue to produce outstanding players and teams from such a tiny population base. Historically New Zealand has been a dominant force in international rugby for ever – they won the inaugural World Cup in 1987 and can point to a winning record against every nation they have played.

The pre-match haka, a Maori war dance which has intimidated even the most unflinching of opponents, is as much of a signature as the black jerseys with its silver fern badge.

So when the All Blacks played at Lancaster Park in Christchurch, the crowd and the atmosphere was on a different plane again. In those days, teams did not disappear into the dressing room for 20 minutes or so. Most of them stood on the sidelines eating oranges.

My most enduring memory of watching them for the first time was seeing Bob Scott, the full back, practising his goal-kicking during the half-time interval – in bare feet and usually from inside the other half of the field.

The Will To Win – 31

In later years Don Clarke also specialised in place kicks from 10 or 20 yards inside his own half. The only person I have seen do that since is Frans Steyn of South Africa.

In the Springboks' final match of the 2009 Tri Nations against New Zealand, his last match with the Boks before his departure for France, he converted two penalties from well within his own half of the field and barely missed a drop goal from midfield and near a touchline.

Sitting at home watching the game live on cable television, which I love to do these days, is a concept which would have been unimaginable to my parents. And even though my rugby playing did not go beyond school days, Aaron Mauger, a distant relative of mine, played for Canterbury, was a four-time Super 12 title winner with the Crusaders, and appeared 46 times for the All Blacks, including the 2003 and 2007 World Cups.

His brother Nathan and their uncles Graeme and Steve Bachop also played for New Zealand.

Because it often is so cold in Christchurch in the winter we usually avoid going back there during the rugby season, but after Aaron and Nathan got in the Crusaders Super 14 team I have been to a lot of the games and the same with the All Blacks. From my racing days, I have always tried to gain knowledge as well as inspiration from high achievers in other fields.

Aaron set it up for me to go to an All Blacks training camp when we were in New Plymouth for the staging of the 2004 World Long Track Championship Grand Prix, and dropped in to Yarrow Stadium for a publicity shoot. He got very good tickets for Kym and myself when the Crusaders played the Queensland Reds.

All of that makes me as much of a sports fan now as I was as a kid. My parents always encouraged my interest and involvement although my dad was quite ill so neither he nor my mum had much to do with me getting into the various teams. Most of that was on at my own initiative.

Dad never talked much about his motorcycle enthusiasm but he did have a 500 side valve Triumph. When he and Mum used to go to the movies on Saturday night, Trev and I would race out to the garage, take the bike into the kitchen, put a sack under it, take off the cylinder head and turn the piston around a few times. Then we put the head back on and returned it to the garage.

We thought we were big-time mechanics then. It was not until years later that we admitted to Dad what we had got up to.

In spite of the big choice of sports on offer, there was never going to be anything to rival speedway. At the age of nine, I knew nothing about it. Within a couple of years, the course of my future career and life had been set.

The speedway scene was excellent in those days with tracks including Invercargill, Dunedin, Wellington, Palmerston North, Hastings and Napier, Gisborne, Hamilton, Auckland, New Plymouth, Wanganui and Whangarei.

The news Christchurch was to have a purpose-built circuit of its own was a big talking point in the Mauger house. As a lifetime dedicated motorcyclist my dad was happy to hear that Alec Pratt, who had run the Taita track in Wellington, was heading up a group to introduce racing at Rowan Avenue, Aranui – previously home to the hurly burley course of the New Brighton Motor Cycle Club.

Les Moore, an Aussie who had raced cars and bikes and in 1946 caught his first glimpse of a Wall of Death act at the Hobart show in Tasmania, was heavily involved in the track construction work.

His adventurous lifestyle had earlier prompted him to construct his own wall of death which he took to Sydney for a season, and then on to Perth. The appearance of his son Ronnie on 'the wall' gave the show an exciting new dimension. Word spread and Les received offers to take the act to South Africa and New Zealand. He chose New Zealand.

So it was that the Moores hitched a ride with a travelling circus for six months, Ronnie was enrolled in Christchurch Technical College and Les tried speedway for the first time up in Wellington.

His association with Alec Pratt led to his involvement with the Aranui project and when the gates opened, it was a fork in the road for speedway history.

Trevor Redmond, Peter Dykes, Kevin Hayden, Bob McFarlane and others who had or were on the way to making a name for themselves were among the first-night attractions – but Ronnie stole the show.

You could legitimately race on the speedway at the age of 15 and despite appearances – he looked about 12 – Ronnie quickly showed he was a man in boy's clothing, so comfortable and confident on the bike. Those hours of throttle control which are such an essential ingredient for riding wall of death obviously had done his ability to ride speedway no harm at all.

Just to give an idea of the excitement created, after the 10,000 turned up for the opening meeting, in future weeks the crowds frequently were around 14,000. Huge traffic jams were the order of the day. Not all of the locals welcomed the track's arrival and all that went with it. But any protests were overwhelmed by the huge popularity of the new facility and its star performers.

The circuit was a quarter of a mile, black cinders laid over clay, and the whole thing was absolute magic. The first time I watched it, I knew I wanted to be a rider. The first time I saw Ronnie Moore on the track, there was no other career ambition in my mind.

YOUNG TALENT TIME – *a youthful Ronnie Moore on a 1932 Rudge, with Jap engine, his first speedway machine*

As visits to Aranui became the highlight of each weekend, the riders were all heroes to us. They were kings, and young boys always wanted to be like them. My mum later recalled how as a kid I would sit in the stand endlessly telling her I wanted to be world champion when I grew up.

The Canterbury team, usually Trevor Redmond, Mick Holland, Jack Cunningham and Art Lamport (who only had one leg) won the Gold Helmet inter-track competition. Other team matches included New Zealand v Australia and South v North Island. In addition to Ronnie, further emerging young guns included teenager Craig (Spike) Jones and Geoff Mardon – both also destined to follow the path to Wimbledon later on.

The prospect of a full season of racing further lifted Aranui's status and 1949–50 attracted plenty of newcomers both on track and on the terraces. A notable new rider was Dick Campbell, who had gone to the UK with a Globe of Death act in 1947 and caught the eye of Belle Vue before heading up to Edinburgh.

An even more notable addition to the Canterbury team was Norman Parker, captain of Wimbledon and England, who introduced a dash of real class and, historically, paved the way for Ronnie Moore to go to England.

Although the legion of kids in short trousers would have disagreed, Ronnie at this stage was not considered ready for inclusion in the Canterbury first division team. But his shining talent was there to see – although few can have imagined just how quickly he would make an impact in the UK.

Watching the overseas riders take on the locals at Aranui was an education. Parker and his Wimbledon team mate Ron Mason swept the board when they led an Overseas team to victory over New Zealand, giving a hint of the gap between established professionals and our home-grown heroes, all of whom had been assumed to be gods up to this point.

The first year or so Aranui was running, Trev and I went with Mum and Dad and Pat in the car and later we started going by bike with mates from cycle speedway.

The thrilling anticipation of going to watch the racing started around Thursday or Friday and we were excited all day Saturday. Then on Sunday mornings we would meet at the cycle speedway track and talk about all the races and who done what and where in every race.

When I first told my parents of my intention to become a speedway rider, my dad said something along the lines of 'you don't want to kill yourself like Charlie Blacklock did'. But once he and Mum had grown used to the idea, they didn't put any obstacles in my way.

Jack Parker was the star arrival in the 1950–51 season. He was Norman's older brother and had dominated in British speedway since riding in the very first meeting at High Beech in 1928.

Regarded as one of the best never to have won the world title – the war years robbed him of his best opportunity – Jack did nevertheless win its equivalent, the British Riders Championship at Wembley in 1947.

But of course the greatest reception was the special welcome home for Ronnie, fresh from qualifying for his first World Final at 17. His success overseas was the catalyst for so many others who wanted to follow in his footsteps.

The idea of going to England first crystallised in my mind at this time. All the cycle speedway kids in Christchurch dreamed of being like him but I was the only one who wanted to go to England.

On Saturday afternoons my mates and I rode our bikes to the corner of Pages Road and Rowan Avenue, usually an hour or more before the riders on the night's programme at Aranui began to arrive.

We were really only waiting for Ronnie. Even in the early days he would have the latest big flash English car with a trailer and two beautiful bikes. When he turned the corner we used to rush into the stadium and go to the bridge that overlooked the pits. For the next few hours we hardly took our eyes off him, studying and absorbing everything he did in the pits and on the track.

There were other locals of obvious talent. Trevor Redmond and Geoff Mardon stepped up the tempo as they prepared to join the ranks of riders headed overseas. A couple of new kids who caught the eye were Barry Briggs, 20 months younger than Ronnie, and Ron Johnston, who came up from Dunedin with a big reputation.

Things were buzzing and soon enough Briggo and several others were joining the exodus of riders seeking fame and fortune on the other side of the world. It was exciting stuff for everyone, and when they were away Frank Ridding, an Englishman who was in the Aranui Speedway Supporters Club, lent me his copy of the English magazine *Speedway and Ice News* which contained details of how the various riders were faring on their travels.

Studying that magazine was to be invaluable to me when I did get to England because it enabled me to recognise most of the riders at the various meetings without having to ask who was who.

Academic learning remained low on my list of priorities but at least my interest in geography was given a workout as we pinpointed various towns and cities around the British Isles. We even learned about trips to exotic new locations including South Africa, where Trevor, Ronnie, Geoff and Briggo blazed new frontiers.

While they were charging around the world establishing their claims to fame, I faced the serious business of how to earn enough money to be able to afford a speedway bike of my own. When at the age of 12, I started my first after-school job, it paid 17s 6d (87.5 pence) and during the school holidays working full-time went up to the princely figure of £3.

The following year I managed to become a regular in the pits at Aranui, helping out any riders who would let me. I used to hang around Mick Holland and Craig Jones and, later on, Ronnie Moore if he was there. He spent the 1952–53 season in South Africa and Jimmy Gooch, who became a good friend when I raced in the UK, was the Canterbury resident rider that year.

My brother and I have always been close and he was very interested in my speedway ambitions. Trev did have friends of his own and other interests but when we were both quite young his mates and mine used to have races down the Rapaki track (behind where Trev and Larry Ross live now) on our cycle speedway bikes.

It is about four miles from the top of the hill at the Summit Road to the bottom and is in a big zigzag. At that time all us kids had some almighty crashes coming down.

I got the idea to run up it for training purposes and quite often I would do so at least twice a week and sometimes more – and occasionally twice on Sunday mornings. I have always had very strong legs since I was 11 or 12 from playing rugby, hockey, running, Olympic Harriers and training.

By now it was not just speedway which had captured my heart. When we were not riding cycle speedway, going to Aranui or attending any one of many sporting events, all the boys in the area were out and about on their pushbikes. I was with my mates when I met Raye. It started out innocently enough as these teenage romances often do.

Raye – Sarah Leslie McPeak Telfer to give her full maiden name – was born in Carlisle, close to the England-Scotland border, on January 23, 1941. She had polio at the age of three which left her with one leg shorter than the other. The Telfers, Andrew and Agnes (Nan) were Scottish and had 13 children, three of whom died very young. Raye was the youngest.

One sister, Emily, died from infantile paralysis at the age of 16 and it was after this her parents decided to emigrate, bringing Raye, two older brothers and another sister. Another brother and sister came out later. Her Dad was an aero engine fitter, belonged to The Church of the Nazarene and was a lay preacher. Her mother came from a Salvation Army background.

A LIKELY PAIR – on Trevor's 350cc Triumph Twin, 1954

The Will To Win – 37

The first time I saw Raye was by the clock tower at the Brighton Pier, across the road from Nicholls Restaurant and milk bar at the corner of Pages Road and Marine Parade, where she worked. She had her right leg in plaster and was on crutches after an operation on her polio foot.

I didn't speak to her then but the following Saturday I saw her again and started talking as she was coming out of the restaurant. We hit it off straight away. In no time I started to ride over to see Raye at her parents' place at New Brighton, half an hour away. Failing that she was always assured of at least one regular customer coming by for ice creams and milk shakes.

We had been seeing each other for a while and it seemed to me that to take the relationship further, some more impressive transport was needed. So when brother Trevor was away on military training I decided to borrow his Triumph Twin motorbike, which was sitting in the shed behind our home, and take Raye for a spin.

I was only 14, not yet old enough to have a motorcycle licence, but that was a minor detail. I was a little lad, too. We had to park the bike in the deep gutter alongside the road, before we could clamber on board.

We had not gone very far along Pages Road, heading in towards the city via the Brighton Bridge, when a car turned out in front of us into Onepu Street. Motorbikes in those days didn't have great brakes – maybe it was a good rehearsal for years to come – and Raye, the bike and I all flew through the air in different directions.

Fortunately we were little the worse for wear but Trev's pride and joy was looking decidedly secondhand. It was a day or two before the bumps and scrapes had been disguised and painted over so I could sneak the bike back into the shed.

We did not have too much time to get into further mischief, though. I was saving up the pennies and the pounds as fast as I could, and spending as much spare time as possible at Aranui.

When the stars returned – especially Ronnie who backed up from his debut season by rocketing into genuine superstar class – the crowds, always enthusiastic, turned out in even greater numbers.

The boy who went off as a promising teen prospect, and to whom it all seemed so easy, matured into a brilliant rider who made it to the World Final every year, was one off the rostrum in 1951 and 1952, placed second in the National League averages in '51 and then was to top the charts in each of the next five seasons.

One of my most vivid impressions of him is watching Ronnie do a celebration wheelie the length of the Aranui straight. Don't let anybody tell you the wheelie craze is something invented by modern-day riders.

NEW CHAMPION – Ronnie Moore after winning at Wembley in 1954

And he didn't limit his talents to solos. It was not unusual to see Ronnie on board his dad Les's Vincent-powered sidecar and, later, on four wheels as he hungered for even more excitement.

One night he pulled a huge crowd who had come to see him ride a rocket-powered bike. It was a bit of a gimmick dreamed up by the promoter and it got a lot of publicity.

It wasn't just that Ronnie was superman. He was our very own superman, who demonstrated that anything was possible, that by winning races you could also get the girls, the flashy cars and the respect and adoration of everybody. He was a household name, the closest thing Christchurch had to a chart-topping pop star.

In 1954, when Ronnie was 21, he became the youngest speedway world champion at Wembley, in spite of needing a brace on his left knee which he had broken in Denmark a few weeks earlier. The injury was forgotten as he swept to a 15-point maximum, and he wasn't short of mates with whom to celebrate.

Briggo was making his World Final debut and Geoff Mardon and Trevor Redmond were in the field too – an incredible quarter of the field who could trace their career progress from their Aranui education.

All kids have dreams and I had been nurturing mine for years. With such familiar role models doing so well on the international stage it was easy to imagine my own career taking a similarly glittering path.

When word came through to Christchurch, the timing was spot on. It was less than a month before my 15th birthday, the long-awaited magic moment when I could have a motorcycle of my own.

I got my road licence the day I was 15 on my brother Trevor's 350 Triumph Twin and about three months later had saved up enough money to buy a Triumph Thunderbird 650cc Twin.

It had a cast iron engine and weighed about 365 pounds (165kg). I was still only an inch over five feet (152cm) so I used to drop it occasionally trying to put it on the stand, and regularly used to break the front headlight.

I would come up the driveway at 50 Isis Street, slow right down and lean the bike against the weatherboards along the side of the house. Those boards had the gouges in them until we sold the house in 1984. Bernie Lagrosse replaced them when he was doing it up to sell.

A few weeks after my birthday I left school and got a full-time job with Lane Walker Rudkin, a big clothing manufacturer whose factory took up the whole block between Durham Street and Montreal Street in Sydenham.

The company later became Canterbury Clothing Company, recognised worldwide as manufacturers of sport and leisure wear and also as sponsors of the All Blacks.

Ken Rees, who I knew via the Aranui Supporters Club – we met up at one of their roller-skating nights – lived round the corner at 31 Bourke Street (off Montreal Street) with his parents Windy and Aggie.

One time when I took Ken for a spin as a pillion passenger on the Thunderbird, we clipped the kerb at the end of the road and fell off, fortunately without too much damage.

My ambition to race and to go to England had not wavered. A regular weekly pay cheque of £10, usually topped up with overtime, meant the start of some even more serious saving. And now I had Raye who was encouraging me all the way.

After getting myself organised on the road, next I wanted the speedway bike which had been a dream for so long. Ken Rees had the answer to that one. His dad, a Welshman, had arrived in New Zealand before the start of the 1952–53 season and announced himself by winning the South Island grass track title, but a foot injury kept him off the speedway until the following year.

He was not a star but he was one of the regulars at Aranui and Ken, a couple of years older than me, had similar ambitions. He was another one who wanted to be just like Ronnie and had recently joined the solo ranks and won a few junior races.

I was really happy when Ken told me to come round to their house and look at the bikes in their garage. There was Windy's machine and Ken's. Like the rest of us kids, Ken idolised Ronnie Moore and whatever Ronnie had on his bike he copied (a bit like Ole Olsen did with me a dozen years later). There was also a spare Jap engine and a spare Jap frame.

The first thing I asked Windy was how much did he want for a bike. The answer was £65. He said the engine and carburettor would be £40 and the rest £25. I had already saved up £35 since I bought my Triumph Thunderbird and it was under the mattress.

Windy said if I could pay that for the engine he would keep the rest of the bike until I could pay it off. With that, I raced home, got the money, borrowed the other fiver from my brother and went back to give it to Windy within the hour.

I went around to his house pretty well every night the following week and Windy and Ken helped me put the engine in, connect up the chains and everything else and we started it up.

Three weeks later I had saved up the other £25 and took it round to Windy so now I had my first bike. Trev had a trailer on his car and we went and picked it up on the Saturday morning and took it home. To give an idea of how big a deal this was, I took that Saturday off work.

I asked Mum to tell Dad, but she wouldn't. Next morning he saw the bike and asked me 'whose bike is that in the garage?' When I told him it was mine, he was OK about it but disappointed that I hadn't told him I had paid for the engine weeks earlier.

A month or so later Trev took my speedway bike to the Brighton beach for my first ride because Windy and Kenny and a couple of other local Christchurch riders were going to be there.

This soon became a regular outing, with Peter Pollett, George Topp and Ron Watkins among the others who came down for a skid. Ron had a 1930s vintage Model A ute and if Trev and his trailer were not available, he would take the bikes.

The Spit was sand and very flat when the tide went out at South Brighton, not far from where later Raye and I bought our first house at Rocking Horse Road.

Dad was unwell and I don't remember him going most of the time but he certainly went on a few occasions, as a couple of photos in my personal album confirm. There is one of him with Trev and me on bikes – his was one he borrowed from Windy or Ken.

For months my whole focus was to practise, train, work, and prepare for the day when I could go racing. There were practice sessions before the

TEN BOB – the first pay cheque from Aranui

TEENAGE HOPEFUL – looking forward to action at Aranui

1955–56 Aranui season started and it was at the first one I confided my intention to head overseas.

I had not talked to anyone about it but before I had even ridden in the novice races, the other riders were sitting around talking about all sorts of stuff. One of them asked me what did I think about riding on speedway. I told them my intention was to ride at Aranui only until I had enough money to go to England.

Waiting for a birthday or Christmas to arrive was nothing compared to my excitement and anticipation as the season opener drew closer.

On Saturday, October 8, just four days after turning 16, I had my first ride in public.

The record books show that I ran a second behind Alby Jordan in the four-lap novice race. It felt like we were racing at a million miles an hour, but a time of 93 and four-fifths seconds for the winner suggests that it probably was more exciting for me than for most of the 10,000 crowd who turned up to watch a 16-race programme of solos, sidecars, racing cars and midgets.

Reg Fearman, later chairman of the British Speedway Promoters Association, was the headline act that night. A year or two ago he dug out and sent to me the newspaper cutting from that day. My own personal souvenir was my first pay cheque, for 10 shillings. I never cashed it and have it to this day.

My first race win came four weeks later and from then on, it was a case of steady progress for the rest of the season. Ronnie and Briggo were in a class of their own whenever they featured on the programme. When the big guns had gone back to England there was more of an opportunity to step up against the best of the rest.

Even so, I recognised I was nowhere near the standard required, but the prospect of hard work did not faze me. Nor did the fact the popularity of the solos seemed to be waning. Some of the initial impetus had gone, and the introduction of cars and various support events promised tougher times for the solos.

The biggest downer of the year, though, was when little Billy Philp died giving a demonstration in his ultra-midget car at a Rakaia Car Club meeting. A very well-known and popular personality, he had been the mascot for the Canterbury team and I also knew his family.

His dad Bill Philp used to do speedway and with Mick Holland, Art Lamport, Jack Cunningham and others from Aranui also rode at the Halswell Domain where Trevor Redmond's Tai Tapu Club ran grass track meetings.

It was there I saw grass track racing for the first time and thought how relaxed it was compared with speedway.

Mind you, it was at one of those Halswell Domain meetings that Ronnie Moore crashed and was hit in the left cheek with his handlebars. From that day to this he has had a ring-shaped scar on his cheek.

FAST COMPANY – alongside Ove Fundin, Ronnie Moore and Brian McKeown at Aranui in January 1957

The Will To Win – 43

There was a grassy earth bank around the outside of the track and Ronnie was passing another rider. His footrest got stuck on the bank and he went over the handlebars, which would have been a pretty rare sight.

I started to ride on speedway at probably what was not the best of times. Spectator interest continued to wane after the boom of the early post-war years. From little bits of gossip it seemed even England was not as good as it was in the late 1940s and early 1950s. I still wanted to go anyway – there never was any question of turning back.

While some of the novelty had worn off with a lot of guys in Christchurch, I was really excited about going. I would stand around and listen to all the riders who had been to England. They didn't know I was listening really hard, but I was intrigued with some of the stories they told.

I made a point of talking to Ronnie but when Briggo first went to England he didn't come back every season as he used to go to South Africa. I didn't have any contact with Barry early on and the first time I met him was not until 1957 at Wimbledon.

At the start of my second season, though, it all stretched out before me. A priority was to accumulate enough cash to pay for my boat fare, and some solid improvement on the Aranui programme, because my ambition extended well beyond being a big fish in a small pond.

Don't ask me how I did it but it was not unusual for me to work from eight until five on the Saturday, dash home to clean up, and then race to Aranui where Trevor would have taken my bike and set things up in the pits.

I was determined to improve and, so confident was I of making the necessary progress, booked a boat ticket to England months in advance. I paid £125 for it and got a passport at the same time. On my passport I was 5ft 2in.

Some of the results at Aranui confirmed there was a fair bit of improvement happening. Winning the handicap final from the always consistent Brian McKeown was one highlight.

Ronnie was racing in Adelaide that night but he was back in town to take on new world champion Ove Fundin of Sweden. The show they put on was stirring stuff but emphasised I was going to have to start going a lot quicker to live with those guys.

I did make an early acquaintance with Fundin after going well enough to be selected for a couple of nominated heats. In the Selected Four race, Ronnie was out front when Brian McKeown dropped it and Ove had to put down his bike. I was right up his exhaust and also had to react in a split second.

He was quick to thank me for avoiding him and asked how I learned to do that so quickly. What he did not realise was that a beginner could not get

PROUD PARENTS – Edwin and Rita Mauger, Andrew and Agnes Telfer, February 9, 1957

a licence in New Zealand before demonstrating the ability to lay it down. The local steward and his assistant stood on opposite corners and had a small stone in a white rag. Riders did not know who was going to throw it out in front of them, and they had to react promptly at both ends before the chief steward would approve the issue of a licence.

Here I was at the start of my career and a few days later, Ronnie shocked the speedway world when he announced that he was finishing with solos because he wanted to go car racing on a full-time basis.

His dad Les was as much of a car enthusiast as he was a bike man, importing a number of flashy racers. As early as 1952, father and son raced in the famous Wigram Trophy. Ronnie crashed after he collided with another car and finished upside down, soaked in fuel and lucky to escape serious or possibly fatal injury. Les drove on to win the event, his second victory in a row in what is regarded as New Zealand's oldest motor race.

The accident did not lessen Ronnie's enthusiasm for four wheels and increasingly in England he had been racing, usually in a Cooper, at weekend meets at tracks such as Aintree and Silverstone, eventually joining Ray Thackwell in the Kiwi Equipe race team.

New Zealand's pioneering world speedway champion may have – temporarily – fallen out of love with the British scene. But my own love affair was burning brightly … and I hadn't been out of the South Island yet!

The Will To Win – 45

Socially, Raye and I did not have any extravagant habits. After she left school and joined me in the workforce, we both saved everything we could. Nothing could have seemed more natural than that we would become engaged and I raided my savings to buy her a diamond ring which cost £55. It does not seem much now but at the time I was getting around £10 a week.

I asked the boss at Lane Walker Rudkin if I could do extra shifts and they were very busy then so I did as much overtime as possible. Sometimes I worked seven days a week for weeks on end to build up the pot of money needed to go to England.

Ideally we would have pooled our limited resources and headed off to England together – but realistically it didn't look as if that would be possible. Raye didn't even get out to watch me race very often because she was working at the restaurant.

So the idea was for me to go overseas, become a star, and return, rich and famous to claim my teenage bride. Then the master plan went astray when we learned we were to become parents.

There was no way I wanted to postpone going to England so I sold my Triumph Thunderbird and bought a ticket for Raye on the SS *Rangitoto*. It was too late to get a twin cabin so I was in a cabin with three other guys and she was in a cabin with three ladies.

I also sold my original speedway bike and bought another one from Mick Holland. who had been one of our local heroes when we were kids. Then he went to England and rode for Cardiff and later Swindon. He was also New Zealand road race champion on both 350cc and 500cc.

On February 9, 1957 Raye and I were married under special licence in the Richmond Methodist Church – one of the oldest in New Zealand – at 311-315 Stanmore Road, Christchurch. It all came and went in a bit of a blur, with about 70 relatives and friends there.

The way Raye tells it we were in a hurry to get away so we could start our honeymoon.

The way I remember it is that we received all the congratulations, said our goodbyes and then at last we were on our way to England.

I took the bike and we crammed our clothes into a couple of suitcases. We didn't have anything else to take.

I also took a tool box I got from Mick Holland which was an ex-war ammunition box. I painted it black and then put on a big white NZ. That tool box later went on every trip to Australia and came with us when we returned to England in 1963. I still have it, a bit scratched but still going strong.

Like us, it obviously was built to go the distance.

Heat 3

VOYAGE OF DISCOVERY

NEW ZEALAND was home, but when I was growing up, you would hear references to 'the old country' all the time.

My dad and many close relatives were first and second generation descendants of immigrants. They spoke often and respectfully of the British Isles, half a world away but apparently full of people just like us.

What we did learn early on was that New Zealand was a long way from anywhere. Even Australia, the closest neighbour of any size or significance, is 1250 miles (2000 kilometres) across the Tasman Sea. The distance to England was 10 times further.

As a schoolboy sportsman I travelled to a few regional centres on the South Island, but I'd never been out of the country. Raye was one up on me, having done the round-the-world voyage as a nine-year-old when her parents moved to New Zealand. She recalled not only the excitement of the trip but also had her memories of what England was like, in and around her birthplace of Carlisle at least.

My awareness of the UK, even though teachers would have preferred me to know more, was limited to the names of various speedway tracks. Miss Saunders at Opawa School had been to England for a couple of years but she couldn't throw much light on places like Wimbledon or Belle Vue.

I knew Wimbledon was in London, which was assumed to be the centre of the universe. I knew most speedway riders came from England, that Kiwis and Australians who went there to race were part of the scenery, and apart from Sweden there appeared to be very few other countries involved.

My sources of information were not school textbooks, but from reading *Speedway Star and Ice News* which Frank Ridding lent me each week. That, and gossip around the stands and terraces at Aranui when an exotic overseas star breezed in to town – from Norman Parker through Ken McKinlay to Ove Fundin, who as the newly-crowned world champion appeared in Christchurch just a few weeks before we set off to England.

Full of excitement and still on a high after our wedding, we took the ferry from Lyttelton to Wellington for our honeymoon. We stayed with Raye's cousin Leslie and her husband Ralph at Karori near Wellington.

After our short stop there, we boarded the New Zealand Shipping Line's *Rangitoto* for our trip to England. The 22,000-ton liner carried 460 passengers, and it took more than a month to circle the ocean via Pitcairn Island, Panama and Curaçao.

KEEP TURNING LEFT – England star Ron How imparts valuable advice at the 1957 Wimbledon press and practice day

48 – Ivan Mauger

Because our tickets had been booked at different times, we had to make do with separate cabins, and that apart, we had plenty of entertainment on board. But we were both impatient to get to England for the real adventure to begin.

The voyage completed, at last we got off the boat, grabbed our belongings and found the train into London. We knew nothing and had little idea of what to expect. Our first impression of England was spotting row after row of identical terraced houses, all with chimneys. We had never seen a double decker bus and didn't know what it was!

Nowadays young kids jet into Heathrow and they know what to expect because hardly a night goes by when there's not a shot of London on the TV, a movie or an English show. They know all about England from five years of age. There's not the same mystique.

The weather was much colder than we expected as it was early spring but we did not let it concern us, then or in all the time we lived in England. We were there for speedway and the weather was not a problem to us at all.

Soon enough we had to fit in the compulsory sightseeing, doing the tourist things like watching the pigeons in Trafalgar Square, and walking round Piccadilly Circus and Oxford Street.

For a couple of nights we stayed in a £1.50 per night guest house Raye's brother and his wife had booked for us. They were the only people in England who knew or cared that we were there.

Of course, Wimbledon was the speedway club everybody knew, because of the others who had been there, and all of that dated back to when Norman Parker – the Dons captain – came out to skipper the Canterbury team each year. He was responsible for Ronnie Moore going there, and Barry Briggs and later Geoff Mardon also wore the famous red breastplate with its gold star.

So if you were a kid going from Christchurch there was only one place to head to, and that's what I had in my mind. I did not know Briggo although I had made it my business to get to know Ronnie the year before and even got to race him a few times.

But unlike the times over the past 40 years when I have recommended and made introductions for scores of New Zealanders, Aussies, Americans and Europeans and connected them to British clubs, none of the Christchurch Wimbledon riders had anything to do with me going to the Dons.

Within a day or two of our arrival Raye and I found the way to Wimbledon by tube train and walked the mile and a half from the station to the stadium, which in actual fact is in Garrett Lane, although it always has been known as Plough Lane. It was an impressive sight.

The Will To Win – 49

The stadium opened in 1928 in time for the great speedway boom in England, and was equally if not even more famed for greyhound racing. The speedway circuit was separated from the viewing area by the dog track. An 8,000-capacity glass-fronted grandstand ran along one side, housing a restaurant and other facilities, and there were covered stands and amenities virtually all the way round the stadium.

When the decision was taken to book tickets to England, it was on the basis that I would fund the trip myself, and take such steps as necessary to get myself fixed up with a team.

I had heard, read and knew about Wimbledon and Ronnie Greene, the legendary promoter. Ronnie Greene had not heard, read or as far as I am aware known anything about Ivan Mauger until I knocked on his office door.

I introduced myself to Mr Greene, told him I was there to be a speedway rider but I needed a job. He gave me a job at the track there and then and took me to the pits where I met Alan McFarlane (always known simply as Mac) and told me to report for work on the following Monday.

I was also instructed to present myself at the speedway press and practice day so he could see how I measured up. The first phase of the learning curve was about to begin.

It never was my ambition at Aranui to be king of the kids. I didn't want to be an also-ran at Wimbledon, either. It was obvious there were stepping stones to be negotiated, but make no mistake, I wanted to be like Ronnie Moore.

And Ronnie Greene wanted me to be like Ronnie, too. His ambition was to establish the Dons as the outstanding club in speedway. Already they had won the National League three times in a row. But suddenly there were huge shoes to be filled when Ronnie decided to quit speedway and go car racing.

Briggo was shaping as a world championship contender. Also on the books were Ron How, Cyril Brine, Cyril Maidment, and an improving Bob Andrews.

But to be fair, two or three of those guys were at a developmental stage, rather than the finished article they were to become in future seasons.

There was a further challenge for Wimbledon and the other big teams. All had to cut their cloth according to a new set-up in which the First and Second Division members of the previous year amalgamated into one 11-team league.

All things considered, the arrival of another ready-made talent would have been the answer to any promoter's dream and Ronnie Greene perhaps was entitled to dream – Moore, Briggs … and then Mauger. That would have had a neat continuity about it.

If you believe half of what you read as having come from the mouths of some speedway promoters, that's probably too much. Mr Greene, though, was one of the legendary figures, a big, imposing man physically and with his force of character. And when he told the speedway press and the fans that the new kid from Christchurch was shaping up to be another Moore or Briggs, they too would have wanted to take notice and believe it.

I wanted to believe it myself, not stopping to consider that when Ronnie had arrived in 1950, bursting with talent and potential, he also had his dad and Norman Parker to look out for him. When Briggo came bouncing along two years later, Ronnie and Trevor Redmond were on the spot to point him in the right direction.

The other big difference was that both of them could ride a bit when they turned up at Plough Lane. I was full of confidence, full of ambition and maybe a bit full of myself, especially after the publicity blitz.

It was a week before Easter as Alf Weedon, for years one of the sport's most famous photographers, clicked and chattered away. Pictures on the

READY FOR ACTION – Wimbledon Dons before taking on Sparta Wrocław, April 19, 1957. Back row, left to right: Ronnie Greene (promoter), Ron How, Cyril Maidment, Ivan Mauger, Gerry King, Cyril Brine, Ted Brine (team manager). Front: Bobby Croombs, Barry Briggs, Gerald Jackson.

bike, off the bike, on the track, with Raye, at the stadium entrance, it was heady stuff. Even more so when we picked up the *Evening News* the next day and saw ourselves presented as the teenage kids who had travelled half way round the world in search of sporting fame and fortune.

It was all rather overwhelming. The greatest shock was seeing how fast everybody was as they raced around the track. I got to England and saw those guys riding round full throttle, going faster than I'd ever thought. I'd always imagined Ronnie Moore was the only one who did that. I couldn't believe it, and had completely underestimated the standard, still less realising that all the best riders were concentrated in a handful of teams.

I was not the only junior on parade, though. Ronnie Greene handed out a team race jacket – which I had coveted ever since seeing Ronnie Moore wearing one back at Aranui – to Gerry King, Bobby Croombs and myself.

The vests were supposed to be for publicity purposes only – but I never gave mine back and I still have it to this day. Mr Greene asked me for it a few times, but I always gave him a smart answer until the stage when he stopped asking.

Alf Weedon, who is over 90 now, never fails to remind me that he took the first photos of me in England. We often meet up with Gerry King at the World Riders Association dinners and occasionally Bobby Croombs. It is always nice to talk to them about our novice days at Wimbledon. Gerry's son Dave was later to make the King silencers which came to be used in every speedway country.

Even though my first laps had not been anything to write home about, Mr Greene told me I would be in the Wimbledon team to face Sparta Wrocław, a Polish touring side, in the first home match of the season on Good Friday.

Against opposition which turned out to be of pretty ordinary standard, I managed one point from two rides as Wimbledon cantered to a 66-30 victory. But it was not enough to earn me a place in the first official team fixture at Rayleigh in the Britannia Shield.

Instead for my next opportunity I had to drive to Liverpool where Reg Duval was putting on a challenge match against Oxford and I filled in for the Cheetahs, again scoring one point.

After that, it was a case of hoping there might be a second half race for me on Monday nights. Other novices and juniors hanging around with a similar hope were Gil Goldfinch, Ken Vale, Tommy Sweetman and Ernie Baker, who also used to do the fuel and oil for Briggo.

Just two more senior appearances came my way that season, at home to Norwich in the Britannia Shield where I failed to trouble the scorers, and a National League visit to Ipswich which produced one third place.

52 – Ivan Mauger

I was spending each day at the stadium, working on the track or in the workshop, earning £7 a week and loving it. By now we had a small second floor bed sitter in Fulham Road – rent was £2 a week.

I used to leave home at 5.30am to be at the stadium by 8am. I would run about three or four miles, crossing Putney Bridge on my way to the tube station. The fare to Wimbledon was cheaper if you started the journey south of the Thames and we had no money to spare.

Then I would run another couple of miles to the track. So I saved money and got in some early morning training.

Almost all the people we met in those first few weeks were very friendly towards us, possibly because we were very young – and married.

After a few weeks we got a little flat at 44 Hayden Park Road, less than a mile from Plough Lane. The first evening I came home from the stadium Raye was nowhere to be seen but Jimmy Hone, who lived five doors down, told me she was in his parents' house having a cup of tea.

Jimmy was riding his cycle speedway bike in figure eights and had recognised me from the Wimbledon second halves – the first person to do so. That moment was the start of what turned out to be a lifelong friendship with the Hone family.

Jimmy is my oldest friend in England and we are more like brothers than just good friends. When we make trips to England we usually stay with Jimmy and his wife Marilyn. They have been over to stay with us on the Gold Coast.

Jimmy's mum and dad Sid and Renee Hone became like second parents to Raye and me. They lived in one of the prefabs put up after the war to house families. They were moved in the early 1980s about a mile or so away to Havelock Road.

The Hones were great friends of all our family in later years and we used to visit them often. When I came to ride at Plough Lane I used to call in and see them. Sometimes I had Jim Airey with me and lots of times I had Ole Olsen with me. They also became firm friends of the Hones.

Sid and Renee came up to spend Christmas with us several times in the 1970s and early 1980s. Sid passed away in 1991 and Renee was still going strong at Havelock Road until she died in April, aged 95.

Wimbledon's race night was Monday, and I had several jobs that had to be done that day. Ronnie Greene was very pedantic and insisted that everything looked good on the night. Every Monday Mac and I had to mow the centre green exactly the same as the Wimbledon tennis courts and the soccer pitch at Wembley.

Another job was to blacken the tyres on the tractor so it was smart and there always was weeding the tulip beds at each end on the infield. There

TRAFALGAR SQUARE – feeding the pigeons at one of London's most famous landmarks

were red and yellow tulips in the shape of a star. I was not allowed to touch the tulips – the gardener did that. I was only allowed to take out any weeds and cut the edge so the flower beds looked just perfect.

There was an angle iron steel star with red and yellow bulbs and the electric socket was absolutely in the middle of the centre green. It was my responsibility to take it out and place it exactly in the centre and with the cross piece of the star precisely parallel to the glass enclosure.

I could hardly reach across and it was heavy. That's where I got my broad shoulders and upper body strength which helped me later on the 1000-metre grass and long tracks in Europe.

On Tuesday mornings we could practise on the track but we had to be off by 8am. I had the key and sometimes I was there going round between 5am and 7.30am. Then the bike had to go in the workshop.

At eight o'clock we had to take the tarpaulin sheets off the grass greyhound track. (I have hated greyhounds since then). We would unhook the speedway wire mesh fence and had to lay it on the ground as the dogs 'did not like the fence'.

Then I drove the tractor and Mac worked the grader. We had to change the grader blade for harrows as Mac would tear the track down to eight inches (20cm) every week. We would attach the blade and he would grade it from the outside and then from the inside back to the outside. After a day's harrowing and grading we had to water the track to put a sort of crust on the top so dust would not blow on to the greyhound track.

(Of course if it was 2010 there would be no need for the sheets as there is no dirt on the tracks now!)

The rest of the week some of my duties included sweeping out the pits and dressing room, then hosing them down and doing the same with the showers and toilets. I had to clean the workshops for Ted Brine, who was the mechanic and team manager, and Bert Dixon, the frame builder.

Every Wednesday Ronnie Greene did his inspection with Mac and myself and everything had to be right. Mostly he was satisfied but he was such a detail man. I learned from his example how to be the same and that experience helped me in later years as I always had a system for my bikes and equipment when racing.

Working on the track was a good learning experience too. I got to know about tracks from the surface down to eight inches below. That helped when I was racing as I understood all circuits and conditions, knew which had been prepared as Mac used to do and those not prepared to that standard.

When other riders stood around and moaned about track conditions I said to myself it was there to be ridden and I got on with it. I had a lot of success at places most of my rivals did not like.

The experience I got from working with Mac helped me win the wettest World Final in history at Gothenburg 20 years later. While most of the guys wanted it rained off I knew the Swedes were going to hold it come hell or high water and could see that the track was not prepared to drain the water off much.

A lot of the riders had a meeting about the conditions. I did not attend and told my mechanics to prepare for a wet one. My guys got extra helmets, goggles, gloves, boots and everything needed out of my big IVECO transporter and got organised for the conditions. I had fresh boots, gloves, helmet and goggles for every race so I was well able to deal with the rain. In my victory speech I thanked Mac for the experience all those years before.

You can't put a price on a good grounding. Cleaning out the pits I learned that someone has to do it – the same with the dressing rooms – and later on I never complained if the pits were not as tidy as I wanted. I simply cleaned my area myself – that's why I always had a big brush with me at tracks where the pits were not cleaned to my satisfaction.

Mac and I usually did not work on Thursday afternoons or Fridays and Saturdays but I spent hours in the workshop helping Ted Brine to clean bikes and engine parts. After a while I helped him with menial jobs on the engines

The Will To Win – 55

and later a lot more on the team members' bikes and motors, although they never knew that.

Ted taught me how to strip and rebuild my Jap engine and used to give me parts he had taken out of his brother Cyril's or Ron How's. Even this was not enough for me. Many's the time the gatekeeper at the stadium had to chase Jimmy Hone and myself out of the place as we were burning the midnight oil working on bikes.

Bert Dixon took pity on me and made me a complete frame and I only had to buy the steel tube from a place in Wandsworth, the next district from Wimbledon. I got to know those people as I went there often to get steel tubing for Bert so they let me have mine very cheap. That was the cheapest frame I ever had until I became a Jawa factory rider in 1969 and started getting them for nothing.

I got to know London very well as Ted used to give me his little van to go to Alec Jackson's, the main Jap dealer in Harrow Road, Harrow, to get parts so he could keep working on engines.

Ted also had me going to Tottenham – to Victor Martin's to get clutch parts and other bits for different bikes and the J.A. Prestwich factory where they made the Jap engines.

At the factory I saw engines from the foundry, to the machining, to the end product being completed. That was another experience money could never buy.

The Australian riders Jack Biggs, Ray Cresp and others had workshops behind Victor Martin's so I always hung around for a while with them looking at what they were doing. I also learned a few things not to do!

That's why I still know my way around London to this day. I used to love to go to those places and collect bits for Ted and Bert. I started to go different ways just to see where I would end up, another reason I learned all about London. If Ted or Bert said I had been a long time I always told them I got lost!

It was all very educational and exciting but the opportunities to ride were few and far between. Even getting second half bookings was a struggle. The big guns seemed like a race apart although the presentation was nothing like it was to become in later years.

This was an era when the choice of leathers was like that for Henry Ford's cars. You could have any colour you wanted as long as it was black. It was even before racy extroverts like Mike Broadbanks and Nigel Boocock shocked everybody in speedway with their red and blue leathers.

Of the Wimbledon riders in my first year Ron How and Cyril Brine were always very helpful. Cyril Maidment was too. He drove a laundry truck and

56 – Ivan Mauger

was frequently in the workshop working on his equipment. I often cleaned his bike for him and got to know him very well.

Riding in the second half at Plough Lane on the second Monday in July, I had an accident and suffered concussion. That meant a couple of nights in hospital under observation which would have done Raye no good as she was due to give birth at any time.

Briggo popped in to see me and then he came back the next morning to say his wife June and her mum Queenie had taken Raye to St Stephen's Hospital in Fulham Road to have the baby. I told Barry to get my clothes, got dressed and left the hospital without telling anyone and he took me round to see Raye.

Julie had been born around 11am and I had missed it all.

I was very conscious of my new-found responsibilities but making ends meet was difficult. Within six weeks, Raye went out to earn a few extra pounds, initially leaving Julie either with the Hones or Mrs Walker, who lived across the road from us. Finally Raye's doctor found a woman to look after Julie in a child-minding centre.

One treat for both of us was going with the Hones to watch a World Final for the first time, a huge experience. But I hadn't come all this way to be a spectator. The problem was that apart from the National League tracks, the only other speedway action was in the Southern Area League, where the standard was quite a bit lower.

Aldershot booked me for a couple of individual meetings, in which I scored three points in the Whitsun Trophy and then six in the June Cup. Seven points in Eastbourne's Championship of Sussex was my best for the year, and there were three matches for Rye House in the SAL.

Rides at Plough Lane continued to be extremely limited. In 15 starts there were four race wins and the season ended with a Junior Cup event in which I scored a single point.

In terms of quantity and quality, the highlight of the year was being invited by veteran rider and entrepreneur Phil Bishop to join a troupe of riders for a four-meeting Dutch Golden Helmet trip, my first experience on the continent. In a week I got more rides, and more points, than in the sum total of my Wimbledon appearances – seven at Hengelo, five in Amsterdam, another seven at Tilburg and four at Sleen.

It was a great opportunity, my first 'international' exposure and whetted my appetite to sample new places and experiences.

One unexpected diversion was cycle speedway, which was going strong. I also still have my South London Rangers cycle speedway jacket. I rode for them in 1957 and again in 1958 whenever I didn't have a Sunday afternoon meeting.

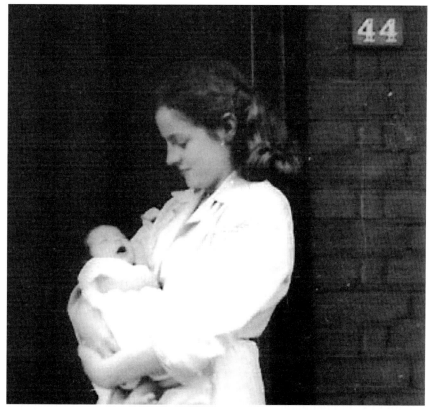

NEW MUM – Raye with Julie outside 44 Hayden Park Road, Wimbledon

In the winter of 1957–58 I got a job as a van driver's mate with the Royal Arsenal Co-op Society in Tooting Bec and went to every corner of London delivering groceries to all their shops.

I had to catch the bus at 5.45am because we started at 6.15am. In those days, before London banned coal fires, there was so much fog or smog so early in the morning it was difficult to find your way. But the job certainly helped me to consolidate my knowledge of the capital.

Raye and I survived our first English winter but it wasn't that much of a big deal. We were used to cold conditions in Christchurch. But with the start of speedway coming round again, I was going to have to take a pay cut and it quickly became evident we were running out of funds, especially with an extra mouth to feed.

We came to the conclusion it would be better for Raye to take Julie back to Christchurch, and for me to stay behind and concentrate all my efforts on making some headway in the 1958 season before my own return to New Zealand. We had to borrow from our parents to help her get home.

58 – Ivan Mauger

Almost a year earlier we arrived to start the great adventure. Now I was watching my wife and baby board the *Rangitoto* at Tilbury to undertake the return journey to New Zealand.

This was a crucial moment not just for my career, but in our life. We had no idea what the future held, no certainty that my second year in England was going to be any more rewarding than the first, no guarantees as to how any of us would cope with a lengthy separation.

What made it worse was the fact it took hours at the dockside to process the passengers – not like the speed of international travel today – and the longer it went, the more upsetting it was.

We were there from early in the morning, with passengers getting on the boat and everybody finding out where the cabins were and so forth. Then came an announcement over the tannoy for all non-passengers to leave the ship.

Even then those who were going would stand at the ship's rail and relatives and friends would be standing on the dock, watching and waving. Finally, the boat slipped its mooring and sailed slowly down the Thames.

I just stood there crying, watching the boat until it sailed out of view. I have never forgotten the feeling, standing there for so long alone with my thoughts. But when the *Rangitoto* was out of sight, I got into my little £15 Ford Thames van and drove back to the flat.

That was when I vowed to dedicate myself to doing whatever it took to become world champion, and that I would never again be in the same position. I said to myself 100 times over 'I'm not going to be in this position next time we come back to England'.

The 1958 season turned out to be another hard road but whenever I asked myself 'what am I doing all this for' I could also answer myself … to be a world champion.

I was not good enough to get into the Wimbledon team in 1957 but I was in 1958. It didn't work out like that, though. With tracks closing, they had a team full of stars, with no points limit those days to curb their success. Midway through the season, Ronnie Moore came back after his flirtation with car racing. The Dons were winning home and away.

I still worked with Mac at the track and those two seasons taught me so much about speedway and what it took to be a professional rider. At last I started to beat several of the team guys in the second half. It was nothing to the promoter but it was everything to me. Unfortunately I don't think Ronnie Greene was even watching. I guess he thought why change a winning team.

My only appearances in the Dons colours in 1958 were in home and away National Trophy matches against Norwich at the end of June. That and 15 second half rides – including seven wins – was the extent of Wimbledon's investment in my development, although it would have been a handful more but for a transport strike which forced the track to close for six weeks in mid-season.

The best tribute I can give to Ronnie Greene is that he was a promoter in every sense of the word, he had very high standards and a very strong personality. There are many great memories and the experience from that period in my career was most certainly a character and determination building time.

To stay in touch with things, if I had the chance to go to an away track with Briggo and Ronnie Moore, Mac would always let me provided I came in early next day to catch up

Ted Brine continued to help out, and even gave me parts he took out of Ronnie's engine. The star guys did not need them again but they were gold to a kid with no money, especially any bit Ronnie had used.

Using those parts always gave me confidence and Charlie Dugard, the Eastbourne promoter, was the man who rescued the season for me. He booked me in for a series of individual meetings on Sunday afternoons, gave

ARLINGTON – Sid Hone with Ivan in the pits and (below) victory in the Eastbourne Silver Helmet, 1958

PHIL'S GUYS – Dutch Golden Helmet contestants (back, left to right) Bertil Carlsson, Noel and Maurie Conway, Gil Goldfinch, Colin Gooddy (front) Bernt Nilsson, Ivan, Pat McKenzie

me every encouragement, and then also included me in team matches at Arlington.

My scores started to become quite respectable until on July 20 I scored my first four-ride maximum in a challenge match against California. Including that red-letter day, I managed to finish the season with double-figure scores in six successive meetings, including a paid maximum against Rye House and another full house which brought me the Supporters Trophy.

Sid and Renee Hone used to come to Eastbourne with me every second Sunday and a lot of people there thought they were my mum and dad. Sid always helped in the pits. Renee used to stand on the mound near the pits cheering for me.

As in the previous year, a high point was travelling out to ride in Phil Bishop's troupe at the Dutch Golden Helmet series in August. It was an exciting departure from normal routine but a bit too eventful as things turned out.

I blew my motor in the first meeting at Den Bosch, the next one at Amsterdam was washed out and after borrowing one of Phil's engines at Tilburg I had a coming together with Ray Harris and broke a couple of ribs. It was my first injury of any consequence, and there still is an indentation on the front of my left side.

There was no more racing for me that day, and I had to pull out of the Hengelo meeting after taking just one ride. When we went back to

The Will To Win – 61

Amsterdam for the last one in the series things were a lot better as my eight-point return suggests.

After the boat deposited us at Felixstowe on the way home, I had a stop-off in Ipswich. One of the guys said Nigel Boocock had a motor to sell. It was my first meeting with Booey and we quickly struck a deal.

I just wanted to soak up every opportunity. As the season went on, my confidence grew. More rides, and the chance to earn some money to top up my stadium wages, meant things were looking up.

The legend built up and circulated that I was a failure in England first time round but I don't buy that. Today, if an 18-year-old comes over and gets a few maximums in the second tier of racing, almost everybody would say he was a wonder kid with absolutely exceptional talent.

For me it was all about learning the trade. Working at Wimbledon Stadium was the best apprenticeship a young speedway rider could wish for. I never looked at it as going to work. I loved being part of the stadium and the speedway, absorbed so much and got to know every corner of London.

A jockey who has won the Grand National or the Derby has not always been a champion. He will have had to do an apprenticeship, cleaning out stables, washing down the horses and all the menial jobs that go with it. He had to learn all about the horses before he got to ride them in races. His first rides would have been training them before daybreak seven days a week.

Mind you, horse racing has been a flourishing industry for centuries. I wasn't so sure about the long-term future of speedway when I went back to New Zealand at the end of the 1958 season. At that stage it looked to be on the slippery slope.

And I didn't really know how things would be when I got back to Christchurch. Very few people had telephones in those days. My mum and dad had a phone but I couldn't afford to make calls to New Zealand and Raye couldn't make one to England.

When she got back she stayed with her parents. Her mother looked after Julie while Raye found work to pay back the money which had been loaned to help pay for their return trip.

From March until November we only wrote letters, just about every day. Not one single, solitary time between her leaving and me getting back did we speak to each other.

When I did get back after the long boat trip, there was a lot of catching up to do. We needed to take stock of where we were in our lives. There were plans to be made, and we had to decide what constituted a 'normal' life in our case. Most immediately, I had to start work to bring in some money.

And then on Saturday nights, there was Aranui. Life, it seemed, had come almost full circle.

CHAMPIONS ALL – with Jack Young and sprintcar ace Bob Tattersall (centre) at Sydney Showground, 1962

MASTER AND PUPIL – keeping Youngie company into the first corner at Rowley Park, Adelaide

Heat 4

BACK TO THE FUTURE

GOING back to New Zealand after a couple of seasons in England was another reality check.

At the end of the 1958 season I returned to Christchurch fearing for the sport of speedway and far from convinced about my future in it.

From the post-war years when crowds came flocking in, things had taken a sharp downward turn, especially in the UK. Tracks were closing, taxes biting, and people were finding new forms of entertainment.

The National League was shedding teams every year and opportunities seemed to be diminishing at an alarming rate.

On the one hand I was looking forward to being reunited with Raye and Julie, excited by the prospect of making plans for our future, happy to see familiar faces and places, family and friends.

On the other there was the very real prospect that a career path which had occupied my thoughts for several years might end up as an increasingly slippery slide into oblivion.

An immediate priority was to make sure Raye and I had enough to live on. She had been staying with her parents at Harewood* and left Julie with her mum so she could go out to work – first at Christchurch Hospital, where she got the sack as her polio right foot would not let her walk fast enough down the long corridors.

Later she got a job in the sewing department of a subsidiary of Lane Walker Rudkin. That paid around £11 a week and meant it was possible to save a reasonable amount.

When I got back to Christchurch I generated some extra cash by selling some equipment. Before I left in the September of 1958 I had bought three bikes and a couple of Jap engines from Eastbourne and Wimbledon riders and sold them for quite a profit to riders at Aranui.

To keep our expenses down I moved in at Raye's folks and worked as a die caster with WL Brown and Co, a foundry in Southwark Street in the middle of town. The owner was Wilf Brown, a top beach racer in New Zealand and a great speedway enthusiast whose sons Allan and Max later went to England to ride.

One of Wilf's mates and former rivals was Burt Munro, a one-time farm boy from Invercargill who was to break the world land speed record for a

---

* The Telfers moved from New Brighton to Richmond, and then to Harewood to be closer to Raye's father's work at Christchurch airport.

motorcycle on Bonneville Flats in Utah in 1967 and was the subject of a 2005 movie *The World's Fastest Indian* starring Anthony Hopkins.

Burt used to come up to the foundry, arriving with boxes of old tractor and truck pistons to make his own moulds and then fashion pistons for his bikes. Wilf let him use the lathes and milling machines to work on and after a couple weeks he would go back down to Invercargill with four or five sets of pistons.

He worked at night when the foundry was quiet for a few hours, and slept for much of the day on the mezzanine floor on a little camp bed from the war disposal shop. Burt had a little primus stove to heat his baked beans and spaghetti, and a long piece of wire that he fashioned into a fork to make his toast near the furnace when it was on.

A wizard with machinery, he often picked up discarded bits of iron and steel and spent hours fashioning them into parts. One day Wilf had a block of steel which was of no use to anybody. Burt took a week or so on the milling machine and without any patterns or drawings made a set of cam followers. It was amazing.

Later Ronnie Moore also worked at the business on and off for many years. He too was a clever engineer and did a lot of experimental stuff for Wilf. Although Ronnie has been 'retired' for several years the new boss from time to time calls him in to solve any tricky machining problem.

Working as a die caster was tough but it kept the cashflow going and there was the opportunity to earn a few extra pounds racing on Saturday nights. Even at Aranui, though, speedway was not so clever. In 10 years since the circuit opened in what was virtually rural surroundings, the Christchurch urban sprawl had crept ever closer. Now the planners were about to take charge of the site for a future development.

My own form on the track was good, showing just how much quicker and more confident I had become in the year and a half away. It was not unusual for me to go through the programme unbeaten, and when far more experienced riders including Briggo, Geoff Mardon and Brian McKeown were there I still managed to give a decent account of myself.

Finishing as runner-up to Barry in the New Zealand championship at Rotorua on New Year's Day 1959 was another big feather in my cap. A decent field was assembled at the A and P Showgrounds for the occasion, and to finish ahead of everybody except for the reigning two-time world champion was something special for a 19-year-old.

Another reason for recalling that meeting was our exciting journey up from Christchurch. We left Julie with my mum and Raye and I were riding up on a 500cc 5H Triumph. I had sent my bike by train with my kit bag and tool box earlier in the week.

ROAD TO ROTORUA – Barry Briggs in his DKW stops to pick up Raye on the way to the 1959 New Zealand titles

Briggo drove in his DKW car with his bike in the boot and when he caught us up just outside Wellington he stopped and said he thought it was too much for Raye to have to travel all the way as my pillion passenger. He promptly directed her to ride the rest of the journey in his car and ordered his 14-year-old brother Wayne – who rode in the UK from 1961–71 and now lives in Spain – to jump up behind me.

The bike was not going too well by the time we got to Palmerston North. But Briggo knew Syd Jensen, several times a New Zealand representative at the Isle of Man TT races, who had a motorcycle shop in the town.

As Syd did not have time to look at the bike straight away, Wayne and I piled in alongside Briggo and Raye, eventually arriving in Rotorua in varying degrees of discomfort and tiredness.

The president of the Rotorua Motorcycle Club had a New Year's Eve party to which everybody who was anybody was invited. Showing the sort of attitude which some people thought was cocky but I always considered to be common sense, we skipped the party and were tucked up in bed by 10pm.

Come the following afternoon I was well on top of the job and very well pleased to be second and best of the rest after Briggo.

Len Jelaca was third and among those who finished further down the field were Bruce Abernethy and Maury Dunn – both of whom had previously won the title – Bryce Subritzky, Goog Allan and Graham Coombes, who was preparing to go to Belle Vue.

In an Aranui season which already had a cloud hanging over it, there was the additional tragedy of a fatal accident in which the very popular Earl Wilde was killed in a midget car crash. Previously Earl was the sidecar king at Aranui.

On a bleak evening on April 11, 1959, the track staged its final meeting. Even with Briggo and Mardon headlining the solos – neither of them at that stage ready to return to England, although both were to do so later – it was a disappointing night in front of a below-average crowd.

It was not the way anybody would have wished a decade of excitement to finish. And within days work was under way to dismantle stands and buildings to prepare the site for its transformation into a construction site.

There was more to think about as Raye was expecting again and we were saving hard to raise the deposit on our first home in Rocking Horse Road, South Brighton. We always wanted to live near the water and from the first time I met Raye her parents had a house opposite the beach, so we looked in that area and found a wooden bungalow we liked and could just afford.

With no further speedway income in prospect for a while, I went back to Lane Walker Rudkin to work on the night shift. After finishing at the foundry at 5pm there was an hour's break before starting my stint in the nylon stocking process plant back at Lane Walker Rudkin. For a few months I worked from 8am until two in the morning

Rocking Horse Road runs through the Spit, a long finger of bone-dry sand between the ocean and the estuary. Originally it was just a sandy track about a mile and a half long with some baches (wealthy people's beach holiday homes). But when we bought it had a really nice wide tar sealed road, although without footpaths on either side – they came later.

The house was about five or six years old and had two extra bedrooms added a year or so before we bought it. It had quite a big garage at the end of the driveway but no fences at all and also no front lawn. We had to do all that ourselves.

Across the road you could walk through the sandhills on to the beach and out the back a couple of hundred yards away was the estuary. When the tide went out it left a huge area of flat sand and that is where I'd had my first ride on a speedway bike. It was handy to have a practice track only a few moments from our back door.

The total cost of the house was £2,750 including the agent's fees. We had saved £750 so we only had a mortgage of £2,000 which Dad suggested we pay off on a 10-year loan. As we were under age, we had to get a court order to buy our first house.

I did those two jobs so we could save up for the furniture including a bedroom suite, kitchen table and chairs. We spent weekends there getting things in order and our parents helped us out with pots and pans, kettles, cups, knives and forks.

Relatives also dug out some old furniture including some antiques, one of which was a wind-up His Master's Voice gramophone and some long-playing records. Along with this we had an old radio and some nights when

Julie was asleep Raye would sit out in the garage and we would listen to the serials like *Dick Barton Special Agent* and *Dad and Dave* while I worked on my bike.

We occasionally grabbed a few hours of leisure time, visiting parents or going for a picnic with our friends. Most of the time they came to us and at weekends the place was never empty. For once speedway was not the only thing in our lives. Those dreams, while not extinguished, were pretty much on hold.

Suddenly, life was turned upside down when my father died on May 16, 1959. He had been ill for many years with emphysema and had a collapsed lung as a result. But there is no way when something like that happens that it is anything other than a shock.

I was only 19 and it is a great regret he never saw my success in later years. He was there when I was struggling and in letters to England in 1957–58 he was always encouraging. That didn't stop him from urging me to remain in New Zealand when I got back there.

Because of his poor health he never got to do all the things many fathers like to do with their kids, but he taught us a great deal. From an early age, my brother Trev and I were advised by Dad never to buy anything 'unless you can afford to pay cash for it'. That message has stuck with us all our lives.

One 'investment' which didn't really pay off was when I had a brief, unspectacular flirtation with a TQ (three quarter midget car) bought from Terry Kiesanowski, whose family had a market garden at Belfast, just outside Christchurch. The idea had appealed to me since Wimbledon started to have midget cars with Jap engines – Ronnie drove one for a while.

Trev and I took the TQ to Aranui several times but it would not start. When John Shaw, the local champion driver, looked at it he said the engine came out of Earl Wilde's sidecar and ran backwards. Earl had two Jap engines side by side and one had to run in reverse.

John came round a few days later and turned the diffy around and it started immediately. But I only ever got to drive it once, at a country meeting run by the Southbridge Motorcycle Club at Doyleston, a few miles out of Christchurch, before selling it.

There had been talk of a new speedway in Christchurch to replace Aranui, but as the months went by it became obvious nothing was going to happen for ages, probably years. I decided to test the water to see if any Australian promoters would give me a go and fired off several letters.

Aranui mates Ivan Crozier and Bernie Lagrosse had gone across to Melbourne and although they did not like it there, kept going until Kym Bonython, promoter at Adelaide's Rowley Park, gave them some rides.

They passed on the address of the record shop that Kym ran, and I wrote to him in August. I told him I did not have much money to spare and he would have to pay return boat fares for Raye, myself, Julie and the yet-to-be born new baby to get us over from Christchurch.

I also dropped in the name of Jack Young, who was the big star in Adelaide. Youngie would remember me as I had been with Ronnie and Barry several times to Coventry, where he was based in 1958, and other tracks.

When Kym wrote back, he said Jack did not know me. But Ivan and Bernie had put in a glowing character reference for me, the deal was on, and he told me to be there for the first meeting which was on Friday, November 6. It was great news and suddenly Kym Bonython was the best bloke in the world.

Apart from Charlie Dugard at Eastbourne, he was the first promoter who had taken more than a passing interest in me and agreed to pay me what was decent money for the time.

CHECK THIS – Kym Bonython, promoter at Rowley Park, Adelaide, and such a great career influence

The Will To Win – 69

Those days until a baby was born nobody knew if it was a girl or boy. Raye and I decided to name the new child Kym if it was a boy or Kim if it was a girl.

We made arrangements to rent out the house, with the payments due to come in more than enough to cover the mortgage. There was the considerable matter of leaving Raye to have the baby in Burwood Hospital, Christchurch – where I was born and then follow on to Australia as soon as possible.

I set off on the three-day boat trip from Wellington to Sydney and on November 1 Raye's eldest sister Margaret sent a telegram to say we had a son. I was still on cloud nine when I disembarked, and made my way to Sydney airport to fly to Adelaide.

There to meet me was one familiar face, that of Bernie Lagrosse, and another who was to become a huge influence in our lives. Kym Bonython was not your usual type of speedway promoter. He turned up on a Moto Guzzi motorcycle specially decked out in yellow, his favourite colour, rather than the Italian bikes' usual red.

Arrangements had been made for us at Mrs Smart's guest house on the corner of Randolph Street and Dew Street in Thebarton, where Ivan and Bernie were also staying along with Swedish rider Kai Forsberg and, later, his fellow countryman Roger Forsberg (no relation). Raye, together with Julie and Kym, were to follow at the end of the month, doing the same sea and air trip as I had done.

Adelaide had more in common with Christchurch than London had done, and we immediately felt at home there. It is the capital city of South Australia, with a lot of British influence evident even today.

William Light, who designed Adelaide, is often (but incorrectly) credited with having also designed Christchurch. It is a very well planned city with good beaches and, not too far away, even better wineries.

The Adelaide Hills and the Barossa Valley, where some of the world's best wine is produced, are always popular attractions.

It also happens to be the driest city in Australia, and the temperature in the summer months often hits the 100°-plus (40°C) mark and stays there for days or even weeks.

Not surprisingly, we spent as much free time as possible trying to escape the heatwaves and fortunately a nearby swimming pool was a perfect spot to cool down.

The heat was a huge contrast to anything we had experienced and bothered Kym more than anybody. After a couple of months we moved into a flat in Windsor Road, Kilkenny, but like Thebarton it was away from the beach and still very hot.

70 – Ivan Mauger

Fortunately we quickly dropped in to a lively social scene. Near neighbours and new friends included Joe and Frank Young, brothers of Jack who as the world champion back in 1951 and 1952 was still the biggest sporting name in town.

Joe and his wife Ruth were very popular because they had the first, and at the time only, television in their street. It was deserted outside in the evenings because they and most of the neighbours would be crowded round the little black and white set intently watching *Eliot Ness and the Untouchables*. The two children would be asleep in the next room.

By day there was always something for them to do – although the heat was a problem. Fortunately there always seemed to be some activity going on. Rowley Park was on Friday nights so Saturday and Sunday were play days. We tried our hand at watersports and were always up for a party or a picnic.

But the reason for being there was to ride speedway, earn some money, and, during the week, to top up the income with a truck driving job Kym Bonython had arranged with John Dring's, a delivery firm about a mile from our digs. Manager Fred Holyoake, who was in the Jazz Society in Adelaide with Kym, already had Ivan and Bernie on the books.

I had an S-type Bedford van and three or four days a week my route included picking up sugar from the Port Adelaide refineries and delivering it to the Arnott's biscuit factory. It was usual for the drivers to sneak delicious free samples of their famous Scotch biscuits to go with morning tea.

The white sugar bags were 70 pounds (32kg) but the raw sugar was 160 pounds (73kg), great training for future speedway riding, not to mention jumping up on the back of the truck 50 or more times a day. There was no need to go to the gym.

Most of the Dring's drivers including me dived into the harbour to cool off while we were waiting for our turn to load up.

Another regular drop was to the Hallett Brickworks where Jack Young worked as a maintenance engineer. I always tried to time my deliveries there for lunchtime so I could grab a chat with the great man although anybody less like a world champion would have been difficult to imagine. He was just one of the guys, wearing overalls and with an ever-present cigarette in the corner of his mouth.

The site close to the River Torrens was dominated by the historic Hoffman 'beehive' kiln, which operated at temperatures of 1100°C and turned out 180,000 bricks a week.

Friday nights at Rowley Park were a real show with a great atmosphere. Kym Bonython was a larger than life character, very much like Ronnie Greene in his attention to detail. All the mechanics in the pits had to have white overalls and the emphasis was on professionalism.

The Will To Win – 71

Kym wore a black and white cheesecutter cap so everyone would recognise who was in charge and he was the trouble shooter. That's where I got the idea for the black and white checks I had on my helmet from that season until I finished racing – and still do, courtesy of Bell Helmets, whenever I do demonstration rides.

To start with I had black and white check tape on my pudding basin helmet, and as soon as I got my first Bell open face helmet had them on the sides and back. Later I started to wear the full face and had the black and white checks all round.

The Bonython family is a big deal in Adelaide. Kym's father was Lord Mayor, and his grandfather owned the *Adelaide Advertiser* newspaper. It probably was not the background you would expect of the man who was to successfully promote Rowley Park speedway from 1952 to 1973.

Kym's great passions included art, jazz and motor sport. He had been a wartime bomber pilot, later owned galleries in Adelaide and Sydney, was at various times an author, broadcaster, dairy farmer, and above all an entrepreneur who loved to back his judgment by encouraging people he thought had talent, and that included me.

Famous Australian artists including Sidney Nolan, Brett Whiteley and Pro Hart benefited hugely from his encouragement when they were unknowns, and Barry Humphries – Dame Edna Everage – got one of his early career breaks when Bonython backed one of his shows.

He put the same drive and enthusiasm into his Friday night show as he did everything else. It was a good atmosphere in which to be racing and the Kiwi contingent enjoyed meeting new friends such as Jack Scott, Geoff Mudge and Rolf von dor Borch.

Plenty of even more accomplished and better-known riders also adorned Kym's programme, with Peter Craven, Ove Fundin, Ken McKinlay, Bob Andrews and Mike Broadbanks all coming in from Europe.

It was great experience for me to rub shoulders with them all, with varying degrees of success. The excitement generated by having the solo stars around also gave Jack Young a fresh lease of life.

He had come back from overseas at the same sort of time as I did and possibly also thinking that there was no great future in British speedway. But once he started mixing it with the boys his appetite returned and he decided to go back to Coventry for the 1960 season.

Youngie quickly became a great friend and mentor. Young riders can get lucky, be well advised, or left to their own devices. I was always super-keen to hear what people who had been there and done that had to impart. Of all those who helped me during the early stages of my career, Jack Young was by far the most influential.

72 – Ivan Mauger

He was a sensation when he went over to Edinburgh, won the world title in 1951 while still a Second Division rider, cost West Ham a then world record transfer fee of £3750 and claimed another world championship 12 months after his first.

In England, I had admired his polished, unhurried style of riding and tried to copy that and the style of Ronnie Moore who was another extremely smooth rider. Now he became a regular source of good advice, and the more he volunteered, the more I wanted to know and learn. He was enormously patient and generous with his wisdom, obviously more than happy to be able to play a part in helping a keen young hopeful advance his own career.

Most of that first season in Adelaide was positive, but unreliable machinery was a regular problem. There were so many races in which things went wrong, and it was very frustrating. The final straw came after Rowley Park had finished. The Australian long track championship was held at Easter at Port Pirie, 130 miles north of Adelaide.

I was leading by a huge margin in the final with only a quarter of a mile to go when my bike seized up. Instead of signing off with what would have been a morale-boosting win in an event which had a lot of prestige, I was left to curse my bad luck.

Kym Bonython must have been frustrated, too. He was always supportive in those early months, finding time to encourage me even though he had a million other things and people to deal with. And he gave me the best possible present by inviting me back for the following summer – on condition I got my equipment sorted out.

In the last few weeks of the season Jock Grierson, who used to ride in England, had been keeping an eye on my engines. Kym said he would provide me with a new motor for 1960–61 as long as Jock maintained and tuned it.

Although the money was to stay the same it was a great deal. That was the first time I had a brand new engine, and Fred Jolly, the local agent, offered to loan me a complete rolling chassis.

We went back to Rocking Horse Road for the winter months, re-acquainted ourselves with family and friends, and I resumed working at the foundry.

At the end of the previous October we had rented the house to a Dutch couple. They tidied up the garden at the back, planted vegetables and put the lawn in the front so it was very tidy when we came back – just as well, as I didn't have much time for gardening.

When the time came to go back to Adelaide, we rented it to Raye's sister Jean and her husband Lex.

HOT STUFF – Ivan (third), Ove Fundin (first), Aub Lawson (second) and Goog Allan (fourth) at the 1960-61 South Australian titles at Rowley Park

After sweltering through the first Adelaide trip we were grateful to Kym Bonython who found us a house in Esplanade Grange, right across from the beach and its cooling breezes and with a huge jetty opposite. This was to be our base for the next 18 months and we had brother Trevor and his wife Bernice with us for the second season.

They decided they wanted to have a bit of adventure and Trevor joined the Dring's workforce, while Bernice got an office job. I was still driving during the week and managed to work my deliveries so I could often pop in to spend time with Raye and watch the midday movie on the TV with her.

Winning races, learning the trade, and gathering as much experience and knowledge as possible was my big motivation. The second season at Rowley Park turned out to be much more successful than the first, with improved results and reliable bikes seemingly going hand in hand.

I was winning scratch races and handicap events, equalled Ken McKinlay's long-standing track record and the bikes kept going. Third place in the South Australian championships, behind Ove Fundin and Aub

Lawson, was an encouraging result at 21 and by January my form was good enough for me to be a back marker in the handicap races.

Given that critics in later years reckoned I was 'nothing but a gater' they should have seen me starting 240 yards back and passing people round Rowley Park.

In the later stages of my time there, Youngie was often 20 or 30 yards in front of me and others such as Jack Scott were in front of him.

I won most of those handicap races. It was a huge learning curve and education for me and taught me how to pass. It also provided the basics which served me very well quite a few times in my career.

Seeing Fundin riding on an ESO was an eye-opener. Fred Jolly was setting himself up to import the Czech bike and I was keen to have a go myself. But Fred insisted on keeping the ESO under wraps until the Port Pirie long track as he reckoned it would be a terrific advertisement if I could win it on the new machine.

When the eagerly-awaited day arrived it was like riding a flying machine. I sliced 11.4 seconds off Gerry Hussey's track record in my first heat race and was feeling full of confidence by the time the final came round.

NORTHERN EXPOSURE – with promoter Ted Price and Ken Cameron at Rocky Showgrounds, 1962

This time I was leading the field by half a lap at the midway stage and the clutch which was on a taper sheared off and hit me on the left leg in almost the same place as my Jap had seized the year before. For the second year running misfortune had robbed me of the Australian title.*

There was one long track win chalked up, though – in the South Australian 350cc championship riding a bike loaned by Laurie Jamieson

Shortly after the season ended, it was time to celebrate as Raye gave birth to our third child, Debbie, in Adelaide's Princess Margaret Hospital on

---

* The same thing happened twice in a 1973 world long track qualifying round. I won virtually all the long tracks in Europe that year so those clutch failures probably stopped me winning the world long track title three times in succession.

The Will To Win – 75

May 5, 1961. I stayed at home to look after Julie and Kym and then had a couple of drinks with Ivan Crozier to wet the newborn's head, so to speak.

We decided to stay in South Australia for the winter and it gave me an opportunity to try another form of racing. Scrambles (now known as motocross) events were popular, testing man and machine up hill and down dale, and I was keen to participate in the discipline.

Rolf von dor Borch, who I met on my first day in Adelaide and became my dope and oil man after his own racing ambitions were spoiled by a knee injury, was friendly with Bob Timms – who, when he wasn't working for Gestetner, dabbled in buying and selling motorcycles and fancied himself as a bit of an entrepreneur.

Bob loaned me a bike for half a dozen scramble meetings, usually within a 40 or 50-mile radius. My best result was to win the 1961 South Australian 350cc scrambles championship.

(I also rode in the South Australian motocross championship in October 1962 and won the 500cc title.)

It was a pleasant diversion and helped keep me fit as we waited for the next speedway season to begin. Kym Bonython was happy with everything and had invited me back on increased terms and Fred Jolly had promised me use of a new ESO engine for the 1961–62 season.

Before Rowley Park re-opened Ted Price, the promoter at Rockhampton, called to invite me to do four meetings in North Queensland in October. On successive Saturdays I raced at Rocky, Mackay, Rocky again and Townsville and achieved fair results considering I was on a borrowed Jap.

The first meeting was the Australian championship, revived for the first time since 1955. It was a huge occasion for Rockhampton, with a big crowd in despite rainy weather. Bob Sharp won the title when he steamed past me on his ESO, and I got second ahead of Keith Gurtner, the original 'little boy blue' so named because of the colour of his leathers.

It was seven days later I met Vic Paivenen from Finland, who was riding on the Mackay programme. We struck up an immediate friendship and Raye and I count Vic and his wife Daphne, who now live at Bribie Island north of Brisbane, among our oldest friends.

The following week I had some measure of revenge over Bob Sharp by beating him in the A grade final. Presenting the prizes that night was Rocky's most famous sporting son Rod Laver, who had won the Australian Open in 1960 and added the Wimbledon title in 1961 at the start of what was to be a stellar tennis career.

By now my own thoughts were again turning to the possibility of getting back on to the British scene. Any and all experience was part of building a case to present to British promoters. I made the return trip south via a team meeting at the Brisbane Exhibition Ground. Then it was back to Adelaide for their traditional season opener on the first weekend of November.

While my second season at Rowley Park had been highly successful, that third summer in Australia was even more of a breakthrough time. I was into it straight away, excited by the return after 18 months of Jack Young, and lining up alongside him and drop-in visitors Ronnie Moore and Briggo in the first meeting.

As the weeks went by I was gaining confidence on the new ESO, and rivaling Youngie for the top spot. We had some great tussles, and it was not long before he recognised I was no longer an anonymous wannabe.

Whenever I could work my driving delivery routes, I still would happen to drop in on Jack just as he was taking his lunch break at the brickworks. He had a great sense of humour, loved to talk and didn't seem at all bothered by the barrage of questions about wheelbases, seat heights, clutch springs, compression ratios and the rest.

He didn't even mind more of the same when we travelled together for interstate meetings. Often we were cooped up in the car for hours at a time as we headed off to Victoria or Sydney for meetings, and then turned round and drove all the way back

Those distances, some of them on dirt roads, didn't bother me at all. They were my chance to broaden my education. Youngie rode speedway in what was described as an armchair style; he was all about control. One of his lessons was to advise that sometimes 'slower is smarter', and a more conservative approach preserved motors and tyres.

I was still a brash young thing, and obviously amused him from time to time with my over-zealous efforts to pass at the wrong point of the track and lack of knowledge. He had a wealth of philosophy, strong mental powers and the ability to focus which had stamped him as one of the great early champions. I couldn't get enough.

An especially memorable moment was at Fred Tracey's speedway at Maribynong in January 1962, when I beat Jack in the Victorian championship. A few weeks later I was runner-up to Brian Collins in the NSW state titles at Sydney Showground.

On Easter Saturday, April 21, I made it at last, third time lucky, in the Australian long track championship. Five miles (eight kilometres) round Port Pirie is quite a journey at any time, and after the breakdowns of the two earlier visits, it was great to last the course and take the title, with Jack Scott second and Don Prettejohn third.

Those five laps were the slowest I had been at Port Pirie. That has been my philosophy ever since. I have only gone as fast as I needed to preserve the engine, chains, rear tyre and other parts of the bike.

THIRD TIME LUCKY – *victory at last in the 1962 Australian long track championship at Port Pirie*

All of these results were building into quite a substantial body of work. Still none of the promoters in either the National League or the emerging Provincial League seemed to care. Youngie had suggested Coventry as a possible destination and by now it was fairly common knowledge in England that I wanted another crack at it.

There was an alternative, which was to spend the southern winter racing in Rockhampton. The weather there was likely to be a lot better than an English summer, Ted Price wanted me as a resident rider on his show, and going back to Christchurch to work seemed nowhere near as attractive as a few months up north and racing.

On Easter Monday Raye and I and the three kids set off in our black Standard Vanguard car with speedway gear, family possessions and even a washing machine on the trailer.

We had no mod cons such as air conditioning, mainly drove from late afternoon to early morning to avoid the heat and spent the days under trees or in motor camps where they had a swimming pool. There was a big mattress in the back of the car so the kids could sleep at night.

The 2400 kilometre (1500 miles) journey across country took three days and when we arrived on the outskirts of Rockhampton, we decided to have a swim in the river and then find a place to have a shower and change our clothes. Everybody was having a great time until people on the bridge above called out to warn us of crocodiles. We were out of there faster than the time it takes to drop the clutch.

Rocky, though, was a very hospitable place with a country town feel. It is the beef capital of Australia, just above the Tropic of Capricorn and 400 miles (650 kilometres) north of Brisbane. The sun seemed to shine every day and we never had so much steak, pineapple and other fresh fruit.

In addition to his speedway interests Ted Price was a bookmaker and well known to almost everyone around town. He lived in North Rockhampton and found us a nice Queenslander house in Macaree Street, with an Olympic swimming pool nearby.

We were never short of entertainment for the kids, or social life. As in Adelaide, I drove a truck during the week when Ted did not run for a couple of months in the 'winter'.

Ted set up the job with the Capricornia Truck Company whose boss was a mate of his – and I did odd jobs here and there. But Saturday night was the one that counted.

The Queensland titles provided my first big win at the track. Keith Gurtner had won the title 10 times in 12 years so it was quite something to beat him. I had been having magneto problems and had to hold my breath in the later stages of the race in case anything went wrong.

The rest of the stay went smoothly enough, with occasional side trips to other northern tracks, usually requiring an early start with Ted, Goog Allan and Bill Bryden along for the trip.

The weather up there is good all year round, unlike the southern states where winter sometimes is not so great. Even so people in North Queensland

CHAMPION – Ivan with Goog Allan, Keith Gurtner and Ken Cameron after the 1962 Queensland titles

HOME GROUND – back on familiar territory at Rowley Park

didn't like to go out so much when the 'cold' nights – less than 20 degrees (68°F in the old money) – kick in.

When the time came to head south again, we left behind many good memories and with a new stockpile of friends. It was such a positive experience, and one which helped form our opinions about Queensland where eventually we were to settle.

On the return trip, we went via the coastal route, and took longer than expected because the car broke down. After it was fixed we took the kids to Currumbin Sanctuary and Surfers Paradise Ski Gardens (later Sea World), and called in on speedway friends Peter Dykes in Brisbane and Bob Sharp at Glen Haven, about 30 miles out of Sydney.

We raced one another in a meeting at Sydney Showground at which I met Jim Airey for the first time. But then we had to keep moving. After all our adventures, it was good to get back to Adelaide, which had come to be like our second home.

My aim was to put in another solid summer at Rowley Park, take advantage of any decent meetings interstate, and hopefully attract some attention from England at last.

A return trip to Rocky for the Australian championships in December 1962 produced another rostrum finish, but one place further back this time. Mike Broadbanks won the title and Keith Gurtner relegated me to third.

Others in the meeting included Goog Allan – who like me was hoping to go overseas – and Victorian Ken Cameron, who went to Edinburgh early

AUSSIE FAREWELL – with Ken McKinlay, Jack Scott and Jack Young before the South Australian titles at Rowley Park, February 1963

in 1963 and was responsible for me meeting Ronnie and Norrie Allan who had a considerable part to play in my life later on.

In Adelaide, I was winning regularly, my continuing friendly rivalry with Jack Young a big feature of the weekly entertainment. And still I hadn't pumped him dry for advice or information!

On our trips to distant tracks, he kept me fascinated with tales of how he had won his two world titles, and earned serious money. The years had made him wise but ultimately, perhaps, not as wealthy as he might have been, not that anything appeared to bother him.

Jack seemed contented enough, didn't hanker for the bright lights or the good old days. As long as he had his smokes, a few beers to sustain him, his ute and his boat to go fishing he was fine in his role as a typically laid-back Aussie.

However, seeing Youngie toiling away in a pretty mundane job at the brickworks, apparently with not too much to show at the end of his career, made me determined to be sensible with whatever money I might earn in the future.

I was still dreaming of getting back to England, still hopeful someone, somewhere, would answer one of my letters. Then Ivan Crozier, who had helped set me up with Kym Bonython, and later went over to ride for

The Will To Win – 81

Newcastle at the start of 1962, suggested I drop a line to see if Mike Parker would be interested in taking me there. At the same time he said he would put in a word for me.

I took his advice and sent the letter. I told Mike Parker I wanted to come to race again in England but would need to have accommodation, equipment, transport and return tickets provided so I could bring Raye and the three children. I said we were coming in any event as we had tickets booked on the *Castle Felice*.

After the heartache of 1958, that was always going to be the minimum requirement of any deal. If nobody came up with the right terms, then we were going to take the family back to New Zealand for the winter.

Christmas came and went and in January it was time to drive across to Melbourne for the defence of the Victorian championship. Youngie and I made the trip as usual and while we were away Raye received a telegram from Mike Parker in Manchester which said 'Terms agreed. Tickets paid for. Collect from Thomas Cook, Adelaide'.

She sent on the good news to Fred Tracey's place and it turned out to be a double celebration as I won the meeting, relegating Mike Broadbanks to second place.

I was buzzing all the way back to Adelaide. Youngie was as pleased for me as I was myself. And Raye being Raye immediately turned her thoughts as to what arrangements had to be made now we were going back to England instead of New Zealand. We had about three weeks to organise everything.

It meant cutting short the season at Rowley Park but Kym Bonython understood it was time for us to go. We had to take the train to Melbourne to catch the ship which was to stop in Auckland on the way. For the first leg of the journey we had my ESO in the goods van to deliver it to Mick Simmonds, who had agreed to buy the bike.

Our travelling party included Rolf von dor Borch. Originally he had been planning to come back with us to Christchurch for a holiday but when he heard of the change of plan he decided he would come to England as well and act as my mechanic for the season. That was the start of another of those lifelong associations which ended only when he died in January 2008.

When we docked in Auckland, there were loads of our relatives and friends who had come up from Christchurch to see us off.

It was like February 1957 all over again, but with a bigger cast, and expectations defined and clarified by our Australian experience.

JUST CHECKING – *where are those guys?*

Heat 5

ROUGH DIAMOND

AFTER Wimbledon and its plush stadium, such an eye-opener for a teenage arrival in 1957, Newcastle was something of a culture shock for a new signing in 1963.

The London we first encountered was still recovering from the damage caused by the war years but in our view it was the most exciting, vibrant city in the world.

Newcastle upon Tyne, my new speedway base, and Manchester, where we set up home, were traditionally industrial northern cities – only a couple of hundred miles or so from London but they might as well have been light years removed.

Brough Park had history. It was one of the first tracks to operate and the incomparable Johnnie Hoskins ran the place before and after the war. However, it always had been basic rather than beautiful, a bit like the city itself which for years had a reputation as being hard-edged and predominantly working class.

At first sight it seemed a grey, unforgiving sort of place and bear in mind during 1957 and 1958 I rarely travelled further north than Coventry!

The north-east of England people, though, are the salt of the earth and once they have accepted you — and you have managed to understand the distinctive dialect of the region — the Geordies are great.

We have fond memories of a six-season association with the Diamonds which, after a few early irritations had been ironed out, began so promisingly, and produced some great occasions for the team and for me as an individual. It is a pity it ended quite acrimoniously, thanks to a falling-out with the man who got me there in the first place.

The fact I left Newcastle in 1968 as world champion, in my opinion, was as much in spite of Mike Parker as it was because of him. In the end the place wasn't big enough for both of us, although from the distance of time it is easy to think I possibly was as great a part of the problem as he was.

Raye and I will always be grateful to him for bringing us and our family to England and Newcastle. When we were last in the UK in 1958 nobody in speedway had heard of him, but in the years we were away he had made a big impact.

Originally a midget car driver, Mike opened several tracks in 1959 to run composite speedway and car meetings, and was a leading light in the foundation of the Provincial League the following year. The man helped change the landscape of British speedway, and as such was one of the

84 – Ivan Mauger

architects of a revival which could not have been much better timed from my point of view.

Very much due to his powerful influence and that of a few others – Trevor Redmond and Reg Fearman among them – the number of British tracks doubled virtually overnight, and signalled the start of speedway's long journey back into the sunshine.

Parker was the new league's chairman and operated at Liverpool, Stoke, Middlesbrough and Bradford in 1960. His interests continued to expand, among them Wolverhampton and Newcastle, whose 1962 team included Gil Goldfinch, one of my former Plough Lane colleagues, and Ivan Crozier, an old friend from Christchurch with whom I had ridden in Adelaide.

It was Ivan who encouraged me to contact Mike Parker, and at the same time urged him to give me a go.

New tracks meant fresh opportunities, and a whole new blast of enthusiasm was running through the sport, especially at this level. All was not so good with the National League, with the traditional big track promoters doggedly clinging to past glories but seemingly challenged when it came to finding a new formula to invigorate a competition which by 1963 was down from the 10 teams of 1958 to just seven.

The league was still being dominated by most of the big stars who were around five years earlier. By contrast, the Provincial League contained plenty of names I remembered and recognised, although few I thought would have improved to such an extent that I couldn't live with them.

The Provincial League had 13 tracks. The Diamonds, after finishing bottom in their comeback year of 1961, had climbed to ninth the following season; and the locals were hanging out for further improvement.

It was against this background that our family unit, now five strong, undertook the 35-day boat trip via the Italian ship *Castle Felice* to Southampton. We took the overnight sleeper train from Adelaide to Melbourne to board the ship. With three active youngsters in tow, barely old enough to understand what was happening but inevitably caught up in the excitement of it all, we were ready for a new beginning.

Before getting to meet Mike Parker in person, we were met off the boat at Southampton by Eddie Glennon*, who was his right-hand man, managed various of his teams and was a very popular and generous personality.

His first connection with Mike Parker was as secretary of the Manchester Midget Car Club. Over time we were to discover that Eddie was a great foil for Parker, who was widely regarded as a tough operator and often gruff with it.

---

* Eddie Glennon died in a car accident in July 1968, returning north after a meeting at Newport where he held the promoting reins on behalf of the Mike Parker organisation.

The Parker base was in Manchester, he owned a lot of property in Whalley Range, and had accommodation for us to rent. Even though it was so far north of London and the people and places with whom we had become familiar on our first visit, and was about a three and a half hour drive to Newcastle, the distance was not something we considered a drama.

But when we finally arrived at 101 Upper Chorlton Road, most of the arrangements hc had laid on were less than ideal. The flat turned out to be a tip, an ex-GPO van provided in the deal obviously had seen better days and a promised bike wouldn't pull the skin off a rice pudding.

Still the big one was that Mike Parker had offered a team place and coughed up all the expenses for Raye and I and the three kids to get to England. For that I agreed to ride for him for a minimum of two seasons on whatever the normal start and points money was in Provincial League.

Because I had signed a contract with Wimbledon for both 1957 and 1958 I was officially on their retained list. When I started to win quite a few championships in Australia and there was occasional publicity in the speedway magazines that I wanted to go back to England, that probably was the only reason Ronnie Greene kept me on the Wimbledon retained list.

Mike Parker had quite a battle with the Speedway Control Board over who owned my contract. But he had a much stronger personality and level of determination than any of those guys at Belgrave Square. They were no match for his powers of persuasion so he got me released without any problem.

We were on a high, just getting a chance to come back. The accommodation was something which could be fixed up. Being located in Manchester was fine as there was reasonable access to all of the tracks. And while the bike he provided was extremely second-hand – Bill Andrew had used it the previous year – I was so grateful he brought us to England, that situation didn't bother me too much.

We didn't really have too many bad words over the car and bike except to tell him that if he wanted me to actually arrive at the track and start scoring maximums I couldn't do either using the bike or the car he provided, so I soon gave them back to him.

My first appearance for Newcastle was at Middlesbrough on Thursday, April 11, and the Bears were all over us, winning 51-26 with Eric Boothroyd scoring a maximum and Johnny Fitzpatrick, another rider I remembered from Wimbledon second halves, 10.

After three scoreless rides, my first points came in Heat 11 when I ran a second to the 18-year-old Eric Boocock, with Ivan Crozier third.

My home debut was four days later, against Wolverhampton. It was my first sight of the 361-yard Brough Park circuit and at a quick glance it resembled the shape of Wembley, my recurring theatre of dreams. No dream

DEBUT – for Newcastle at Middlesbrough, April 11, 1963. Left to right: Mike Parker (promoter), Ivan Mauger, Brian Craven, Pete Kelly, Ivan Crozier, Mike Watkin, Jack Winstanley, Bob Duckworth, Maurice Morley (team manager)

start here though, as the bike packed up in my first ride and next time out I trailed in behind Tommy Sweetman, another one-time Wimbledon second half opponent.

Then things got better and two heat wins later I was starting to feel more confident. Newcastle picked up their first victory of the season and it was clear to me that on proper equipment the way forward was going to be better still.

Long-term, the biggest plus on that initial home meeting was within the first half hour when I met Gordon Stobbs, who was a track raker. He and his wife Margaret started going to away meetings on their 500 BSA and Gordon later became my full-time mechanic – he was with me until I retired at the end of 1985.

They became great friends of all our family and have visited us on the Gold Coast in Australia. Raye and I stay with them when we are on our UK northern trips and even in recent times Gordon has come to help out at some of my training academies.

Over many years Gordon was absolutely the most loyal mechanic in speedway. He knew my moods, likes and dislikes and he got to know if I was going to win a meeting or just do some experimenting for future meetings.

The Will To Win – 87

We could go to a track in Europe for the first time and he would attend to the gear ratio, the wheel base, ignition settings and other details which were accurate nine times out of 10. Gordon usually got to those cities several hours before me and one of his jobs was to make sure we got rooms on the quiet side of the hotels.

All of this was way in the future, though, and at this early stage I needed a good machine before I needed a good mechanic. I asked a few people including Ted Brine at Wimbledon if they knew where there were any good bikes for sale. Ted said his brother Cyril had retired and he was selling his bike.

That was enough for me. With Rolf von dor Borch, we jumped into my newly-purchased £100 Bedford Dormobile – it had three rows of seats and space in the back for a couple of bikes, tool boxes and all the other gear – and went down to Wimbledon to buy the bike for £125.

The payback was immediate. Next Monday, I got a maximum, Newcastle disposed of Edinburgh in the Northern Trophy and my Heat 5 win over Wayne Briggs was in a new track record time.

A decent machine meant I could start doing the business on track, and there was another boost for the family (especially Raye) when we moved next door to 103 Upper Chorlton Road, where the accommodation was bigger and better.*

When the league matches started, my form just kept improving, and for most of the next several months I was around the top of the averages. At Brough Park in particular I had the measure of most riders and no less pleasing was finding the ability to go to away tracks for the first time and win races on a regular basis.

In 24 league meetings there were 13 maximums and an average of 10.80 was enough for me to be top of the Provincial League averages in my first season. I held the Silver Sash match race title for a couple of months.

The team improved steadily, too. In the end sixth place was the best we could do, although just one more win would have pushed us up to second spot behind champions Wolverhampton.

Given the lack of interest from National League promoters when I made it known I wanted to come back to England, it was quite funny to have several of them scrambling to use me as a fill-in rider – Oxford, four times, Southampton twice and even Wimbledon on a couple of occasions – and then fielding suggestions they would like to take me on board the following year. I had great delight in telling them all to get stuffed.

* We stayed there until we went to New Zealand at the end of the 1968 season.

In those eight league and KO Cup appearances I scored 59 points at an average of 7.37, including 11 for Wimbledon at Swindon where Peter Moore beat me in my last race to spoil my chance of a maximum.

Every man and his dog it seemed wanted to have a say about whether I should or shouldn't be allowed to ride. It was the same sort of argument and debate repeated years later when riders like John Louis, and most recently young Australian prospect Darcy Ward, were top of the pile in the lower division and scoring big points as a rent-a-guest for a succession of teams in the top flight.

Several additional opportunities came my way in Provincial League select teams booked to ride on National League tracks. I even beat Peter Craven in my first race at Hyde Road. The Belle Vue riders started 10 yards back but that could be an advantage as it carried more momentum at the first corner. Peter was beside me in the first turn but I got better grip on the exit and rode away from him to win a fraction outside his track record,

A few weeks later I scored paid seven from four rides to help Oxford beat the Aces, a result which threatened to spoil their charge for championship honours.

In another source of controversy, not that any of us took that much notice of it at the time, Mike Parker was starting to flex his muscles in what would prove a long-running battle with officialdom. He was warring with his fellow Provincial League promoters over the signing for Wolverhampton of Rick France from Coventry.

There was increasing talk of operating outside the jurisdiction of the Speedway Control Board, threats of a breakaway. Most riders were aware of some of it, but few had any idea how the relationship between promoters and the governing body was about to fracture so dramatically.

Of course I kept an eye on what was happening in the National League, and was sad when Ronnie Moore broke his leg in a crash at Plough Lane. Ronnie was one of the 'big five' – Briggo, Peter Craven, Björn Knutsson and Ove Fundin were the others – who were doing it the hard way, starting every race off a handicap at that stage.

His accident occurred in a last-heat decider in May when Bob Andrews and Swindon's Martin Ashby came off in front of him as he was trying to make his way through the traffic. Before the season was over Ronnie had announced his retirement, for the second, but as it happened, not the final time.

The worst accident of the year, though, was a fatal one – Peter Craven, riding for Belle Vue at Edinburgh in a challenge match in September, collided with the safety fence trying to avoid the fallen George Hunter. He never regained consciousness and died four days later in hospital.

It rammed home the dangers riders face every time they get on a bike. Everybody accepts speedway is dangerous and there always is the potential to get hurt. But little Pete, against whom I had raced in Adelaide only a few months before, in an inter-league event at Hyde Road in April and at Middlesbrough later in the season, was such a huge star, and yet such a good bloke, it was shocking to think he had gone.

The Provincial League Riders Final at Belle Vue on September 28 started with a two minutes' silence for Peter who had died four days earlier. It was a sombre way to go into one of the biggest meetings of the year.

For weeks I had been building myself up to prove I could do the business in the league's showpiece occasion. Normally I was as healthy as any young bloke, and fitter than most because I took physical training and conditioning pretty seriously. But in the days leading up to the PLRC I was feeling very ordinary, suffering bad headaches for the first time in my life. I put that down to some kind of tension going into the big meeting.

The last thing I needed on the night was a mini-riot, stirred up by riders who took exception to the 24-heat formula. The traditional 16-rider, 20-heat world championship format was ditched and instead two dozen riders contested the meeting, taking four rides apiece, with the top four scorers to qualify for a grand final.

HAPPY DAYS – Ivan and Raye with Mike Parker, Provincial League Riders Final, September 1963

90 – Ivan Mauger

Nothing revolutionary about that in more recent terms, but it was an innovation which did not please the purists and threatened to go pear-shaped when five riders tied on nine points. Jack Kitchen of Sheffield and I were safely into the decider with 11 points each from our four rides, but George Hunter, Ross Gilbertson, Ray Cresp, Clive Featherby and Maury Mattingley were locked together.

After a lengthy delay it was decided to put all five into a run-off – at least Hyde Road was big enough and plenty wide enough for an extra rider on the starting grid. Gilbertson and Hunter duly joined us in the final, and my chances looked shot when I drew the worst gate. However it was Hunter who turned out to be the unlucky one. He made the start but packed up at the beginning of the second lap, allowing me to take the lead which I held to the chequered flag.

Many people in the full stadium gave me the reception which often goes the way of a fortunate winner, but the massed ranks of Newcastle fans didn't care – and nor did I. It was in all respects a champion feeling.

A couple of hours later, though, I was much the worse for wear, and not because of any celebration. After the meeting a group of us went back to a pub in Bolton where the owner was a friend of Newcastle rider Jack Winstanley. Mike Parker, Eddie Glennon and most of the other Diamonds riders were there along with their wives.

I had an extra strong headache by the time Raye and I arrived and the owners took us through into the lounge where I lay on the couch and was not involved with all the celebrations out in the bar.

The owner called a doctor but before he bothered to come out to see me he'd had a few beers in the bar so obviously he didn't think there was anything seriously wrong. Raye was sitting in a chair next to the couch and he looked at her and asked 'does he take any drugs'.

Raye said 'the only thing he takes is glucose in the orange juice I mix up for him at the tracks and then he takes vitamin tablets that you buy from the chemist'.

Anyway the doc was convinced I was on some kind of drugs and he left us and just went out to the bar and started drinking more beers.

When we got home I was in a bad way. Raye has always had medical books and when she looked up my symptoms she decided I had meningitis. First thing in the morning she walked down to Dr Friedlander, our family doctor who was a couple of blocks away.

Fortunately he came to see me and immediately called for an ambulance to take me to the Monsall Hospital in the middle of Manchester.

They promptly put me in an isolation ward and I was there for over a month, missing all the remaining meetings of the 1963 season. It cost me a

The Will To Win – 91

lot of money, a KO Cup Final appearance against Cradley Heath and more besides. For several weeks I was so far out of things it was not until later that the full impact of it all hit home.

Dr Friedlander and the other doctors at the hospital told Raye it would take up to a year to get rid of the symptoms and that she should never let me get tired.

By this time it was mid November and Raye made me go to bed about nine o'clock every night. It was winter anyway and it was not until well into the new year I was able to go to the workshop and tinker around on my bikes for a few hours at a time.

Fortunately Guy Allott, who had been forced to retire after suffering serious injuries when he fell off the tractor grader during a victory parade at Sheffield, was getting into engine preparation and tuning. It was reassuring to know he was working hard to get my motors prepared for the next season.

I started on my recovery, training and running at the Manchester YMCA where the facilities included an indoor track. It took a long time before my health was anywhere close to what it had been, and a night at the pub with Rolf did not speed my rehabilitation.

He thought he was doing the right thing by getting me out of the house to unwind, but a couple of beers knocked me flat again. Raye was not at all amused.

With the season a few weeks away, there was another huge cloud on the horizon. The Speedway Control Board tried to coerce Mike Parker into moving Wolverhampton into the National League, accelerating a long-running dispute into open war.

There was talk of strike action, the Provincial League promoters voted to operate outside the official channels, and the SCB warned riders they would be suspended if they rode on unlicensed tracks.

Most of the PL tracks were attracting excellent crowds and there was great racing because most of the boys had a lot of ambitions, whereas the National League numbers had been on the slippery slope for several years.

West Ham were added to the ranks, replacing Southampton, but in spite of the quality in the top division, the quantity still wasn't there. They simply did not have enough tracks or offer sufficient meetings to appeal to a lot of riders.

The bottom line is that Mike and other PL promoters had a meeting with the league's top guys at Cradley Heath a couple of weeks before the start of the 1964 season to tell us they were going to run 'black' and without being licensed by the Speedway Control Board. That meant we also would not have licences. But they assured us that it would 'all blow over before the world championship qualifying rounds'.

I wanted to believe what we were being told. I told Mike that I owed my loyalty to him because he had brought me over while there had been no contact or response from the National League promoters such as Ronnie Greene at Wimbledon and Charles Ochiltree at Coventry, who had never even answered my letters.

To shore up the arrangement Mike voluntarily offered what was at that time quite a good guaranteed prizemoney arrangement for each meeting which I accepted and gave him my word for two seasons.

Later we realised there was very little intention of linking up with the SCB. The PL promoters were doing well financially without paying licence or permit fees and did not have anyone outside their group telling them what they could and could not do.

The first year Mike would often drop in to see me. He rented the upper floor at 81 Upper Chorlton Road, he (and Eddie Glennon) had offices on the ground floor and my workshop was out the back. He knew I had tea on most of the day. But from about May 1964 he rarely looked in – the promised truce had not materialised, and he knew I was angry at having been misled.

Nevertheless I had a great time in 1964, starting with 10 maximums in 11 Northern League matches; only a fall at Glasgow cost me a perfect record. I was top of the Provincial League averages, defended the Silver Sash against all comers from May to September, and again won the PLRC at Belle Vue at the end of the season.

What very few people knew was quite often I had to have a sleep in the afternoon. I left home a couple of hours early to go to Newcastle each Monday and had an hour or so flat out on the couch in the speedway office before just about every home meeting

There were a few changes in the Provincial League with Stoke, St Austell and Rayleigh all gone from the previous year, but new teams in Sunderland, Glasgow and Newport.

The arrival of Sunderland promised a fresh local derby rivalry but the Saints, who signed new Aussies Jim Airey and Gordon Guasco, operated for only a few weeks before closing down.

The two of them then went to Wolves who immediately became a serious threat, bracketed with ourselves and Hackney – who had Colin Pratt and Roy Trigg – as likely honours challengers.

As far as we were concerned, Newcastle would be the team to beat. Brian Craven had retired, but the returning Bill Andrew, the jockey-turned-racer from Palmerston North, was a decent replacement, Goog Allan was another recruit from New Zealand, and the signing of the veteran Ken Sharples after Sunderland closed gave us an added edge in the second half of the season.

FIERCE RIVALS – Ivan and Cradley star Ivor Brown clash at Brough Park

Fans who had been watching for years reckoned these Diamonds had enough about them to bring a league title to the club for the first time.

I hardly put a foot wrong, although there was one memorable time when Ivor Brown, who dished it out but appeared to regard himself as untouchable, did get the better of me and hung me out to dry when Cradley Heath came to visit Brough Park in June.

He was my challenger for the Silver Sash but hardly put any effort into it. In the second half final I warned Mike Watkin and Bill Andrews to stay out of the way in the first corner. Ivor ended up going through the pit gates.

From a personal viewpoint my league and KO Cup results could not have been much better – 293 points from 24 matches, an average of 11.49 and 15 maximum scores.

Newcastle was an unforgiving circuit, usually on the rough side, and we made the most of it as a home track. We also had the ability to win six out of 11 away from home, finally clinching the championship with a 49-29 home win against Edinburgh. In the end we had a three-point margin over Hackney with the rest way behind.

Celebrations in the north-east went on for days and at the end of the week, winning the individual title at Hyde Road for the second year in a row was another highlight.

TITLE TIME – Newcastle, 1964 Provincial League champions. Back row, left to right: Bill Andrew, Russ Dent, Mike Watkin, Mike Parker (promoter), Goog Allan, Ken Sharples, Pete Kelly. On machine: Ivan Mauger (captain).

TWO IN A ROW – PLRC winner again in September 1964, flanked by Roy Trigg (Hackney, third) and Charlie Monk (Glasgow, second)

The Will To Win – 95

After dropping a point to Roy Trigg in my first race, and another to former Adelaide rival Charlie Monk (Glasgow) in Heat 12, I finished on 13 and needed to beat Charlie in a run-off for the championship.

As we were the only riders with a figure above 11 for the season, it seemed a fitting result. I would have been disappointed with anything less, but it was a tough night.

Belle Vue was packed, the meeting attracting more fans than any other at Hyde Road that year. The atmosphere was brilliant, although by all accounts thousands of fans were angry when programmes sold out an hour before the start.

The point was not lost on those who were following the continuing split between the 'official' National League and the 'black' Provincials. The Speedway Control Board suspended Belle Vue's licence after they staged the PLRC, but relented a few days later, shortly before all parties were to meet in the first step towards reconciliation.

It took many weeks in the off season, a great deal of wheeling and dealing. When everybody had given their input the Shawcross Report into the state of speedway eventually brought together all the feuding factions.

All of this was still in the melting pot when the season ended but this time I was determined not to let anything get in the way of my preparations for the following year and my world championship ambitions.

Raye and I and the kids again stayed in England that winter. Julie and Kym were established at school and doing well and we wanted to have five or six months quality time in one base during the winter to get really organised for the following season.

In addition I had made the conscious decision to start my year's preparations on January 1 – an ideal time to start a new campaign – and I have always kept to that plan even today.

I was in my workshop for a few hours most days during November and December, just cleaning things up and starting to make a plan with Guy Allott as to what we should do with engines and so forth the following year.

Not being able to ride in the championship rounds had occupied a lot of my thoughts in the weeks after the end of the season. When Mike Parker eventually got around to coming in to see me shortly before Christmas it probably was the first time he and I ever had hard words. He was a very strong-willed person and so was I and that made it inevitable we would have our problems sooner or later.

He started off by telling me his plans for the formation of the British League which meant the National League and Provincial League amalgamation was going to happen. He was keen to talk about a new deal but I wasn't ready. It was good to know the two competitions were coming together but I had fulfilled the two years agreed. He and I both fully understood that there was no loyalty now after his lies in 1964.

Mike was very much a visionary for speedway and one of the first people who could see a join-up had to happen. He was more forceful and had a stronger personality than any of the other promoters and that was a huge factor in how the BL got started – just as he was one of the first group who had a vision for the Provincial League a few years before. But I also knew I was coming from a strong bargaining position.

I told him as one of the hot properties in British speedway, after cleaning up the Provincial League in 1963 and 1964, I figured I could ride for pretty well whoever I wanted. By staying loyal I had wasted a year of world championship rounds. In that instant I could not have cared less whether I rode for him again or not. Discussion stalled at that point so I locked my workshop door and went home.

Raye and I discussed everything for a week or two. We had made many friends up at Newcastle and we loved all the people; they were great supporters and very friendly, as they are today. I really wanted to stay there – but on my own conditions.

We decided upon exactly what I wanted no matter who I rode for in 1965, Newcastle or anybody else: good guaranteed money, better transport vehicles, better bikes and better accommodation. Only then did I go back to the workshop.

When Mike next came in he asked me if I had calmed down and asked if I wanted to ride for Newcastle. I said 'yes, let's go up to your office and I will tell you what the deal is.'

I started off by telling him it was his turn to make the tea and provide the chocolate biscuits. We sat in exactly the same place as we had done 10 months before when he called me in to tell me that the Provincial League promoters and riders were going 'black' and offered me the financial guarantee to continue with him in the PL that year.

I told him I could not forget how all those assurances about the dispute being settled quickly had been shown to be false. I again said I could ride for whoever I wanted and in particular Belle Vue, who had made no great secret about wanting to get me to Hyde Road from the first time I had been on the track.

After I outlined all the conditions Raye and I had worked out he was silent for quite a long time and I was determined not to speak until he did. People in Newcastle had told me Mike was desperate for me to ride there particularly in the first season of the new competition which was his brainchild. I also knew he had done some deals with other promoters when he was trying to get the new competition started, and Morris Marshall, the chief executive officer of the entire Belle Vue complex, was top of that list.

The Will To Win – 97

It followed that Mike did not want to get into a fight with Belle Vue so I told him I would ride at Newcastle home and away and open meetings for a guarantee of £100 a meeting plus double travel money. Any challenge matches I could negotiate with the promoters for a higher guarantee. Any individual meeting at home I kept whatever prizemoney I got plus the guarantee.

That was good money in those days. Briggo, who was world champion in 1964, only got £35 for open meetings. But I didn't have any doubt I was worth that sort of money to Mike Parker – not that I expected him to immediately agree. Anyway, after a while he said that was too much and that no club in the country would pay that and also he wouldn't give me a transfer to another club.

I was wise enough to know at that stage that his ambitions of being chairman of the BSPA or certainly number one promoter in the British League with several tracks would play a part in his thinking. All the other promoters wanted me to be in it and Mike had upset so many people any arbitration court at the RAC would defeat him.

I gambled on the fact that his ego would not allow him to be publicly defeated so I was confident that he would come up with my requests. After about another half hour of silence during which time Mike made more teas, he said he thought I was completely ungrateful after he had brought my family over and I should reconsider.

My reply was that I had fulfilled my loyalty of two seasons which when I made that agreement and committed to that loyalty never included being excluded from the world championship for one of those seasons.

Mike could sense I was determined and also at that time I thought he was figuring out how he was going to tell the people at Newcastle that I was leaving. After a while he asked me to come back the next day.

When we got together again we haggled and compromised a bit, part of which I did not get any travel money at all! But obviously he had cleared his thoughts overnight and done the sums because we did the deal there and then.

The prospect of earning £100 several nights a week was quite attractive as the average weekly wage was in the region of £13 and petrol was less than two bob a gallon.

As with every deal I did with Mike, all it took was a handshake and he paid every penny.

As the start of speedway's new era dawned and everybody in the UK was getting very excited about the formation of the British League, I was as jazzed up as anybody.

98 – *Ivan Mauger*

For two years in the Provincial League things had gone extremely well for me. My results were consistently good, my confidence was high. The drama of meningitis behind me – although never forgotten – I felt I was ready for the challenge.

Plenty of people had doubts about how the former Provincial League guys would fare up against the gun riders who had been stars in the National League. Among them were those who seemed to take a delight in reminding anybody who would take notice that Ivan Mauger and all the rest of them had everything to prove, because none of them had cut it in the big time.

And it was true. But thanks to several years of increasingly tough competition, to a greater or lesser degree all of us were now serious contenders. If the biggest criticism to be levelled against us was that we lacked experience, well now was the time to bring it on!

At least I'd had the benefit of racing against some of the star names before coming back to England, and handling myself more than adequately. I knew too that I was a far better all-round rider than say, two years before when the Newcastle adventure kicked off.

My analysis of the teams for the new British League was that the overall strength would not be that much greater than the Provincial League had been. Of course the big stars like Briggo, Nigel Boocock and company would present a whole new challenge but they were only one man in a seven-man team.

What remained to be seen was whether good domestic form could be carried over into the world championship rounds. After being dudded out of the opportunity to compete in 1964, this was a high priority.

It was good to be able to get into detailed planning for the months to come, although it was not the case for all the riders who were going to be involved in the new set-up. There were pay disputes, threats of tracks shutting down and various other loose ends to be resolved before the new British League lurched into action.

When all the talking and argument was over, Coventry, one of the traditional big guns, met Cradley Heath, one of the ex-PL clubs, and 14,000 people turned out at Brandon to give the bold new era a fantastic start.

Newcastle were one of the later-starting tracks but we had a challenge match at Sheffield and I kicked off my season with 13 points. Then there was a gap of more than a week before Newcastle were due at Wolverhampton on Good Friday.

In between times I had a very bad bout of flu which put me in bed for a few days. But of course Mike Parker wanted me to me to ride at Monmore Green – another of his tracks – so against my better judgment, I got out of bed and went.

You can ride with injury, and put up with the pain, but I wasn't thinking clearly because of the flu.

In my second ride I rode a lazy first corner, came down, and Gordon Guasco ran over my left foot and broke my ankle and leg really badly.

It wasn't Gordon's fault and you couldn't say directly it was Mike Parker's fault, but the bottom line was for a second year in a row it looked as if my world championship hopes were in huge trouble – through trying to help out.

There was so much more besides. As holder of the Silver Sash, which I successfully defended for weeks in 1964, I was keen to hold on to it for a while. There was talk of being nominated to challenge Briggo for the Golden Helmet, the most prestigious match race championship in speedway. There was a Test series coming up against the Soviet Union, history to be made, and I fancied my chances of getting a run in that too.

Brian Brett

As a speedway rider you have to accept there is a possibility all the best-laid plans can be wrecked by injury. All forms of racing have that element of risk attached, which can be minimised by engaging the brain before twisting the throttle. But by its very nature, motor sport is dangerous, as the warning on all the programmes and posters used to say.

And that is precisely when injuries made a mess of my season.

Doing myself serious damage was shattering in more ways than one. In over eight years I had never had anything worse than a bit of concussion in 1957 and broken ribs in 1958, but this was something else.

The most immediate single consequence was the way it made a mess of my hopes in the world championship. Carlo Biagi*, speedway's 'miracle doctor' did patch me up any number of times over the next few months to help me through the qualifying rounds, then the British semi-final. But my hope of getting all the way to Wembley was pretty much doomed.

---

* Carlo had almost legendary status because of his work at Peel Hospital, near Galashiels. In 1982, he was awarded an honorary fellowship of the Royal College of Surgeons – a tribute normally reserved for distinguished international visiting surgeons and almost unheard of for a surgeon at a small hospital such as Peel. In 1990, he was presented with an MBE at Buckingham Palace for services to orthopaedic surgery.

100 – Ivan Mauger

Provided you are not too squeamish, you can read about that in more detail in the next chapter in which I expand upon the nature of my ongoing mission to make an impact at world level.

After missing 16 meetings in the first couple of months of the season, I managed to get some reasonable results but the British League proved tougher for the Diamonds than might have been imagined.

Newcastle were good enough to win 14 and draw one at home but managed only two away victories in 17 road trips, at Edinburgh and Long Eaton in my first few weeks back in action.

Bill Andrew had gone from the previous year, replaced by the returning Brian Craven. After my Good Friday crash, Mike Parker talked Brian Brett out of a short-lived retirement, and then had to battle with the other tracks to hold on to him after I was fit to come back.

He won that fight and for a spell the team strung together some consistent results before the injuries struck again. In the end 12th place in an 18-strong league was the best we could do and seven of the teams who finished behind us the previous year now jumped above us on the table. Former National League clubs West Ham, Wimbledon and Coventry made the running for the big prizes.

I managed to be 0.01 ahead of Bretty in the averages when the line-up was announced for the first British League Riders' Championship, which was allocated to Belle Vue after their earlier success with the PLRC.

This was one last chance to salvage something from the year and my only time at Hyde Road in 1965. It also was the start of a sequence of tremendous occasions which signalled the end of the UK season.

Most riders loved the space and speed of the track, they enjoyed the atmosphere of the old Zoological Gardens which for so long were a massive attraction in the north-west, and the buzz created when a full house packed into the stadium was very special.

I hoped for something good with which to sign off, and won my first race, but fell next time out, again aggravating the ankle, and collected five points from my three remaining rides.

Briggo blasted through the field with 14 points, collecting the first of what turned out to be six consecutive titles, and my mid-table scoring just about summed up my year.

In spite of all that, everyone in Newcastle was complimentary about the way we had tackled that first British League campaign. At the end of season function at the Mayfair ballroom, 1600 turned up and made our night by presenting me with an illuminated scroll to acknowledge my efforts.

We even managed to have a civilised end-of-season conversation with

Mike Parker. The speedy upshot was agreement on another two-year deal, with improved terms and built-in provision for price index rises.

For the first time in more than two and a half eventful years, the family set off for a trip to New Zealand – our first by plane. We flew via San Francisco and Fiji.

I hadn't intended to ride much, but those intentions lasted only a few days. Promoter Russell Lang persuaded me to race on the Saturday night programme at Templeton.

I was keen to build up my fitness and just as I had done as a kid years before, went off to Rapaki hills to do some running. But after a few sessions I was getting terrific pain from the ankle.

It turned out that I had been pushing myself so hard that the screws in the ankle had bent over and were rubbing against the bones. Dr McFarlane, a specialist in Papanui Road, Christchurch told me it was best to have the screws removed and that turned out to be a simple and painless procedure.

Within a fortnight I was back in action and building up for our return. After falling sick at the end of my first season with Newcastle, struggling for fitness the next year, and having 1965 blighted by injury, it was desperately important for me to go through an English season with a clean bill of health. At last in 1966 I managed that,

In the league I upped my average by half a point, from 8.93 to 9.46, I scored the first seven-ride 21 point maximum at Poole in a KO Cup match, and it was a much improved year for Newcastle.

Only one home defeat, some decent results on the road, with Peter Kelly and Brian Brett – despite some injury problems – doing a good job and a hard-working supporting cast, helped pin down fifth place.

It was no accident that my good form in the British League, and selection for the World Team Cup and Great Britain teams, also coincided with the first consistently successful world championship campaign. That too, is something charted in greater detail in the next chapter.

Winning the European Final at my first meeting at Wembley, and qualifying for my first World Final, were achievements I would happily have settled for going into the year.

At last I felt I belonged and proved I could go well in the very highest company. It had been years in the making, and eventually everything started to fall into place. Good for me, good for Newcastle.

But it also provoked another argument with Mike Parker. While the disappointment and deception of 1964 still rankled, this was the beginning of a bigger rift which ultimately meant a parting of the ways would be inevitable.

Heat 6

DOWN WEMBLEY WAY

IT was more than nine years after my first ride in England before I finally made it to the greatest stage of all – Wembley. The wait seemed worthwhile when in my first meeting at the track, I was crowned the 1966 European champion.

While Aranui was the eye-opener which convinced me I had discovered my career calling, Wembley reinforced and defined my ambition to become world speedway champion.

As a nine-year-old watching my first meeting I was immediately swept up with the excitement of it all. Aranui wasn't the greatest venue of all time but it sowed the seed.

But nothing in my experience can compare with a first sighting of the world's most famous stadium. When Wembley opened in 1923 more than 200,000 tried to get in to watch the FA Cup Final and thousands more were locked out. It's part of sporting folklore.

When I glimpsed those famous twin towers in 1957, attending the World Final as a spectator with Raye, I felt as if I had gone to sleep and woken up in heaven.

Wembley possibly was beginning to look a little shabby at the edges, certainly by modern standards. This, remember, was almost half a century before a £757 million makeover dragged the old place into the 21st century. But I was dazzled.

One of the first impressions was of the enormity of the place, the terraces stretching high into the sky, a vast concrete temple set in 100 acres in north-west London. Built in just 300 days at a cost of £750,000, for the British Empire Exhibition, it was later and for almost all of its first 34 years associated with chairman Sir Arthur Elvin.

Despite its spectacular design and ambitious opening the stadium quickly went into liquidation and Elvin, a First World War flier who had been a stallholder at the exhibition, bought everything for a knockdown £127,000.

He brought in Johnnie Hoskins to introduce speedway at the stadium in 1929 and Wembley became the spiritual home of the sport, hosting the major individual events such as the Star Riders' Championship and, from 1936, the World Final.

ONE NIGHT IN SEPTEMBER – Wembley Stadium, the theatre of dreams and original home of the speedway World Final

104 – Ivan Mauger

(In the first three seasons after the war, the world championship was not staged but the success of its equivalent, the big end-of-season British Riders Championship, preceded the return of the World Final from 1949.)

Crowds were enormous, often 60 or 70-odd thousand for league matches, and at Elvin's insistence the Wembley Lions were the most notable of the glamour teams, winning the National League seven times between 1946 and 1953. The one year they missed out was when they had to race home matches at Wimbledon because Wembley was staging the London Olympic Games of 1948.

Like everywhere else, declining attendances and climbing bills brought the glory days to an end. Even so, speedway was in shock when the Lions pulled out of league racing only weeks after Elvin died at sea on February 4, 1957 (five days before Raye and I got married) while on a trip to South Africa.

Of course as a youngster I was only vaguely aware of the facts but it positively reeked of history; all speedway people (and football fans too) spoke of it with reverence and pride.

This was where Ronnie Moore had become world champion and the ghosts of other greats roamed. It was a national icon and, to me, more exciting than seeing Buckingham Palace or the Houses of Parliament for the first time.

Sporting royalty lived here and the weeks before the 1957 World Final were full of excitement and anticipation. Ronnie Greene provided us with tickets and when the great day dawned, Raye and I went to Wembley with the Hones, our 'second' family. Julie, at seven weeks, was left behind in the care of Mrs Walker.

We sat along the front straight and had a perfect view. The date was September 21, a Thursday, which was the norm back then. Although the record shows there was a disappointing crowd of 50,000, to me it seemed closer to 100,000.

People were coming from all directions, thronging along Empire Way from the Wembley Park underground station, in cars and coaches from every part of the country, all in good humour and good voice, decorated with scarves and banners, carrying the rattles which were as essential a piece of equipment as an air horn is at Cardiff these days.

In the time before there were rounds all over the place, the British and colonial riders had to do their qualifying in England. There were 10 World Final places available in 1957, the field completed by half a dozen riders earning a spot at Wembley via meetings in Scandinavia and Europe.

I hadn't even been close to being in the entry of 72 which nine UK qualifying rounds whittled down to 32, and then the top five riders from each of two semi-finals, at Poole and Coventry, made it into the night of

FIRST TIME – Barry Briggs celebrates his 1957 World Final win with Ove Fundin and Peter Craven joining him on the tractor ride

nights. I went to help Briggo at some of the rounds and he got a chance break a few days before Wembley.

He ran out of petrol on the way back from a Wimbledon match at Southampton, parked the car on the side of the road and with June and his brother Murray started to walk to find the next petrol station.

A truck hit the parked trailer and Barry's car and his bikes. Fortunately with the insurance he was able to buy two new bikes from Alec Jackson's in Harrow Road, Ted Brine prepared the engines on both of them and he set off for Wembley with the best equipment.

History records he went on to win the first of his world titles, beating Ove Fundin in a run-off, a perfect outcome for him and a dream outcome for me, just great.

Just being there as a spectator gave me a sense of how dreams can become reality. This was the real thing – Wembley with all the bells and whistles and the greatest atmosphere of any World Final I have attended, including those I won.

Eight countries were represented, a record, and other riders in whom we took a special interest were Ron How, making his big night debut, and Dunedin's Ron Johnston who was such a fine performer for Belle Vue.

While nothing had happened in my first few months in England to seriously advance my own chances, it all further fired my imagination and ambition. My first small step on to the world championship stage as a rider was 10 months down the track. At least there was a place for me in the qualifying rounds the following year.

At Ipswich, where local favourite Peter Moore went through the card, I had two engine failures, missed another ride, and had a third and then a second place to show for my efforts around what was then a big, pacy 440-yard circuit.

Things went much better for me two nights later when I collected nine points at Coventry, where once again a home team man won with a 15-point maximum. Jack Young had been tempted back to British speedway after missing the previous year and he was all class, although Ken McKinlay and Arthur Forrest also had their moments.

A dozen points from those two rounds was never going to be enough to secure a passage into the semi-finals but from my perspective it was all gain, all positive.

AVID LISTENER – with Ronnie Moore on the way back from a meeting at Swindon in 1958

Winning races in the Southern Area League, as I was doing for Eastbourne, provided no guarantee of success against National League riders.

This was all highly competitive, but encouragingly, probably for the first time I was able to mix it convincingly with much more experienced and credentialled performers.

Among those who finished behind me at Brandon were Cyril Brine from Wimbledon, Maury Mattingley who would become the Veteran Riders' president almost half a century later, and Reg Trott, one of the few riders who went on to become a top referee.

Most of the usual suspects were up at the top of the qualifying lists, which were followed again by semi-finals. Ronnie Moore was back in the mix after he made a mid-season return following his extended flirtation with car racing.

I tried to get to his and Barry's championship rounds and helped out in the pits a few times, savouring the atmosphere. With both of these great role models qualifying, it added an extra dimension to Wembley's 1958 big night and once again I saw Briggo take the prize. He was not headed and victory over the previously unbeaten Fundin in the last heat before the interval effectively clinched victory.

Again my vantage point was along the front straight in pretty much the same position as before. This time Sid, Renee and Jimmy Hone went with me, together with Mac.

As on my first visit, the Wembley atmosphere was simply electric. While a handful of rides in the qualifiers in July had fuelled my belief, it took a ringside seat at the sport's greatest occasion to provide the most spectacular incentive to further progress.

Even during the next four 'missing' seasons, England remained the land of hope and glory, and the opportunity to race at Wembley the holy grail. Just as well I didn't know then that I would have no further contact with the world championship until 1963, it would be another three years before I set foot in Wembley, and all up eight long years would elapse before my World Final debut.

But when we headed back to join Newcastle in 1963, it was in the knowledge that in the intervening years Plough Lane contemporaries such as Bob Andrews and Cyril Maidment were now qualifying for World Finals. If they could do it, surely I would be in with a sporting chance.

The big difference was that now Provincial League tracks held a series of qualifying rounds, designed to find 16 riders to contest a final eliminator before the big guns of National League came into the reckoning.

Then followed the more usual National League meetings, culminating in a semi-final stage in which riders rode in two of four meetings and had to place in the top 10 to make it to Wembley.

Under no illusions about the size of the task, I went into the early rounds full of confidence, winning at Newcastle and Wolverhampton before taking out the Provincial final at Edinburgh against opponents including a former World Final qualifier in Eric Boothroyd and four future finalists – Brian Brett, Eric Boocock, Reg Luckhurst and Colin Pratt.

The next stage, however, was as starkly unsuccessful as it was possible to imagine. Three rounds – at Southampton, Oxford and Swindon – in the space of four days produced scores of five, two and six to show for a great deal of endeavour but little joy against the likes of Briggo and Craven.

In the Southampton meeting I came a cropper first time out, won in my next race, but it was pretty much all downhill after that. It was not the ending we had been hoping for, just another reminder the top guys possessed that extra edge and experience, a situation only time and more hard work could turn around.

Even so, I felt confident of my ability to put the lessons learned to good effect in 1964, and capable of not only going further, but being able to acquit myself much more convincingly the next time I was up alongside National League riders.

This belief was an important factor which helped me in the UK winter of 1963–64 as I recovered from the meningitis that knocked me sideways after that first Provincial League Riders success. Getting myself healthy was a priority and increasingly I felt good and ready to take on the challenge of meeting the top guys.

Being badly misled and let down by Mike Parker and other promoters who assured me their dispute with the National League and the Speedway Control Board would be all sorted in no time at all was an enormous disappointment.

BACK STREET BOYS – Goog Allan, Jim Airey, Ivan, Gordon Guasco and Bill Andrew at 81 Upper Chorlton Road, Easter 1964

The Will To Win – 109

I allowed myself to be taken in. Although up to this point Mike Parker and Newcastle were entitled to the commitment I had promised them when I signed, it should have been a two-way street and, clearly, it wasn't.

It would be wrong to say 1964 was a wasted year because so many other things did go well for me but the biggest of all, the world championship, was a total washout.

All the riders who rode 'black' were denied the opportunity to appear in the qualifying rounds and when it became clear there was to be no outbreak of peace between the warring bodies, it was hugely frustrating.

That meant I couldn't ride in the world championship, which was one of my main reasons for coming back to England. I told Mike Parker I had come to be world champion, not to ride in the Provincial League at 'black' tracks. While I owed a loyalty to the man he would never have been in any doubt about my wanting to be in the world championship.

Coming up to the start of the season he told me not to worry because, by May or June, the Control Board would give the Provincial League clubs licences as they couldn't do without them. Parker even lined up his promoting buddies to assure us the situation would be quickly resolved, certainly within a short time after the season got under way. The message was that I and other ambitious boys in the League like George Hunter who wanted to enter the championship, would be able to ride

Parker, Ian Hoskins, Pete Lansdale, Trevor Redmond, Allan Martin and Morris Jephcott were among the track bosses who met with a group of us at Cradley stadium to head off any rebellion. Reg Fearman was not there, having recently fallen out big time with Parker.

I went down from Manchester with Goog Allan. Other Newcastle riders there were Ken Sharples, Brian Craven, Ivan Crozier and Jack Winstanley, along with George Hunter, Dougie Templeton, Colin Pratt, Pete Jarman and several of the other Wolves boys. It was only later we realised we had been taken for a ride. I have always felt we were deceived and resented losing that year out of the championship.

As it turned out, 1965 was another desperately unhappy year for my ambitions. The formation of the British League, the amalgamation of the two competitions into one big happy family, has been widely described as the beginning of a whole new era for the sport. For me, in many ways, it was a false dawn.

Being injured in my second meeting of the season threw a massive spanner in the works but I was not prepared to write off yet another world championship year without a fight. There were two months to go before the rounds, after all.

But the doctors who attended to me in hospital at Wolverhampton said I didn't need to bother thinking about a return to racing for months. My ankle

110 – Ivan Mauger

was operated on with two huge screws inserted to hold it together and it was set pointing downwards.

The surgeon told me he would look at it in three months but it would be four or five months before I could walk on it. They wanted me to stay there for a week but I got sick of it after two days and discharged myself. It was itchy in that plaster so stupidly I put one of Raye's knitting needles down to scratch it and ended up getting an infection.

Dr Friedlander sent me to the Manchester General Hospital and I was there for 10 or 12 days. A nurse used to come round at about five or six in the afternoon and give me an injection of morphine in the thigh. It only took a couple of minutes and the pain was completely gone.

After a few days of the injections they started giving me morphine tablets which took about an hour before the pain went away. As far as getting myself right in time to ride in the world championship rounds, however, the medical people in Manchester were no more encouraging than those in the Midlands had been.

As with any hospital I have ever been in I quickly became impatient and true to form discharged myself three or four days before they wanted me to leave – and made a call to seek the opinion of Carlo Biagi, the man they called speedway's 'miracle doctor'. The problem was with a foot in plaster I was not in a fit state to drive.

Fortunately the neighbours were good! Goog and Ursula Allan were living in one of Mike Parker's places nearby and Dave Gifford and a load of other Kiwis were in another house Mike owned in Whalley Range.

It so happened Goog and Dave had a meeting at Cowdenbeath, an open licence track outside Edinburgh, so they took me to Galashiels to see Dr Biagi on the way up.

On that first visit he told me he could get me ready to ride in six weeks as I needed – but it would hurt!

Of Italian heritage, but as Scottish as they come, Carlo had a terrific reputation which grew when he saved the life of Bob Duckworth at Southampton where he was the track medico from 1959. After that he was responsible for patching up many riders. In 1963 he constructed a plaster cast which Ove Fundin wore to protect a broken foot and won the world title.

Soon after that Carlo headed back north and for a quarter of a century he ministered to all and sundry from the tiny Peel Hospital in the border country. He was the track doctor at several of the Scottish tracks for years. He made things happen that others assumed to be impossible. In the days before sports psychology became fashionable, Carlo was the original 'can do' man.

SPECTATING – at Cowdenbeath, with Carlo Biagi. That's George Hunter in the front row of the VIP box and Wayne Briggs at the back

His great skills with people were hugely appreciated by speedway riders. Carlo treated us like responsible adults who knew what we were doing, unlike many medical people who simply regarded motorcycle racers as complete idiots who deserved no sympathy if they happened to hurt themselves.

Certainly he didn't overdo the sympathy but he did tell it as it was. He was a great believer in getting on with things, and if you wanted or particularly needed to ride a couple of days or a week after suffering the sort of injury which might have sidelined others, he was your man.

Carlo would explain what the consequences could be. More often than not, he would give every valid reason to get back on the bike sooner rather than later and that, of course, was what I wanted to hear from him.

Goog and Giffy were both riding for Newcastle and for the next few weeks took me back to the doctor every Monday. We would leave Whalley Range early and drive up to Galashiels before going on to the meeting at Brough Park.

From that Good Friday crash to my scheduled first world championship qualifier at Newcastle on June 14 was eight and a half weeks. The foot got better and my ability to move it improved but I still couldn't put weight on it without pain.

Each visit to Carlo he would take off the plaster, manipulate and reposition the ankle and then put on a new plaster. He bent my foot up a little bit more until it was at an angle that I could use. Then he made me a plaster cast as strong as possible and we made a steel shoe to fit directly over the plaster.

Ready or not, it was showtime. Carlo rigged me up with a pair of crutches, and I was all set. Many people thought I had no chance and others thought I was mad to try, but never say never. There is no telling a young and ambitious sportsman what he can and can't do.

After all those weeks of pain and frustration, I was determined to have a go and struggled in to the Brough Park pits on that Monday night feeling much less optimistic than I was willing to admit.

In spite of the discomfort I cobbled together 11 points, running second to Charlie Monk first time out, followed by a couple of race wins. My fourth ride lasted three and a half laps in close contact with Brian Brett before I

MAN OF STEEL – Ivan with his special protective plaster, racing Dick Fisher in his 1965 comeback world championship qualifying round

The Will To Win – 113

ended up on the track, fortunately with my pride hurt more than my body. Another win to round out the night was followed by the luxury of three days off before my next round at Glasgow on the Friday.

Charlie ruled the roost again on his home track, and Aussie Bluey Scott – who these days lives not far from our Gold Coast home – was close behind. My contribution was steady, three seconds, a third place and a win to finish, a further 10 points in the kitty.

Another 12-point score at Edinburgh 24 hours later gave me a total of 35 from my three qualifying rounds, a comfortable pass mark. That was enough to answer the doubters, and to reassure me the effort had all been worth it.

Even better was the fact there was a four-week interval before the second of the British semi-finals, again at Glasgow. That meant there was time for more meetings in which to step up my race fitness, and the opportunity for Carlo to oversee more work on the ankle, which continued to develop increased movement.

With eight British Final places up for grabs, I was comfortable with my 11 points at White City, a steady as she goes effort with four second places and one win. Charlie Monk, whose form was one of the stories of the year – he stunned all the big boys by winning the Internationale at Wimbledon – confirmed his outstanding transition from the Provincial League by winning the round. He beat Trevor Hedge in a run-off after both had scored 14 points, one more than Brian Brett.

Things seemed to be getting better and going my way as I got back into regular action but three weeks later, after scoring a maximum for an Overseas team in a nothing challenge match at Newport, I was in trouble again. In the scratch race final I was out wide and smacked my right hand on the Somerton Park safety fence, cracking several bones.

Sore and sorry, I was determined to ride for Newcastle at Wimbledon the following night. It was not the best decision of all time. After an unsatisfactory start left me alone at the gate in Heat 10, I parked the bike in the starting area, and then Ronnie Greene tried to wrestle me and the bike off the track. It must have looked very undignified, especially for the promoter for whom perfection was never enough.

Things went from bad to worse in the last race. Newcastle needed a 5-1 which would have produced a 39-38 win. Bretty and I were out front, trying to team ride, and touched handlebars. I highsided at the end of the straight, breaking eight bones in my right foot. Once more it looked as if my world championship was jinxed.

It was a complete fluke that the British Final at West Ham, scheduled for the following Tuesday, August 24, was washed out.

114 – Ivan Mauger

But it did give me a few more days in which to try to get myself as ready as possible for the last big push.

Newcastle were at Halifax on the Saturday and, determined to prove to myself I could do it, I rode – quite poorly and painfully as it turned out. I had a last, two seconds and a win but all that achieved was to aggravate the injuries in my hand and leg.

With six World Final berths on offer, the British Final was going to be a tremendously competitive meeting for anybody, never mind a seriously incapacitated first-timer. I turned up with a bag of goodies provided by Carlo but the West Ham track doctor took one look at the telltale marks on various parts of my body and refused to give me any more injections.

This was not the only thing which did not go according to the script. There was more rain which threatened the meeting and then a lengthy argument between a group of riders and promoters over the terms agreed for the meeting. All of this went on for maybe three quarters of an hour and was a further distraction.

When it was sorted out and the other riders eventually went out on parade, I was in the ambulance room injecting myself in my heel, between the toes, and the fingers of my right hand in the forlorn hope of masking the pain.

Briggo as usual led the qualifiers with 13 points. I scuffed around and scored five points but at no time was there much danger of finishing among the top six. In fact the more experienced ex-National League riders dominated a night on which Newcastle's joy was limited to cheering Bretty to his first World Final.

I simply didn't have the stomach to attend the final at Wembley. In those days all the riders in every team received two passes for the big night. After investing so much into it and suffering so much grief and frustration, I'd had enough of the world championship that year and gave my tickets away.

When we got back to Christchurch after the season ended I set about stepping up my fitness. Twice a day I trained at the Rapaki track which was quite a steep climb. I purposely strained my foot and ankle forward because the screws inserted at Wolverhampton restricted the upward movement and I needed that upward movement for my steel shoe.

(I tell all my training school pupils that your steel shoe should be like a snow ski or water ski and how they need to have their left foot tilted upwards and the steel shoe tilting upwards in the front).

But it was giving me huge pain every day and night. The surgeon in Wolverhampton had told me the screws would stay in my ankle indefinitely. When Dr McFarlane in Papanui Road X-rayed my ankle he told me one of the screws had bent over, so no wonder it was painful.

SEEING THE WORLD – in Wrocław for the 1966 World Team Cup Final with Colin Pratt, Barry Briggs, Terry Betts, Nigel Boocock and Charles Foot

The doctor said he could take them out, no problem. He looked after the All Blacks' ankles and I trusted his version of events so a few days later he performed the operation and the problem was solved.

I had two big scars up either side of my ankle and he cut both sides only an inch or so, took out the screws and put the ankle in plaster for about a week. So I only have those scars now and not any others. Then I went back to see him again and he took off the plaster and just bandaged it up.

He told me I had to walk three or four times a day, starting off with a mile and building up to four or five miles. I was under instruction to do that for about a week or 10 days before I could run up the Rapaki track again. I have had absolutely no pain in it since then.

Staying healthy was uppermost in my mind as the 1966 season approached. A year older, a bit wiser, a great deal more committed than ever before, and batteries recharged after those few months in New Zealand, I was desperate to make this the long-awaited breakthrough year.

If that was to happen, it meant successfully negotiating the longest haul British and colonial riders had been asked to endure – seven meetings, 35 or more races, with something over four months between the first qualifying

EUROPEAN CHAMPION – a first-time win at Wembley in 1966 with Barry Briggs second and Antoni Woryna third

rounds in May and the final in Gothenburg on September 23 – its latest staging date.

Modern observers talk about the Grand Prix being a marathon rather than a sprint. Those who refer to the old one-off World Final can easily overlook the fact that even in those days, a rider had to be close to the top of his game over an extended period just to get through a series of qualifiers to the night of nights.

This time I got my campaign off on the right foot by going through the card at Newcastle followed by 12 at Long Eaton and 11 at Hackney. So far, so good.

The draw put me in the British semi-final at Halifax which looked like being a pretty tough meeting, and so it proved. Briggo at his most dominant romped round The Shay and peeled off five victories but it was a dogfight for everybody else. I was happy enough to cobble together nine points and George Hunter and I took the last two qualifying places.

The British Final at Wimbledon, with nine to qualify for the next stage, was more comfortable going for me, although a very hard-fought affair further downfield. Again Briggo topped the pile and I was second on the night, a point behind him.

At Sheffield 10 days later in the newly-created British-Nordic Final, it was the same one-two finish. Barry took no prisoners and collected a maximum. I got 13 and felt my confidence gathering.

Norway's Sverre Harrfeldt was the only one of the Scandinavians to make the top seven, but the occasion had an interesting footnote, the first appearance in England of Ole Olsen. The 20-year-old Dane scored five points.

And so to Wembley and the European Final. The top 10 would be rewarded with a passage to the World Final in Gothenburg. I was winning my fair share of races in most meetings. A couple more shouldn't be too much to ask for. Surely my time was coming.

When I went down with Goog Allan for practice day on the Thursday it was the first time I had been in the world's most famous stadium for eight years. I remember how I felt driving into Wembley – so proud to even be riding there as that seemed such a distant ambition on my previous visit.

Guy Allott at Buxton spent hours preparing my bikes. We had two bikes ready but I had a clear idea about the one I preferred. When Goog and I set off on the Saturday morning, everything was organised, and the mood was good.

As to the meeting, it was fantastic to be in that unique atmosphere and part of the Wembley scene. The whole experience was as I had imagined it when I saw Briggo win the world title there in 1957 and 1958 – the crowds, huge waves of noise, multi-coloured scarves from all the tracks, rattles whirring.

And at the end of the night, I was the new European champion.

As with all those qualifying meetings I went to the track to make it to the next stage. If I got eight or nine points in my first three rides I would then try to either win the meeting or place as high as possible.

For once Briggo did not carry all before him. He beat me in our first race but after that everything went my way and I won the title with 14 points, relegating Barry and Poland's stylish Antoni Woryna to the minor placings.

It was a great feeling to win my first meeting at Wembley – but not an end in itself. I was through to a World Final at last.

AT LAST – Ivan Mauger, world champion, 1968, a decade after the first attempt, two years on from a World Final debut in Gothenburg (below)

Heat 7

THE MAKING OF A CHAMPION

MY life and career has been closely bound up with the world championship, and a list of successes I am very proud to have achieved.

On reflection, those six world titles were a payback for years of hard work and attention to detail, the rewards all the sweeter following the struggles and many disappointments which littered my first few years of racing.

Winning my first world crown in Gothenburg on Friday, September 6, 1968 was a moment I had been waiting for half my life, since that first ride on the beach as a schoolboy hopeful.

A month short of my 29th birthday, I was the oldest first-time winner since England's Tommy Price, who was 37 in 1949, the first post-war World Final.

I thus became the first 'newcomer' outside the circle of the 1950s and '60s 'big five' – Ronnie Moore, Peter Craven, Ove Fundin, Barry Briggs and Björn Knutsson – to take out the title since Freddie Williams had his second victory in 1953.

Much has been made of the fact that my breakthrough was a long time coming, whereas Ronnie won his first world title at 21, as did Craven. Ove and Briggo were only 22.

However they were not exactly overnight sensations. Their successes were some years in the making, really.

As often as not, comparisons are made between the three guys from Christchurch who scaled the heights. Ronnie qualified for the World Final as a 17-year-old in his first season in England which of course was exceptional and never repeated.

But don't forget he had been on his dad's Wall of Death act at the age of seven and riding motorbikes from an even earlier age. His 1954 Wembley win came towards the end of his fifth full season of racing in England.

Barry came to motorcycles much later, and 1957 was his sixth National League campaign.

When eventually I climbed on to the rostrum in Sweden, it was almost 12 years since my first competitive ride but I had done less than four seasons in Britain's top flight, the first of them wrecked by injury.

So in racing terms, probably we were about even. A handful of races in 1957 and 1958, then two Provincial League seasons, had been the extent of my UK apprenticeship before the birth of the British League in 1965.

120 – Ivan Mauger

If the rides and the opportunities had been forthcoming, who knows, I might have got to world championship contention a lot earlier, but I don't feel my career suffered from it – in fact it may well have benefited.

Certainly I worked for and appreciated everything that eventually came my way, and retained an appetite and enthusiasm for it all over many years. That is not to knock or downplay what the other guys did in any way.

Ronnie was the original talent, and the records do not do justice as to how good he was. Part of that is because he took time out although he was such a natural he always came back with a flourish.

Barry on the other hand had to battle a bit more. He's still absolutely in love with speedway, though. At our ripe old age I am very selective about where and when I get on a bike these days.

The modern-day followers and speedway historians classify Briggo as a four-time champion yet tend to overlook he was one of the favourites going into the 1972 World Final in which he copped a bad hand injury and, frankly, was never quite the same again.

I am grateful not to have damaged myself too much in the pursuit of the title, and in the early times when progress was desperately difficult would happily have settled for just a fraction of the success which my two role models accomplished. In the final analysis, I kept on racing and kept on winning because once I discovered the knack, it would have seemed wasteful not to carry on.

The glamour and excitement of racing overseas is part of the journey, but getting to the World Final and better still, winning the championship, was the crock of gold at the end of the rainbow which inspired me and, no doubt, many others since.

After winning the European title at Wembley, I gave myself a chance of winning in Gothenburg in 1966.

It's not right to say it didn't happen because I was denied the chance to practise on a track I had never seen. But the fact Mike Parker refused to let me go in time to size up the place certainly didn't help.

I was really excited about qualifying for the final, in the best form of my life – after the injuries and frustrations of the previous year, my second British League campaign brought me 388 points, a 9.82 average, eighth overall, and 11 maximums in 36 meetings.

Although Brian Brett had an injury-marred season the Diamonds climbed to fifth in the league. Hardly anybody could touch us at home, Pete Kelly and Graham Coombes from Auckland made handy contributions and there was a buzz in the air.

There was almost three weeks between Wembley and Sweden, in which all the usual anticipation was building by the day. Most of the forecasters were tipping a likely three-way tussle between Björn Knutsson, the defending champion, his old mate Barry, and the dangerous Göte Nordin, one of the few riders to get remotely close to Briggo in the averages.

The fact Knutty was no longer racing in England was not seen as a mark against him; a few weeks earlier he had come over with Vargarna and looked pretty sharp when he scored a maximum at Newcastle.

Nordin, though, was very much on the British League scene and beat just about everybody who was anybody – except me – in the Internationale at Wimbledon on Whit Monday. I wasn't invited. Perhaps Ronnie Greene had mislaid my contact details.

It didn't bother me at all that most of the pundits hardly mentioned me in passing. After 10 years in waiting, I felt good and ready to have a real crack. Often a rider's best chance is the first one, when other people's expectations are not that high, and it is generally assumed that nerves and inexperience will play a big part.

Briggo would not have underestimated me. He has said my European Final win was a turning point, because up to that meeting he usually expected to beat me and he thought I probably expected it as well. Certainly it was something more than just a stepping stone to a World Final.

But when Mike Parker would not let me go to the Wednesday practice at Ullevi, it punctured the mood. Even for the World Final, riders had to get permission from their promoter to ride in FIM meetings in other countries.

The boat left Hull on Mondays and those days most of us only had two bikes, both of which were needed at the practice. Parker refused to let me go because to have done so would have meant missing the Monday night meeting at Newcastle.

There was little option but to cop it sweet, and by the time I arrived in Gothenburg, everyone else knew more about the track than I did. As the new boy I just absorbed the atmosphere and prepared to do my best. Bob Hall and Gordon Stobbs were with me in the pits and for the first and last time in a World Final we guessed what gear to pull at the start of the meeting.

Björn Knutsson

122 – Ivan Mauger

Not having seen the place did me no favours because after two rides on the big night I had scored a third and a second, and with three points to my name found myself behind seven other riders. With the benefit of practice I would have pulled a higher gear which could well have made a big difference.

Possibly the only rider who was more dejected at that stage was Björn Knutsson. The reigning champion, carrying so many of the hopes of the Swedish crowd, managed a single point from his first two outings. His title defence, and, as it happened, his world championship career, was all but over.

I did manage to get my act together and take two wins and a second from my remaining rides, but 11 points took me no further than fourth place.

The entire outcome was settled in Heat 9 when the previously unbeaten Briggo, Sverre Harrfeldt and Toni Woryna met. The 1-2-3 finishing order was also how they ended the night.

In a way my debut performance slipped under the radar. Apart from the obvious recognition of Briggo's dominance and the outstanding efforts of the other placegetters, much of the talk revolved around how disappointing Knutsson had been, how unlucky Nordin was after having his gear stolen a couple of days before the final.

And as far as many observers were concerned, if they had glimpsed a future world champion on parade it was Torbjörn Harrysson who took their eye. Despite being shocking off the start, the little-known 20-year-old collected 10 points on debut with five eventful and exciting second places.

Alan Ashall had kept the program for me at the European Final but Peter Oakes was my stats man at Ullevi – and was to continue to do so at all my World Finals and other important world championship meetings.

It was another piece in the organisational jigsaw. I usually was pretty aware of who was doing what and kept on top of my progress and that of the other riders, but having somebody as cluey as Peter on the job was always reassuring.

It is impossible to say what difference there may have been had I been able to practise in Gothenburg. I don't think I would have won the meeting, but very possibly could have done better.

The fact my promoter had given little thought to my championship ambitions did nothing to improve our relationship. It is not uncommon for organisations and bosses in all walks of life to expect loyalty from people but conveniently forget loyalty is a two-way street.

It meant we finished what had been my greatest season so far on something less than cordial terms. Having made an agreement to stay on, I was not about to go back on it. But I did suggest to Mike Parker that as world

No.4 and European champion, I should be worth a bit more than he had contracted to pay me for the next year.

He did agree to buy me a new ESO machine which turned out to be a mixed blessing, but we could not have anticipated that. It's fair to say, though, that in the off-season I was not unhappy to have as much distance as possible between myself and Mike Parker.

It so happens that teammate Goog Allan and I put a few thousand miles between ourselves and British speedway in February 1967, when we went off to ride in the world ice-racing championships in Siberia. On the basis that it's fine to try anything once, I did just that but had no great ambition to try it again!

The Russians had been awarded the title with the proviso that riders from other countries would be included, and when I heard about it I told the Speedway Control Board I would be interested in going. When I mentioned it to Goog, he thought it would be a good adventure.

Rounding out the official Great Britain party for that ground-breaking trip was a third New Zealander, none other than Trevor Redmond – TR the NZ Star as he liked to be called – who came along as our team manager.

We flew from Heathrow to Moscow, and then set off on the 55-hour Trans-Siberian Railway journey to Novosibirsk.

The Russians and Swedes in particular took their ice-racing very seriously and they all seemed very accomplished and confident. When we went out for the parade, we could hardly stay upright on the ice. For us it was a case of learning on the job.

Goog adapted quite quickly to the peculiar racing requirements but I found the whole experience so far removed from conventional speedway I must have looked the complete novice I was. I scored a single point on each day of the two-day semi-finals and in retrospect was quite happy to get out of there in one piece.

Nevertheless it was an incredible couple of weeks, not least attending the after-meeting party at which the truly experienced ones demonstrated their ability for knocking back shots of vodka in traditional Soviet style.

Back at Newcastle for another season, 1967 was in many ways similar to the previous year – 387 British League points, a 9.32 average, eight maximums. It wasn't great but it wasn't bad either, especially as I spent a lot of time going to and fro trying to decide whether to stick with the Jap or go with the new ESO motors.

The bike Mike Parker had bought for me seemed a better bet if the tracks were rough which, increasingly, some of the British circuits were. But Briggo, who had won the world title on the Czech machine the previous year

NEW KID – Ole Olsen listens attentively at 1967 Hyde Road training school

and was now importing the bikes into Britain, reckoned they could eventually surpass the Jap for all-round performance.

Time was to prove him right. My own early experience, however, was anything but promising. The Jawa kept misbehaving and costing me points, and when I went back on to the Jap that developed some major problems too.

Exasperated, I told Mike Parker I needed a replacement engine for the league visit to Swindon. He provided a Jap motor for me to use but it turned out to be completely useless. I blew my top and walked out of the meeting at Blunsdon. It was not a good reaction and it brought a whole storm buzzing around my head.

It didn't help when the local paper and the Diamonds programme made a number of references to my problems which suggested to the public that I was not on top of the job. In fact I was spending every spare hour known to man working with Guy Allott to try to sort things out and I didn't take at all kindly to inferences suggesting otherwise.

The team slipped to a mid-table position but we were good value, especially at home. A surprise loss against eventual champions Swindon – coinciding with my worst meeting of the season – ended up costing us about four places on the table but there were some positives, including the contributions of fellow Kiwis Goog Allan and Dave Gifford. Probably the most significant happening, though, was the arrival of Ole Olsen.

Brian Brett decided he had had enough of commuting up from his Hoddesdon base every Monday and made tracks for Cradley Heath, a much more central home location. Mike Parker and I were not best buddies by now but at least we managed to agree on one thing – Ole had the potential to be a handy replacement.

The more experienced Kurt Bøgh was the rider Mike fancied signing, but Ole had impressed me in a training school Mike had organised and I ran for a party of Danes at Belle Vue a few weeks earlier, before the season got under way.

Ole had a rubbish bike and just the tyre that was on it, but soaked up every morsel of advice he could. I was impressed by his enthusiasm and even took him back to stay with the family after the first night because the accommodation organised for the Danes, surprise, surprise, was anything but five-star. Ole was the only one who could speak English so we got on immediately.

Kurt Bøgh looked a better rider to Mike because he and several others had bought new bikes and spare wheels with new tyres. But Ole had a new bike waiting for him in Denmark and I told Mike I could help him a lot more. With Mike's permission I called Ole and he agreed immediately to come over. I told him he could stay with the family, use my workshop and travel with me.

The other promoters, always mindful of the quota of foreign riders coming in to the British League in its early days, took their time before agreeing to sanction the signing. Eventually the DMU, the SCB and everybody else was happy and rubber-stamped his contract. As soon as they did, the Diamonds had an extra sparkle about them.

I went to Harwich to pick him up and for the first couple of years we shared my car and travelled up and down England, Scotland and Wales. We slept in the car when we were too tired to drive any further, we shared rooms

126 – Ivan Mauger

at bed and breakfast places all over Britain and sometimes when we were late booking in we had to share a double bed.

When we were driving to and from meetings he used to ask me a hundred questions about setting up bikes, what compression for what type of tracks, ignition settings, throttle control, where to ride on what tracks, what were the best gates at different circuits – all the questions I used to ask Jack Young on the nine hours each way Adelaide to Melbourne haul a few years earlier.

Ole was very receptive and would then go out and do what we talked about on the track. In 1967 and 1968 we would practise a lot of nights after the meeting at Newcastle and sometimes at away tracks.

We both had the same determination to be world champion but different ways of going about it and quite different values in life. But the common denominator was winning the world championship and the fear that we would fail to do that. That fear was what made us both successful.

My first advice to Ole was that Newcastle was very bumpy, had long straights and tight corners and would teach him to ride really well after the big round tracks he was used to racing on in Denmark and Germany.

He ended up averaging 7.52 in his first season – and 9.23 in 1968 – and his presence not only helped the team to be pretty competitive, it certainly gave me an extra push as well.

One bonus in 1967 was that the route to the World Final was not quite so lengthy as the previous year. My championship campaign got off to a great start with a maximum and a new track record at Hackney, followed by a patchy 10 at rainy Cradley Heath the following evening.

Bad weather rubbed out the scheduled home round at Newcastle but after a week's delay I scored 15 at Brough Park to post 40 from my three qualifiers. That was comfortable enough, and a 10-point haul in my British semi-final at Wimbledon was sufficient to guarantee further progress.

Briggo blasted out his own message by going through the card, and did the same in the British Final at West Ham. My own form was decent enough, 13 points and second place on a night Eric Boocock, Colin Pratt, Rick France and Ray Wilson qualified for a World Final for the first time … and Nigel Boocock, who had been in four in a row, missed out.

At least there were no problems in the run-up to Wembley. I won the Northern Riders title at Sheffield a couple of nights after the British Final, put together some of my most consistent scoring in the league and had a fair amount of quiet confidence building. The critics didn't burden me with too much by way of pre-meeting predictions and that suited me just fine.

Bob Hall, Chris Macdonald, and Ole were with me in the pits and we knew things were much more organised than they had been a year earlier.

The Will To Win – 127

HELPING HANDS – Barry Briggs and Ole Olsen offer their advice at Wembley, 1967

ON THE ROSTRUM – happy to be a Wembley medallist, even if it's bronze behind Ove Fundin and Bengt Jansson

128 – Ivan Mauger

After winning my first three races, at the interval I was level with Fundin, a point ahead of Bengt Jansson and Igor Plechanov.

This time it was Briggo, a raging favourite for the title, who had the slow start, three points from his first two rides. He wasn't going to be coming back from there. Then Ove lost to Jansson and Plechanov beat me so with four rides gone, four of us were on 11 points.

My Heat 18 clash with Ove was going to be critical. But my challenge had barely begun when I was dumped on my backside after Bernie Persson had bowled into me in the first corner. He was rightly excluded but spent 20 minutes arguing and carrying on, just the sort of situation to suit the Swedes.

I didn't have the experience to blank it from my mind, and when Fundin beat me in the re-run, Benga also won his last ride and Plechanov ran a third. I had to be content with the bronze medal, and watching the wily old Swede use all his psychological powers to see off Jansson in the run-off.

I felt great standing on the rostrum but disappointed not to have got into the run-off. It did help concentrate the mind, though. As the crowd roared their appreciation and Mrs Nelson Mills-Baldwin, wife of the SCB chairman, presented the prizes, it made me determined to win it the next year.

It opened Ole's eyes as well. He was with me in the Wembley pits and no doubt the whole occasion made a massive impression upon him. If he was unclear about his ambitions before that night, they dropped into place there and then.

These were early days for him but I sensed I was getting close enough to take a real shot at the title. Less certain was what the next 12 months might bring. Thanks to my improving reputation, my ability to pick up good appearance fees for continental bookings was increasing all the time. At the same time the relationship with Mike Parker was deteriorating.

But both of us saw the benefit of coming to another agreement for 1968. I also wanted to find out if my increasing world status might be attractive to one of the manufacturers. The Jap was still going strong but Jawa were starting to mount the beginnings of a challenge.

Riding in Europe on a regular basis, I had heard suggestions the Czech factory might be interested in bringing me on board as a works rider.

But I heard nothing from them, and decided to try my luck with George Greenwood, the Jap agent. With the British engine still favoured by the majority of riders, he did not see any value in offering me anything and I couldn't imagine that situation changing.

So I decided to continue with both, while favouring the Jawa for world championship meetings. Right from the off, it appeared not to matter what

I rode, I couldn't stop winning. The results kept coming, my confidence was soaring, and there seemed no good reason why it should not continue.

The world qualifiers started with a 15 at Belle Vue, then another maximum at Newcastle, and 13 the next night at West Ham.

Those 43 points were not enough to put me on top of the list of qualifiers, though – that distinction went to Briggo and, more surprisingly, Martin Ashby who was really beginning to hit his straps after a winter rider control-directed move from champions Swindon to Exeter. They both got 44.

Then I won the British semi-final at Poole with 14 points, heading off Ashby in a run-off.

The British Final at Wimbledon was even better, a 15-point maximum which included Briggo's only defeat of the night, and then another five-ride full house in the British-Nordic Final at West Ham on a track affected by rain.

Publicity or the lack of it didn't unduly bother me but it was amusing to have more attention generated by Barry's uncharacteristic six points at the Custom House than anything I did on the night. He had been troubled by a broken thumb since before the British Final and even after taking a rest from

STEPPING UP – British championship winner Wimbledon, 1968, flanked by Eric Boocock and Briggo

racing to help it to mend, it looked as if he would be out of the championship after 14 World Finals in a row.

As events turned out, reserve Norman Hunter (flu) did not travel to the European Final in Wrocław, and then last qualifier Eric Boocock was ruled out by doctors after suffering chronic airsickness. Relieved and reprieved, Barry rode after all and with nine points safely negotiated his way through to the final.

The Polish trio of Pawel Waloszek (13), Antoni Woryna (11) and Jerzy Trzeszkowski (11) led the way but from my viewpoint, 10 points and fourth spot represented a more than satisfactory job done.

Going to Poland was regarded as the toughest of all possible tests. The Iron Curtain was still in place, trips to Cold War territory were usually nervous affairs. This one was all the more so as the Russians had invaded Czechoslovakia a few days earlier and Europe was a very tense place.

To give an idea of the thinking of the time, some western-based pundits had gone so far as to suggest that all five Poles and three Russians could qualify from the Wrocław meeting. During the practice none of the British-based riders were going any good, and I said to Guy Allott:

'I am going to have to ride like the Poles and Russians if I am going to qualify, otherwise none of our western guys are going to make it.'

I went out in the next practice, perched my bum on the back mudguard as the Poles and Russians did and was amazed that it all went OK.

Everybody expected the opposition on the day to be fast and ferocious and sure enough they were all over us. But I stayed tuned in, picked up points along the way, won my last race and got the track record so I must have been doing something right.

The meeting was also memorable for a horrific crash which wiped out Sverre Harrfeldt and the Norwegian suffered injuries which took more than a year to mend.

The irony was the Norwegian federation had told Harrfedlt and Reidar Eide not to go because of the political situation. They ignored the advice and Harrfeldt ended up in a Polish hospital with a broken pelvis, thigh and ankle injuries.

While Wrocław at that point remained a venue which westerners had yet to crack, Gothenburg seemed like familiar territory. I hadn't been back since my debut there two years earlier but felt full of confidence in my ability to go well.

Most of the season had gone like clockwork. In the British League I scored 23 maximums in 36 meetings, totalled 449 points and averaged 11.37.

Newcastle began well enough to be talked of as a title chance, only to fall just short. Fifth was a big effort nevertheless, only three points behind Coventry who pipped Hackney on race points.

Ole made massive improvements and our friendly rivalry was a big factor in pushing both of us to greater heights. And Gary Peterson, the latest Kiwi connection, a 22-year-old from New Plymouth, looked a great little prospect in a handful of appearances. He also helped me out with workshop jobs and came on a few weekend trips to the Continent.

However at times Newcastle was not a happy camp and it was no secret my relationship with Mike Parker was deteriorating fast. I could win a dozen races on the trot, then have a problem in one and cop criticism for it.

Just as in the previous season, there were comments in the programme and the local press which questioned my professionalism and they all had the Parker stamp on them.

Reporters always have the opportunity to make up their own mind, but when they were being fed with this sort of stuff, obviously it made the headlines they often find irresistible.

Things blew up following one especially uncomplimentary report which appeared after I'd had a couple of less-than-flash international matches. I didn't have to be asked twice to give my thoughts. It was a situation in which I needed little encouragement to blurt out some of my own frustrations, including the fact the Brough Park track was usually rough and better suited to riding scrambles.

I quit the captaincy and told people I wouldn't be riding for Newcastle after the end of the season. Just about the final straw was when once again I wasn't allowed to go to the practice in Sweden. All that achieved was to make me even more fired up to win the title and crystallised my determination to move on.

If the promotion had changed I would have been happy to stay with Newcastle to the end of my British League career. But that wasn't going to happen. This was when I put in a request for a transfer to Belle Vue. Maybe it was not ideal timing, with the World Final looming, but this was something which could not be bottled up any longer.

Contrary to opinion I never fell out with Mike Parker over money. He paid me excellent money for the years I was at Newcastle, the other riders never complained either and this was a promoter who never owed any of the boys a thing. Most of the conversations we ever had concerning money were pretty well agreed in 10 minutes.

It is on record how Mike was one of the promoters who got the Provincial League started and was also the prime mover in the formation of the British League. Speedway really took off and was great for the next 20 years or so.

132 – Ivan Mauger

The sport probably could do with another Mike Parker, a man never afraid to tell the authorities and the other promoters exactly where they were going wrong and what they should do to get it right. He was also very much a visionary and knew where he wanted the sport to progress. I accepted all that but I still needed to get away from him.

This time I was one of the clear favourites for the world championship. Briggo had been struggling with fitness – although his Gothenburg record alone stamped him as a huge threat. Fundin was back to defend the title and there was no telling what someone like Toby Harrysson – by now a top man in British League – might do.

In my mind, the title was there to be won and that's how it turned out.

Raye's mum Agnes had come to stay with us on what was her first trip back to England since 1950. She was not at all interested in speedway and was the ideal choice to babysit the kids when we went off to Gothenburg.

Raye told her mum she would call after the meeting to tell her the results. It was great that she could ring and say that I had won for the first time with a 15-point maximum.

Kym and Debbie were asleep but Julie, who was 11, was allowed to stay up. Julie has often recalled how she and Agnes both danced in the lounge room to celebrate the news.

After the first four races I was ready to do some dancing of my own — two points ahead of Briggo and three points ahead of Gennadi Kurilenko, the young Russian who was in his first final.

I won my last race to wrap up my first world championship. Briggo got a second in his final outing to finish as runner-up on 12. Poland's crew-cut kid Edward Jancarz came from a point behind Kurilenko and won his last race so both finished on 11. Jancarz beat Kurilenko in the run-off for third.

The Swedes have always been big on presentation and among the goodies handed up to me as I surveyed the view from the top of the rostrum was an enormous bouquet. A few minutes later I was able to hand it over to Raye, who had made her way through the crowds, and we shared a private moment which celebrated all the years of sacrifice.

When it comes right down to it, a world champion has to find from within whatever it is to get the job done. At the end of the day, it's something you have to accomplish all by yourself. But of course nobody can win a world title without a lot of help from a great many people.

I was happy to share the moment with the Newcastle fans who had supported me, cheered me, comforted me in difficult times and cheerfully celebrated the good ones. But I definitely had a problem observing Mike Parker basking in the reflected glory and seemingly wanting everyone to give him equal credit for my success.

LOVELY – savouring the 1968 World Final win with Mona Samuelsson, Sweden's Miss Speedway

When I got back to Newcastle for the Monday night match against Halifax and what should have been a celebration, we had our last massive fall-out. The mayor was there to give me a full civic reception on the centre green.

Mike congratulated me and said that he'd brought me over to Newcastle and helped to make me world champion. Then he handed the microphone to the mayor who said some great things before handing it to me.

I put the mike behind my back and said to him: 'Don't believe a bloody word he said. Actually, he's hindered my chances of being the champion.'

Mike was standing about a foot away and his face was turning purple. Then I told the crowd it had been great but I would only ride the rest of the season at Newcastle. When I had fulfilled my commitments, it was the end. I said that the only way I'd continue for the club was if they had a new promoter.

I couldn't believe how angry he was getting but that was how I felt. It was all a matter of principle and over what I thought he had done to my career – especially the way he treated me over the World Finals.

We never had another conversation. He never tried to get me to change my mind. My attitude was that if I didn't get another club in the UK then I would concentrate on riding overseas, especially in Europe where almost every weekend was a big payday.

It was a risky thing to do because I didn't have a track to go to although there had been unofficial approaches from several who were ready to talk. I gambled on the fact that as the new world champion, the British Promoters' Association would eventually want me back.

The Speedway Control Board were sufficiently concerned to ask Mike Parker and myself to attend a meeting at the start of October to clarify the range of disagreements which had prompted my transfer request.

Nelson Mills-Baldwin, chairman of the Board, asked me about claims that I did not like the Newcastle track, that association with a Monday night promotion hampered my increasing continental commitments, and that other tracks had offered me large inducements to move.

It was not difficult to answer – sure I had been critical of the state of the Brough Park circuit, but my record of success there including countless wins and the track record made a nonsense of suggestions that the track was a problem. I had no dramas getting to Newcastle from wherever I had been racing in Europe on a Sunday. And money was never a factor in my wishing to leave.

If Mike Parker paid me 10 times what I received in 1968, it wouldn't have been enough to persuade me to continue riding for the man. Our relationship had well and truly passed its use-by date.

MY HERO – Raye joins in the victory celebrations at Ullevi

The drama still was not quite over because before the end of the season I had to send my equipment back to New Zealand. That meant borrowing a bike for each of the last two fixtures, when old mates Ken Vale and Pete Jarman helped me out.

Despite the fact I top-scored in both meetings, at Wimbledon and Wolverhampton on successive evenings, Newcastle reported me to the Speedway Control Board for supposedly breaching the contract which stipulates it is a rider's responsibility to supply a machine in proper working order for his own use.

If officialdom did not realise the extent of the bitter rift before then, that should have convinced them. It was a sorry way to end a six-year association with a club where I really enjoyed riding.

Raye and I made lots of friends with whom we still keep in contact and visit whenever we go up that way. Newcastle was so much a part of our family's life.

I've mentioned Gordon and Margaret Stobbs but there were many others. Jack and Eileen McClurey and their family became very good friends. Bob Hall who ran the Lowry's Shell Garage in Church Street, Walker was a great help to all the team as was Les Cummings.

Bob and Tony Shelley came with us to my first win in Gothenburg in 1968 – along with Gordon and Chris Macdonald – so it was very much a combined Newcastle effort.

The years at Brough Park were great. The Geordie fans were encouraging to all the boys and we could all feel it. There was great team spirit in the 1960s and the stadium was always buzzing on Monday nights. Eddie Glennon was an excellent team manager who had a rapport with all the boys. The team changed a bit but there were several riders who were around in all those years.

The *Evening Chronicle* used to have a special race night edition every Monday with two back pages. They used Spencer Oliver's photos and Sam Brooks's reports. Then come Tuesday morning there was half a back cover. Spencer would go home after the meetings, develop his photos and take his selection to the *Chronicle* and Sam would do the story.

Tom Graham Snr became Mike's right hand man in Newcastle, George English Snr and his wife Joan with Jack Hewlett ran the supporters club, and Ivan Stephenson was the pit marshal. Those were good times.

Mike Parker was not everybody's favourite by the time I left Newcastle but he did do a lot of good for speedway. You can never take that away from him. But, from a personal point of view, he gave me my chance and then held me back.

ACE OF CLUBS – the pride of Belle Vue

Heat 8

ACES HIGH

ONLY a handful of clubs have managed to dominate British speedway for several seasons in a row. Nobody did it better than Belle Vue in the four years I was there.

One of the key elements when the British League was formed was the understanding between promoters that for it to succeed, there needed to be a reasonably even distribution of talent.

Various forms of rider control have been applied, either by committee or, in later years, by a succession of points limits. Some have been more successful than others, almost all have been controversial, none perfect.

The one thing most promoters agree upon and most supporters disagree over is the need for any sort of control or regulation.

A huge number of professional sports have survived because they do impose some such rules, whether by a salary cap or some other device. The survival of the fittest is fine in theory but the survival of the sport is why speedway clubs have been subject to this type of control.

In a world where only the strong survive, and the weak are allowed to go to the wall, the numbers and competition will contract. In the end the big guys are left with only themselves to play against.

However it is essential that those with enterprise and ambition are given the opportunity to develop their own resources and aspire to greater heights.

The flip side is that speedway, like any other sport or entertainment, needs its headline acts, its star attractions who can be guaranteed to pull the biggest crowds. Requiring the most successful teams to contribute to the greater good remains one of the most hotly debated aspects of British speedway.

The principle and the reality of rider control helped me to get to Belle Vue in 1969 and was the underlying reason behind my departure four honours-laden seasons later.

I was happy riding for Belle Vue and would have continued to do so for the rest of my British League career. They were great days and after helping to turn Newcastle into a club that could win, I wanted to do the same and more for the Aces.

That ambition was more than achieved. I went to Hyde Road as the world champion, left as the world champion, and in the intervening period led the team to three titles in a row, something which has never been equalled in the modern era.

138 – Ivan Mauger

Belle Vue had a tremendous name in speedway, but for a few years they had done little after winning the National League in 1963, posthumously honouring Peter Craven's contribution.

The fact they were one of the pioneering tracks, and dominated during the 1930s, kept the flag flying in the wartime years, and were one of the diehard members of the top flight, gave them a reputation more recent performances had done little to uphold.

In the first two years of the British League, they did not win an away match. Their placings from 1965–68 were ordinary, and apart from a spell in 1967 when Ove Fundin turned out as a replacement for the injured Sören Sjösten, they hadn't had a top name.

When Dent Oliver was appointed as manager things started to take a turn for the better. Dent had been a star rider after the war, and at 42 was still a rival to be respected in my first Provincial League season, when he rode for Sheffield.

His great contribution though was to take over the Hyde Road training school and devote himself to unearthing and polishing raw talent. His early charges formed the nucleus of the Belle Vue Colts team which won the first Second Division in '68.

So from all those points of view, the Aces were once again a club on the rise. But nobody could have predicted just how much success would come their way over the next four years. At the time, I just wanted to get myself away from Newcastle, sorted and settled.

Geographically, Belle Vue was perfect for me. The facilities were ideal. The racetrack was the best in the world. And they wanted me, big time.

I got on well with managing director Jack Fearnley and Dent Oliver and both knew my relationship with Mike Parker was falling apart.

Belle Vue, owned by Trust House Forte, had a reputation as a very professionally-run outfit and you couldn't miss big, booming Jack, who had been a rugby league player of some reputation. He had been a fixture at Hyde Road for 27 years in a variety of increasingly important roles so when he spoke, everybody listened.

Strictly against the BSPA rules (but it goes on all the time) from the early part of the 1968 season we started talking seriously about me joining Belle Vue in 1969. So even before Gothenburg we had a deal pretty well agreed and about the only thing that changed was the price went up when I won the world championship.

When I put in for a transfer, Newcastle couldn't really oppose it because from the Control Board down everyone knew I would not go back there. I told the BSPA in a letter that if I couldn't ride for Belle Vue then I would simply step up my continental meetings and concentrate on riding in Europe.

Jack Fearnley

It was a bit of a gamble but I was sure all the other promoters would want me riding in England in 1969 and none of them were great friends with Mike Parker.

Raye and I and the kids returned to New Zealand at the end of the 1968 season and everything went quiet for a while. Then the BSPA started to sort out their set-up for the next season and the formation of teams and movement of riders, then as now, occupied a fair amount of time.

Ronnie Greene was the chairman of the BSPA and he telephoned a few times. In one call he said there had been a management committee meeting which approved the transfer request and had allocated me to Hackney.

I had no problems with Len Silver who was running Hackney, but that was never going to be a satisfactory move for me. If the BSPA put me at Belle Vue, that would be great and I would make arrangements to come back. Otherwise the message was that I was quite happy at home in New Zealand doing what I was doing.

Then I got another phone call, this time saying I had been allocated to Coventry – whose promoter Charles Ochiltree had not bothered to reply when I was trying to plan my return to England six years earlier. I don't think so.

The next week Ronnie Greene rang to say I had now been allocated to Wimbledon. It was my pleasure to tell him he had passed on the chance to put me in his team on merit in 1958 and no way was it going to happen now I was the world champion.

Meanwhile either Jack Fearnley or Dent would talk to me at intervals and at one stage they were getting concerned. Because they were pinning their hopes on me joining Belle Vue they were not taking any other riders that would be likely to go into the number one position.

The affair seemed to be dragging on for weeks and Ronnie Greene in an attempt to push me into a decision in 48 hours said that if I didn't go where I had been allocated, the positions would be filled and I would be left without a track.

Historically, however, what the BSPA deem to be impossible before or after Christmas is all of a sudden possible a week or two before the start of the season when teams haven't finished their rebuilding. In the event a few days before the start of the season came the call to say it was all systems go for Belle Vue.

It was a rush to pack up everything in Christchurch and get ourselves back to Manchester – so much so I missed the season-opening home and away challenge matches against Sheffield.

In addition to New Zealand to England return air fares, Belle Vue were paying a decent guarantee, were to provide me with two bikes (which I retained) and a spare engine, and pay Guy Allott for all the tuning work,

They were also to buy us a house as after renting for six years we wanted to put down permanent roots. In the meantime they provided a place for us at 61 Windsor Road, Denton, a few miles from the stadium, where we lived for five months before finding one we wanted.

When we chose 62 Abingdon Road in Bramhall, one of the more expensive places to buy a house in and around south Manchester and rather more than they had anticipated, we compromised. We paid a slice of the purchase price and Belle Vue ended up giving me a higher guarantee for the second half of that season and all of the next to make up the difference.

HYDE ROAD – a great racing venue sadly consigned to history

The Will To Win – 141

They must have been satisfied they were getting good value because after being in the bottom half of the table for the first four years of the British League, in 1969 we were runners-up to Poole.

Not only did the Aces win all 18 home matches, there were five away wins which was more than there had been in the preceding four years put together. My own scoring was even better than it had been the previous season, 461 points, an 11.67 average and 25 maximums in 37 meetings.

From a personal perspective everything seemed to be going like clockwork. I was totally in the zone and just couldn't stop winning races. It was good working with Dent Oliver and I was happy to be providing input and having some influence on how the team was performing.

Belle Vue wanted me to get involved in this way – it was part of the contract and became a standard condition of every deal I did with them and the clubs I was to represent in later years. There were challenges, though.

Tommy Roper, the captain, was someone I had known for a few years and he was happy Belle Vue had managed to get me there. He supported me when I suggested team changes and gave my opinions about pairings to Dent.

We tried different things away from home, where some of the riders were not as convincing as they were at Hyde Road. Towards the end of the season Tommy suggested I take over as captain because he felt I was good at assessing riders and had the ability to gee up all the boys.

I also changed around the pits arrangements which were very unprofessional. In the first few weeks riders were all over the place although the away team always parked together. Unfortunately I put Tommy and Sören Sjösten next to each other because early in the piece I didn't know they did not get on.

They were paired in the second to last race at home and regularly used to carve each other up, come back in the pits and start arguing about who was where and what had happened. It became a regular occurrence for them to come in and start scrapping. Fuel tins got knocked over and sometimes bikes got pushed over. It was even more colourful if they happened to be out in the same second half heat.

Like me, Sören used the Belle Vue workshops and we got to know each other quite well. He was a likeable guy, always jovial, and his wife Yvonne, who he met when he first came to Manchester, was a lovely person.

He was a really sharp rider and very good from the start. His style was to go very fast into the corners, come to a bit of a stop in the middle of the bend, make a turn and then exit the corner at speed – a bit like Hans Nielsen would do in the 1980s and '90s.

142 – Ivan Mauger

At lunchtime he often would go to the local pub and have a few pints – although never on race days. Sadly, after he finished riding he became an alcoholic and used to hang around with all the winos in central Manchester, often sleeping under bridges. After he went back to Sweden he died of alcoholic poisoning.

Dent was a workaholic, one of the old guard, and commanded widespread respect. He didn't get into speedway until the end of the war, but made three World Final appearances, and was loved by fans at Belle Vue and Bradford as a tough, uncompromising rider. After several years out of the saddle he made a comeback at Frank Varey's invitation at Sheffield in 1963 and 1964.

His great contribution when he went to Hyde Road was to oversee the emergence and development of some outstanding youngsters. Sometimes brusque, always passionate, he was always at the track in his trademark tartan cap for the practice sessions on Monday nights when the kids were riding round and a couple of them, Chris Pusey and Eric Broadbelt, were already making an impact.*

Chris was a flamboyant, bubbling personality, originally a top grass track rider. He became a favourite with the fans because halfway round the corners he would leg trail and it was spectacular to watch. In later years Briggo and I had him on our World Series several times and took him to California for that reason.

On and off track he liked to make a fashion statement. Chris had blue polka dots down the side of the legs and arms of his leathers and quickly became known as the 'polka dot kid'.

It wasn't difficult to identify his peg in the dressing rooms. He would come in decked out in smart jeans, mod suit, flared shirt and natty shoes. After the meeting he put on all the gear and headed off with his mates to the Liverpool night clubs.

We had all these characters and Belle Vue was a good place to be. The kids thought it was great as it was so close to home. Raye often took them to the Zoo in the afternoon on Saturdays before racing started. If their attention started to wander during meetings and they wanted to have a look around she would take them into the fun park next door.

Belle Vue was an exciting track to ride round and very fast. It got you going because of the miles per hour you could work up although I was used to doing high-speed long track racing on the continent as well and comfortable travelling a lot faster than some riders.

---

* Dent Oliver died at his Disley home in December 1973, aged 55, after suffering from heart problems.

WALK TALL – Val Doonican hands over the 1971 British League championship trophy to Aces Alan Wilkinson, Dent Oliver, Peter Collins, Ivan Mauger, Eric Broadbelt, Dave Hemus and Chris Pusey.

There were a number of small track riders in speedway then, and there still are today, who are very good at a certain speed but they don't want to go 10 miles an hour faster. You could do that extra speed at Belle Vue if you could handle it so it was quite an advantage.

I always loved the big, fast, sweeping corners and for several years as a Newcastle rider (and even after I left the Aces) a succession of Belle Vue people let me test bikes there on Wednesday mornings.

I had a bike with a big fuel tank and a big oil tank. I could do 22 or 23 laps full throttle, then refuel and do the same twice again, adding up 66 to 68 laps on the trot. It did not matter what the weather was like. I did it (occasionally) in sunshine but more often than not in all kinds of weather. Sometimes it was typical Manchester pouring rain but I still did those laps whenever the time permitted.

It meant going out to do just four laps in a normal race was a doddle. I could sprint four laps. Yet even these days when everybody and everything

144 – Ivan Mauger

is supposed to be that much more professional, you often see even top-class riders tire and lose concentration on the last lap.

When we first lived in Manchester the manager was Harold Jackson and he and team mechanic Wilf Lucy were at Belle Vue all week. Until Stuart Bamforth bought the track in the 1980s there was quite a comprehensive workshop and Harold and Wilf had always let me use the machinery and other facilities.*

It was a big advantage to have that sort of set-up available, and it generated confidence. Occasionally a little over-confidence crept in, and I had a spell when I sometimes forgot to turn on the fuel tap and had to go like a bat out of hell to make up lost ground. That was something you could do at Hyde Road.

That oversight cost me the track record one time and Gordon Stobbs would almost invariably check the tap was on after that. It took about another 18 months before I finally knocked off that record which had stood at 69.8 seconds since Peter Craven set it back in 1958. And that was after failing to turn on the fuel once again!

But for that I reckon I would have taken a couple of seconds off little Pete's long-standing time instead of 0.2 seconds. This was in heat six of the 1970 KO Cup Final against Wimbledon. It put the icing on an even more successful second season with the Aces, who won the championship, a whopping 11 points clear of Coventry.

My contribution was 475 points in 40 matches, an 11.18 average and 19 maximums. For the third year in succession I was the top points scorer and top average rider in the British League, something I was to repeat in 1971 which was a source of considerable pride and pleasure.

These were special times in Manchester. After the drama and distractions at Newcastle, we were happy and settled.

At the end of the season we were on the move again, but only a few miles – selling up in Bramhall and moving to a much bigger house and ground at 446 Chester Road, Woodford.

After the first league title, it was a good time for Belle Vue to start filtering in more of their outstanding youngsters. Rider control wanted to take away Tommy Roper but we managed to hold on to him for half the season because Chris Pusey, such a fast improver, had a lengthy spell on the injured list.

But the conveyor belt kept producing exciting fresh talent. Alan Wilkinson stepped up as a lively likely prospect, and after a while, Peter

---

* When Bammy knocked down the workshop, Harold Jackson called me as I had used the flat plate since 1963 to sand my clutch plates. All the famous Belle Vue riders had used it from 1928. He said it was mine if I wanted it so I raced over to get it – and I still have it.

PIT CREW – Chris Macdonald and Guy Allott on duty at Hyde Road

Collins demonstrated that he was good and ready after some spectacular performances at Rochdale.*

I first saw PC at the Monday night training school, then in one of his early meetings at Rochdale and straight away wanted him at Belle Vue. It brought me into immediate conflict with the board of directors who wanted, and expected to win both leagues.

I told them if the Aces were to continue winning we had to keep introducing the new young riders and I couldn't care less whether Rochdale won or not – my job and contract was with Belle Vue.

* Belle Vue Colts were Second Division founder-members in 1968 and continued to race at Hyde Road until 1970. Then the promotion decided to operate the team from nearby Rochdale, where Collins, 17, was an instant first-year success.

Rochdale was started as a training track. It gave youngsters the experience of being part of a team and going to away tracks. During some quite heated exchanges I reminded the board of that fact.

My pitch was that we couldn't win the league again without Peter in the team.

So he came in but that wasn't the end of my problems. PC came into the middle of the side but some of the other senior riders weren't happy because he was moving them out of the way to go past and win races.

They didn't like a young rider coming in and going faster than them. They fronted me up after a few meetings and said: 'You got him into the bloody team so he can ride with you.' And that's what happened. PC rode with me for a while.

His inclusion gave us the impetus we needed to push on for the 1971 title which eventually was achieved with five points to spare over Coventry. Opposing teams respected us, and promoters loved us because we would fill up their stadium and take hundreds of supporters to away matches.

HOME SWEET HOME – the family at 62 Abingdon Road, Bramhall

A rare sour note was on what should have been and almost was the perfect end to the year. The British League Riders Championship had been a Briggo benefit for the first six years of its existence and it niggled me that this was one significant meeting which so far had eluded me.

The good outcome was that this time, I rattled off four convincing victories and the fact Barry beat me to the flag in our last race was too little, too late for him. The downside was that officials had allocated the riders' wives some of the worst seats in the stadium, showing no respect to the people without whom there would have been no 25,000 crowd and no bonanza pay day for the BSPA.

I wasn't popular when I went on the mike and criticised the organisers but I felt it was a classic example of speedway taking for granted its most important resource – the riders. I even gave the crowd BSPA chairman Reg Fearman's telephone number so they could call him personally to add their opinion.

Probably it was not a great idea to antagonise the hierarchy because Belle Vue's successes did provoke a certain amount of jealousy. It's the oldest story in sport and life in general. Lots of people love you when you're on the way up and like to see somebody new winning the prizes, but if you dare to make a habit of it, they can turn very quickly.

Somehow the Aces again managed to go through the winter team moves relatively unscathed. PC moved up full-time to join Pusey, Wilkie, Eric Broadbelt and Ken Eyre which meant five of the seven had been home grown and graduated from Second Division which had been set up for precisely that purpose.*

Sören Sjösten was coming up for his sixth successive season and I was heading into a fourth, so by now everybody knew everybody. We were a really tight-knit unit and the desire to do well and keep winning was stronger than ever.

The test was whether we could maintain our league championship domination and, perhaps, add the 1972 KO Cup to the honours list. The answer was an emphatic 'yes' as we lost only two matches and took 63 points from 34 league outings.

For the fifth year in a row I averaged more than 11 points a meeting both home and away – although my final tally of 350 points at 11.37 was fractionally down because I missed a handful of meetings through injury.

Even then, the boys were capable of keeping the pot boiling nicely and to win the championship with 11 points to spare, ahead of Reading and

---

* In later years Wilkie would be a brave, full-on captain of the Aces. The 1978 racing accident which left him paralysed and in a wheelchair was one of the tragedies of speedway.

UP FOR THE CUP – the Aces with the 1972 Speedway Star KO Cup, back, left to right: Eric Broadbelt, Peter Collins, Ivan Mauger, Chris Pusey, Dent Oliver (team manager). Front: Ken Eyre, Alan Wilkinson, Sören Sjösten

King's Lynn, was a spectacular effort. And we did ice the cake this time by seeing off Hackney in the cup decider.

We all finished elated with our efforts, confident there could be more success to come – especially as the nucleus of the team was made up with very young riders. If ever there was a side which could stand the loss of one of its top riders it was this Belle Vue team, packed as it was with young tyros aiming for the top.

From a personal angle, at the end of the year I had added three world speedway championships to the one I collected at Newcastle; there had been consecutive world long track titles and everything was looking rosy.

But I never was one for sitting still and a month after the season finished we went down to McLarens, the New Zealand-owned and operated motor racing team who had their headquarters at Colnebrook, just behind Heathrow airport.

Raye and I stayed with Denny and Greta Hulme for a week or so and he showed me all the details of the Formula One tracks, the lines to take and so forth.

The Will To Win – 149

Denny and the manager Phil Kerr, another Kiwi, were keen to have me driving for McLaren and there was a lot of publicity around that I was going to retire from speedway in the near future and go into Formula One.

The truth is I was a bit keen to do it and even got measured up for an F1 car but the lure of two wheels won out in the end. Belle Vue though put two and two together and concluded there was a strong possibility I would only do another season or so – if that.

Another angle was that although Belle Vue were good to me, I was earning a lot more money in Europe than I was in England anyway. I was 32 and other than Sjösten – who had joined Belle Vue as a kid – the future at Hyde Road obviously revolved around the young guys. In addition to those who had already stepped up there were more in the pipeline with Chris Morton tipped as the next big thing.

It was not hard to understand that the directors were anxious to keep hold of those riders with long careers in front of them. A friend who knew what went on in the boardroom meetings told me it was suggested Belle Vue would announce to the BSPA that if they proposed to take any of our riders then they should try to take Ivan Mauger and see how they got on.

This situation was sort of germinating during January and February and it got to be early March, only a couple of weeks before the season started, when the BSPA called Belle Vue's bluff and made the decision that I would be the one to leave.

By now I was halfway to getting used to the idea that perhaps I wouldn't be in British League at least for a year or so, so I began making alternative plans. My European manager Wilfried Drygala in Bremen started taking a lot more bookings around Europe than I normally would commit to with the normal quota of British League meetings to fulfill.

The national newspapers and the speedway press have never liked the idea of riders being moved on and my stance with them was that if I could not continue with Belle Vue then I would not ride in the British League. By now I had just about resigned myself that I would not be staying with the Aces.

It was very disappointing. I felt I was instrumental in helping to get those youngsters under way in the team and the next thing it seemed the board were getting rid of me because I was 32 years of age.

I can't say I made them into riders but I gave them a lot of help as a senior rider, telling them where they had to go on a track, what they had to do and what standard of professionalism and performance was expected of them because they were at Belle Vue, rather than some third-rate team.

HAPPY DAY – champion of the world for the third time in a row

Heat 9

GOLDEN RUN

AFTER making a world championship breakthrough at last in Sweden, if anybody had told me I would follow up my first world title by winning again in 1969, 1970 and 1972 it would have been difficult to believe. Four seasons as a Belle Vue rider coincided with the most productive run of my world championship career.

Of course my confidence was enormously boosted by becoming world champion. But only three riders, Jack Young (1951–52), Briggo (1957–58) and Ove Fundin (1960–61), had managed to win back-to-back World Finals.

Nobody had achieved three in a row. Some considered it could not be done. And certainly most observers thought a Western rider had little chance of winning in Eastern Europe.

In the circumstances, I considered my win at Wrocław, Poland, in 1970 the absolute best that I had ever raced, and I still do.

The Poles and Russians were the emerging force in the 1960s and began to produce riders who were capable of beating anyone, anywhere. They seemed able to adapt to racing in Great Britain and Sweden better than our boys could cope with conditions behind the Iron Curtain.

Trips out there were often very intimidating, the environment and atmosphere quite forbidding. A lot of the Eastern European tracks had a bit of an adverse camber on them and were very wavy.

Their riders had a technique of sitting right over the back wheel in the corners and their front wheel was just floating over the waves. The Westerners used a completely different technique, especially going into the corners where we needed to be over the front wheel.

I had been at Wrocław in 1966 for a Poland-Great Britain Test match, followed by the World Team Cup Final – without much joy. But in 1968 at the European Final I got 10 points, finished fourth and broke the track record. Psychologically that was something of a breakthrough meeting for me.

Defending the world title for the first time was another new experience but by now other people's expectations did not bother me. As long as I was comfortable in my own skin, happy with how I was riding and the bikes were working, it was a question of getting the job done.

I knew I could handle the pressure and all I had to demonstrate to myself was that this was another year, another opportunity. And there was no need to venture outside England as the always alluring goal of Wembley was waiting at the end of the championship road.

152 – Ivan Mauger

The switch from Newcastle to Belle Vue had gone exceptionally well. I stopped in my fourth ride on my slightly delayed debut for the Aces in a challenge match at Halifax and that blip apart, had 50 races without defeat.

The first three world championship rounds produced 14 at Poole, 12 including a new track record at Wimbledon and 15 at Hyde Road so that was a satisfactory way to start the campaign.

A return trip to Plough Lane brought second place in the Internationale, won by local favourite Trevor Hedge after I had crashed in a run-off for the prize, a new bike. There was a bit of controversy when I went off to the showers and was starkers when someone dashed into the dressing room to tell me the presentations were going ahead without me.

Some people took it as a snub or assumed I was having a hissy fit but it wasn't the case. Mentally I was in the best place and underlined it by scoring maximum points in my next eight team meetings, and winning the Supporters Trophy at King's Lynn.

Going to Sheffield for the world championship semi-final was another good day at the office, 14 points and victory over the fast-improving Ray Wilson in a run-off.

The odd point was dropped in July, the one race which disappointed me most being in the Peter Craven Memorial Trophy which cost me a shot at a title which would have meant a lot to me to win. I was the first winner of the trophy in 1967 and it would have been nice to get it again. This was one of a few occasions when the occasional technical glitch was starting to give cause for passing concern.

A melted piston in a KO Cup tie at home to Sheffield brought more grief and 48 hours later – the day before the British Final at West Ham – I was still working to solve those problems and decided to put my energies into the workshop rather than going to Newcastle for a Northern Riders Championship qualifier.

But next night, proceedings momentarily got off on the wrong foot when I ran a last first time out. It was a pretty competitive field, one which some pundits reckoned would not have disgraced the final itself so I needed to get my finger out to rustle up 11 points and a place in the top six who qualified for Wembley.

To illustrate the quality of the line-up, among those who didn't make it were England internationals Ray Wilson, Eric Boocock, Martin Ashby, Trevor Hedge, Roy Trigg, Jimmy McMillan and Australian Charlie Monk, all of whom were averaging close to or above double figures at the time.

Happily, the qualifiers, headed by another rampaging 15-pointer from Briggo, also included Ronnie Moore, celebrating his first season back in the UK after a six-year absence. Even 'honorary Kiwi' Howard Cole made it through.

There was some damage done in the European Final in Olching which accounted for a few favoured riders, notably Bengt Jansson who had done so well at Wembley in 1967. Even so, anything could happen in a one-off World Final and Russia's Valeri Klementiev rubbed in the point when he headed Briggo in his first ride.

My first four rides all went like clockwork. By the interval it was all looking good, and after four races I was still unbeaten on 12 with daylight between myself, Nigel Boocock on nine, Briggo and Sören Sjösten with eight.

That meant the relative luxury of needing just one point in my last ride to be champion again. Sjösten was in that race and beat me to the first turn. Having seen plenty of him in Belle Vue matches, I was a bit wary of him because of his habit of coming to something of a stop going into corners, especially on the tighter tracks, so I was quite content to stay out of his way and protect second place.

A world title is a world title and 14 points was more than enough to do it for me, a three-point winning margin for the second year running. Much to the despair of English fans Booey could do no better than a third in his last ride.

Barry and Sjösten finished on 11 and New Zealand had one-two for the second time in a row after they had a run-off for silver.

CONGRATULATIONS – Ivan looks on as 1969 third placegetter Sören Sjösten shakes the hand of Barry Briggs

154 – Ivan Mauger

If Nigel had made it on to the rostrum for the only time in his life I would have joined in the congratulations and celebrations because he had been a mate as much as a rival for some years. But Sjösten was a good guy too and it was all credit to him that he got to that situation.

Some of the Brits, especially the Coventry followers, were disgruntled that in playing it safe, I had incidentally put my Aces team mate in a medal position. But I wasn't there to look out for anybody's interests except my own.

What added to a special occasion was that not only was Raye there again to witness everything, but Julie, Kym and Debbie were up in the stands. So was my mum Rita, absolutely electrified by her first overseas trip and blown away by what possibly was the most exciting occasion of her life.

Double world champion had a nice ring to it. Most of the noise which swirled around Wembley had a suitably happy note to it and the Belle Vue people thought all their Christmases had come at once. I enjoyed the sensation of winning once more sufficiently to make a mental note to do it again some time.

At the same time it was widely thought the chances of a British-based rider winning behind the Iron Curtain in 1970 were somewhere between poor and impossible. There was a lot of negativity attached to the whole thing and if I hadn't had that glimpse of light in the 1968 European Final then I might have bought the whole story.

The myth that the Poles and Russians morphed into supermen in their own back yard had its origins several years before. British and Swedish visitors to Poland routinely came home with their tail between their legs, never more so than the 1966 World Team Cup which was just a picnic for the home riders.

The Poles also won the team title in 1965 and 1969 and they were developing some seriously talented riders. The Russians too seemed to be breeding a convincing new generation to replace the pioneers such as Igor Plechanov and Boris Samorodov who created such a flurry when they rocked on to the scene in the early 1960s.

As if all of this was not daunting enough, it was another of those years of apparently unending rounds. After the British qualifiers there would be a British-Nordic Final to deal with, this time significantly spiced up with the inclusion of the Swedes.

For all who negotiated that tricky passage, a European Final in Leningrad lay in wait. Not many of our guys had even been to Russia but you could tell most of them didn't fancy their chances.

Whether subconsciously this accounted for the attrition rate through the rounds it is impossible to say. At Wembley the UK representation was down

RUSSIAN CHAMPAGNE – victory in the 1970 European Final in Leningrad, with Gennadi Kurilenko (left) and runner-up Vladimir Gordeev

to an Englishman, a Scotsman and a Welshman* but joking aside, only one Brit was destined to make it through to Wrocław a year later.

Trevor Hedge thought he was gone after finishing two places off the pace in the British-Nordic Final at Coventry. He snuck back almost by default after Bengt Jansson (broken wrist) and Ove Fundin (visa problems) were ruled out of the European Final.

My own run through fortunately was a lot less agonising than the doomsayers had predicted. A few problems in the Belle Vue round were soon forgotten, overtaken by maximum scores at Exeter and West Ham.

The British semi-final at Leicester yielded another full score, and the trip back to the Custom House for the British Final produced a chart-topping 14 – one better than Ronnie who was flexing his muscles nicely and enjoying his speedway again at Wimbledon.

He showed he could still be a contender with another sharp performance at Coventry in the British-Nordic final where all three Kiwi world champions made it through. But the honours at Brandon went to Sjösten, riding with spectacular nonchalance, and Ole Olsen took second place.

* Nigel Boocock, Ken McKinlay and Howard Cole were the only 'true Brits' in the 1969 World Final.

156 – Ivan Mauger

Leningrad was sure to be a scrap and a big test of nerve. Predictably enough the Russians put on a show but I was calm and confident, dropping only one point on my way to another European title.

Between July 18 and September 6 there were seven weeks to get ready for the first World Final to be held in Eastern Europe. Seven weeks to test machinery, check and re-check, experiment with different ideas, hone everything to perfection.

Seven weeks too in which to maybe freak out at the prospect of tackling the Poles and Russians in a hostile environment, on a track far better suited to their racing style, in front of a hugely partisan crowd eager to see the invading Westerners cut down to size and hanging out for a historic home-town victory.

Seven weeks in which to reflect upon the achievements and lessons of a world championship campaign of seven meetings and 35 races – compared to that of the six seeded Poles who we learned were to be headed by Toni Woryna, a third placegetter in 1966, and the very experienced Pawel Waloszek whose 10 points from his last four rides at Ullevi in 1968 had not gone unnoticed.

They were likely to be the standout challengers, along with Briggo, although such was the nature of the meeting there was no way the contenders could be limited to those guys. Andrzej Wyglenda and Henryk Glücklich promised to be tough to beat and the Soviets had heaps of faith in Klementiev and Kurilenko.

My mood in those weeks fluctuated from serene to snappy. One day I felt entirely in control of my own destiny and far more relaxed about my chances than everybody seemed to think I should be. Then on other days I was quiet, pensive, away in a world of my own and liable to bark at anybody who interrupted my thought processes – including Raye and the kids!

By practice day I was sufficiently tuned in to have a bit of fun with the Poles. They were always especially curious to see what we had on our bikes, which were usually decked out with more chrome and sponsors' stickers whereas they still had the bog standard basic Jawa blue paintwork on the tanks and mudguards.

A lot of it was purely cosmetic but they were not to know that. Of greater importance was getting to grips with the race conditions. Their officials and riders were hugely interested to see what we were doing so I hammed it up on the track, tried different lines and generally tried to disguise my real thoughts and intentions.

The Olympic Stadium in Wrocław qualifies as a bit of a trivia question. Any student of the Summer Games will tell you Poland has never hosted an Olympics. But in 1936 Breslau, as this Baltic port was then called, was part of Nazi Germany and the stadium did house some football in what history records as 'Adolf Hitler's Games'.

I had history of my own in mind as the 65,000 fans took their places and my helpers went about setting up our pits position. My allocated spot was in the heat of the afternoon sun, so we decided to relocate round the corner, behind a big concrete pillar which gave some relief from the heat.

Traditionally there is plenty of frantic activity and a lot of worried faces around at this time but Gordon Stobbs and Chris Macdonald didn't put on a new tyre or fire up a motor until the parade was under way. Told by pits officials they couldn't continue, they took the three bikes round the back of the stadium to warm them up away from inquisitive eyes.

They were in on the mind games as well and any casual observer might have wondered just what was going on in the Mauger camp. At least we knew what we were doing. We knew the Poles would pull any stroke they could to gain an advantage for their guys, like calling for the riders to come to the pit gate for the next race and then leaving them there stewing in the sun while their riders were taking their own time to come out.

We overcame that by having a system whereby Peter Oakes kept an eye on what they were doing and then gave a signal to Gordon, Chris and Guy when they were ready. Ronnie Greene, who was in charge of the British delegation, was flustered when the officials tried to hurry us out but it was important for us to stay on top of the situation.

It was shaping up as a meeting in which it was easy to see anybody beating anybody but everything seemed to be going according to script when I beat Briggo first time out.

There were threats lurking around every corner but Glücklich and Wyglenda were duly dealt with, and a win in the last race before the interval put me up there on nine points with the only other unbeaten riders, first Waloszek, then Woryna to come. And Woryna laid down his marker by winning the first race after the break to jump to 12 points.

Hedge had been helped off after crashing in his previous outing, which opened up the possibility of hard man Edmund Migoś coming in as reserve in Heat 15, my fourth ride. None of us fancied the scenario of Migoś doing his bit to help Waloszek so Ronnie Greene persuaded Trevor he should do his duty and go out for the race to forestall that possibility.

Some critics over the years labelled me 'just a gater', conveniently and unfairly overlooking the work I put in to ensure I was a consistently good starter. In the right circumstances, or even the wrong ones, I felt very good about my chances of winning races from the back if necessary. But this was one in which a convincing start was crucial.

It could hardly have panned out better. It was probably the best gate I made all year and once I had beaten Waloszek to the first corner the job was

TELLING IT AS IT IS – grabbed by Polish television for an interview seconds after clinching the 1970 world title

The Will To Win – 159

three-quarters accomplished. He was a wily one, Waloszek, but probably not the greatest at coming from behind.

That still left Woryna to deal with in Heat 17. Of all the Poles, many of whom in the 1960s were death or glory merchants, Toni was the most stylish and technically gifted. His career highlight to this point had been four years before, when I was making my World Final debut in Sweden.

He hardly put a foot wrong that night, but had to yield to an irresistible Briggo and went home with 14 points and a silver medal. The Polish fans were urging him to go one better this time, but I blocked out everything, concentrated all my energies and snapped off another dream start.

Four laps of a quarter-mile circuit can appear to be a long haul. Every step of the way demands a clear mind. But the journey passed completely without incident – no buzzing challenge from Woryna or anybody else, not a missed beat of the motor. All over. World champion. Again. And they said it couldn't be done.

This was and remains my ultimate moment in speedway. The bumps, the back-slapping, all the usual outpouring of emotion and celebration felt fantastic. Polish television whisked me off for an interview. That duty done, I was able to greet Raye who had come down from the stands, her white coat streaked with grey dust from the track, and we reflected silently for a few seconds on the enormity of it all.

In some ways, the effort which went into winning this one might have caused a slight but significant case of burnout which kicked in 12 months down the track. My results in 1971 were very much on par with what had gone before but in the final analysis there was a tiny ingredient missing.

The season kicked off with seven maximums in 16 days and a track record at Halifax before the unusually early British qualifying rounds of the world championship. I won at Reading, Belle Vue (after a run-off with George Hunter) and cruised at Wolverhampton with 40 points ample for progress to the British semi-finals.

With a victory in the Internationale in between, it was business as usual with first place in the Sheffield semi (14 and a run-off win over Ray Wilson) and the British Final at Coventry (14 again, one ahead of Briggo) before the trek up to Hampden Park for the British-Nordic Final.

With eight to qualify there were hopes the Kiwi trio might get to play an encore but this is where the road ended for Barry. He had a night to forget, and fell a couple of points shy of the qualifying mark.

I topped the pile, a point in front of Wilson, and Ronnie, so unlucky the previous year, also made it to the next stage but we both felt the disappointment of our dejected compatriot.

When a hugely respected opponent and mate comes up short, there is a small voice inside which tries, usually unsuccessfully, to rationalise it all. Better him than me, says the voice, and of course, that's one less genuine contender to worry about.

Then competition mode kicks in and preparations are under way for the next phase, in this case another European Final appointment at Wembley. I never tired of the place and the challenges it posed. Winning the title for a third time was undeniably sweet although it should have been Ole's night.

A fast and accomplished racer, hardly recognisable from the young hopeful who spent two years under my wing at Newcastle, he switched to Wolverhampton when Mike Parker pulled the pin on first division racing at Brough Park. Ole then qualified for his first World Final in Poland and had five points from his first two races before fading.

From the start of 1971 he had displayed great form, knocking over track records and prompting some people to start tipping him as the next big thing. At Wembley he showed just how well he was going by ripping to four wins before a broken rocker arm while leading Heat 18 robbed him.

Another really unlucky rider on the night was Ray Wilson, who referee Georg Transpurger controversially excluded from Heat 12 after a tangle with Jerzy Szczakiel. That blip cost him because just like Ole he won his other four rides.

European champion again, for sure, but under no illusion about how tough the World Final defence in Gothenburg might be, I got ready in the

ANOTHER ONE – a third European title, at Wembley in 1971 ahead of Ole Olsen and Ray Wilson, with actress Julie Ege and Sunday Mirror sports editor George Casey in attendance

The Will To Win – 161

usual way, or I thought I did. Probably I did not realise how much pressure there was on me, or had been defending that No.1 ranking for three years.

You can't go into a World Final feeling flat mentally, but deep down I think I wasn't quite there. After a first race win, I was hampered when Szczakiel got in a tangle off the start of Heat 7, caught Sjösten, but could not reel in Wilson who had avoided the traffic.

Ole meanwhile was going like a train and arrived at the interval unbeaten with me a point adrift – and we had to meet in Heat 13. I trapped on him but the former pupil came underneath me on the final turn. That was the instant in which I could see the title disappearing and I suspect Ole viewed it as a bit of a turning point in our rivalry.

Now all he had to do was to finish the job which he did by completing a 15-point maximum, almost all from the back, in a very emphatic display. My 12-point return was never going to be enough, although I did beat Bengt Jansson in a run-off for the silver medal.

For once, I hadn't been able to lift myself for the big occasion. I'd won six out of seven rounds leading up to Gothenburg and come up short when it mattered.

For a few minutes, it almost was a relief. In one way it was better to see Ole win than someone I didn't rate so much as a rider or a person. And then the disappointment kicked in.

They say you don't appreciate some things until you lose them and it was not long before I came to realise that if it was a case of choosing between the pressures of being the world champion or the disappointment of losing it, there was only one course to take.

Belle Vue's continuing charge to the championship helped me maintain some momentum and winning the BLRC again did provide some kind of satisfaction. I never considered it the best measuring stick but the fans always voted with their feet to pack out Hyde Road and it was a matter of honour to sign off the season with a flourish.

It didn't matter who it was, I decided I didn't want anybody to get in my way in 1972. Wembley was the goal, a fourth title the target. The quest got under way with another Belle Vue maximum, and a point dropped to Arnie Haley in the last race at Sheffield.

Then I beat Ronnie Moore in a run-off at the Internationale. But a crash in the World Best Pairs Final at Borås in Sweden a couple of nights later threatened to derail my progress.

Ronnie and I were attempting to repeat our 1970 success and after the programmed rounds, we were level on points with the English boys Ray Wilson and Terry Betts.

In a run-off to decide first place, I was leading when the bike lifted, I came down and Willy clattered into me. I was not aware of it at the time but finished up with broken fingers in my right hand, a cracked scaphoid in the other.

The extent of the injuries did not become apparent until Doc Brown, the Belle Vue track doctor, suggested I get X-rays done because the pain wouldn't go away. The hospital plastered both hands and said to come back a month later.

That was no good to me with a Leicester world championship round coming up, the British semi-final at Sheffield a fortnight after that, and the start of the Inter Nations tournament. So for several weeks I had the hands taped up for racing, and carried with me a bag of syringes with which to inject myself before meetings.

I got past Leicester, went through the card at Owlerton, and had a another five-ride maximum as New Zealand beat Australia at Hyde Road. There was a lot of discomfort but if riders were to pull out of meetings every time an injury was playing up, there wouldn't be many meetings.

In any case, there was the long track title to be defended in Germany. As usual Carlo Biagi levelled with me and helped make up my mind about what I could and could not do. He fixed me up with a special cast and all the effort was worth it as I won at Mühldorf.

After that we decided to lay off the heroics for a while and Raye, I and the kids took off for a fortnight of rest and recreation in Majorca. It was an ideal break and gave me the idea to take a mid-season spell in future years to help recharge the batteries.

I came back with a full score in a Northern Riders qualifier at Belle Vue but then had to pull out three rides into the next round at Glasgow a couple of nights later.

The signs were not great, Raye wasn't even aware I was having to do the injections, and the British Final at Coventry was only a few days away. To complicate matters, this was looming as one of the toughest meetings of the year, with just five places open. Fortunately only Eric Boocock got the better of me and with 14 points I was back in the winning groove.

There was another potential distraction which revolved around the pay rates for the World Final. Three years had elapsed since the last Wembley staging, interest was running hot and ticket sales suggested it was going to be a bonanza occasion – for everybody except the riders.

Briggo, no stranger to this sort of thing, and I put the case for improved terms to the Speedway Control Board and for a while they stonewalled us. Eventually somebody acknowledged it was ridiculously unfair for the stars of the show to be paid little more than the standard start and points money which applied in domestic meetings.

The Will To Win – 163

August was otherwise a good month. The injury problems were something which could be managed and I could feel my confidence and anticipation building. But nobody was taking anything for granted. Briggo had been in some vintage form, John Louis from Ipswich took a lot of people by surprise as he stormed through to Wembley and Ole clearly was not going to relinquish his crown voluntarily.

The pressure, though, bit him hard when he dropped it in his first race. After missing the start he poured everything into an attempt to catch and overhaul Christer Löfqvist, overdid it and opened the door for the rest of us.*

An even bigger misfortune befell Briggo who excited his followers by beating me in our first race. Then he was caught up in a shocking crash which left him stricken on the track nursing a lacerated finger. He was rushed to Mount Vernon Hospital and fate decreed it was to be his last World Final appearance, 18 years after his debut.

Some observers were unhappy with Bernie Persson's role in that incident although in the end it was the Russian Valeri Gordeev who clanged into Barry, and took off towards the dog track in spectacular fashion.

Persson was a tough, strong competitor, the white-jerseyed hope of truckloads of fans of under-achievers Cradley Heath. Locked in the memory bank was 1967 when his antics at Wembley played a part in my finishing third instead of at least making it into a run-off for the title.

Despite a solid British League record, he was more hustle than sophistication and while he wasn't ordinarily their favoured one, everyone was aware how badly the Swedes wanted a successor to Fundin as a genuine title candidate.

After the incident with Briggo he did not let his concentration falter and was the leader with 11 points after everybody had completed four rides.

Despite being on the wrong end of a couple of unsatisfactory starts, and dropping points to Barry and Ole, I was on 10 and knew I needed to beat Persson in Heat 19, which would put us both on 13 points and set up a run-off for the championship.

He certainly wasn't an opponent to whom I would have wanted to give an inch.

And for once in my career it wasn't me who was the bad guy, the crowd seemingly more inclined to support me rather than Persson.

It required a lot of visualisation and pre-planning before that race to make it off the unfavoured outside gate but I managed to get off the start and across. I was too busy concentrating on winning the race to know

---

* By winning his other four rides, Olsen finished runner-up on 12 points.

MOMENT OF TRUTH – the start of the 1972 run-off against Bernie Persson

where Bernie was but he got the second which he needed to ensure there was a decider.

Anything can happen in a two-horse race, so it would have been stupid to underestimate him. My focus was to try to ensure as far as possible proceedings moved along at my pace rather than his.

The track staff pushed our bikes up to the starting gate and we walked side by side from the pits to the starting line to do the toss for gate positions with John McNulty, the Speedway Control Board manager. I won the toss and took gate two, which in theory put Persson on gate four.

I could tell Bernie was really really nervous and was anxious to get on with the run-off. Scandinavians sometimes don't like delays. He was first up, and I thought the longer I left him sitting at the gate the better so I went under the tapes and slowly rode a complete lap of the track before coming to the start.

In such a situation, no matter who it is, you have to block out everything other than how you plan to execute. The delay wouldn't have suited Persson.

He moved across the grid to around three and a half to be sure of positioning himself in a good bit of dirt. But I got settled on one and a half in another decent bit of dirt so it was tit for tat.

At such a moment, what you need is self-control and self-belief. I knew what I had to do. When we finally came into line, everything went sweetly. I was quickly away from the tapes, able to choose precisely where I needed to be and to cover any move.

World title wins are like kids. You love them equally, for different reasons. This, my fourth in five years, the third in four seasons as a Belle Vue rider, certainly felt pretty good. It had been a tough and often painful ride this time, but winning again was the best possible way to make it all worthwhile.

Heat 10

THE WORLD'S MY OYSTER

WHATEVER it takes to be regarded as a citizen of the world, I've been there and done that.

I have always been excited by travel, and grateful for the opportunity to see how people live their lives in different countries.

Much of the journey was tied in with my world championship dreams and it wasn't just the quest for individual success which brought me a lot of joy.

Collecting those titles was the pinnacle, but featuring in World Team Cup and World Pairs victories was right up there – not to mention three world long track championships.

From early in the piece, colonials were included under the British banner and it was an honour to be associated with World Team Cup wins in 1968, 1971 and 1972. All that changed in 1973 and it still rankles to have been wiped from the reckoning after being good enough to pull on the Union Jack race jacket on those and many other international occasions.

The standing of the Brits at world level had come a long way in a few years and sadly, memories were short. It does not diminish from my pride in what was achieved but it certainly ensured I look back on those years from a particularly personal viewpoint.

For many years there were millions of people around the world who were delighted and comforted by their British heritage and traditional connections. The Brits thought of New Zealanders and Australians as being best-friend, much-loved cousins.

Since the United Kingdom joined the European Community in 1973 – taking the number of member states to 10 at that time – those ties, once so strong, have been loosened. Kiwis and Aussies, and others, have become increasingly marginalised and old alliances, forged by a shared history in wartime and peace, systematically weakened.

It is a consequence of the way the world political map has been redrawn. There are 27 European Union members now, with more in the queue to join. The much-prized right to work and live in the UK is taken for granted by citizens of Slovenia, Latvia, Bulgaria and countries who down the centuries have had absolutely no connection with the British Isles.

On the one hand, I am extremely fortunate to have been able to go to many locations and race in more than 30 countries where I have been

THAT BIKE – Ray Bokelman and George Wenn present Ivan with his world-renowned gold bike in California

168 – Ivan Mauger

enthusiastically received. Raye and I have countless friends in all of those places and great memories.

On the other side, my forbears came from the Channel Islands and always spoke of 'the old country' with pride, affection and a sense of belonging. Raye was born in England, it was our main home for more than a quarter of a century, our kids were raised and educated there.

We love the place, we have so much connection with it even now. It was completely natural for me to pull on the Union Jack breastplate and go out to do battle in the World Team Cup and Test matches as a representative of Great Britain. Commonwealth citizens had stood side by side in some of the defining conflicts of the 20th century and those of us engaged in the sporting equivalent were proud to do so.

Never, ever, did we feel anything but wanted, respected, loved and excited to be in such a privileged situation. But when Prime Minister Ted Heath took the Brits into Europe it almost immediately coincided with the end of an era and the scrapping of a relationship which had been part of the fabric of international speedway.

And I went from being an automatic choice for those big 'British' occasions – World Team Cups, internationals, and, soon afterwards, the UK rounds of the world championship – to, not a foreigner exactly, but no longer a 'home' rider.

In many ways, it was logical enough. As the sport became ever more international, it was right for New Zealand and Australia to have their own qualification processes. But that old special relationship between the Brits and the Anzacs has been put under enormous strain, not so much in a sporting world, but certainly in the political sense.

There still are plenty of ambitious hopefuls from the southern hemisphere anxious to follow their dream and come to the UK to race, just as there are thousands of youngsters who want to have the chance of the rite of passage and life experience that travelling overseas has always been.

Rules and regulations have tended to make it much harder than it ever was and I'm not alone in thinking it is a bad thing and a sad development. The world moves on, everybody recognises that, but we know people in Britain who were not even born in 1973, yet right or wrong, they still think of us colonials as being just like them, apart from the funny accent.

And in speedway terms, followers of the sport who are of the latest generation, never mind the oldies from years gone by, almost invariably categorise their more recently-acquired European chums like the Swedes, the Danes, the Poles and others as 'foreigners'.

Riders such as Briggo, Ronnie, Geoff Mardon and Peter Moore had turned out in British Commonwealth and Great Britain teams in the mid and late 1950s; and in 1960, the first year of the World Team Cup, both New

Zealand and Australia fielded a team in the four British qualifying rounds staged to supply one team to the final.

England did enough to progress but finished a distant second behind Sweden and the following year – after winning what was a three-way qualifying series – they were even further downfield in third spot.

The biggest international events of 1961, though, involved the rising stars of Sweden. The Commonwealth connection of Briggo and Ronnie was considered an essential part of the team selected to face them, and made the sort of top-scoring contributions expected of world champions.

It was a commonsense step for the World Team Cup selection criteria from 1962 to include both of them and by the time I was in a position to claim a place it was accepted as part of the natural order of things.

Between 1966 and 1972 I was an ever-present. After a mind-numbing debut in Poland when we scored just eight points, I helped play a part in breaking the drought and then featured in three cup-winning sides as Great Britain became the team to beat.

It was not a promising start. The smashing the Poles administered in the first of those finals in Wrocław was part of the folklore which for several years freaked out most visitors to the country. They were so far ahead of us, it was embarrassing.

Briggo had been there before with mixed success but he was no more on the pace than the rest of us. Nigel Boocock had plenty of experience too, Terry Betts and Colin Pratt were regarded as genuine international material – and we mustered eight points between us.

It was not just the manner in which the home riders outpaced everybody, the extent of their organisation seemed limitless. Every rider had a couple of bikes at his disposal, with more spares and changes of tyre available than we had ever seen. By comparison we all looked like complete novices.

The Russians were all ESO-equipped and tooled up as well and the only westerner to come away from the experience with any credit was Björn Knutsson. He dropped a single point to maximum man Marian Rose and scored half of Sweden's 22 points – even Ove scored only a couple.

Eric Boocock and Ray Wilson, both of whom had just qualified for the individual final for the first time, came into the side for the 1967 staging at Malmö. Again it was home team benefit night, although the Swedes had only a six-point margin over Poland and the best of British finished a further seven points adrift.

So far, no good. But 1968, with the final allocated to Great Britain for the first time, we got ourselves on to the honours board at last. The ghosts were laid to rest as I got a maximum, Nigel, Martin Ashby, Briggo and reserve Norman Hunter all produced winning form and Wembley rang to

THE FIRST TIME – World Team Cup winners at Wembley, 1968, Martin Ashby, Ivan, Barry Briggs, Nigel Boocock, Norman Hunter and team manager Ronnie Greene

the rafters – not quite as it had done when England won soccer's World Cup in 1966, but for speedway followers it was a pretty satisfying occasion.

The Swedes provided a serious challenge for a while and Fundin, usually at his best at a track which held so many great memories for him, dropped just the one point. A winning margin of 19 points was comprehensive, though. The next question to be answered was whether we were progressing sufficiently to win on foreign soil.

Not yet, as 1969 in Rybnik demonstrated. Poland won it again with 31 but Great Britain finished only four behind on 27. The signs suggested our time was coming. But the following year, back at Wembley, was a disappointing step backwards.

Fundin, in his last gold medal-winning world championship appearance, produced a vintage display and Bengt Jansson, Anders Michanek and Sören Sjösten supported him to the hilt. Sweden won with 41 points and finishing 10 points behind was a kick up the backside because Great Britain had been widely expected to win again.

Reversals can trigger all kinds of response and the British victory in Wrocław in 1971 was far and away the best to that point – and a highlight of my association with the team.

Russia, Poland and Sweden were well matched. But none of them got close to our determined, emphatic all-round effort. Longtime Aussie mate Jim Airey shone, and Ronnie Moore as non-riding reserve at 38 years of age jumped around the pits like a teenager supporting all the guys.

The occasion will be best of all remembered for Ray Wilson's maximum, the first in a final by an Englishman, the performance which earned him the nickname 'World Cup Willie' and in hindsight, a moment in history as far as the self-confidence and identity of English riders was concerned.

In 1972 Willie added another world title to his resume when he and Terry Betts helped themselves to the pairs crown.

With Briggo injured I was the lone Kiwi in the camp when Great Britain successfully defended the Team Cup at Olching.

In a display which had all the conviction of the previous year, and a 15-point winning margin over Russia and Poland (21), Willie and Bettsy were joined by the fast-rising John Louis and they all did well and looked the part. My 11 points was the only double figure score on the day, a second behind Henryk Glücklich in the last race the only blemish.

The Union Jack was flying proudly again and my record in the competition stood at 56 points from seven appearances – not a bad tally as

GREAT, BRITAIN – *victorious in the 1972 World Team Cup at Olching, left to right, Terry Betts, Ivan Mauger (captain), John Louis, Ray Wilson, Ronnie Moore*

172 – Ivan Mauger

the first couple had produced a meagre five points. My total stacked up ahead of everybody else bar Briggo whose 10 WTC outings produced 71 points.

From an early stage, even going back to those first trips to Holland years before, I always enjoyed the challenge of racing against different opponents and taking part in meetings which had some kind of international label.

League matches in the UK were the bread and butter for many years, before increasingly speedway began to cross frontiers. Racing eventually took me round the globe several times, and apart from taking a rider out of his comfort level and broadening his experience, it is difficult to think of a more exciting way to see the world.

Many mainstream sports like cricket and football allow elite sports people the opportunity to sample new experiences. As often as not, though, travel, hotels and all the other arrangements are made for them by a squad of officials and support staff.

It is a much more solitary existence for golfers and tennis players but generally the top ones have an entourage of helpers to ensure everything goes smoothly. For riders, especially in the 1960s and 1970s, trips to the Continent and further afield were often tinged with adventure of one kind or another. When foreign riders and teams came to England, they were a bit of a curiosity and for a long time we provoked a similar reaction in return.

My first competition match in England had been against a team of Polish tourists so it was a coincidental twist that my first full international experience should be on a Great Britain tour to Poland in 1966.

The day we were leaving Heathrow there was one ticket missing and I drew the short straw and had to go the following day. When I arrived I had to share a room with the Polish team manager Charlie Puzio and the bus driver.

It went downhill from there. Our best result of the series was a rain-off at the halfway stage of the fifth Test at Czestochowa! The Poles played horses for courses and blitzed us in the other four matches, with only Briggo and to a lesser extent Nigel Boocock looking capable of scoring decent points. My total of 19 from the series was not an auspicious beginning.

Briggo, who was the Jawa ESO importer, supplied bikes with very small Jap carburettors because in his opinion they were better for English tracks. I was still winning most of my races on a Rotrax Jap in England but decided to take the Jawa to Poland. That was a big mistake.

Our bikes were slow and most of the time we were racing each other while the Poles were half the length of the straight ahead of us.

Just about the only bright spark on the trip was having Cyril Maidment in the team. Maido was a very funny guy and a laugh a minute.

The Will To Win – 173

No matter how down the boys were after the meetings he could always get everybody laughing.

We first crossed paths at Wimbledon in my early days in England. Later he rode for Belle Vue from the start of the British League until I went there in 1969. He often came up from his south London home to Manchester early in the day and had lunch with us before going off to race.

We ate better than on the 1966 Test series in Poland, when I took a load of Mars bars and otherwise lived mostly on cheese or ham rolls. The best meal of the day was at breakfast when they had ham and eggs and we got that served to us in a little frying pan.

There was much more for the boys to enjoy when the Poles came over for a three-match return series in England a few days later. This time Great Britain prevailed 3-0. I rode at Hackney without much joy but got paid 15 from six rides at Sheffield where Briggo, Booey and Trevor Hedge all were undefeated by an opponent.

The Poles were much more convincing visitors the following year and the series was level at 2-2 before we smashed them at Newcastle, and I was able to enjoy some home advantage, dropping just one point to Andrzej Pogorzelski. This was better than a series against Sweden had been the previous month, in which the Brits were beaten 3-2 and it wasn't a great experience for me.

I had another very ordinary (and losing) series against the Swedes in 1968, suffering a lot of problems on the back of which came plenty of adverse criticism, specifically from the direction of Newcastle where one or two relationships were becoming increasingly fractured.

It didn't go much better for me in the World League, an FIM competition involving Great Britain, Sweden, Poland and Russia which was not finished because of fixture problems. The Brits won all of their six matches but not because of any great contribution from me.

It was quite a different story in 1969 as Great Britain beat Sweden 5-0 and at last I had something to do with it, topping the charts for the series and scoring my first international maximum at Wimbledon, followed by another 18-pointer at Leicester.

I was still looking for my first maximum on foreign soil and went close with 17 in a 54-all draw in a one-off Test against Sweden in Malmö a couple of days before the World Pairs in Stockholm.

Sweden was always a good trip enjoyed by most of the riders. One time, though, I couldn't get anybody to share my enthusiasm for country music so while the rest of them were out on the town, I went on my own to a Johnny Cash concert. It was a great night.

Great Britain dished out another 5-1 beating to the Swedes in 1970, with Briggo and me leading the charge, and broke new ground by winning a three-match series in Sweden for the first time. It was good to play a leading role – 18 at Gothenburg in the opening Test and 14 at Målilla and Stockholm.

One of the features of visits abroad was having Charles Foot as the team manager. Everybody thought he was a great guy. After the matches Footy usually wanted to dine with all the dignitaries from the town and when I was captain he gave me a big roll of notes and instructed me to make sure the boys had a good dinner and whatever they wanted to drink.

Ronnie Greene

He never told me how much money was in the roll but as he was an accountant it was fair bet he would have known. I did the right thing, only paid for the meals and drinks, and gave the remaining notes back to him the next morning.

The Poles were back in 1971, and left on the wrong end of a 5-1 scoreline. I was unbeaten in three of the four Tests in which I was selected. After the coatings we had received at the hands of the Poles over the years that was pretty satisfying.

There was one night at Sheffield when Ronnie Greene was team manager and we were beating the Poles in a big way. He came to me when there were a few races to go and asked me to let the reserves have a few rides to make it a little more of an even contest. Needless to say that suggestion didn't go down well and he was firmly advised not to press the matter.

That was pretty much the last time I had any significant involvement as a Brit and already there were the seeds of a switch of emphasis. In 1969 and 1970, after Ronnie Moore had returned to British League, there were three-match series between England and New Zealand; and around that time there were Tests in New Zealand too against the touring Lions.

Because of distance and the comparatively small rider pool, New Zealand was never going to be a big player on the international stage. That didn't stop Trevor Redmond from drumming up a great deal of enthusiasm and pushing the barrow for representative-type matches wherever he could from the early 1950s. He was a fantastic pioneer and ambassador.

The Will To Win – 175

We were proud to wear the New Zealand colours on a variety of occasions but to be turning out in official Test matches in England was something else. We won the '69 series 2-1 but with Ronnie out injured, lost all four matches the following year even though I scored a maximum in three of them and Briggo was also going like a train.

With the Kiwis capable of being a legitimate international force, and the start of the emergence of nations such as Denmark, the British promoters floated out the idea of an Inter Nations tournament in 1972 – because of injury I rode in only one of New Zealand's four matches, scoring the lot against Australia at Hyde Road – and it grew into the Daily Mirror International Tournament a year later.

With seven teams contesting 24 matches over just short of three weeks at 18 British League tracks, and a final at Wembley, it was the biggest and most ambitious series ever staged and one of the BSPA's greatest successes.

Ronnie Moore and Jim Airey, both recently retired from British League, were brought over for the tournament. Never mind what people say about Australia and New Zealand and the traditional sporting rivalry between the countries, Jimmy stayed at our house, rode a couple of my bikes to represent Australia and kept Gordon Stobbs occupied for the duration.

He took Jim to all the Australian matches, took me to the New Zealand matches – but only had to do one five-minute trip when the teams met at Hyde Road. During Jim's stay there was a call from Sydney to say his wife Ronda had given birth to their son Shane.

The New Zealand challenge started badly with a rain-off against England and defeats against the combined Denmark-Norway side and then Sweden. Then we got our act together and I got the lot in wins over Poland, Australia and USSR which put us in the semi-final.

England were too good for us at Belle Vue, and went on to beat Sweden in the final at Wembley. That result, coming as it did on top of the emergence of Ray Wilson and the spectacular rise of Peter Collins, was probably the defining moment for promoters, press and riders who were beating the England drum.

A few weeks later Wembley was to host the World Team Cup Final – and the selectors decided to choose an all-English team of Peter Collins, Ray Wilson, Terry Betts and Malcolm Simmons with Dave Jessup as reserve. The move paid off with another victory which had the flag-waving fans raising the roof of the old stadium in celebration.

It was the beginning of a changed dynamic as far as those generations-long colonial ties between New Zealand (and Australia) were concerned, especially after Great Britain went into the Common Market.

The swell of public opinion was understandable. From a speedway perspective, Briggo and Ronnie were now gone from British League racing, and nobody knew how much longer I would be on the scene. Nevertheless, it was hurtful and disappointing to be dumped and it wasn't until six years on that one afternoon at White City finally squared the ledger.

But Kiwis are nothing if not resourceful. At least we were not stateless. And while there were not enough riders around at any one time to do more than scratch at the surface of team success, it was a different story when just two were required.

An opportunity to fly the flag had arisen when the FIM endorsed the World Best Pairs, elevated to the status of the third most prestigious event on the international calendar – according to the words of John McNulty, the 'crazy professor' who was the secretary of the Speedway Control Board.

A scholarly, rumpled man, an unlikely candidate to be associated with professional motorsport, he was on hand in Stockholm in September 1969 for the first staging of the World Best Pairs which previously had been a strictly unofficial Scandinavian event.

My partner for the ground-breaking meeting was a pretty improbable player, too. Bob Andrews, once a Wimbledon colleague, and a World Final qualifier and former Great Britain representative with a distinctive London accent, got the nod because Barry Briggs and Ronnie Moore were unavailable.

HISTORIC PAIR – Ivan and Bob Andrews, winners of the inaugural World Best Pairs in Stockholm, 1969, flanked by Martin Ashby and Nigel Boocock (Great Britain) and runners-up Göte Nordin and Ove Fundin (Sweden)

Ronnie had broken his leg earlier in the season and Briggo, after partnering me to semi-final success at Wimbledon, decided he would not go to Sweden. He had legal action pending there after some scathing media accusations had been made about his off-on qualification for the 1968 World Final and declared he would not ride in the country again until it was satisfactorily sorted out.

Bobby, despite his Edmonton upbringing, had decided in 1962 to emigrate to New Zealand and was a naturalised Kiwi with a citizenship certificate to prove it. He continued to travel back to England to play out what were by now the later stages of his league career and by this juncture was a seven or eight point man at Cradley Heath.

I figured our chances were best served by me winning as many races as possible and whatever points Bob picked up would be a bonus. In the event I got 18 and five times in six races we got a 5-1 and Fundin and Nordin were a point behind us with Great Britain, represented by Nigel Boocock and Martin Ashby, a further six back in third.

Briggo joined me again the following year when we won a semi-final at Belle Vue, but once more he opted out of the final which was to be held in Malmö. Instead a fit Ronnie Moore came in and it was one of the greatest nights of my life as we scored 28 and took the title.

A TITLE TO CHERISH – Ivan and Ronnie, World Best Pairs champions 1970

178 – Ivan Mauger

The Swedes again provided the toughest opposition, Ove and Bengt Jansson finishing three adrift and England's Boocock brothers Nigel and Eric were next.

When I first went back to New Zealand as world champion some of my old friends and acquaintances behaved as if it was no big deal. As far as they were concerned I was still just Ivan who used to run with the Olympic Harriers and then had some rides at Aranui speedway. Maybe they just wanted to make sure I kept my feet on the ground.

The funny thing is that it all changed after I had partnered Ronnie to that pairs title. Suddenly I was someone who had done something. That gives a hint of just how big time Ronnie was, and how his reputation in Christchurch endured.

How it would have been had Briggo and I ever managed to win the pairs can only be imagined.

At last Barry and I did get together for the 1971 Final in Rybnik, after winning the semi-final at Leicester. The night before the final we went to the movies.

Neither of us noticed a guy who came and sat in the row behind us until he tapped us on the shoulder and said 'the only way you can beat Szczakiel tomorrow is you have got to ride very wide and when you go to the first turn especially you must keep going and ride very wide'.

We didn't know who he was but we thanked him for the advice and said we would do just that. We were laughing when we got back to our hotel room and decided we had got to get halfway to town before we turned left in the first turn.

But it didn't make much difference and the laugh was on us as New Zealand's chances of a third successive title win were blown away by the Polish pair of Szczakiel and Wyglenda. They revelled in the occasion and placed one-two in every race, finishing six ahead of us.

With the next year's final to be held in Borås, Ronnie and I again qualified as semi-final winners, at Wimbledon, and fancied ourselves as strong candidates for another victory.

Things didn't go quite according to plan as Wilson and Betts matched us on 24 points, and took the title after I crashed in the run-off against World Cup Willie. The Swedes missed out yet again.

They finally broke their drought at Borås a year later, when the New Zealand challenge was irretrievably damaged by the absence of Barry and Ronnie. Both had opted out of British League racing.

With Graeme Stapleton in, New Zealand finished last in the 1973 final and to all intents and purposes that was the turning point in a competition in which we went close but never again managed to win.

It was fun while it lasted but I wasn't short of other commitments or opportunities to see the world.

From 1967 I was fitting in additional meetings on the Continent, usually on the 1000-metre tracks, and sampling grass, sand and shale in a whole lot of new locations which sometimes were challenging and occasionally quite exotic.

Most were on an individual basis, there was the ice-racing jaunt with Goog Allan to Siberia, and in 1969, I accompanied the Belle Vue team to Leningrad for an end-of-season trip.

My contract left it to me to decide if I wanted to do additional away meetings and this was a chance to visit somewhere unusual even if the conversion rate of roubles to pounds was pretty ordinary. Part of the deal was for Sören Sjösten, manager Jack Fearnley and I to fly out. We lost the teams match 40-38 but next day I won the individual meeting for the Leningrad Gold Cup.

When Jack Milne – who I met on my first trip to the United States after winning my first world championship – heard we were going he asked if I could buy a Russian-made 'over and under' double-barrelled shotgun he wanted for his already large personal collection.

On the practice day I told a couple of officials from the Neva club that I wanted to buy the gun and they said after the meeting they would take me to the right place to buy it.

Most of the Belle Vue team went by train to Helsinki on the morning after the match but we were not going back to Heathrow until the following day as there was a function to attend in Leningrad. After we had put the boys on the train I told Jack and Sören what I was doing.

Sören had a wallet full of money that had to be spent in Russia and announced he would buy another of the guns because he could sell it in Sweden. The club officials came to the hotel and took us to the shop to buy the guns.

Modern travellers will find this hard to believe with all the checks nowadays but we went through security at Leningrad with the guns under our arms as we did not want to check them in. We walked through without being stopped although no one was in any doubt about what we had – the guns were even pictured on the outside of the box.

We were diverted to Brussels because of fog and exactly the same thing happened there. It was a similar story when we got a connection to Heathrow and the same again going on the shuttle back to Manchester.

A few days after the BLRC, Raye and I, Briggo and June, and a few others went to Los Angeles and it was exactly the same going out of Heathrow and coming in to LAX. Not one person at any time challenged

180 – Ivan Mauger

me. Jack and Harry Oxley were there to meet us at the airport and I handed the gun to Jack.

Mind you, much has changed in 40 years. When my continental career started I would leave home in the early hours of Sunday to drive to London. Flights went out of Heathrow at seven o'clock or later to the likes of Frankfurt, Munich, Copenhagen, Amsterdam, Paris and Brussels.

At the other end there was often a wait of up to a few hours until there was a connection to an airport close to where the meeting was – and it was commonplace to be dashing in to a meeting after a hectic drive, in time to jump on a bike which Gordon or Wilfried Drygala would have warmed up in the meantime.

Some of it was a bit challenging for Gordon, not least when we drove back as we often did. By instinct he is a 60 miles an hour man and hurtling down the autobahn in a V8 Mercedes doing 200 kilometres an hour was not his idea of fun.

The first of my individual continental meetings was in 1967 at the Golden Key of Bremen, which was staged on May 1 every year. Wilfried, who controlled his father's truck depot in the northern German city, contacted me for the previous year but it didn't eventuate.

The delayed debut worked out as I got second behind Sweden's PeO Söderman and that really kicked off my European career. A lot of promoters and club presidents attended meetings every Sunday because most had only one or at the maximum two international meetings a year.

Wilfried spoke perfect English and when some of those club bigwigs came up to ask me about doing their meeting on such and such a date Wilfried did all the arranging.

Soon afterwards and to this day he became my European manager. Memory tells me I got 600 marks (about £200) for that first meeting and my travel and expenses had to come out of that. It was not long before the asking price went up and I would only ask for a flat fee.

A lot of other riders wanted a guarantee, with flights, hotels and incidentals on top. I worked out all of those costs and gave the promoters an all-inclusive price. It may have been a bit more than most wanted to pay but they all knew exactly what was the cost to put me on their track.

Soon there were invitations to do a couple of grass tracks and long tracks which meant buying a long track bike. After a meeting at Wimbledon I stayed overnight with Sid and Renee Hone and went to Alf Hagon's shop at 350 Leyton High Road and bought one of his Hagon sand racers. I had a spare Jap engine and put that in it.

Long track appealed to me since the first time at Easter 1960 when I saw the mile track at Port Pirie. I could not wait to get on my bike and go fast

FLAT STICK – going for it in a world long track championship semi-final at Scheeβel in 1972

down those big long straights. Although the long track is not as spectacular to watch for spectators, from a riding point of view it is definitely more exciting. And money-wise, it made a lot of sense to do more meetings.

Wilfried had taken over his dad's company and had trucks going up and down Germany and to other countries in Europe. He took me to the depot and offered me the use of the end workshop which was quite big and spacious. We cleaned out some of the truck stuff and my speedway and long track bikes were to stay there from halfway through that 1967 season until I stopped riding in Europe at the end of 1985.*

The money increased over the next two or three years as I had a reputation of winning most of the international speedway meetings, did well in international long tracks and won my fair share of international grass tracks. At the worst way I got into the finals which made the promoters

---

* There was so much equipment there, Gordon Stobbs and I went over from England to collect it all. We went in my big IVECO transporter and had to take the trailer. At one time there were four or five speedway bikes, three or four of my best long track bikes and three grass track bikes as well as numerous spares.

182 – Ivan Mauger

happy, as Ray Cresp, the Aussie who I first met in 1957 and '58 when he had a workshop at the back of Victor Martin's had told me it would.

Bremen gave me a good kick start – it was a meeting I won six times in a row from 1968–73 and would win again in 1975 and 1976. It was the start of proving to myself and the various promoters that I was good value on the Continent. Three long track and three grass track wins also in '68 set the bar at a level I continually sought to improve upon.

The going rate also went up over a period of time because of my successes on speedway, long track and grass tracks. The Europeans were not used to that because they either had guys who were specifically speedway riders or long track riders or grass track riders. Finland, Norway, Sweden, Germany, Czechoslovakia and France all had very good long track riders and Germans in particular and some French and Dutch were very good on the grass track.

Things took off when the FIM sanctioned the official world long track championship in 1971. It previously existed as a European championship and I twice qualified for the final but did not ride in either. The money was really bad but European long track champion had a ring to it and would have nicely matched my European speedway champion status.

A 'world' tag was even more attractive and justified as increasing numbers of top international guys were riding in the European championship. Participation meant scheduling rounds and preparation to fit around speedway and other commitments, but we got everything organised and the first world long track final turned out just fine – in the end.

Second place in my first qualifying round at Scheeβel in May was followed by victory in the semi-final at Mühldorf a month later. The final was in Oslo on September 1 and I won that after having to withstand a protest.

I needed to win the final because Manfred Poschenreider from Germany was only a point behind me. I was having trouble with my factory Jawa and borrowed Don Godden's Jap in the decider – it was very fast and reliable. I won the final and Manfred was second ahead of Runo Wedin from Sweden.

Celebrations were put on hold when Poschenreider's father-in-law Sepp Giggenbach (who reportedly was Hitler's personal driver during the war) protested because he said I did not ride Don's bike in practice and therefore should not be allowed to ride it in the final.

Steward of the meeting was Wladyslaw Pietrzak from the Polish Motor Federation, and later President of the CCP. He told Giggenbach no rule existed and therefore the result would be upheld.

In 1972 as world champion I was seeded direct to the semi-final at Scheeβel and won it. The final was at Mühldorf on September 9 and I won with a 30-point maximum. It remains the one and only time the world long track championship has been won on a maximum.

From what at first was unfamiliar territory around Europe I also returned to ride in meetings in Australia and New Zealand in the southern summers, mostly on a one-off basis as an individual. Later the idea to form a troupe of top-name riders came together. That part of my career developed to a scale which couldn't have been imagined back in the early Aranui and later Rowley Park days.

The ultimate frontier, though, was America. Speedway had made an impact there before and after the war, Jack Milne, Wilbur Lamoreaux and Cordy Milne were 1-2-3 in the 1937 World Final, and all sorts of motorcycling disciplines had their followers in the States.

During 1968 I was at George Greenwood's Jap shop at 106 Harrow Road, London when Bill Kitchen came in. Bill had ridden against the Americans in that Wembley final and subsequently captained the Lions and England. Like all the old riders, especially those who had ridden on either side of the war, he had such great stories to tell.

WELCOME TO AMERICA – with Cordy Milne, Pete Coleman, Jack Milne and Ted Tinsdale in California, November 1968

Bill had recently come back from a holiday with Jack Milne at Pasadena. Coincidentally speedway had just re-started in California and that tickled my attention. He gave me Jack's home phone number and also the number at his motorcycle shop.

Next day I called Jack and asked what was the possibility of me riding in California after the British League Riders Championship Final at Belle Vue at the end of October. I was going to Sydney in any event and there would be time to do a couple of meetings in Los Angeles on the way.

Jack sounded very enthusiastic, said the season went to the end of November and he would contact Dude Criswell, the Whiteman Stadium promoter, on my behalf. The track was in the district of Paicomo, not too far from Jack's shop at Pasadena.

When he called back, Jack had negotiated a fee of $500 for each of my two meetings. Later on, only a couple of weeks before the trip, he phoned again to say that Criswell had decided he did not want to pay a guarantee and that I should ride for prizemoney as all the other guys did.

Jack, who had been a promoter after the war and until the mid 1950s at Lincoln Park, said he felt he had a responsibility to me and that he and his parts manager Harry Oxley would promote the two meetings when I was there. Harry and his wife Marilyn also provided accommodation at their house at Sierra Madre.

HI GUYS – first appearance at Whiteman Stadium, 1968, Back row, left to right: John Carter, Ivan, Eddie Mulder, John Hateley, Chuck Jones, Steve Scott, Jack O'Brien, Elliott Schultz. Front: Dwayne Keeter, Paul Conserary

The Will To Win – 185

The flight was late getting in to LA and Pee Wee Cullum, another pre-war name, had his son Don pick me up and we had to go straight to the track where the meeting had already started.

Jack had arranged for me to ride a bike prepared by the ex-Norwich mechanic George Wenn. The American riders were nitro methane-mad and I practised for three laps on the bike before it seized up with too much nitro. Fortunately, George had a couple of other bikes and I won the four races that I had that night.

The American boys were riding Class C style which was similar to long track and had turned down handlebars. Their tyres were pumped up to maximum pressure and they had full face helmets. I had my own bars to put on each of the bikes, an open face helmet and a completely different take on the tyre pressures and attracted a lot of sniggering and ill-concealed amusement from the home riders – until I started winning and broke the track record.

Harry Flanders, father of Bruce who later did the announcing at Costa Mesa and other southern Californian tracks, had a handlebar company. Harry got the Flanders company to make about 50 pairs of my handlebars and sold them to all the riders. I ran a couple of training schools during the week and all the riders wanted them.

Word spread quickly. Johnny and Jeannine Roccio* called Briggo in England and told him what was happening. He promptly hopped on a plane and arrived in time for us to ride together at the start of the second meeting where we had three match races together.

As was common practice in demonstration events we won one each and raced for the third one, which Briggo won. Then we went into the normal heats and semi-finals and I got him back in the final.

Those meetings were the catalyst for the great resurgence in American speedway, with many riders who were just kids devoting all their energies into becoming accomplished performers.

Harry and Jack got the idea of starting a new speedway after their experiences at those two meetings, looked for some venues and ended up at Costa Mesa.

They promoted it for the first five years with Gene Rhyne and then bought his shares and ran it together for many years until Jack passed away in 1995. Then the Oxleys ran it and when Marilyn died and Harry went down to live in Mexico, their son Brad took over the longest-running speedway in the United States.

---

* Brothers Ernie and Johnny Roccio rode for an American team which toured England in 1951.The following year Ernie was a member of the Wimbledon team alongside Briggo, and died following a crash at West Ham.

186 – Ivan Mauger

Raye and I were to go back to California for the next 20 years and more. We owned a condominium in Garden Grove – the next district to Anaheim where Disneyland is situated – for much of that time and had a Buick Park Avenue car with NZ1 on its registration plate.

Many strong and lasting friendships were forged in the States.

It was fascinating to watch the development of the sport and the emergence of so many talented young racers. And it was great to be associated with some tremendously enthusiastic people who had been in and around speedway for years.

Gene Rhyne was Jack and Cordy Milne's mechanic from 1928. He talked a little bit like Mr Magoo and had some great stories to tell from the 1930s when they rode 'back east', a reference to New York and the states in and around that area. The Milnes raced five or six nights a week in the summer and then they came home and rode a similar schedule at the southern Californian tracks.

Cordy worked at Milne Motorcycles and his speciality was rebuilding wheels. I used to spend hours sitting out in the workshop drinking coffee and just talking to those two guys and never tired of listening to their stories. Jack often came out to join in although he must have been one of the most modest world champions of all.

After I won my second world championship I had a big V8 Mercedes and Mercedes wheels on my trailer with two factory bikes on it. I got a picture to take over and give to the guys.

Gene took a look, and said he had a picture pretty similar to that from 1929. He wandered off to his back room and come out with a picture of the latest Model T Ford in 1929 with a trailer and Model T Ford wheels and Jack and Cordy's two bikes.

The opportunity to link the past and the future set the stage for more speedway activity. The enthusiasm of promoters, riders and supporters made for exciting times, as if the USA wasn't exciting enough!

From 1969 onwards I had two speedway bikes that stayed at George Wenn's house and also a long track bike. I needed the long tracker because occasionally there were half mile events at the Ascot circuit in Gardena.

When Jack and Harry were drumming up publicity to promote a Costa Mesa show it so happened fellow Kiwis Denny Hulme and Bruce McLaren were racing their big Can Am series cars at Riverside the following weekend.

A joint press conference was organised at the Dodgers Stadium with Briggo, myself and the two race drivers in attendance The LA media thought it was great that four New Zealanders with high profiles were in town at the same time.

The Will To Win – 187

Alan H Seymour III was the press officer who arranged it. He was quite a character who said 'there is no first or second' – he just liked the idea of tagging 'the third' to the end of his name and usually would only respond if you called him by his full title.

We had my 1969 world championship machine on display (Briggo's was not exactly tidy enough to put up on the stage) and the MC said it was the best-looking speedway bike he had ever seen. At that, Ray Bokelman – whose wife Ethel owned the first bike provided for me at Whiteman – said if I were to win the triple crown in 1970, he would gold plate the bike at Orange County Metal Processing.

When we got back from Wrocław after the 1970 Final, Ray called and asked where was that bike? Gordon and I took it to Manchester airport freight depot the same day. Ray picked it up from LAX freight a few days later and it took about 18 months to complete. George Wenn pulled it to bits and he and Ray rebuilt it after it had been gold plated.

So many people in California could never do enough for us. When we were there for another series of meetings we got to hear that Elvis Presley was appearing at the Hollywood Forum. Tickets were like gold dust but good old Alan H Seymour III had plenty of contacts around town and got four great seats close to the stage for Raye, June and Briggo and myself.

Raye and I have a wide taste in music and still consider that concert the greatest live show we have seen. It was an unforgettable experience. They were black market tickets and very expensive but it was money well spent. We were so keen to see Elvis, we didn't even ask Alan H the price when he said he could get us some.

It was only later we realised we were due to go back to England two days before the show. We had cheap excursion tickets from London to LA return but couldn't change the date. That meant throwing away those tickets and buying new singles which were more than double what we paid for our excursion return.

It was still a small price to pay.

LONG WALK HOME – on the way back to the pits after such a costly breakdown in the 1976 World Final in Katowice

Heat 11

FROM FEAST TO FAMINE

BETWEEN September 1968 and September 1972, I rode in 16 world championship finals – individual, team, pairs and long track – and won 11 gold medals.

In the 39 months from June 1973 I rode in a further 10 finals and it was not until the last of them, the 1976 world long track, that I struck gold again.

It was a long time between drinks, long enough to convince some critics Ivan Mauger was a spent force, still a tough nut to crack but almost certainly over and done with as far as winning the big ones went.

I never believed that. History was to prove I was right not to believe it. They were tough times, defending a reputation which had been so difficult to achieve. Yet throughout that period, I never considered myself anything other than a legitimate contender for world championship honours.

The closest call, and probably the most remembered silver medal of all, happened in Poland, a country with which there was more than a passing thread of triumph and disaster during my career.

Moving from Belle Vue to Exeter at the start of the 1973 season necessitated a few changes in my travel arrangements and a bit of revision to my commitments, but otherwise it was business as usual.

The British qualifying rounds produced wins at Belle Vue, Exeter and Ipswich and the only point dropped was to Tony Davey in the last of those rounds. I beat him in the run-off for first place. Another 14-point winning night saw me securely through the Leicester semi-final. The point lost there was to John Louis although he had to break the track record to beat me.

Ray Wilson made his presence felt at the British Final at Sheffield, when he became the first UK-born rider to hold the title since Peter Craven in 1963. Despite being excluded for tape-breaking in my last ride I went through comfortably enough, and from the British-Nordic Final at Coventry which Anders Michanek won in some style.

Mich was again the man in the European Final in Abensberg, responsible for the only point I dropped there. That gave me and everybody else a fortnight in which to gear up for the World Final. For the first time it was being held at Katowice, a massive stadium in the coal mining area of Silesia. It was a new venue for all of us.

Poland played many of their home international football matches at Chorzów, at least in part because they had developed a tremendous record there and the crowds were as passionate in their support as at a Liverpool or Manchester United.

190 – Ivan Mauger

There was a great deal of anticipation with a speedway world record crowd of 130,000 expected. Many of the lingering suspicions which had accompanied visits to Poland in past years had been dispelled, first by my win in the 1970 final, and then the World Team Cup victory of the following year.

The seeded Polish riders – the veteran Pawel Waloszek, experienced Jan Mucha and big movers and improvers Edward Jancarz, Zenon Plech and Jerzy Szczakiel – looked certain to pose a lot of problems. Most were rightly regarded as being quite capable of challenging for the title, and all rated as serious spoilers at the worst.

Even so, there was much more optimism from the Western contingent than there had been in the past. I liked the look of my chances, no doubt Ole and Anders fancied theirs quite strongly and Ray Wilson and first-timer Peter Collins were riding on a high.

What none of us took into account was the enormity of the occasion, with the massive crowd on terracing which seemed to reach up to almost touch the sky. The locals were pumped at the prospect of crowning one of their own as champion, but few of them, or indeed anybody else in speedway, could have dreamed how the script would play out.

Michanek, one of the favourites, was first to buckle when he ran a last in the opening heat and I was happy not only to win my first outing, heading Plechy, but also to see Ole relegated to third with Wilson taking a fall.

Poles won five of the first nine races, Szczakiel coming out of the woodwork to claim three of them including one in heat eight when he and Waloszek allowed me no way through.

A third to first victory in Heat 11 got my adrenalin flowing and confirmed it was possible to be patient, plan moves well in advance and generate plenty of pace. Two more wins put me on 13 but only too well aware that if Szczakiel won Heat 18 then he would have 14 points and it would be all over for me.

That wasn't all. Zenon Plech had 10 points from his first four rides and was out in Heat 20. The Polish fans and officials were beside themselves in anticipation of one or other being crowned world champion. Just to add to the intrigue the explosive Russian Grigori Chlynovski was in exactly the same situation.

The Western union stuck together as Ole Olsen – who like me used a long-stroke engine – did me what could and should have been an enormous favour by getting out ahead of Szczakiel and putting himself in precisely the right position to run the race.

So there we were, both on 13, both aware Plech or Chlynovski could join us by winning the last heat. As it turned out Plech got dumped big time

SECONDS TO DISASTER – the start of the 1973 World Final run-off with Poland's Jerzy Szczakiel

by Chlynovski, and being awarded two points got him on to the rostrum, whereas exclusion for his opponent ended the Soviet challenge.

This sparked off a tremendous kerfuffle with officials, riders and the referee arguing and debating the toss for half an hour. It gave me time to reflect and, I hoped, time for Szczakiel to get nervous. I was keen to get any edge going, just as in the run-off with Bernie Persson a year before.

Szczakiel had been a surprise finalist, his overall record was not remotely as convincing as that of Plech or Eddie Jancarz, and the PZM officials always gave the impression they thought his temperament was fragile.

Even so, this was a rider who had scored a six-ride maximum in the 1971 World Best Pairs Final in Rybnik and looked unstoppable on that occasion. After winning his first three rides in such confident manner it was clear to all that he was a huge chance.

My preparations were interrupted by a call to the pits telephone. It was referee Georg Transpurger, the man who had his finger on the button at

Wembley in 1972. Apparently he remembered my tactics prior to the deciding race and was kind enough to tell me that if I did the same again, he would exclude me.

Szczakiel's winning ride, and my crash, is one of the most-played speedway clips off all time. I don't have to see it again to be reminded that this was a world title chance I managed to screw up all by myself.

Speedway followers tend to regard Jerzy Szczakiel as the 1973 world champion by default. Not so. He probably is the one-off World Final winner who would have struggled most to win a title under the modern Grand Prix system, but his victory at Chorzów was entirely worthy.

Sure, I crashed in the run-off and instead of adding to my record of four wins in five years had to eat dirt and suffer what many regard as the most spectacularly disappointing world championship moment of my career.

It was not an enjoyable experience and does not get any better when the subject is broached, or the old video is replayed. What television commentator Dave Lanning described as 'the biggest sensation in the history of the world championship' makes for a memorable entry in the otherwise slim Szczakiel career highlights package.

It was nobody's fault but my own. Never one to agonise too much over defeats, but always anxious to analyse mistakes so they didn't happen again, I have had ample opportunity in my mind to re-write that race.

A DAY TO FORGET – unless your name is Jerzy Szczakiel. Ivan and third-placed Zenon Plech look suitably detuned on the Katowice rostrum

The facts are Szczakiel got the sort of start to dream of in such circumstances, and I misread the track conditions to such an extent that in trying to reel him in, I was going too fast, too soon and in the wrong place.

Katowice was a big, fast circuit and offered the opportunity to do lots of things you couldn't do at, say, Wembley or one of the smaller British tracks. Using a long-stroke two-valve long track engine with a higher gear than most of the other riders, I was prepared to forfeit speed from the starts for a set-up which allowed for more power and greater momentum,

Especially after my third ride I was confident of being able to pass, particularly going wide around the first and second corner which generated tremendous grip and speed off the second turn all the way down the back straight.

When Szczcakiel bolted out of the start in the run-off it was obvious I was going to have to summon up all my experience to get past him. My mistake was to have failed to take into account that the track was still slick on the inside from the previous race, with plenty of loose dirt on the outside.

As a result I caught Szczakiel three quarters of a lap sooner than I expected. The plan was to catch him by the start-finish line on lap three, and then line up and go past him on the outside down the next straight.

Instead I found myself charging up on the inside going into the third turn on lap two, gaining ground and going so much faster than him. He heard me coming, turned left as he was entitled to do to block my charge, and I highsided over his rear wheel.

Riders can bang into each other going into the corners and if they are going a similar speed they don't fall off. But Szczakiel was going much slower than me and when I ran into him it was like hitting a wall.

Would I have done things differently? In an ideal world, of course. But if I or any of the current GP riders were faced with that situation, we would all go for the huge gap on the inside.

So the outgoing world champion was sprawled in an undignified heap by the safety fence as the new champion completed the formality of the last lap and a half on his own.

I didn't expect the referee to stop the race. He was never a fan of Briggo's from when Barry rode in Germany years earlier and they had a lot of arguments. I was branded as Briggo's mate so Mr Transpurger definitely was not a fan of mine either.

Jerzy Szczakiel has never got the credit he deserved.

I made the mistake, he didn't.

Critics have complained that he was just a fast starter who counted correctly, anticipated when the tapes were going up and reaped maximum

THRILLER – Peter Collins savours his 1974 European Final run-off victory over Ivan and Ole Olsen in the company of actress Nerys Hughes

benefit on a day when most of the starts were pretty ordinary; that the whole occasion was stage-managed for the benefit of the Poles.

Again, not so. He did all he had to do and he did it well. His misfortune was that he never came close to doing any such thing again, and many British fans, in particular, seemed to have been personally offended.

He had a nightmare meeting in the World Team Cup at Wembley a fortnight later, a shocking tour with Poland, and has been widely and for many years damned as the worst rider ever to win the world title.

It is an unfortunate tag for a pleasant, unassuming man who not only was a whole lot better than that reputation suggests, but legitimately earned himself a place in the record books which hundreds of other supposedly better-credentialled riders never achieved.

Normally I would have been able to switch attention from speedway to the long track final, but not this time. I was winning just about every long track meeting in Europe by a country mile and in my first qualifying round at Mariánské Lázně in Czechoslovakia won my first two races and twice broke the track record.

I was leading my third ride and the clutch came off (shades of the 1961 Australian long track championship at Port Pirie). The two-speed Jawa gearboxes had the clutch on a taper and Standor Dvorak, the factory mechanic, put it back on in the track garage.

The two wins meant I had 10 points. Then the clutch again came adrift in my next race so I did not even qualify for the semi-final. It was a bitter disappointment as having won the speedway championship three years in succession I wanted to do the same on the long track.

Ole took advantage of my absence and won his only long track world championship in Oslo.

Shrugging my shoulders and telling anybody who would listen 'there's always next year' would have fooled nobody, least of all myself. But part of the job description requires the ability to put on a fresh face, get stuck into the next challenge, and that for me was, and always was, to demonstrate I could win again.

On speedway, increasingly I wanted to do what was necessary in the seven meetings along the way in 1974 and then try to be to be ideally prepared for the one night which counted, in Gothenburg. Victory in the Exeter qualifying round at the start of the campaign was followed by double figures at Poole and King's Lynn and a spot in the Leicester semi-final.

The English boys were busy knocking themselves out trying to outdo one another at every stage and I quietly gathered together sufficient points to move through to the British Final at Coventry and beyond.

The newly-created British-Nordic-American final in Fredericia was a departure from the normal and Ole Olsen made his fellow-countrymen very happy by winning the first big-time world championship meeting in Denmark, with me a point behind.

The European Final at Wembley came next, offering no fewer than 11 riders the passport to the World Final. It turned out to be one of the most keenly-contested and enthusiastically watched meetings of the season.

Peter Collins, just out of his teens by now, produced another of his Wembley party pieces by winning the title. He, Ole and I all scored 13 points but PC couldn't help himself and gave the British fans more evidence of his credentials as a genuine title chance.

Realistically it was a bit early for him and on the grounds of experience, Ole – such a brilliant winner at Ullevi in 1971 – and I were the favourites going into the final.

Nobody really knew how the Swedes would go. They had a dreadfully poor record at the track, and most of them had spent the season out of British League after one of the periodic anti-foreigner purges by the BSPA. The one

196 – Ivan Mauger

exception was Sören Sjösten, married to a Manchester girl, based in England and still at Belle Vue.

The one thing which could be relied upon when a World Final was staged in Gothenburg was bad weather. That apart, it turned out to be night of surprises. After expecting the 1970 and 1973 finals in Poland to be tailored for the home riders, nobody anticipated something similar in Sweden.

But a few races into the meeting, the Swedes were all over everybody. Several had spent their time away from England experimenting with different set-ups including four-valve conversions, and they all seemed to be on flying machines.

Between them the home riders won 12 of the 20 heats and when consistency was the key, Anders Michanek was the master. After years of beating everybody everywhere except in World Finals, he suddenly discovered massive self-confidence and powered his way to a 15-point maximum.

Most of the visiting riders were shell-shocked and well off the pace. My own contribution was four second places and a solitary win, the least convincing or competitive display in any of my individual speedway finals up to that point.

Managing to head of Sjösten in a run-off for second was small consolation. We had been ambushed. But I got out of there in one piece, more than could be said for Ole who crashed in his second ride and broke his leg.

Many of the riders in Ullevi had little time to catch breath, because the FIM had scheduled the long track final less than 48 hours later in Scheeßel, near Hamburg. It was poor planning by the CCP members who were well aware of the increasing number of the top speedway riders contesting both championships.

The closeness of the two finals had played havoc with the normal preparations. In the run-up to Gothenburg, Gordon and I had to go to Bremen to prepare the long track bikes, which included a quick trip down to the Jawa factory at Divišov in Czechoslovakia to rebuild a couple of engines.

We had to get back to England to be ready for Exeter on the Monday night and then go in the transporter all the way up to Gothenburg the next day because the flights got in too late for the practice on the Wednesday.

After the Friday night speedway, none of the guys who were in the long track could stay for the traditional World Final dinner as we all had to get down to Scheeßel in time for practice by one o'clock the next day.

Even so, I approached it in a reasonable frame of mind, having won my qualifying round at Gornja Radgona in Yugoslavia and the semi-final at Mariánské Lázně in Czecho.

SPLASH HIT – Anders Michanek was in a class of his own at the 1974 World Final in Gothenburg. This was the closest anybody came to him all night

Wilfried Drygala and a couple of guys from the Bremen club who used to help me during the week took the long track bikes to Scheeβel. Gordon, Chris Macdonald and I made the overnight trip in the transporter, taking turns to grab a few hours of sleep.

After being sandwiched between two Swedes in Gothenburg, I was a silver medallist once again when Egon Müller took out the long track title with his German compatriot Alois Wiesböck third. Egon twice beat me by about 30 or 40 metres on his Otto Lantenhammer-prepared Jap.

It was Müller who got me thinking. He had finished last the previous year but was unstoppable that day, winning races as he pleased. Egon was a fitness fanatic, not a big guy to start with but one who had slimmed down until he had the body of a whippet. He was a stone or more (six or seven kilos) lighter than me. What was more, the bike on which he won weighed only 77 kilos, compared with my 94kg Jawa which did not have the same horse power.

Prior to the start of the next season I paid nearly £5000 for my best four speedway bikes and best three long track bikes to be lightened and to have titanium bolts made with dural nuts.

Gary Hansen, who had bought a Bultaco trials bike from me a couple of years earlier, had an engineering business and did the work. My bike at the 1975 World Final was 81 kilos because we did so many other things to lighten it.

Most riders with ambitions of being at or around the top paid attention to their fitness and I spent several years training with Manchester City Football Club. Some of the young guys would rag me but that simply spurred me to do more. I might go home and do a few hundred press-ups, come back next day challenge them to a contest. None of the other riders trained that hard.

Employing a rigid diet I also lost a lot of weight and finished up a couple of kilos lighter than Egon. In the run-up to Wembley and the long track final a fortnight later, I went on an even stricter diet which consisted of fruit

YET ANOTHER – Ivan collects the 1975 European title at Bydgoszcz, from Ole Olsen and Phil Crump

The Will To Win – 199

and water one day and cereal and water the next. It left me looking like a real mean machine but eventually came back to bite me for overdoing things – and it all started because I was trying to beat Egon in the long track championship.

Although my face was all lined with the weight loss I felt OK in myself and for weeks it seemed nothing could go wrong. The scores were flowing in England.

Three qualifying rounds, three victories without dropping a point – at Exeter, Wolverhampton and Swindon. Next came the Inter-Continental Final in Gothenburg, and another win, followed by the European Final in Bydgoszcz where I beat a recovered Ole in a run-off.

My former protégé had a long time to reflect on his 1974 disappointment and put it to good use by coming back firing. I'd tried to analyse all the lessons and thought I had come up with most of the answers.

But I was to learn that a hungry fighter, supposedly the meanest contender of all, can end up being too hungry. My mission in this year had been to go for everything, to take no prisoners, and to use Wembley as the stage to show I was still made of world champion material.

In five rounds I had dropped two points and if the Grand Prix system had been in operation then they might as well have given me the title without the bother of going to Wembley.

Unfortunately because of unusually warm weather in the lead-up to the final and problems with track preparation, this was not the usual Wembley. The stadium people did the track and despite their best efforts, the conditions left a lot to be desired. It got to a stage where spectators even got the hoses out and started watering the track so it was very patchy.

Ole meanwhile came back into the spotlight like a man possessed. He won every race and blasted away all the frustrations he had been forced to endure for four years since his first title.

After winning my first, I misread the track in the next race and came third behind Ole and John Louis. Defending champion Anders Michanek had suffered a similar fate but he came past me in Heat 9 and my second place left me well behind although not completely out of the reckoning.

I ended up with a dozen points, enough to get into a run-off with John Louis for third, and physically and mentally I was shot. Third, fourth, it really didn't matter at that moment, as either result was a million miles short of my expectations.

Anders was to regret his poor start because winning the next four races put him a couple behind Ole. And Peter Collins, the people's choice and a big popular favourite for the title, controversially ran a last after winning his first two – right after the impromptu hosedown by those angry fans.

200 – Ivan Mauger

To add insult to injury Reg Fearman described me as a 'has been' in what was supposed to be a tongue-in-cheek speech at the official function, which caused BSPA, SCB and FIM officials to cringe. Several of them came up to me afterwards to apologise for his ill-chosen remarks.

It was a rare moment to have so many of the sport's top brass siding with me and although they insisted Reg had been joking, it went down like a lead balloon with everyone present. It's fair to say I noted it in the back of my mind and looked forward to the day when he, and any and all my other detractors, would have to eat their words.

The long track campaign ended disappointingly too. I finished second in my qualifier at Jübek in North Germany and won the semi-final at Mariánské Lázně, so often a happy hunting ground.

But in the final I had to settle for runner-up at Gornja Radgona. Egon Müller proved he was no lightweight when it came to performance, picking up his second title in a row, with Ole behind me in third.

By this time he and a lot of the Germans were on four-valve Weslakes and I was still on the two-valve Jawa, albeit one which now weighed only 81kg Egon beat me twice that day but only by a couple of metres. In the circumstances it was quite a good effort to run him so close.

But overshadowing almost everything in this year was the death of Gary Peterson, the young Kiwi prospect who was beginning to look as if he had a big future in the sport. Gary was a neighbour in Manchester for some years after he arrived from New Plymouth and was a house-sitter for us at Upper Chorlton Road when we went back to Christchurch one winter.

He had a lot of talent and was very brave but had bad luck with accidents. When out of action Gary often helped me and Gordon at meetings and in the workshop and he got on famously with Raye and the kids.

My brother Trev and his wife Bernice were holidaying with us in England and we heard about Gary's accident on the radio as we were driving home from an end-of-season meeting at Newport. When the report came over, we were quite close to Wolverhampton and dashed to the hospital but he had died from injuries received in the crash.

It was speedway's second fatal accident of the year. Wimbledon's Tommy Jansson died after a prang in a world championship qualifying meeting in Sweden in May and the sport mourned the passing of a popular and accomplished rider who seemed to have the world at his feet.

Contrasting with such tragedy, there was a stunning reminder of what happiness and reward speedway had brought me. I was awarded the Member of the British Empire (MBE) in the New Year's honours list, after being nominated by the New Zealand Government.

When we landed in Auckland with the World Champions Troupe there was a big welcoming committee, all of whom seemed to know the news.*

The 1976 speedway championship route started earlier but involved less by way of qualifying rounds than ever before. The FIM decided there would be an Australasian Final in Auckland in January – with the top four to qualify for the Inter-Continental Final at Wembley in June.

It wasn't as routine as it might have appeared as I had to work hard to prevent an Aussie whitewash. John Boulger, Billy Sanders and Phil Crump occupied the first three places and I needed to beat Phil Herne and Mitch Shirra in a run-off for the last berth.

The top eight at the Inter-Continental Final would go forward and it was like old times as PC beat me in a run-off for first.

Just how tough a night that was can be gauged by the fact that the eight non-qualifiers included Ole and Mich, world champions in the two preceding years, as well as the likes of Bengt Jansson and Bernt Persson, both of whom had been desperately close.

It did not mean the World Final, in Katowice again, would be any cakewalk. The Poles did not have quite the depth but they had at least a couple of likely suspects. Phil Crump could beat anybody on his day and Scott Autrey, my Exeter teammate, was capable of being in the mix.

I still regard this as a title which got away, and to have won it would have been my absolute greatest victory. I was the only rider on a two-valver as Jawa did not have their four-valvers ready in time. The other 15 were on four-valves which were far superior to my bike.

This was the dawn of the Weslake era and Peter Collins and Malcolm Simmons were on super-tuned engines that had twin carburettors and special camshafts manufactured particularly for that track. Crumpie was on the new Street four-valve conversion that had a downdraft carburettor and all the goodies.

As in 1973 I was on a long-stroke engine and as on that memorable visit, I was using a much higher gear than any of the others. It meant being a bit slow off the start but I still rated my chances as I was happy enough about the prospect of having greater speed overall. The long track motor generated so much drive out of the corners.

From everything that happened in practice, I felt sure I had a great chance of winning. One two-bob component ordained otherwise. It was possible to count on the fingers of a man with no arms the number of breakdowns I had suffered in a World Final – 54 races without stopping once

---

* The Queen presented the MBE to me at Buckingham Palace on July 28, 1976. My mum, Raye and the kids were all present so it was a very special occasion.

WHERE'S IVAN – Peter Collins (centre) Malcolm Simmons and Phil Crump, 1-2-3 in the world championship that got away

– until heat five in Poland, where I won my first race and was well in the lead in the next.

Then a jet block in my carburettor broke. Crumpie was behind me and stopping in that race didn't just wreck my chances of winning; I did not even get a run-off chance to get on the rostrum. The three points Phil got while I was sitting on my bike on the centre green took him a point ahead of me and put me fourth overall.

My only souvenir from that day is one half of that jet block which today is sitting in the medal cabinet at home. The other half went to Jan Křivka, who was the director and main man at Jawa.

By the time I beat PC in the last race he was like me in 1969, needing only to score a couple of points to win the title. Malcolm Simmons, who finished up with the silver medal, took a couple of rides to get into a winning groove and had finished with 13.

I should not have expected sympathy and I didn't get much – most of the British reporters who were at that meeting did not even care that I had made such a challenge on a two-valver because for the first time since 1962, they had an English world champion and also an English runner-up.

At least the run of outs was destined to end at Mariánské Lázně a week later, when I salvaged something from the year by collecting a third world long track championship. It wasn't the speedway title I so wanted but it was another world championship, and a hard-won achievement.

I negotiated the rounds at Mühldorf and Scheeβel but had to threaten the Jawa factory before they got their act together and provided an engine for the final that was man for the job.

I was so angry with Jawa after the speedway final and told them I intended to get Dave Nourish to do a Weslake for me with the twin carbs for Mariánské Lázně. They were not happy with that. Everyone in Czechoslovakia and elsewhere knew I was a factory rider so the last thing they wanted was to have me riding a Weslake.

It stirred them into action, though. In quick time they finished off five engines – which should have been done so I could compete on even terms with the others at Katowice – and gave one to Jiří Štancl, Zdeněk Kudrna, Ole Olsen and myself, all of us being factory riders.

Briggo was disgusted. He was the Jawa agent in the UK but they did not do one for him. Instead the fifth engine was in a bike to be available as a spare to the four works riders.

When we tested them on the Friday morning, the magnetos were misfiring at the end of the straights. The factory guys and Jan Křivka took them back to Divišov that same afternoon and said they would change all the magnetos to generators which had an outside coil and could take much higher revs. They came back ready for the practice on the Saturday and this time all went well.

READY TO GO – Ivan manouevres into position at the start of the final of the 1976 world long track championship at Mariánské Lázně, with Ole Olsen (9) and Jiří Štancl (6) also in shot

Come the day I finished a point ahead of Ole with Egon (on his Lantenhammer-tuned Weslake with twin carbs) and Wiesböck a further four points adrift. At the end of almost four years of frustrations, it was a sweet and satisfying result, FIM gold medal number 12.

Incidentally, the FIM Technical Department banned two carburettors on speedway or long track at their Autumn Congress at the end of October 1976.

After being dropped from the British attack on the World Team Cup three years earlier, realistically the only other championship on offer was the Best Pairs and this had also been a source of frustration over several seasons.

Since crashing out in the 1972 title run-off, I finished seventh back at Borås the following year with Graeme Stapleton as my partner, third at Belle Vue with Barry in 1974, and fifth, again with Briggo, at Eskilstuna in 1976.

The first few years New Zealand had a side in the World Team Cup served up a few more disappointments. It got off on the wrong foot in 1974 with a huge row when Briggo and I didn't ride at Ipswich.

We turned up to a jam-packed Foxhall Heath for the scheduled opening round but the weather was foul and the meeting could not go on. John Berry, the Ipswich promoter, very successful but very autocratic, told us the re-

DROUGHT OVER – world long track champion for the third time, with Gordon Stobbs and Wilfried Drygala at Mariánské Lázně

staging would be the following Sunday – the first time it had been suggested that any new date would be anything other than Ipswich's official Tuesday alternative race night.

Barry and I had SCB permits to race in FIM-inscribed meetings at Copenhagen and Schwarme respectively on the Sunday and were quick to tell him there was no way we intended breaking those contracts. The BSPA and Ipswich had six days of the week in which to organise themselves and come up with a workable date but John Berry fancied his chances in an argument and tried every which way. When he finally accepted that we meant what we said he then tried to get us both banned.

It was childish, petulant, self-interested behaviour of this kind which too often put promoters and riders at odds with one another. John Berry didn't forget and he didn't miss us a couple of years later when the qualifying round was again allocated to Foxhall Heath.

This time the problem was the original date set was May 30, so Briggo and I kept that Sunday free. Then the BSPA decided to switch the meeting to May 16, the day Ole Olsen had a big individual meeting at Vojens for which both of us had been booked months before.

When we said we would be fulfilling our commitment in Denmark and would not be able to ride at Ipswich, we were accused of being disrespectful to British speedway, disloyal to New Zealand and all kinds of treachery. Pressure was brought to bear through the Speedway Control Board and we were told if we didn't ride in the World Team Cup, we would be banned from appearing anywhere else on the same day.

Perhaps John Berry considered that meant he had won his little battle, but the end result was that we didn't ride – so nobody won, both events suffered, the fans lost out, Ole and his Danish fans and sponsors lost out. The whole affair did nothing to convince me that I should be giving the event much thought in the future.

I was getting too long in the tooth to be wasting my time and energies fighting with officialdom. Not so ancient that the competitive fires were cooling down, mind.

There was a year to go on my Exeter deal, a year in which there was room for one more serious attempt to be world speedway champion.

Mariánské Lázně, and reminding myself of the pleasure of standing on top of the pile on such an occasion, was the spark to start the motor running on another championship road.

GLORIOUS DEVON – good memories in a five-year association with Exeter

Heat 12

FLYING WEST

AFTER winning the world speedway title for a fourth time, leading Belle Vue to three British League championships and a KO Cup victory, and securing a second successive world long track crown, I was riding high.

Little did anybody realise that within a few months I would be contemplating life without British speedway.

My customary good intentions and all the resolutions took an immediate hit when I damaged ligaments doing a 6am limbo dance at a New Year's party at Woodford – shortly before flying to Perth.

The hands which had been such a problem for much of 1972 had recently been operated upon and up to that point I felt my fitness was coming good.

My future in domestic league racing, though, appeared to be under some kind of a cloud. Belle Vue had won everything the year before and it was an open secret the BSPA rider control committee would be looking to the Aces to release somebody. One whisper doing the rounds was that they might be looking to release me.

I was the oldest rider on their books, and the most expensive. Good youngsters kept coming off Dent Oliver's training school conveyor belt. When calls started coming in to ask where I stood with it all, I said I was staying at Belle Vue.

But I wasn't dependent upon riding in the British League because the diary of meetings in Europe was packed. One minute Belle Vue were telling me they would fight to the death to keep me there, the next they were telling the BSPA to try to take Ivan away!

The BSPA were no more consistent. First I was going to have to be the one to go. Then I could stay and Sören Sjösten, who had been a one-club man and a Belle Vue rider for twice as long as anybody else, was to be the sacrificial offering.

After getting over the knee problem I was thousands of miles away, in New Zealand and then Australia. I read in a Perth newspaper that I was being allocated to Wimbledon of all places. Cyril Maidment, who had packed up riding and taken over as their front man after Ronnie Greene retired, listened to what I had to say about that and said his directors would not be pursuing their interest.

The promoters association didn't let things rest, though, and said there were other clubs who would take me, including Coatbridge, 180 miles (290

208 – Ivan Mauger

kilometres) north of my Manchester base, and Exeter, which was 200 miles (320 kilometres) south.

Neither seemed particularly practical or appealing at first, although I always believe in listening to what people have to say. I didn't tell the Belle Vue board but things had got the point where I decided I didn't want to ride for them any more, and whatever happened would happen.

We came back to Woodford uncertain what the future might hold. I had a couple of training schools to run – I'd done one at Exeter the previous year and this time Stoke and Weymouth wanted me to do something along the same lines.

As far as racing was concerned, I was in limbo but some people still wanted to know me. I got a great reception when Alderman Edward Greer, the Lord Mayor of Manchester, hosted a civic function for the Belle Vue boys who had done so well the previous season. And I had some fun on four wheels, finishing second in a celebrity race at Brands Hatch, despite spinning off at one point.

Then the people who made the *Blue Peter* television programme asked me to bring down my gold-plated world championship-winning bike and appear on the show. That too was an enjoyable diversion although it went pear-shaped afterwards. The suspension on my Mercedes broke and I had to ask the BBC if they could keep the gold bike in the vaults at Wood Lane until the car was good to go the following day.

Meantime the season, and the Aces, had got under way without me. A couple of nights later, I was at home and getting ready for bed when Wally Mawdsley, the Exeter promoter, rang to say his Falcons needed strengthening and to ask if I would ride for them.

Unlike Belle Vue, who had the reputation and trappings of a glamour club even though they were doing it tough in the years before I went there, Exeter had never been considered anything other than unfashionable. But that didn't disqualify them from my thinking.

I knew Wally as a well-respected promoter who had interests in a number of tracks. He was involved in the Provincial League from the start, had been Second Division chairman for a few years, and among a variety of tracks he ran, had been longer at Exeter than anywhere.

I liked the County Ground circuit – after riding on long tracks, its speed did not bother me – and invariably had done well there. There had been a string of victories in the individual meetings such as the Westernapolis and the Westward TV Trophy to which I usually received an invite.

Peter Oakes, who was my manager from the mid 1960s, had a fair amount of contact with Wally, and the three of us teamed up to run a season of open licence meetings at Barrow in 1972. It was my first dabble in promoting, although because of racing commitments I was for once pretty much a 'silent' partner.

The venture was not a huge success and we were happy enough to sell to George Graham, a local businessman,

Wally's involvement at Exeter was much more long-running as he and Pete Lansdale had been at the County Ground since 1961. It was one of the first places in England to stage speedway, but the Falcons were never a 'big' club. Because of its location down in the south-west Exeter had always been regarded as a bit of an outpost.

Attracting top riders was often a problem and apart from 1968, when rider control took Martin Ashby there from Swindon, the previous year's champions, they rarely challenged for honours. Mid-table or below was the norm.

The big, fast track was 443 yards, banked, bumpy, very narrow and on the outside of the rugby union pitch. It was considered pretty daunting and not many visitors fancied their chances there. Racing up close to a steel fence is not every rider's idea of fun. Some like big tracks, others prefer the smaller, trickier circuits. I enjoyed both types and Exeter was a lot of fun to ride around, especially if you were on top form.

Wally was prepared to offer me a lot of money but the big obstacle seemed to be their Monday race night. Just getting there was difficult at the best of times and in my case, after racing on the Continent on Sundays I got in to Heathrow any time from 10am to 1pm depending where I was in Europe. Then I got a connection to Manchester airport.*

I told Wally I would have to get a vehicle only for Exeter because of the miles run up in the Mercedes or my transporter to get there and back to Woodford. It would require Gordon to meet me at Heathrow and the journey was a hassle. The M5 ended at Bristol so it was the A38 all the way to Devon.

It was fine for a tourist with time to admire the scenery but hopeless for a speedway rider in a hurry. There were loads of small towns to go through, most with traffic lights. The A38 was narrow and windy so if you got caught behind a truck you were there for many miles before you could pass.

It didn't look as if it could work, but the conversation got me thinking. Even if Belle Vue couldn't sort things out, at least somebody wanted me.

The following Monday, Wally was on the phone again. Exeter had dropped a point in their first home league match and were still in the market Not much had changed in my situation, though.

---

* Unlike the present day when riders easily trip between Britain and Europe, regional airports such as Luton, Stansted and Manchester had few if any continental flights in 1973.

However, next morning John Richards, Wally's partner at Exeter, called to say he would double the deal Wally had offered. Suddenly it started to look more reasonable.

I told John and then Wally the terms Belle Vue had paid me and apparently this did not deter them. Publicly I was telling the media that it was still Belle Vue or nothing but I was warming to the idea of the move, especially if Exeter improved upon the terms.

The following Monday was the breaking point for the Falcons and a turning point in the negotiations. They had Bob Kilby carted off to hospital after a first race crash and went down 50-28 to Belle Vue, their biggest British League defeat at home.

JUST SIGN HERE – Ivan puts pen to paper watched by Wally Mawdsley and the County Ground fans

Wally again called me after the meeting. This time I told him I was thinking about their suggested offer but felt it still was not enough to justify the hectic rush back from Europe on Mondays.

John was on the phone a few hours later and this time it was the real deal. He upped the money, and said he would arrange transport to take me from Heathrow down the M4 to White Waltham airfield nearby where his personal pilot would give me a ride in his Cessna 182 to Exeter. From there John would pick me up in his Rolls Royce and drive me to the track. After the meeting it was another plane ride in the Cessna, taking me back to Manchester airport.

In a few short weeks I had gone from being the rider Belle Vue had to lose to the rider Exeter had to have. And the net worth of my new contract was about four times greater than it had been at Hyde Road.

It seemed almost too good to be true. After the months of indecision I didn't want to bind myself into an agreement which was still going to incur problems, so I contacted the BSPA and asked to meet members of the management committee.

My position was that I didn't want to be messed around again and I wanted to own my contract. I didn't want to be subject to rider control and run the risk of being punted around again as had just happened. To my amazement they agreed.

The Will To Win – 211

An announcement was put on hold for a few days because I had to go to Denmark for a weekend meeting. I rode in the meeting, stayed overnight with Ole Olsen's parents in Haderslev, and then jumped on a plane in Copenhagen the next morning.

Peter Oakes had organised a lunchtime press call at the Sportsman Club in Tottenham Court Road, London. It was attended by many Fleet Street reporters and the speedway media guys. They all fully expected me to announce my retirement from speedway. None were ready for the announcement that I had agreed to ride for Exeter.

After the press conference Wally, Peter and I dashed across to Paddington to catch the train down to Exeter. By the time we arrived at the station, the Westward TV news had broken the story and we were met by a pack of reporters, television, radio and a huge number of fans.

At the County Ground, the reception was similarly frantic. For a while I could imagine what it must have been like to be a George Best or touring pop star. I signed my contract on a card table in front of the grandstand before the meeting against Leicester and then retreated upstairs to see Exeter lose 35-43.

The result emphasised the extent of the job ahead. The Falcons had now lost four and drawn one of their first five matches, and were looking like candidates for the wooden spoon.

Things had to get better, and they did. On my first appearance in the Easter Trophy match against Poole the following Monday, 10,000 people turned up, we won 43-35 and only a broken throttle cable robbed me of starting with a maximum.

Wally and John were right. The team did need a lift. Fortunately the results continued to improve, and the arrival of Tony Lomas in an exchange deal which took Bob Kilby to Oxford was one important change.

The real plus however was provided by teenage American Scott Autrey, who I had recommended to the club some months earlier. Kevin Holden, an ever-present in his first full season, was another exciting prospect and Frank Shuter, from Christchurch, was an invaluable behind the scenes contributor and could always be relied on to win a race when we really needed it.*

The team eventually finished eighth in the 17-strong First Division and in spite of my late start I kept my average at 11.29, and had 17 full scores in 26 British League meetings.

There would have been more but for a few incidents, particularly at Coatbridge and Oxford, where unsatisfactory starts robbed me of points.

---

* Frank was killed a few years ago in a road motorcycle accident going to his factory in Los Angeles.

The starting procedures in so many meetings were going from bad to worse, with many referees lacking the personality to get a grip. At some places it was a case of 'green light, go' but there was no consistency and little discipline across the board.

I'm not saying the riders were saintly in their approach or tactics, myself included, but it was a big problem for the sport.

At Exeter, though, the word 'problem' hardly existed. I didn't drop a point in 12 home league meetings, the first time I had achieved a perfect record after going close for several seasons in a row.

As far as the international calendar went, this was a year of ups and downs. The BSPA and PZM arranged a three-Test series in Poland but I missed the first two because they were on Sundays on which I had already completed and signed contracts to race in Europe.

The Poles won easily in Wrocław and I was due to go to a grass track at Holzwickede the next weekend when the second Test was on at Rybnik.

National team manager Charles Foot, the BSPA treasurer, Poole co-promoter and my accountant, said they wanted me to ride so they could put on a better show.

When I told him my FIM permit for Holzwickede had been OK'd, he assured me that in fact it hadn't and so I was free to ride for Great Britain. I dashed about to undo all my arrangements, apologised to the German promoter, and agreed to lend my best long track bike to Briggo so he could do the meeting.

Then the Speedway Control Board told me the Holzwickede permit had been approved, which didn't go down well with Footy and the other British promoters, but at least meant I could fulfil the original commitment. The problem was all the travel and transport arrangements had to be reorganised yet again.

As chance would have it the British team won in Rybnik to level the series, so presumably they didn't miss me – and when I turned out in the decider at Gorzów a few weeks later, got absolutely thrashed!

I was having a few dramas on my travels as this came hard on the heels of a World Pairs Final disaster at Borås, where my gear was mislaid by the airline – as it had been at the corresponding meeting in 1972 – although at least this time I got out of the place in one piece.

The Daily Mirror International Tournament which occupied three weeks in the middle of the season provided an interesting diversion. Even though Briggo and Ronnie rode, it was always going to be a tough one for New Zealand. We did get to the semi-final but England were too strong for us, winning 48-30 at Hyde Road.

It was enjoyable flying the Kiwi flag but of wider consequence was a gathering division between the Brits and the colonials. There was talk that New Zealand and Australia might organise their own championship rounds, a suggestion which grew wings when Briggo – who had opted out of British League racing in 1973 – was denied the chance to ride in the qualifiers.

With Ray Wilson crowned as the first home-grown British champion in years, and then my dumping from the World Team Cup, it seemed as if New Zealanders and Aussies were under threat of becoming 'them' rather than the 'us' we were used to being for so long.

A season which had contained so much drama and eventually so many positives associated with the move to Exeter got seriously worse when my long track ambitions ground to a halt. Then crashing in the World Final run-off in Poland was a real low point.

I got back to England, won the Welsh Open at Newport, and then crashed and hurt myself in the first race at Ipswich the following night. Another fall at Wolverhampton's Brew XI Trophy 24 hours later left me feeling even more sore. By the time I got around to having X-rays the medical people told me I had a broken left shoulder and a broken bone in my arm.

A fortnight's break in Cornwall helped the injuries and the mental hurt to heal. There was a month of the season to go and while it would have been too easy to extend the rest, my instinct was to get back on the bike and starting doing what I do best.

FLYING FALCON – by air or road, this is the way to travel, courtesy of John Richards' Cessna and Rolls Royce

CHAMPIONS – Exeter at the start of their 1974 British League-winning campaign, back row, left to right: John Richards (co-promoter) with mascot, Kevin Holden, Scott Autrey, Tony Lomas, Frank Shuter, Peter Thompson, Chris Julian. On machine: Ivan Mauger (captain)

A late flurry of form gave the last few weeks of the season renewed impetus and to top it off, the fixture list showed two visits to Hyde Road – one with Exeter and the other for the British League Riders Championship.

Wet weather interfered with the plans and both meetings ended up being rearranged. Not that a rehearsal was necessary, but a five-ride maximum neatly rounded off the League fixtures and the following week, on November 3 – after the official season-closing date – the BLRC provided a perfect send-off to this less than perfect year.

I felt sharp, confident and in control, won my first four rides and – after Ole Olsen had been excluded – needed only to stay calm for the fifth, coming in behind Anders Michanek but satisfied I had given everybody at Hyde Road something else by which to remember me.

It was a relief to be preparing for my second season with Exeter without any of the uncertainty which surrounded my arrival there. The deal with John Richards and Wally Mawdsley was intact for three years, we had started to sort out the riders and ensure we had whatever home advantage we could by making subtle alterations to the track and pits arrangements.

I liked the idea of leading from the front – to the extent that my picture was on the programme cover with my sponsors getting full bang for their buck, down to being involved in all aspects of the team and how we went about our business. As with Newcastle and Belle Vue I fell out with a few

SPARKLING FINISH – Lawrie Quayle of Westward TV pours the bubbly as the Falcons prepare to toast their title triumph

people and their hangers-on but that was a necessary evil to get the team to have any success.

Nobody could match us round the County Ground and winning away became a pleasing habit, all the more so as it traditionally had been the downfall of earlier Falcons teams. Peter Oakes was like an eighth man – as team manager, he was always ahead of the game, and we planned everything like a precise military operation.

I scored better away from home, and one or two blips at Exeter took a bite out of my figures, but a final British League average of 11.15 with 18 maximums in 29 matches indicated a decent job for my employers. When we clinched the title, relegating Belle Vue to second place, the promoters broke out the champagne and as far as I can remember, we all agreed I had been a good investment!

One of the most satisfying of feelings after getting your own job done is to see others learning and absorbing valuable lessons to advance their careers. Nobody picked things up faster than Scott Autrey whose elevation to genuine heat leader status was a big plus.

He was the first of the new wave of Americans to make a success of racing in the British League. A few others with a big reputation in California – the most notable of them being Steve Bast – had been, seen and gone home again. Scotty was determined to learn and to do whatever it took to make the grade.

We rode together in the last race at away tracks and several times went into Heat 13 and scored a 5-1 to win 40-38. We had a perfect understanding and mutually decided who was going off which gate.

Always there was a plan A and plan B, the first dependent upon one of us making the start and plan B was what we would do if we both missed it. Our understanding was almost telepathic and we rarely missed doing the complete race according to our game plan.

Tony Lomas and Kevin Holden were good value and the signing of Australian champion Steve Reinke was the additional factor which helped turn the team from challengers into British League champions.

Reinke was a hard-riding action man from Ipswich, west of Brisbane. Although he broke a collarbone early on, when he recovered he contributed some significant scores which tipped the balance in a number of meetings.

The Australian connection was boosted for 1975 when Exeter signed John Titman and Mike Farrell, two more Queenslanders, to replace

ONE OF THE BEST – Scott Autrey was a super signing for Exeter, a valued colleague and friend

Tony Lomas, who switched to Leicester, and Frank Shuter, who moved to Los Angeles.

It all looked promising on paper but somehow the team did not fire up quite as efficiently as in the championship year. Kevin Holden was injured and Steve Reinke went home, neither of which did much for the hopes of retaining the title.

My own results were up – from 1968–72 I had an 11-plus average home and away and for the first time in three years managed that double again. The overall average was 11.45 and 18 full scores matched the strike rate of the year before.

However a season in which I had plenty of success also finished up as one in which the big prizes, individual and team, proved elusive. Exeter had to settle for fourth place. Ipswich won the British League for the first time, and thereby hangs another tale.

For most of the year it looked as if Belle Vue were going to take the title. They had a so-so year immediately after I left, went close in 1974 and finally it looked as if their home-grown boys were going to bring the championship back to Hyde Road.

I was still a fan of the Belle Vue people. Raye continued to go to the Supporters' Club meetings with the kids on a Tuesday. Even though I was an Exeter rider, I went along whenever I could to meet old friends.

As the fixtures panned out, Exeter had to meet the Aces home and away in the closing days of the season. We were at Hyde Road on the Saturday night and Belle Vue were due at our place on the Monday.

They needed to win their last two matches to pip Ipswich and I knew they were capable of beating us at Exeter. The fracturing of a beautiful relationship played a big part in denying them the top spot.

Belle Vue fans loved me in the four years I rode for the Aces. I led them out of the doldrums so I couldn't believe my ears when the same fans booed me when Exeter were there.

When the last race came round, we were in a position to win the match. As the tapes went up, my primary chain broke and I was left stranded – which produced the biggest cheering of the night.

I was so angry. Without thinking I bent down to pick up the chain which was red hot. It burned through my glove and ruined it and started to burn my hand and fingers as I was walking back to the pits.

But I couldn't give the crowd the satisfaction of seeing me drop it in front of them. I thought these people had no right to boo me after everything I'd done for the club. I carried that chain all the way back to the pits – and we lost the match.

218 – Ivan Mauger

I called all our riders together in the pits before we left and told them I'd be ringing them on Sunday morning. I was absolutely determined to do everything I could to beat them on Monday and stop them winning the title.

When I phoned them on the Sunday I told them to get to the track an hour earlier than usual. I wanted them all in the pits before the Belle Vue boys even started turning up.

Exeter never cleaned the pits until before a meeting so it was always full of rubbish, paper cups and stuff from the previous match when we arrived. I told the guy who swept up to deposit all the rubbish out of the Exeter pits into the Belle Vue side and leave it so it was a mess when they came in.

I didn't tell anyone else this but there were eight lights on the visiting team's side of the pits and I took out five of them. It was October so it was pretty dark over there as well as being a mess.

I arranged with Wally Mawdsley that we would dispense with the usual pre-match parade. We didn't tell anyone. I wanted the Belle Vue riders to get prepared for it.

When they went to get changed the Exeter boys were primed and warming up their bikes. You could see the Belle Vue team wondering what was going on.

We were prepared for battle. The pit marshal called the riders out for the parade and Belle Vue walked out on to the track. But we stayed put, ready to race. Wally went and told them there was no parade and that it was time for the first heat.

They had to rush back while we pushed off for the starting gate and their riders for the first race were put on two minutes to get ready in the half dark among all the paper cups and old rags.

By the time Belle Vue had got themselves sorted out we had taken a comfortable lead and our win meant that Ipswich had won the title. I got off my bike and went straight to the speedway office to phone Ipswich promoter John Berry and congratulate them on becoming the champions.

And all that came about because the Belle Vue fans booed me and cheered when my chain broke. They paid a high price for it.

Armed with a new two-year deal, I was keen to help keep the Falcons to the fore in 1976. As things panned out, the Witches again were too good for everybody, including Belle Vue who finished seven points adrift and Exeter, nudged into third on race points.

For the first time in years my average slipped a fraction below 11 (it was 10.95 in the league with 19 maximums) but it was good enough to put me on top of the charts, always a good feeling.

Scott Autrey was developing into a rider approaching world class and John Titman started to hit his straps. A great asset, he was always capable of

NERVE CENTRE – brother Trevor and Gordon in the workshop at 446 Chester Road, Woodford, in 1975

scoring more than his share of points and was also very valuable in the pits doing work for the team which fans never saw.

Tito could be relied on to help with any mechanical problems, usually had a fix-it solution and many times was solely responsible for different riders finishing the meeting on their own bikes and scoring extra points.

Mike Farrell was another very popular member of the team and a huge trier. His efforts used to get him into a bit of trouble, especially at the end of the back straight at Exeter. He wasn't the world's fastest starter but he used to catch up to some of the visitors as they did a bit of a wobble after going over the bump that was always on the entrance to turn three.

I lost count of the times he went end over end at that part of the track. As a consequence he hurt himself a few times and in 1976 missed a big part of the season. He came up and stayed with Gordon Stobbs at Bramhall and worked for me. Mike was always good in the workshop and had some ingenious ideas and we all enjoyed having him around.*

---

* In recent years Mike built his own classic road race bikes using a modified two-valve Jawa and won the Australian Classic Road Race Championship. He has a great workshop in Brisbane with all the best equipment and has done a lot of the engine work for riders in my speedway and long track series.

220 – Ivan Mauger

With the addition of promising recruits Steve Koppe, another North Queenslander, and Peter Prinsloo, who had impressed when our World Champions troupe raced in South Africa and Rhodesia, there were hopes Exeter could make a stronger challenge for honours.

Kevin Holden went to Poole but the signing of Václav Verner, always a tough competitor on the Continent and one of several very accomplished Czech riders making a name for themselves, went down big with the fans.

I met Václav several times at Prague and Slany when I was testing Jawas and set things up to get him to Exeter. He made an immediate impact and was an absolute blast at home.

Sure enough, we stepped up the tempo and finished second in 1977, a couple of points behind White City. With Scott Autrey and Václav going like a train there were slim pickings for visiting riders and more than ever it was always likely away form would separate the champions from the rest.

Yet the match which ultimately cost us the title was when Belle Vue ended our run of 26 consecutive home league wins and beat us 46-32 in June. I had just had a fortnight off because of injury and had bike problems but almost all of the team under-performed and there were some angry words afterwards.

Fortunately there was an opportunity to immediately rectify matters. All the boys acknowledged their individual and collective responsibility; 24 hours later we went to Leicester and we won easily, although I had another average night.

At the start of July, it wasn't just my machines which were struggling. My body and mind were craving a rest. The Exeter promoters were not impressed, but Raye and I decided there was nothing for it but to take a few days off on the French island of Bendor, owned by Ricard, one of my sponsors.

Apparently John Berry – such a big fan of mine – urged the management committee to ban me as an example to discourage such a reckless avoidance of duty. Presumably he was still dirty about our World Team Cup disagreements and also that I had missed another couple of scheduled visits to Foxhall Heath.

I wanted to limit the fallout but when we returned from the break Wally told me I was to be disciplined by the club and would have to miss the home league match against Leicester. It wasn't exactly the news I wanted to hear.

The truth is at this time a lot of people around Exeter were concerned about the amount of time and money Wally and John appeared to be pouring into their new Bristol venture. There was a widespread impression they were more bothered about their Eastville operation which was expensive and riddled with difficulties – and it caused a lot of tension.

NICE ONE SON – Kym, Raye, Rita and Wally Mawdsley salute the 1977 world champion

All of that was pushed to one side when I went to Gothenburg and won a fifth world title (see Pages 242–246). It was redemption for me, one in the eye for my critics and I was touched by the amount of genuine joy and pleasure it brought to Exeter supporters who had waited for ever without having anything remotely like this to celebrate.

That sort of enthusiasm is quite humbling. Most riders are running on close to empty by the time the last few weeks of a season comes around. After all the exertion and emotion attached to the World Final I was in that category. My tank was further drained by a flying visit to the FIM congress in Caracas, a five-day side trip between meetings.

But part of the deal is that you keep yourself going, and without achieving quite my normal consistency that's how the season finished.

Exeter signed off with a thumping home win over White City, who many felt were able to call themselves champions in large measure because they had been granted a rider replacement facility for the absent-all-year Dag Lövaas.

In all the sentiment of end-of-season farewells, I looked forward to nothing other than that I would be back at the County Ground the following season and for a while after that.

Ivan's

GOLD ALBUM

SPEEDWAY TITLE NUMBER SIX – Ivan and Raye on the podium, Katowice, 1979, with runner-up Zenon Plech, bronze medallist Michael Lee and fourth-placed Kelly Moran

FIRST AMONG EQUALS – Ivan Mauger, 1968 world champion, flanked by runner-up Barry Briggs and Antoni Woryna

WROCŁAW 1970 – Pawel Waloszek, Ivan, Antoni Woryna

NO PLACE LIKE HOME – Wembley 1969 and Ivan is crowned champion for a second time

FAB FOUR – Wembley 1972 with Bernie Persson, Ole Olsen and actress Alexandra Bastedo

TOP AWARD – the FIM gold medal awarded to Ivan in 1987

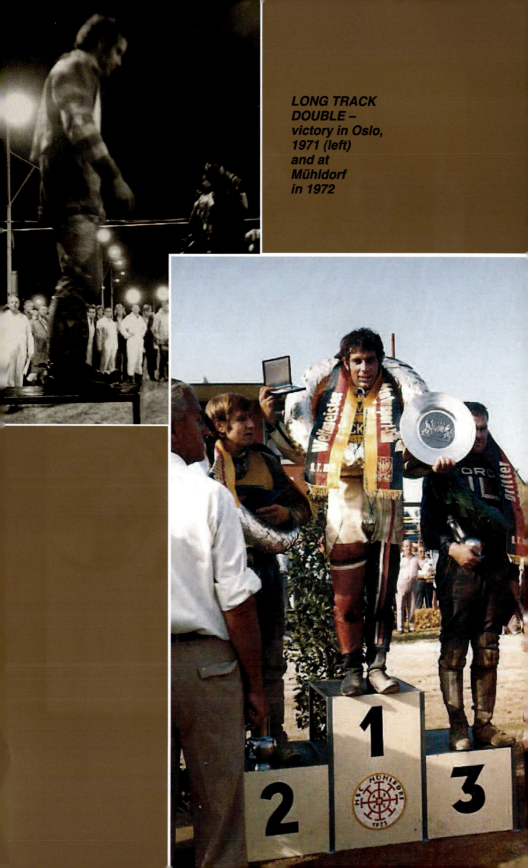

LONG TRACK DOUBLE – victory in Oslo, 1971 (left) and at Mühldorf in 1972

MAKE IT THREE – another world long track title in Mariánské Lázně, 1976, ahead of Ole Olsen and Egon Müller

SINGING IN THE RAIN – speedway sweet success number five at Gothenburg in 1977

THE WORLD'S FASTEST – setting a world long track speed record of 144.6

at Alexandra Park, Auckland, in February 1986 .... the record still stands

WEDDING DAY – Ivan and Raye at Richmond Methodist Church, February 9, 1957

TOP THAT – after receiving the MBE from HM The Queen at Buckingham Palace in 1976, with Kym, Raye, Sid and Renee Hone, Julie, Rita and Debbie

FOND FAREWELL – with Jack Young and Kym Bonython at Wayville, February 1986, Ivan's last meeting in Australia which he won

AND THAT'S IT – fronting the riders in his final competitive meeting, at Waikaraka Park, Auckland, back, left to right: John Cook, Gregorz Dzikowski, Ryszard Franczyszyn, Kym Mauger, Neil Evitts, David Bargh, Olli Tyrväinen. Front: Mitch Shirra, Einar Kyllingstad, Ivan, Bobby Schwartz, Armando Castagna

BAYSIDE – Ivan and Raye taking it easy at home at Runaway Bay

OLYMPIAN – running a leg of the Olympic torch relay before the Sydney Games in 2000

STUNNING – Mount Taranaki, overlooking the World Long Track Grand Prix which Ivan hosted for the FIM in 2003 and 2004

THAT'S AN ORDER – receiving the Order of the British Empire from New Zealand's Governor-General Sir Paul Reeves at Government House, Wellington, 1989

CITIZEN – awarded the freedom of the City of Christchurch by Mayor Garry Moore, 2007

Heat 13

FIVE IS NOT ENOUGH

THERE is nothing better than achieving something after almost everybody has decided that you can't do it.

Winning a fourth world speedway title a month short of my 33rd birthday, I never doubted my ability to add to that total.

It wasn't a question of trying to outdo Briggo, who signed off with four, or catch Ove, on top of the all-time pile with five.

It was all about continuing to race because in my heart of hearts I knew I still possessed the desire and the capability.

HISTORY BECKONS – leading Ole Olsen and Peter Collins in the 1979 World Final

That was the case for five years from Wembley, 1972, right up to the moment coming off the final turn of my last race in the 1977 World Final in Gothenburg ... with five digits aloft to remind the doubters that I was now a five-time winner, and counting.

While Peter Collins was unfortunate to hurt himself at the wrong time, it was a case of luck evening itself out in my mind. I still hadn't got over missing out in Poland 12 months earlier when my bad luck got only a fraction of the press coverage devoted to Peter's shin injuries.

Once the result is in the book, further debate does not achieve much. But even as I savoured the joy of winning in Sweden, I knew there still would be critics who dismissed it as a flash in the pan, the last hurrah for an ageing warrior.

Which meant five still would not be enough.

From my perspective, winning another world championship at Ullevi was confirmation my own self-belief through some difficult times had been entirely justified; and I enjoyed the moment sufficiently to like the idea of doing it again.

Sure enough, when title number six materialised in Poland in 1979, I did again enjoy the uniquely personal and by now familiar sensation

NOT TOO OLD – John Boulger, Phil Crump and Billy Sanders bow the knee to Australasian Final winner Ivan Mauger, Sydney Showground 1977

of delight, relief and fulfilment that routinely accompanies such a meaningful achievement.

Clinching a third long track title in 1976 after a long dry spell was one of those occasions which reminded me what winning a world championship is all about and how it feels. The fact Jawa had at last got around to producing a competitive four-valver was a further source of encouragement.

It was with that memory to sustain me that I went into my 1977 speedway campaign in a committed and focused frame of mind.

A maximum in the South Island championship in Invercargill was followed by the New Zealand Final in Auckland. My magneto packed up in the opening race and after that four wins safely secured a place in the Australasian Final.

Several of the so-called experts in Sydney were quick to dismiss my chances of doing anything in the meeting. They wrote that Ivan Mauger was too old and the Sydney Showground was not his favourite track – a contentious call considering I had ridden there only two or three times in my career.

The Sydney Showground was not a place for the faint-hearted but at the end of a fiercely-contested meeting I was the champion, having beaten local guns Phil Crump and John Boulger in a run-off after we all had scored 14 points. It was satisfying to make those experts eat their words.

There was a six-month wait before the Inter Continental Final at White City and what a drama that turned out to be. Peter Collins raced away from me to take out the first heat in a track record time – and kept on in similar vein all day.

I ran a last next time out, and in my fourth ride had a tangle with John Davis after which he was excluded. If referee Günter Sorber had seen that incident differently I would have been in real strife. I felt he called it correctly but there were many in the crowd who voiced their disagreement.

In situations like this it's a question of holding your nerve. I managed to do that and in the end scrambled together nine points, enough to put me in the top seven – and into the World Final.

There is a saying 'you have to be in it to win it' so from that point of view it was mission accomplished. It was not the most comfortable entry into a title decider but I wasn't about to fret over that. Others could read into it whatever they chose.

I went to Gothenburg as well prepared, as organised and ready as for any World Final. Nobody could have faulted my attention to detail. Guy Allott had worked every waking hour to ensure the Jawa motors were purring perfectly.

244 – Ivan Mauger

The press were talking up PC, they were in raptures over the qualification of Michael Lee, confident Ole would bounce back from his disappointment of the previous year.

The four seeded Swedes could all be dangerous and five Continental Final qualifiers included one or two potential dangers. It is wise to respect any and all opponents. Even so, I was not fearful and a rich vein of form in the lead-in was good for my state of mind.

The memory of my missed opportunity in Poland was another factor. I was absolutely determined to make up for it this time. My expectations were high although many people would not have been confident to tip me. Even so, if I managed to slip under the radar, there would come a moment of reckoning, and so it turned out.

Most of the attention was on Peter Collins, who had badly gashed his shin in a fluke accident at Belle Vue the previous weekend. Riding around in a second half race, he caught a drain cover which had not been properly replaced at the side of the track. It flicked up and smashed into his left leg.

There was the usual speculation about whether he would ride, but of course if it was a World Final, that's what you do. I had plaster casts on both wrists at Wembley in 1972 and my injury situation just made me all the more determined to do well. It was no surprise to me to see Peter grit his teeth, grab his crutches and get on with his title defence.

He started with a couple of wins. I was a point behind him after being the victim in an awful start to my second ride and eventually coming through to finish behind Finn Thomsen.

Come the interval, PC, Ole, Michael Lee and I had all dropped a single point and the rain, which seemed to be a traditional part of almost every final in Gothenburg, was threatening to become a real factor.

There was a stroke of good fortune in Heat 13, which had to be re-started after Egon Müller had crashed. This time I got the better of Peter and had myself 11 points in the bag while other contenders still needed to get out there and deliver.

Michael faltered, Ole did not and the draw found the three of us in Heat 18 with all to play for. By this stage the scores were: Mauger 11, Olsen 11, Lee 10 and Collins – due out in the last heat – also on 10.

That meant Ole or I could wrap up the title by winning, and Michael was right in the mix. PC meantime could only sit and wait to see from the outcome of this race if he was still in the hunt.

By now the rain was really sheeting down, the track surface was a skating rink, and, typical of the distorted thinking which can apply at major sporting events, if it hadn't been so important the obvious and only decision was to call a halt and send everybody home.

But that was never going to happen. Sure, it was a lottery but I figured I had a better idea than most of what the winning numbers might be. If ever there was a case of summoning up all my experience and calling upon the lessons learned over 20 years, this was it.

Then along came Johnny Boulger to momentarily upset the apple cart. The cheery Aussie, making just his second World Final appearance in 11 British League seasons, was a good competitor but the way he jetted off the inside gate he could have been mistaken for a superstar. Then unbelievably he rode out wide in all the slush and equally unbelievably, Ole, off two, was right on his pipe.

Both were going too fast for the conditions. At the end of the back straight JB aquaplaned through the spray to disaster and Ole, close behind, put it down a split second later.

Boulger was correctly disqualified and the rest of us were left to pick ourselves up, clean ourselves down and prepare for a re-run which almost certainly would decide who was to be the new champion.

We were all plastered with mud and slime and so was our machinery. Ole looked like a train wreck victim and his bike, which had clattered into the fence, was in a bad way too. Both Michael, who had missed the start completely off four, and I were filled in and similarly soaked.

Michael's crew got him organised quickly but I could see Ole taking a while to get everything ready. Meanwhile Guy, Gordon and Kym were helping me put on a dry pair of boots and changing my helmet, gloves and all my top goggles. People told me afterwards the track announcer had called two minutes in Swedish but there was such pandemonium in the pits none of us were properly aware of it.

Norway's Tore Kittlilsen was the referee and it was common knowledge that he and Ole had been mates for years. I gambled on the fact Tore would not disqualify Ole if he was over the time allowance – and I certainly wasn't going to go on to the track before him.

Meanwhile Michael was first around to the start and ready to go, much as Bernt Persson had been in 1972. The King's Lynn kid and new British champion was 18, in his first final, and couldn't wait to get going.

I was in no such hurry. Situations like this were right up my street. Briggo often said the longer Ivan and Ole took to get around to the start the greater the odds Ivan was going to win the race, and he turned out to be a good judge.

This time I made a dream start in the re-run and the four laps were almost a formality. Once I was gone not even Olsen or Lee would make any impression on me. Coming off the last corner, I saluted the crowd and felt the emotion wash over me.

BUBBLING – his record equalled, Ove Fundin flavours his congratulations with champagne

As if I wasn't wet enough, the next drenching I got was from Ove Fundin, whose record of five wins I had equalled. He poured a bottle of champagne over my head and Kym, in the pits with me for the first time at a World Final and not yet old enough to drink, copped half of it.

Ove was generous with his congratulations. He alone knew exactly how much hard work had been involved. His fifth title also came after a few unproductive years during which every man and his dog had written him off as a spent force.

A lot of people in the sport seemed a bit shell-shocked to realise they had been so wrong to underestimate my chances. Peter Collins, who won his last race and finished on 13, collected silver but was feted like a champion. It had been a gutsy effort all right.

Like it or not though, I was the champion again, and for once, it got me a free pass to the Inter Continental Final stage of the 1978 titles. At one time, years before, a world champion was seeded directly to the final to defend his title, but that didn't last for too long.

Being seeded to ride at Fredericia in July allowed the unprecedented luxury of being able to pace myself through the first half of the European summer. It didn't do me any harm and with seven places on offer I rode with

The Will To Win – 247

confidence, scored 13, and didn't place any significance on the fact Ole delighted the home fans by winning a run-off with me for the title.

I wasn't in sensational form. There were obvious adjustments to be made and a few loose ends to be tidied following a winter transfer from Exeter to Hull. But I still felt optimistic of making a good strong title defence in what was British speedway's much-celebrated Golden Jubilee year.

The sport had achieved a high profile during the 1970s and with the final back at Wembley, the stage was set for a memorable occasion. The biggest concern for many people seemed to be the fear that an unpopular old five-time champion might spoil the party and win again.

They reassured themselves that there were at least half a dozen contenders whose record suggested they had a better shot than I did. Ole, despite, or maybe because of his declared intention to finish with British League, was winning all over the place, top of the averages, and leading Coventry on the way to a league championship. He was the favourite.

Michael Lee – British champion for the second year running – Dave Jessup and Malcolm Simmons were all scoring consistently as well so there was a great deal of expectation firmly directed on those guys. Scott Autrey was going like a train too so there were plenty of popular choices to succeed me.

I wouldn't say I was public enemy number one exactly. But there was no doubt many sections of the speedway public as well as highly-placed officials did not have me at the top of their popularity parade.

Just as well I never let it bother me. I had long come to the conclusion that if there were to be a choice between being popular or being a winner, I'd take winning every time.

In a dozen years as a World Final qualifier, I had learned to block out distractions and not be affected by outside considerations or incidents before or during the meeting. In my first couple of finals there had been one or two opportunities missed because of my relative inexperience at such a level.

Older and wiser, I now felt capable of producing my best whatever the circumstances but Wembley's Golden Jubilee did not go according to plan. Sadly, hours before the sport's great showpiece occasion, BSPA President Charles Foot died and I have no doubt that adversely affected me that night.

Charles was my accountant for many years, we had been together on numerous international trips, and of all the senior promoters with whom riders came into contact, he probably was the most popular, best respected and greatly loved.

He was in his element at major events and being around all the other dignitaries and delegates at Wembley would have been right up his street.

248 – Ivan Mauger

He had attended a big function on the Friday night and we heard on World Final day that he had died in his sleep.

It was very difficult to feel upbeat or motivated for racing. Getting properly prepared and putting yourself in the right frame of mind no matter what is what racers do but as I looked out from the pits to see the thousands filling the stands, my thoughts were elsewhere.

If there were any subconscious suspicions that this would not be my night, they were confirmed all too quickly. My first race was Heat 4, off gate two, with Ole inside me, John Titman off three and Gordon Kennett, making his World Final debut and celebrating his 25th birthday, on the outside.

After the usual kidology games with Ole I made the start and led for more than two and a half laps. Kennett continually buzzed me up the inside and Ole had the outside run but could not quite get all the momentum he wanted.

Running into the pit turn for the third time and with the yellow/black flag about to be displayed, Kennett applied the pressure once more. My engine, which was getting slower each lap, seized and I ended up sliding across the corner on my backside.

My championship defence was over almost before it had begun. A lot of people blamed Kennett for my crash but he had nothing to do with it – the engine tightened up at the wrong place and I had no alternative but to bale out.

It was while I was lying on the track by the pit gate that I got my mind power working and vowed to myself things would be different in 1979.

World titles are not usually won with a 12-point score – the only time it happened was when Jack Young achieved it in 1951 – so after that race I was going to be chasing shadows.

Ole pounced to seize the moment and, as it turned out, put himself on the way to 13 points and his third title. I did win a couple of races, but eight points was my lowest score in all of my World Final appearances.

Kennett ended up having the best meeting of his life and took the runner-up spot. Nobody had seen that coming. On my night of disappointment, it did give me some pleasure to shake the hand of Scotty Autrey, who got third after beating Jessup and Jerzy Rembas in a run-off.

It's amazing what a difference losing makes. Hordes of supporters wanted a piece of me afterwards. I must have qualified for the sympathy vote because the queues of autograph hunters and well-wishers seemed endless. It was ages before I could get away to the official banquet.

My appetite was not at its best. But my hunger for another winning night was still intact. Defeated champions invariably say 'I'll be back' after a

OOPS – leading Gordon Kennett (left) and Ole Olsen seconds before a costly fall which meant the 1978 World Final bid was over almost before it had begun

defeat and I was no different. The thing is, I meant it. I was absolutely determined to give one more supercharged effort to the 1979 campaign.

The road to Poland started in January with the New Zealand Final at Ruapuna Park in Christchurch, a comfortable exercise for Larry Ross. I dropped a point to him in the first race, won three others and stopped in one with magneto problems – 11 points more than enough for a place in the next round.

Three weeks later, at Rowley Park where so much of my early career started to come together, the Australasian Final held no terrors. Billy Sanders ruled the roost as once again bike problems rubbed me out of one race. But 11 points from my other rides guaranteed a passage to the Inter Continental Final at White City in August.

There were nine qualifying places up for grabs from a meeting with a line-up which would not have disgraced the World Final. My form was back to something approaching its best but there were a lot of guys going well so nothing was guaranteed. More than ever this was one in which safety came first, glory second.

Michael Lee and Peter Collins jousted with one another for the win, which the King's Lynn youngster secured in a run-off after both had scored 14 points.

250 – Ivan Mauger

As things turned out it was a reasonably comfortable afternoon for me, one which provided the opportunity to effectively pick my spot at Katowice.

Finn Thomsen, Dave Jessup and I all finished on 10 points and that required an extra race to sort out the finishing order. For the first time the FIM had done the draw for the World Final and I knew if I managed to finish third in the run-off and fifth on the day, that gave me number 15 in the line-up in Poland.

I went out, made the start and led the race but then pulled up on the last corner. Almost everybody who was watching thought I had been unfortunate enough to suffer bike problems. In reality it was simply taking care of business, giving me a reasonably well-spaced schedule in the final.

Of course in an individual meeting run on the traditional 20-heat, 16-rider formula, everyone has to meet. It's down to luck where your races fall, where your toughest opponents may be, and how the gate positions go. But when a world championship is at stake, why wouldn't you eliminate some of the element of chance if possible?

I wanted to avoid No.13 (which the winner of our run-off would get) because that could sometimes involve a panic and quick changes between heats four and five, a point at which referees were usually strict on the two minutes.

No. 15 allowed for an even spread of races in heats 4, 7, 10 and 16 before backing up in 17. I won a few big finals with two on the trot later in the programme, by which time officials were not so pedantic on the time allowance, so that wasn't going to bother me.

A World Final in Poland was no longer quite the daunting prospect it had been, yet there was no avoiding the fact the line-up this time contained anything up to 11 or 12 riders quite capable of lifting the title. It really was that wide open.

On the basis that you respect anybody and everybody who has got there, it would be foolish to discount any opponent – although realistically there had been plenty of finals which were only ever going to be contested by a handful of the usual suspects.

This time, though, the experts were well and truly divided. Collins and Lee were the bookies' favourites, Olsen was trying to win back-to-back, the Poles were rooting for Plech and Edward Jancarz to bring home the prize, and there were plenty of supporters for Dave Jessup, rated the unlucky guy at Wembley the previous September.

I felt relaxed about my chances. My preparation had been excellent, my second year at Hull back to the good old days of averaging around 11-plus in the British League. Vikings promoters Ian Thomas and Brian Larner were on hand, pumped up and loving the big occasion.

Phil Pratt had taken over the tuning of my engines with Guy Allott deciding to take a back seat and they had been going sweetly. Practice, with Larry Ross among those offering his thoughts – we had ridden at the Katowice track the previous year in the World Best Pairs – went almost without a hitch.

It was a bright, clear, exhilarating autumn day in the sunshine. There were friendly, supportive faces all around – including Barry Briggs, with whom there was so much shared history. All the signs seemed promising.

The cards quickly dropped my way with victories in my first two races. Ole and Billy Sanders did the same. Michael Lee dropped a point to Zenon Plech in his first heat but beat me so I had eight after three rides, sharing the lead with Michael and Ole after he, too, had lost to the great Polish hope.

Things tightened up when Sanders was pushed back to third in that one which meant he and Plech both had seven at the interval and any one of the top five had a great opportunity to take the title.

Zenon kept winning but Heat 15 proved disastrous for Ole and Michael, with Jessup and the steadily-improving Kelly Moran taking first and second. This was all good news for me provided I could see off Sanders in Heat 16.

That mission accomplished, there was work to do as the track was given an extra grading between Heats 16 and 17 – the start of the last block of four races. In the pits, Kym, son-in-law Mike Shawcross (assisting at a World

ALL EYES ON THE START – up go the tapes in Heat 10 of the 1979 final, in which Michael Lee inflicted Ivan's only defeat of the day

Final for the first time), Gordon and Norrie Allan, who had seen it all before, and I went through the last-minute routines of checking and preparing.

Meanwhile, around the stadium, thousands were totting up the scores and referring to the programme to analyse the various possibilities. As always Peter Oakes had the sums done. For many, it may well have come as a bit of a surprise to find that after what had been for the most part a close-fought meeting it could be all over if I wrapped up Heat 17.

My score was 11, Plech had 10, Ole nine, Sanders nine, Lee eight, Moran, three weeks short of his 19th birthday, had eight, and even debut-making Czech Zdeněk Kudrna, on his 33rd birthday, was on eight. Mathematically, seven guys were still in with a shout. Any number of permutations remained possible. One win, though, and I could wreck it for all of them and put myself beyond reach.

It wasn't exactly a case of stealing under the radar, then, but all of a sudden for me it was a simple equation, a clear-cut chance to get the job done. I had been here before, felt calm and in the zone. Four copybook laps later, I saw the welcome sight of that chequered flag signalling my successful entry into the record books.

The huge crowd seemed to be shocked into near-silence although the locals rediscovered their voices soon enough when Zenon Plech zipped out for his fourth win and made sure of second place.

ALL EYES ON THE CHAMP – *the gentlemen of the press, headed by ace photographer Alf Weedon, capture the moment*

The Will To Win – 253

There followed the rarity of a four-man run-off for the bronze to sort out one of the most crowded leader boards in world championship memory. Young guns Michael and Kelly prevailed with Sanders trailing and Ole failing to finish the course.

You might think after having been there and done that a few times, the sensation of pleasure and the emotion would be relatively low-key. You would be wrong. I couldn't have been more excited or delighted. Soon enough Raye, Julie and Debbie, from high up in the stands, were making their way down to join the throng of well-wishers.

These moments always tend to pass in a blur. So many hands to shake, so many congratulations to receive. Through it all there was the clarity of realising I had passed Ove Fundin and become the first rider to be a six-time world speedway champion.

Christoph Betzl, a German long track specialist, friend and rival, who had made it through to his solitary World Final, had worn the number six race jacket. Fortunately he was only too delighted to lend it to me and that is how I was able to hold aloft the significant 'six' from the podium.

It remains one of the most familiar images from my career, and I never tire of seeing it. Two titles in three years should have been sufficient to demonstrate I was not a spent force, so that added to the satisfaction.

Over the same period I was keen to win again in the long track – but came up short. No matter how consistent you are, sport can be like that. Nine days after winning in Gothenburg in '77, I finished eighth in the 1000-metre final in Aalborg, where Anders Michanek got the verdict.

The build-up had been routine, a qualifying round win at Mariánské Lázně in May and fifth in the Mühldorf semi-final in August. But the all-important decider in Denmark turned out to be a bit of a disaster. I didn't get into the final and finished up in eighth position.

Bikes could pass inspection at FIM meetings in every country in Europe but in Denmark, scrutineers regularly managed to find something wrong. Maybe the ignition cut-out was not right and there could be any number of other niggles.

Traditionally Danish riders were able to pass the noise control tests but other riders with exactly the same megaphones did not. Aalborg was no different.

Ole and Kristian Præstbro had the passing paint on before the rest of the riders arrived for the Saturday practice. The machine examiners said they had been at the track the previous day to do some publicity (code for private practice) and had been approved. We believed it only correct for their bikes to go through with the rest but both refused.

Although we had on the same mufflers, none passed the decibel requirement until three quarters of the way through official practice when we were sticking wire brushes in the exhaust pipes to deaden the noise.

It backfired on the Danes because Anders won after he changed his muffler for his last couple of rides. He had a few points in reserve so he had to put on the one with the passing paint because after the Final the bikes go into a park ferme in the centre green.

Going back to Mühldorf in 1978 was a case of near and yet so far. The record book does not immediately tell the story of a final I was in pole position to win and yet eventually ended up not even making it on to the rostrum. It rates as probably my most disappointing long track campaign.

It all started brilliantly with a convincing qualifying round victory at Herxheim. Fourth in the semi-final at Mariánské Lázně indicated I was on the pace and my chances of a fourth title looked good.

In one of the most closely-contested finals, Egon Müller beat countryman Alois Wiesböck after both had scored 26 points and PC beat me in a run-off for bronze after we had collected 24 apiece.

In the first few races my Jawa was flying and I had the measure of everybody, beating Egon twice. He was the danger man and with only two to go on the six-race format my title prospects were getting better by the minute.

This was a year the FIM decided to change the formula and run six-man races so all riders met twice. After we had done four races I was five points in front.

Then it all went wrong. I was leading my fifth ride by quite a margin, lost power and had to pull out. I thought the primary chain had broken.

Back in the pits the chain seemed fine but a bit loose so we figured it had jumped over the chainwheel. We put on a new chain and tightened it, I tested it on the gravel road behind the pits and everything appeared to be fine.

I still only needed fourth place in my last race to win the long track for the fourth time and was leading down the back straight on the first lap when the same thing happened.

Later we discovered the main shaft George Wenn in LA had made for me with splines instead of the taper had broken. It must have happened in my fifth ride but had partially welded together with the revs I was doing. It was OK on the gravel road but on the track with all the grip it failed again.

It was shattering at the time. Gordon took it even worse than me. He had to walk away and did not come back to the pits until an hour or so later.

The Will To Win – 255

HYDE AND SEEK – Ivan and Larry Ross lead Peter Collins in the 1977 World Best Pairs Final at Belle Vue

Mariánské Lázně, another of my favourite tracks, was the stage in 1979 and my chances looked decent. I had a fourth place finish in qualifying at Gornja Radgona and got seventh in the semi at Scheeβel.

But I must have been suffering from a bit of a hangover from the previous weekend's World Final in Poland, scoring only eight points which put me down in 11th place. It was my worst placing in any long track final.

Wiesböck got up to win his first and only title, a point ahead of Michanek with Ole a further point adrift in third.

My continuing relationship with the World Best Pairs followed a somewhat similar pattern to my experiences in the long track – good days punctuated by some disappointments.

I scored a six-ride maximum in a semi-final at Lonigo and looked forward to the 1977 final at Belle Vue, always one to be relished. But although in such familiar surroundings I got another 16, Larry Ross couldn't get going and Peter Collins and Malcolm Simmons justified their favouritism by running away with the meeting.

At Chorzów a year later, Larry and I both rode really well and at the end of 21 heats we were locked together with Great Britain (Simmons and Gordon Kennett) on 24 points.

256 – Ivan Mauger

Simmo won the run-off and for the second time an Englishman had turned my dreams of gold into silver.

The 1979 final in Vojens was wholly forgettable as far as Larry and I were concerned, finishing sixth of seven. However it was memorable for one of the most controversial refereeing decisions in the history of the sport.

Not for the first time, Tore Kittilsen of Norway was the man in the middle and made what most saw as a 'home town' decision.

For the third year in a row Simmo was one half of a title-challenging pair although this time it was with Michael Lee, who scored 15 points in a total of 24.

Ole Olsen and Hans Nielsen had to get a 5-1 in the all-important Heat 21 to overtake them, a 4-2 to force a run-off. But they ran into a determined Polish opponent in Edward Jancarz.

Steady Eddie had already put a dent in England's chances and now he challenged the Danes all the way. As far as just about every observer in the place was concerned, he split the Danish pair and narrowly won the race.

A lengthy delay in announcing the result gave the first hint something was up. After what seemed like several minutes came the call, placing the Danes first and second, handing them the title.

This, remember, was in the days before instant replays and video analysis. The evidence of one television camera, which was not officially available to the referee in any case, was little better than making the decision with a naked eye.

Apart from the celebrating Danes, though, there were very few people who considered justice to have been done. Of all the big meetings in my career, this was one which contained possibly the greatest injustice – at least to that point.

Simmo later sent me a video given him by Dickie Davies of ITV's *World of Sport* which clearly showed what a shocking decision it was.

For the first time in seven years, I rode in all four world finals in 1979 and winning the World Team Cup at White City in September was New Zealand's outstanding achievement at team level. The victory incidentally enabled me to become the first rider to collect gold for two countries.

After the colonial connection was discontinued the British boys had embarked on a highly successful run, four wins in five years punctuated only by Australia's surprise success at White City in 1976. Then Denmark, still widely considered a small-time speedway force, got into the act.

Even allowing for those form-busters, few would have given New Zealand much of a chance of going the distance when we suited up for the first qualifying round in '79.

The Will To Win – 257

I had not ridden in the event for three years, during which the Kiwi impact had been almost invisible. We had only 14 riders in the UK. Larry Ross, Mitch Shirra, Bruce Cribb and I had a fair bit of experience between us, and Roger Abel at Eastbourne was the only other rider in the top division.

Roger, from Christchurch, had been battling to make an impression for three or more seasons and midway through this year went on loan to Canterbury. In the lower division there were emerging riders such as Wayne Brown, 19, and David Bargh, 17, as well as Graeme Stapleton, Mike Fullerton and Roger Wright who had been around for a while.

With such a limited talent pool, at one stage there was some doubt as to whether we would even field a team. Then we beat the Danes and won an international four-team event in Kempten, and Trevor Redmond, as usual, did not need much to fire his enthusiasm and then transmit it to all around.

The same team went to Reading for the Overseas Final in May, unfancied but determined to give it our best shot. It was a bleak, wet day, and conditions were so bad the meeting should not have gone on, not that anybody in our camp took too much notice.

We were up against a strongly-backed Great Britain team which included Peter Collins, Michael Lee, Malcolm Simmons, Gordon Kennett and Dave Jessup – all of whom had been prominent players in their recent successes as well as top-rated riders individually.

It was an awful day but all the British boys voted to start the meeting and that was their biggest mistake. Simmo pulled out after just one ride complaining the track was too wet and the out-of-sorts Brits managed only 22 points.

New Zealand, who almost everybody expected to be there simply to make up the numbers, won the round with 30 points. The USA scored 26, joining us in the Inter-Continental Final.

America, at the start of a swift rise to the top, had Bruce Penhall, Bobby Schwartz, Kelly Moran and Steve Gresham.

Australia fielded four of the guys who had won the event three years earlier, plus big improver John Titman who had demonstrated his capabilities by qualifying for Wembley a few months before. They mustered only 18.

But the big talking point was the failure of the home side. It was such a blow to their expectations, team manager John Berry was later dumped from the job.

Three weeks later at Eskilstuna, we did even better. Denmark, the holders, were expected to be a big threat and so it proved. But Sweden, on their own soil, never got their act together.

The scoreline, another memorable one, was: New Zealand 39 (I got 11, losing to Bruce Penhall) Denmark 27 USA 22 Sweden 18.

UNBELIEVABLE – Trevor Redmond checks it really is the World Team Cup, with (back) Roger Abel, Mitch Shirra and Briggo, (front) Larry Ross, Ivan and Bruce Cribb

Surely it was beyond the bounds of imagination to be third time lucky, to go all the way?

We had our own ideas. In the three months before the final we kept in regular touch, and all the boys recognised there would never be a better chance to capture glory for New Zealand.

For the first two rounds we had insisted on having everybody work together, turning up early, walking the track, checking and re-checking machinery.

Our self-belief was hugely boosted, and TR and I turned the whole thing into a crusade.

Roger Abel had seemed to be the best of the rest at the start of our campaign and he stayed at reserve all through – even though he didn't get a ride. But he played his full part and on the big day, almost all of the other New Zealand riders were there, along with any and every Kiwi who was in the country as a mechanic or helper.

Briggo, who had been through so many experiences, was as pumped as if he was racing. The support crew helped reinforce the tremendous spirit of togetherness, something the Aussies had managed on the way to their shock win in 1976, and later the Americans were to do so effectively.

I wanted to leave absolutely nothing to chance so I told the riders I would take six bikes to Wood Lane. Any or all of them could use my machinery if they had any problem or even if they thought my bikes were a better option

The Will To Win – 259

than their own. In making the offer, I didn't anticipate my bikes would be out in 14 of the 16 races.

Our strategy was to consider every point vital that afternoon and to get ourselves on the score sheet in each race. As it turned out while Cribby, under instruction to score at least a point each time, was picking up the crumbs, Larry and I won three races, Mitch two, and we had it won with a heat to spare.

Against all the odds, we were the champions and the scenes of enthusiasm after Heat 15 must have caused my concentration to lapse. I took a tumble in the last race and was in the ambulance room while Ole matched Briggo's 1963 performance of scoring a maximum and finishing on a losing team.

The history books recorded our stunning victory: New Zealand 35 (Larry Ross 11, Mitch Shirra 10, Ivan Mauger 9, Bruce Cribb 5), Denmark 31, Czechoslovakia 19, Poland 11.

It was an unforgettable occasion, the day everything came together, a day never to be forgotten or repeated, for that matter. The partying went on late into the night – helped by the fact SWAPA, the Speedway Writers' and Photographers Association, were holding their presentation dinner at the Strand Palace.

The boys and most of the support team were in attendance. Naturally all the talk was of the meeting and New Zealand's triumph ... and then something even more remarkable happened. The British media had not always been my best friends over the years, so it was a surprise, a very pleasant one at that, when Phil Rising and Dick Bott got up to present me with the association's annual award as their rider of the year.

To be honoured in this manner, and to finish up with the individual and team speedway gold was not a bad way to prepare for my 40th birthday a couple of weeks later.

The prolonged party continued when the family took over the Bavaria suite at Belle Vue, and over 200 people turned out to help me celebrate. Among them were Wilfried Drygala, over from Germany, my former Belle Vue boss Jack Fearnley and Hull promoter Ian Thomas.

There were rider friends such as Bert Harkins, Bruce Penhall, Mick McKeon, Billy Powell, all of whom distinguished themselves by dressing up for a Drag Queen competition.

Just to prove it wasn't all a dream, Peter Oakes, Phil Rising and Dick Bott represented the friendly face of the media.

A great deal of good Russian champagne was drunk, and a certain amount of table-top dancing rounded out a great evening's entertainment.

Being a world champion was never more fun.

Heat 14

TAKING CARE OF BUSINESS

NO matter what walk of life you are in, the one item of mail most people fear is a tax demand.

Imagine my reaction at the start of the 1979 season when a letter from the Inland Revenue dropped through the letterbox at Woodford, asking for £184,668 and giving me one month to pay.

Racing around the world with a great deal of success and being decently rewarded for some years meant we were in a comfortable position. Although we never forgot our time on Struggle Street, those days seemed like something from another life.

But £184,668 ... they had to be kidding, right? 184K was a lot of money in early 1979. It would be almost 700 grand (sterling) in today's terms.

Apparently not. Revenue officials had been conducting one of their investigations and identified speedway, especially promoters and a high-profile rider such as myself, as an area worthy of close inspection.

How they arrived at that figure for me was based on some painstaking research. Officers had scoured through newspapers, magazines, match reports and heat details, done their sums and concluded that I owed them thousands in supposedly unpaid taxes.

Like anybody else, I was keen to hang on to as much of my earnings as possible, but I wasn't in the business of defrauding the tax department. That's why for 15 years, since returning to England in 1963, we had used the services of Charles Foot, one of the most highly-respected accountants in the country.

He was the company secretary at Poole, had been involved with speedway and riders for ages, looked after the promoters' association finances, and rightly enjoyed a reputation as a man who believed in adhering to the highest professional standards in everything he did.

All the speedway boys knew Footy through his involvement as a co-promoter at Poole and particularly in the position of team manager or chef de mission of Great Britain teams home and away. In places like Sweden and Poland he was the best-known of all the British promoters.

Sadly, he died on the eve of the 1978 World Final at Wembley and seven months on, I needed a new accountant, and fast!

Professional footballers usually had good contacts in that field, and this was at a time when I was regularly training with Manchester City. After one morning session we were sitting in the big bath at Maine Road and I asked if anyone knew a good accountant.

262 – Ivan Mauger

I told them about the letter and the demand for 184 grand from the tax department. A couple of the players straight away said Reuben Kaye in Deansgate, Manchester, was the man who handled the financial affairs of Mick Channon, an England international striker (46 caps and 21 goals) City had signed in a big deal from Southampton.

As soon as I got home from training I called Reuben Kaye's office and made an appointment with him in the next couple of days.

I will never forget the first time we met. Reuben was not the usual type of accountant who had filing stacked everywhere. He had a massive office, and a huge polished desk with not one single piece of paper on it. Files were all over the room, against the walls and on the floor in neat heaps with their little tags.

When he asked me what the problem was I slid across the letter from the tax people. He was quite a small person and had a disabled left arm so he shuffled everything around with his right hand.

Reuben studied the document for a while and then looked up and said 'the tax office only send you these things to frighten you' to which I replied 'well, they have succeeded'.

Reuben said it appeared Charles Foot had not been putting all my tax details in to the tax office. For the first few years when Footy knew the New Zealanders and Australians were a bit short of money it seemed he didn't put them in at all. Reuben and I concluded he had thrown them in the bin and we could have done that ourselves.

Then Reuben asked me to give him all the details of any cash payments I had received from promoters or sponsors and every other detail of my income. He said he could only help if he knew the extent of what I had been doing and what money had been received.

So I told him everything from start to finish and what cash I was paid to do open meetings and by some of my sponsors. He asked how much cash there was at home and I told him what we had in the safe. He said 'any fool can have a load of cash in his safe but if that is the case you have got to be careful how you spend it'.

He also asked what we had at home we would not want the tax man to see if he walked in unexpectedly. For a long time I used to buy new Mercedes cars in March every year from their Sindelfingen depot in Stuttgart, which was the foreign buyers' group. I had bank accounts in Germany, Switzerland, Guernsey and the Isle of Man and always paid cash for the Mercs.

Three weeks before meeting Reuben I had bought a new 450 V8 SEL Mercedes from Sindelfingen and I told him that except for that particular car everything at home – including Raye's Merc sports car – was quite legal and bought from British League earnings.

GREAT MAN – Charles Foot, at the rear, in his element at the 1971 World Team Cup Final in Wrocław

His professional advice was to get rid of the 450 immediately. Our Mercedes were always serviced at Stratton's, the Merc dealers in Wilmslow. They often wanted to buy vehicles from me – they knew where they were from and how I was able to bring them into Britain through Dover on my New Zealand passport.

They had to be sold on within 12 months to avoid paying the VAT and customs duty. A couple went to Stratton's that way and others were sent to Australia and New Zealand where they fetched a lot more money.

On the way home to Woodford from my appointment I called in at Stratton's and negotiated a price for the new car.

264 – Ivan Mauger

At 10am next day Raye followed me to the showroom in her Mercedes Sports. I got out of the 450, was handed the money that I negotiated and drove out with Raye. Stratton's obviously had a cash buyer waiting.

On my next visit to Reuben a couple of days later he told me he would find out who was the instigator of the enquiries into my affairs. When I went back to see him he said it was the special branch at Walsall and he had contacted the officer who wanted to come up and talk to us.

Reuben delayed that meeting for about a month and eventually the official came up and produced lots of documents, including a pile of photocopies from the *Speedway Star* magazine. He pointed out several meetings that I had won – British championships those days paid about £250 for the winner, for example – and asked what had happened to those cheques. I told him they had all been banked.

He wanted to see my bank statements which I told him I would produce on the next visit. Fortunately Raye kept all our statements from the beginning of 1963 and we still had the originals. I used to send photocopies down to Footy at the end of each financial year.

From what he produced I figured the taxman did not know anything about second halves because the magazine only had results of the matches. All the open meetings he assumed were at the usual start and points money. I always told promoters I wanted the normal start and point money to appear on the pay sheet so that was a smart move.

He never asked if I got cash or appearance money for those meetings and Reuben and I did not tell him. Nor did he ask me what had happened to the new Jawas which were prizes at the Internationale in 1970, 1971 and 1972. (I sold them all for cash so I would have been in trouble if he had asked about them).

Enquiries and answers went back and forth and Reuben strung out the next scheduled visit for a couple of months. But the guy was getting impatient by mid October so we had to see him again. He wanted a meeting in November to finalise everything and arrive at a decision as to what I needed to pay.

Meanwhile Reuben got to know through his contacts at the tax department that this officer was getting a promotion in January 1980. He told me his intention was to delay things until the day before Christmas and cited my extensive travelling schedule which included trips to many countries as a reason why it was not possible to get together earlier.

He said the special tax inspector would not have liked the person who took over his files to know he had not completed his investigations. Reuben also gambled that he would want to get back to the Midlands by mid-afternoon to spend Christmas Eve with his family.

December 24 loomed and the meeting was arranged for 9.30am. Reuben wanted to see me an hour earlier so we could plan our strategy and what to tell him. Everything was detailed to the extent that if either of us wanted to go to the loo we should go one at a time so as not to raise any suspicions. Lunch would be fish and chips at the office desk, brought in by his secretary.

Reuben emphasised that he would answer most of the questions but occasionally the special branch guy would ask me directly. He did not want me to have a pen or paper in front of me and said I should be ready to stop talking instantly if he dropped his pen on the table. That was the signal for him to take over the conversation in case there was a danger of me dropping myself in it with an ill-chosen admission.

This went on from about 9.30am until 1.30pm, including the fish and chips at lunchtime. The tax man had to catch a train at Manchester Piccadilly at 2.20 but it was a 15-minute taxi ride to the station. That meant to be on the safe side he had to leave Deansgate by 1.45.

After our lengthy session he seemed to be satisfied and as he went he told Reuben he would be in touch on December 27, and that I needed to pay whatever was agreed before the 31st.

Reuben Kaye was quite right in his estimation. The guy wanted everything cleared before he took up his promotion at the beginning of January. In the end I had to pay about £30,000 tax and another £13,000 odd in fines for not putting in the correct tax returns for a number of years.

As soon as we had that decision, I took a cheque in to Reuben's office and he posted it to the special branch at Walsall.

WHEELS WITHIN WHEELS – *if you have to travel thousands of miles, you might as well do it in style*

266 – Ivan Mauger

I guess you could say it was a case of all's well that ends well, and it was a great deal different to the early days when Footy looked after the accounts for a number of riders and promoters.

From 1964 I would get a bill from the British Tax Office wanting £1000 at a time when I didn't have £1000, or certainly not to give it to the tax people. One call to Charles is all it took. His favourite line was 'don't worry about that, son – just send it down to me and I will take care of it'.

When we heard nothing more we figured Footy was 'taking care of it'.

Peter Oakes, Gordon Stobbs and Raye were the only people aware that if I was eventually not able to ride for Belle Vue in 1969 the Plan B was to link up with Poole as Charles Foot was one of the directors there and we had such a good relationship.

I kept him in the loop, told him what Belle Vue were offering and he said Poole would match that and supply a sponsored van to do all their home and away meetings.

In 1967 when I started to race in Europe on a regular basis he helped me set up a company in Guernsey. All my European bookings went through that company and I received a very nominal booking fee paid to me in England. That was always banked and declared to the UK Tax office and was quite legal.

Of course that was a fraction of the total amount I earned on the Continent and most of it was banked in Germany or Switzerland. My fees gradually went from 500 marks up to 5000 which was average those days and from the early 1970s it took off.

Then the Deutschmark slipped against the British pound and over the last 15 years of my career I was getting maybe £2000 to £2500 a meeting in Europe on Sunday and occasional midweek meetings.

Jason Crump once said to me if there had been foreign riders in the Polish League in my racing days, I would never have won the long track world championship because the money in Poland would have outstripped anything on offer in Europe.

The fact is crowds at those meetings all over Europe were on par with anything that happens in Poland today. Not many riders going to Poland these days could buy a brand new Mercedes after a handful of meetings but for a decade I bought a Mercedes every year from the proceeds of four or five long track meetings.

They were ordered in January or February through Cable Price Ltd, the Mercedes agent in New Zealand, with a 10 per cent deposit. Wilfried Drygala sent that down to Sindelfingen.

The car would be ready to collect early to mid April and I sat there with assorted Arab sheikhs, a lot of Mafia-looking guys with dark glasses from Italy and other dodgy-looking people.

Instead of putting my appearance fees and guarantees in the bank each Monday morning after a meeting, Wilfried used to keep it so I had a briefcase full of cash, just like all the others sitting around there. There were several windows, very much as you might find in a bank, from which a buyer's name would be called.

The procedure was to slide the note with the deposit across the little counter. The teller would say how much had to be paid to complete the purchase and like all the others I slid the cash across. They handed over the receipt and another envelope with a stamp already on it which was the VAT document.

The cars had about three or four kilometres on the clock from the road test and then they were driven around the factory to the foreign export depot. After the financial business was completed, the proud new owner went outside where a person called Instructor in a white coat explained where the blinkers were, demonstrated where the hand brake was, where the headlights were and gave you the log book. That took about two or three minutes and you were off.

All that remained was to have the VAT documentation examined by German customs at the border point at Aachen and when they were satisfied the envelope had to be deposited in the post box at the border. With typical German efficiency the VAT would be back in the bank within 14 days.

One year I bought two Mercedes, a 450 SEL for me and a sports car for Raye and we drove them all the way back to Manchester. It was an experience Raye decided she didn't want to repeat. She has never been worried about all the cash deals but definitely did not relish sitting in that waiting room with all the dodgy-looking types. I told her I was one of them at that time!

When I turned up at continental meetings in a Merc it did not attract that much attention. But in the UK, where they were rather more of a rarity, there were people who thought of me as Flash Harry. It certainly was a world removed from the days when I rattled in to a stadium car park in a Ford Thames or ex-GPO Morris Minor van.

It made sense to travel in some style and comfort. Charging up and down motorways and autobahns was an inevitable but never ideal part of what had to be done to get to and from race meetings. Being able to do so in one of the safest and most efficient motor cars ever manufactured was an investment in good sense, not a 'look at me' luxury.

268 – Ivan Mauger

As the schedule got busier and spread across more countries we added a big transporter to the fleet of vehicles. Originally Volkswagen sponsored me with a few transporters but from 1979 IVECO trucks sponsored me with one of their vehicles.

That was great, because it was possible for several people to travel in comfort, eat and sleep in it as well as accommodating bikes and equipment behind a bulkhead – quite a few years before Tony Rickardsson set the trend by hauling around in his 1990s version.

For me it was a considerable step up from 1963 when a Bedford Dormobile was our vehicle of choice and Raye and the family crammed in alongside the bike, spare wheels and tool box for what seemed like an interminable trip from Manchester to say, Newcastle, London or Swindon.

As things got busier, especially after I started to win world championships, Peter Oakes helped to sort out my British diary and Wilfried Drygala kept on top of the continental arrangements. While all this was going on, trips to the United States or Australia and New Zealand were in the planning stage. By the time I was doing 150 plus meetings a year it required organisation of almost military precision, not to mention equipment and mechanics dotted around the place.

At the start of my first season at Newcastle, I had the one second-hand bike bought from Ted Brine. It came with a Dixon frame and was difficult to ride on the long straights and tight corners at Newcastle. I quickly changed to a Rotrax frame and stuck with them all the way until a month or so before the 1968 World Final when I bought a Jawa from Briggo. Mike Parker bought me one in 1967 but it was no good and kept seizing so I got rid of it and went back on to my Japs.

Halfway through that first year I invested in a spare Jap engine from Brian Craven. When there were particularly important meetings Ivan Crozier came with us and brought his bike as a spare. He had handlebars which were very similar to mine so it was never a problem to switch if need be.

Before the start of the next season I purchased another new Rotrax frame from George Greenwood in Harrow Road, London, and put in the spare Jap engine. Now I was in the big time, with two complete bikes. Later I bought another spare Jap engine from Ken Sharples. From then until the time I got off Japs I only had those two bikes and a spare engine.

Things really started to change when my European diary filled up and my ability to be covered for all eventualities owed a great deal to my association as a factory works rider with Jawa from March 1969 until 1982.

Over most of that time, there would be seven or eight speedway bikes, a couple of long track bikes and two grass track bikes at our house in Cheshire. At my workshop in Bremen were another half a dozen speedway

SUPER TROUPERS – Jim Airey and Briggo putting on a show at Stratford in the 1975 World Series, an enterprise which stood the test of time

bikes, four or five long track bikes and a similar number of grass track machines.

I did not ride the long track bikes on grass because generally the grass tracks were too bumpy and it was an easy way to twist frames and do other damage.

The speedway bikes also came into different categories – bikes for nice smooth well-prepared tracks such as Sheffield, Belle Vue and Halifax and others for places such as Newcastle and Exeter which were rarely up to the same standard. Those type of tracks put dents in the rims and ruined centre and rear frames. All the time I rode for Exeter I had three bikes each season that I only ever used there.

Not only was there my own stable of machines but for any big meetings especially in Eastern Europe the Jawa people would take speedway bikes or long track bikes depending on the event. My mechanics would bring the preferred machines and the factory bikes would be there as spares; I trusted my engine tuner in England (Guy Allott) more than I trusted the factory mechanics.

270 – Ivan Mauger

Back in New Zealand, I always kept at least two complete speedway bikes at our Christchurch house. Once America took off there were a couple that stayed at George Wenn's place as well as a long tracker, because occasionally we did long tracks on the half-mile track at Ascot in Gardena. Later on there usually were three or four speedway machines and at least one long track bike at our condo in LA.

January and February could involve up to 20/25 meetings in Australia and New Zealand, with a side trip to Houston thrown in. I had two bikes in Perth, two more in Melbourne, two in Sydney and two in Auckland. Most did not have motors fitted as I would check in two engines in plastic boxes at Heathrow. It was an hour's job to unpack an engine and fit it into a chassis, and half an hour to reverse the whole process and pack them away for the next city.

When my Australian commitments were at their peak I would do a couple of Fridays in January at the huge Claremont track in Perth, with a four-hour trip down to Bunbury sandwiched in between. Claremont started at 7pm and the bikes were on first before any car races took place, so the big final was at about 8.30pm.

The flights to Melbourne or Sydney left at 11.25pm. There was time to pack the bikes into a van, have a shower and get ready to go to the airport. Quite often I did the Saturday night in Melbourne or Sydney followed by Mildura the following evening, and then on to New Zealand which for a while had plenty of midweek meetings.

Then we used to go to our place in LA and do the Spring Classic series, followed by probably three or four meetings elsewhere in California. For a couple of years I rode for Kawasaki so we would go to Daytona and ordinarily we were back in England in time for the start of the season.

For many years the first long track of the European season was at Plattling, just south-east of Munich, usually on the third Sunday in March. From there we motored through to Czechoslovakia, arriving next day to pick up some of the bikes for that year. During my Exeter years I was otherwise engaged on Mondays so Gordon and later Norrie went by themselves.

Gordon had been part of the team from Newcastle since the first meeting there but Norrie did not come on board until much later – although he and his brother Ronnie were among the first people I met when we came back to the UK in 1963.

Victorian Kenny Cameron, my mate from Melbourne and Rockhampton days, rode for Edinburgh and boarded with the Allans' grandmother one street from Old Meadowbank. After racing there, we stopped overnight before coming back down for a Newcastle home meeting, and Ronnie and Norrie, both still at school, offered to clean our bikes in the morning at the stadium workshops.

Ronnie soon started to come to Manchester during school holidays, travel to meetings and spend time with the Kiwi contingent. Several of us had a regular Tuesday night out at the Princess Theatre Club in Wythenshawe to see the comedians and strippers perform.

Raye didn't want us to take Ronnie because he was too young but we assured her he would be fine. As he was under age he was not allowed in and from time to time I would pop outside to take him an ice cream or a Mars bar while he waited.

Years later he went to work in Bristol where he got a really good sales rep job with Bulmers Cider. Eventually he repaid me for all the ice creams and Mars bars because he took a position with Ricard. It was through his influence they gave me a generous sponsorship for several years.

Subsequently he and his wife Linda went to live at Clevedon. Ronnie also became a top referee – brave enough to exclude me at Exeter one night – and for a while was secretary of the Speedway Control Board (now Bureau).

When my schedule became so busy in the 1970s Norrie came down and worked for me and stayed with Gordon and Margaret in Bramhall. Norrie,

MISTER FIXIT – Norrie Allan was an invaluable member of the organisation for years

272 – Ivan Mauger

a confirmed bachelor, did a lot of the European meetings which allowed Gordon to concentrate on British League and individual events in England.

When there were any big qualifying rounds for speedway, long track, pairs or world team cups in Europe they both went and often Chris Macdonald and Wilfried Drygala were there too.

Initially Frank Baldan, an American who was a junior rider at Bremen, helped me a lot during the week but eventually I simply had to have a permanent mechanic based in Europe. Norrie went full-time with me from the start of the 1977 season and he loved being in Europe, often staying there for weeks on end.

When there were big meetings in England he came back to assist Gordon, Chris Macdonald and Guy Allott. Other great, honest and reliable helpers included Kiwi Gerald James, who came over with Gary Peterson, and my brother's mate Geoff Sullivan. If things were very busy Geoff often met me at London airport or took the van to Exeter when Gordon and Norrie couldn't get back from the Continent in time.

Norrie was a bit of a dealer in spare parts and he got to know my sponsors Nigel Bower at NEB (clutches), Henry Rosenthal at Renthal (alloy handlebars), George Sartin at Talon (hubs, wheels and spokes) and Chris Ventris at Venhill Engineering (cables).

We allocated space for Norrie in the transporter and he kept his parts under the bottom bunk. Our arrangement was that whatever he was selling it had to be all done and dusted before I arrived at the tracks on Sundays. Mostly Norrie was there by Saturday afternoon so he did most of his deals then or the next morning so it was never a bother to me.

One time Norrie and a couple of the other regular transporter drivers had a contest to see how many people they could sneak on to the ferries without paying – we regularly travelled in considerable numbers as promoters would ask me to help arrange for other riders to come across from England.

Norrie claimed the record of 13 after a grass track at Saint-Macaire in France. Security and safety regulations brought in after the 1987 Zeebrugge ferry disaster meant such a stunt would not have been possible in later years.

Peter Collins had the record for sleeping. There was a cupboard above the driver's and passenger's front area where sleeping bags, pillows and jackets were kept. After a long track meeting at Jübek in North Germany everybody went for a meal and PC climbed up to the cupboard at about eight o'clock at night . He was still asleep at 10.30 the next morning when I woke him for breakfast at the Blue Boar on the M1 near Coventry.

Norrie came further afield on the farewell series in Australia in 1984–85 and New Zealand in 1985–86. He also did several trips to the USA with me.

Gordon was married with a young son so he didn't go so far from home although he did a couple of the shorter trips to America.

When I retired Norrie got a pub at Downend near Bristol with Ronnie and Linda but hated being tied and went back on the road, helping Shawn Moran with his long track commitments. That relationship collapsed when Shawn failed an alcohol test before a long track round at Esbjerg.

Norrie loaded up the bikes, drove back to England, parked the van outside Shawn's house in Sheffield and got on the train back to Bristol where he had a house opposite the pub. Mark Loram was at that meeting and later he and Norrie got together, doing Sweden and Poland. In due course Norrie became his manager and looked after him well.*

Norrie's wheeling and dealing was nothing new. When riders started to make more frequent trips in the 1960s most had an eye open for the chance to make a little extra. I was no different and regular travelling companions such as Gordon, Guy and Chris Macdonald helped keep the wheels of finance turning.

My association with Chris, like Gordon, goes back to 1963. He went to work for National Provident Insurance and quickly moved up the rank. When he started playing golf I never could figure out which of the two was his main priority because for years he came to meetings and would be at my house any time from lunchtime on.

Almost invariably he had been out and sold a bit of insurance and had a round of golf. We never could work out how he could play in amateur tournaments when he was supposed to be working for NPI. When he started coming on European trips he always had to be back in England on the Monday to sell insurance and play a round.

In the old Communist days, no matter where we went our clothes and vehicles identified us as Westerners. There never was a shortage of Eastern Europeans wanting to do some business.

After the European Final in Wrocław in 1968, Gordon and Chris took my transporter over and there were a couple of Russians who were obviously keen to get hold of Western currency. In the boot of their Lada cars they had several bikes, engines and spares which they were eager to trade.

We had a cloak and dagger meeting behind the bushes and started loading the gear by torchlight when a security van came along. This frightened the hell out of the Russians who thought they were about to get

---

* Mark Loram became world champion after topping the score charts in the 2000 Grand Prix. I helped Mark by phone a few days before each GP just to get his mind power working and to motivate him. Norrie subsequently assisted Coventry's two-time British champion and 2007 British Grand Prix winner Chris Harris over the course of several GP and European seasons.

CZECH MATES – leading Jan Verner, Milan Špinka and Zdeněk Majstr in the 1971 Luboš Tomíček Memorial meeting at the Markéta Stadium in Prague, on the way to the first of three consecutive wins in this event

into trouble with the police and took off. In the event we gave the security guys a fiver and a bunch of stickers and they went off as happy as could be.

There was another drama with an impromptu clothing sale after practice for the 1971 World Team Cup final, again in Wrocław. Gordon, Chris and the other mechanics joined the team when we decided to take a walk around the city before dinner.

All of us except Jim Airey had brightly coloured sponsored jackets from Bell Helmets and other American companies. These really stood out as all the locals had drab clothing. Then a couple of Polish spivs approached us and wanted to buy our jackets. It was getting a bit chilly and we didn't really want to sell so we quoted a stupid price thinking that would be the end of it.

Instead they readily agreed to pay and handed over a big roll of notes. Then they hung around to do a deal for Briggo and Ray Wilson's jackets and the price went up, and it went up even more when it came to negotiating for Ronnie Moore's jacket.

Jimmy was an interested spectator but as he had a plain zip-up cardigan he was unimpressed to miss out as he watched the huge roll of notes getting bigger by the minute. We thought we had struck a fantastic deal but when it came to checking the cash it turned out the two Poles had been sleight-of-hand experts with a couple of high denomination notes disguising that most of the others in the pile were only a few zlotys.

When we realised we had been conned everybody had a good laugh, nobody more so than Jimmy because it turned really cold and he still had his cardigan while the rest of us were walking along wearing just T-shirts. We decided we were not going to sign any autographs the next day for any Polish spectators wearing a bright red Bell jacket.

Bikes, motors and spare parts were the most common international currency. When I first went to Pardubice in 1967 I met Evžen Erban and bought a couple of hundred Jawa ferodo clutch plates from him. He became an instant friend and we have done deals ever since.

In later years I gave him lots of bike bits made in England such as gold metal flake mudguards, alloy handlebars, alloy tanks, short seats, English chain guards and so on for his bikes. Later Evžen became the main owner of the Jawa factory after the fall of Communism in the early 1990s and they have remained as one of my sponsors.

Briggo was the first Jawa agent in England, importing the bikes and operating his dealership from Southampton. Barry did not appreciate some aspects of the way riders traded with the Eastern European guys. Eventually he fell out with the Czechs when the factory guys were told he was bringing parts to America where they already had an agent called Josef Kubíček.

Some of us were so busy charging around the world it was a wonder anybody had time to do anything other than jump on a bike to race.

The modern GP scene has put some new places on the map but even back then there were international meetings in a dozen or so countries for either speedway, long track or grass track. After the British season we were usually in California for a couple of weeks to do the Autumn Classics and then have a holiday somewhere in Spain with the kids.

The end of November and early December was taken up visiting sponsors in England and Europe and going to Sportsman of the Year dinners and other functions. The rest of December was spent getting ready for Christmas with the family and the whole thing started again in January.

It made sense to combine business and racing with benefits deriving from both. Sponsorship and back-up support was an essential ingredient in my career. One thing led to another and a lot of the contacts which came about as a direct result of my riding eventually translated into benefits which stretched in many directions.

Of all the business and sponsorship arrangements, none was more significant than the tie-up with Jawa, who started to make their presence felt with the ESO machines in the early 1960s.

276 – Ivan Mauger

I had been a consistent winner on my Rotrax Jap until shortly before the 1968 World Final when I bought a Jawa from Briggo. He had told me several times that the factory people were not too happy I was beating guys on Jawas in big championships.

A couple of weeks after my win in Gothenburg, he called and said Jawa wanted to see me. I flew to Prague and met Jan Křivka, the boss of the factory for speedway bikes and CZ motocross bikes.

I arrived at the old Prague airport early in the morning and he and Madam Hušáková, the interpreter, drove me to the Jawa factory at Divišov, about 45 kilometres to the south-east.

They took me on a tour through the factory with all the engine building and frame making sections and to the race development area. As they were showing me round it was clear they did not want me to get back on a Jap.

But I was not presented with a contract at that point as they said they had to go to Motokov, the import-export agency, for it to be formalised and approved.

Jawa put me up in one of the biggest hotels in Prague in Wenceslas Square (so now you know where Good King Wenceslas came from). At seven o'clock next morning Mr Křivka and Madam Hušáková collected me and took me to Motokov for the contract.

At first the offer was one complete speedway bike and a spare engine and enough spare parts for the entire 1969 season. I told them I needed two complete speedway bikes and a spare engine, two long track bikes and all the spares I needed.

I threw in the fact I had two complete long track Japs tuned by Josef Hofmeister which I could use if they did not want to give me Jawa long trackers.

After more discussion they agreed to almost everything but only wanted to give me one long track bike. I told them I need two because I always took at least two bikes to international meetings. In the end they agreed and it took about an hour for them to rewrite the contract. When they came back in I signed it immediately and so commenced a relationship in which we were willing participants for years.

We had a contractual agreement of one form or another for 14 years, which finished because they wouldn't build the type of engine I wanted for the long track.

After 1979 I still hungered after another long track title. A top speedway rider could still fancy his chances on the long track where you did not need to be quite as sharp or as fit. Speedway riders tended to be smarter in the first corner than most of the pure long track riders.

HOSPITABLE – Madam Hušáková and Jan Křivka of Jawa Motorcycles

The factory people and myself remained good friends and that is the situation to this day, long after the whole structure of the factory changed when the Berlin Wall came down and Eastern Europe became open.

After signing that first deal Mr Křivka and Madam Hušáková accompanied me on a sightseeing tour around Prague. One of the sights was the Markéta Stadium, which in recent times has been the venue for the Czech Grand Prix. We were back at the airport to catch the five o'clock flight to Heathrow.

Jan Křivka was my boss in all the years I rode for Jawa and Madam Hušáková was always present at any meeting with them either at the factory or Motokov. She was there too whenever I had to test bikes, either at a track at Divišov, at the Markéta, Slany and several speedway venues in Czechoslovakia. We tested the long trackers at Mariánské Lázně, up near the East German border.

I came close to falling out with Jawa in 1975 and 1976 because they would not build a four-valve for a couple years after the Weslakes and Phil Crump's four-valve conversion started to point the way in engine development.

According to Briggo, the factory reckoned Ivan and Ole – also a works rider by this time – were winning everything on two-valvers so why would they need to go to the expense of building a four-valver. Usually to the point, he told them Ivan and Ole were the best riders in the world and that's why we were winning.

278 – Ivan Mauger

At the 1975 European Final at Bydgoszcz the two of us tied on 14 and had to have a run-off that I won. Phil Crump was third and the rest, all on four-valvers, were behind us. It was at that stage Ole and I asked Jawa for four-valve engines and the factory guys asked why, we had just beaten all the others.

Later I contacted Ivan Tighe, the mechanical whiz in Brisbane who had a lot of input into the Neil Street conversion used by Crumpie. He told me to send over a couple of engines and he would modify them.

I sent a short stroke and a long stroke long track motor. The short stroke came up best; I used it from time to time in 1976 and had it as a spare at the World Final. The long stroke never got going but I still have both engines. In fact I have all the bikes on which I won individual world championships.

Everything came to a head with Jawa when I was trying to win in Katowice against the massed ranks of four-valvers. To give a bit of power off the start Gordon bored out the centre of the carburetor as far as it would go. I was leading one race by a long way and the carb jet block broke. Pulling out of that heat when Crumpie was behind me eventually dropped me down to fourth.

When you are leading races by a long way in a World Final and have engine trouble that is what I call bad luck. But often you make your bad luck in the workshop. That's what we did this time but it was a necessity to try to compete with the four-valvers.

Even if they were reluctant to accept all my requests and suggestions, my role as a Jawa works rider entailed consultancy on design, development and testing of all their engines and chassis for speedway, long track and grass track. The benefits were two-way.

As our association continued Jawa supplied me four or five new speedway bikes each year, a couple of spare engines and three or four long track machines as well as all the spare parts to keep me going.

The Jawa stable was topped up as one of my deals with Belle Vue was that they supplied me with two bikes and necessary spares for League and Knockout Cup matches. That happened in each of the four years with the club. They also paid Guy Allott to tune the engines all the time I rode for the Aces.

It was a bit of an irony that this all came about following my years on the Jap. I went from buying and paying to maintain my own bikes from 1957 to 1968 to getting bikes and spare parts supplied free from Czecho for almost the remainder of my career.

When I did leave Jawa, Michael Daniels at Weslake was only too willing to give me bikes and spare engines. And for the last couple of years on the long track Don Godden gave me engines through Hans Zierk, his European agent.

International corporations were my greatest supporters, although the list of national companies who supported me during my career would fill a chapter on their own. Sometimes it required quite a juggling act to keep all the balls in mid-air.

When I was in California early in 1978 Ian Thomas called to say that he had secured Lada sponsorship for Hull and he wanted me to have their logo on the sleeves of my leathers. I told him that could not happen because Volkswagen were backing me with big transporters fitted out with bunks, fridges, a bulkhead and room for half a dozen bikes.

Ian took this back to the Lada guys who told him they would pay for the Volkswagen as my contract was only for three years. When he called me I said I need a new transporter each year because of the thousands of kilometres clocked up in Europe and England. Lada agreed to that and it was the start of a relationship which led to them backing the Wembley indoor meetings from 1979–82.

Lada Australia later sponsored my Australian Long Track Grand Prixs at Bathurst from 1989–91.

Another huge personal tie-up was with IVECO, who have built a reputation as world leader in the manufacture of commercial trucks. Based in Turin, they are a subsidiary of Fiat and most of the focus of their support for me was in Europe. They provided transport and financial backing which was invaluable.

They did though commission me to try to unearth a British world champion and at one stage it looked as though Kenny Carter might be the man they and I were looking for.

IVECO were the main sponsors of my Farewell to Australia and also supported my New Zealand series.

Another big connection was with Ricard, the globally-famed French organisation renowned for their pernod and pastis liqueurs. Raye and I have never been big drinkers but one of the perks was we had to go to Paris each year to work out the details of the sponsorship. They put us up in the top hotels, took us to the Folies-Bergère and all the sights.

They owned Bendor, an island off Saint-Tropez in the south of France. Only 11 people lived on it most of the year but there were two very exclusive hotels which were full most of the summer. It was a fantastic place and I got in trouble with officialdom a couple of times because I took time off in the middle of a season.

As part of the sponsorship Ricard paid for flights from Manchester, accommodation and food. We could not even pay for a Coca-Cola.

It certainly made a pleasant change from the distant days when we couldn't afford to buy one.

Heat 15

ONE MORE TIME

IT was not quite a case of *déjà vu* when I moved from Exeter to Hull. Yet in many respects it was a scenario uncannily close to the one of five years earlier when I left Belle Vue.

At the finish of the 1977 campaign I was world champion again, had piled up a truckload of points for Exeter and the Falcons had been transformed from also-rans into one of the most consistently successful teams in the country.

At the same time the promoters had some fast improvers on the books, with both Scott Autrey and Václav Verner looking capable of vying for the No.1 spot.

And they faced the dilemma of how to fit in everyone and properly fund their County Ground operation – as well as preparing for pending High Court action over their controversial new enterprise at Bristol.

This may well have contributed to Wally Mawdsley's statement to a BSPA meeting in London shortly after the end of the season when, according to Ian Thomas of Hull, he said Exeter was up for sale and so were all the riders.

Speedway regulations prohibit promoters from talking to riders who are contracted to another club, although Belle Vue had tapped me when I was still at Newcastle and everybody knew such things went on.

But on the strength of Wally publicly declaring his riders were available, Ian Thomas, being the entrepreneurial type of person he is, telephoned immediately after that meeting and asked me if I wanted to ride for Hull.

He asked if he could come over to my place next morning and talk about a deal. He duly arrived with his co-promoter Brian Larner in tow. We had some general discussion with Ian doing most of the talking. It was agreed we would get together again the following day and go through points I had raised.

My memory of Brian's contribution was he drank a full bottle of my best brandy during those two days and a fair bit of whisky too. There is no doubt he contributed in full to the partnership but it was Ian with whom I'd always had most dealings and that would continue to be the case.

Speedway first became aware of him when he (and Jeff Brownhut) opened Workington in 1970. He then brought Hull into the British League in 1974 and resurrected Newcastle as a second division (New National League) venue in 1975 with outstanding success.

HUMBERSIDE HERO – undisputed king of The Boulevard

Ian quickly gained a reputation as one of the sport's sharpest minds and what he did at Brough Park for a few years, by all accounts, was as exciting as almost anything that happened there previously.

The challenge a possible move to Hull presented was a familiar one. Here were promoters who wanted to revamp the image of their team, to start winning things if possible, and were not afraid to have a star name at the top of the bill. It wasn't exactly new territory for me.

Much of the time we talked about all the changes I would want at Hull including the pits arrangements and where my position would be. The entrance on to the track was never wide enough, there was only one pit gate and attention to the track and the dressing rooms was needed.

We discussed money for a short time before we agreed on the deal. Ian did not want to talk about guarantees per meeting and we settled on a figure for the entire season. He did not want anything to do with bikes either – which had been a component in earlier deals – so we agreed a bit more in lieu of machinery.

We nutted out a three-year contract initially and I told the Vikings promoters what I had said on my two previous moves – give me the responsibility for the team and who rode with who home and away and who we wanted to get and who we wanted to get rid off, don't worry about upsetting a few people, and I would help them achieve success.

They were so keen to have me on board they agreed to pay Exeter a £12,000 fee. To this day I still don't understand, because Exeter got me for nothing via rider control when I was world champ and I left Exeter as world champ. As I had established with the BSPA in 1973, I owned my own contract so I should have been able to change clubs for free.

Obviously it suited Hull to have me signed and sealed early in the off-season and to be able to tell everybody, including riders and sponsors. I believe Ernie Park, a potato merchant who had been a great supporter at Belle Vue and never got over them letting me go, put in some money to get the deal done.

We kept it all quiet over Christmas and Dick Bott, the northern journalist who did great publicity work for Ian for many years, organised a press conference at the Piccadilly Hotel in Manchester on Tuesday, January 3, which happened to be Ian Thomas's 36th birthday. He later described the signing as 'the most expensive birthday present I ever bought myself'.

I actually signed the contract in the studios of Yorkshire Television in Leeds a few hours later.

In the event Hull was to be the only track with whom I didn't pick up a league championship but we gave it a hell of a shake. It couldn't have been closer than it was in 1979, when the British League title came down to the last match of that second season.

The Will To Win – 283

VIKING CONQUEST – signing for Hull with Ian Thomas, Ernie Park and Brian Larner in attendance

Coventry beat Hull 42-36 in a winner-take-all decider, a match we had to undertake without California kid Kelly Moran who had been the discovery of the season.

Kelly was just 19, averaging 8.60 in just his second year in England, and finished fourth in the World Final to underline what unbelievable talent he possessed.

Unfortunately he broke a collarbone in a second half crash at Wolverhampton 12 days before the big one at Brandon. Maybe it would have been a different outcome to the championship had he ridden. We will never know.

Coventry took no prisoners that night in front of a swaying, heaving audience. The boys gave a fighting display which had them at full stretch and the crowd of around 12,000 on tenterhooks. In the end Ole and company had just a bit too much in the tank and as their fans danced with delight there were a lot of dejected Hull fans around the stands and on the terraces.

Ideally, we should have been able to say at the end of it that it was bad luck, well done boys, hopefully next time.

It wasn't like that, and there never would be a next time. At the end of the 1981 season the Thomas-Larner promotion was shown the door by the rugby league club, their landlords at The Boulevard. It was the end of Hull in the top division and it coincided with what I thought was the end of my British League career.

Knowing there probably would not be many better chances, after finishing third in 1978 and spending most of the following summer hot on the heels of the fast-starting Bees, the team had produced some outstanding performances.

Nobody relished coming to Hull, and for the second successive season nobody came away from the place with so much as a point.

HE'S BEHIND YOU – Ivan keeps Ole Olsen pegged behind him in the 1979 Coventry-Hull British League title decider at Brandon

By the end of the '79 campaign the sequence of consecutive home league wins was 36 and rising.

As is usually the way, though, titles are won on the road, and we lost this one, not on October 13 in front of a packed house, but on a much more low-key night in south London two and a half months earlier.

We were due at Wimbledon, one of a pack of chasing clubs who had pretensions of their own. Plough Lane at the time was almost as much of a fortress as Hull, although Coventry had nicked the points on their visit a month before. It made our visit all the more important, with a real possibility of snatching a win which would leave the Bees in no doubt that we were right there with them.

That ambition was critically dented when Bobby Beaton, Graham Drury and Frank Auffret failed to show up, reporting they had broken down on the motorway.

Now I know people do break down, and from time to time speedway riders have tended to break down more than most, particularly en route to a distant destination which by coincidence they didn't much fancy.

What happened to these three I don't know, and still don't. Ian told me later he understood they never left home. But there is little doubt their absence was a huge reason why we lost 41-36 on the night with a patched-up team. In the final analysis, that was the occasion those championship hopes were fatally wounded.

Beaton was a very experienced rider of heat leader quality, and the other two were usually good for half a dozen points. Even on a bad night they still should have been up to making a contribution to get us over the line. Dennis Sigalos had a great meeting at reserve with a paid 15 points from six rides – his first big score in England – but it wasn't enough.

If we were flat that night, the Hull dressing room after the defeat at Coventry was blue with the rage of frustration. It was a bitter pill to swallow and at the very moment we should have been congratulating ourselves on a great effort and looking forward, angry recriminations were the order of the day.

The anger came tumbling out with Brian Larner and me leading the charge. While Ian was the more calculating half of the partnership, Brian usually wore his heart on his sleeve. He was big, loud and usually happy go lucky. Most of the time he was lucky enough to be associated with success and happy to be in that position.

This time he was neither lucky nor happy and he let everybody know it. I couldn't disagree and had my say too. Six months of effort had failed to deliver the prize. So much went right for me in that year, so I should not be greedy. The fact is though that this was a great opportunity wasted and there is a ring of truth about the old saying that nobody remembers the runner-up.

SO CLOSE – the Hull Vikings who just missed out on the 1979 British League, standing, left to right: Ian Thomas (promoter), Graham Drury, Dennis Sigalos, Joe Owen, Frank Auffret, Brian Larner (promoter). Front: Bobby Beaton, Ivan Mauger (captain), Kelly Moran

Except, of course, those of us who went so close remember – all of us. It was as tight, as exciting and as fiercely fought a league championship as British speedway has ever seen. Never mind the disappointment, it deserves to be remembered as such.

On balance, there were many positives about what turned out to be four seasons with Hull. It was not an obvious destination for me when the Exeter years came to a close, but Ian Thomas had a reputation as being able to charm anybody and Barry Briggs had spoken warmly about the couple of years he did with the club.

Even so you would have to say Hull has a reputation as being one of the least lovely cities in England and many people considered the speedway to be in the same category. The 423-yard circuit was narrow, probably illegally so; the place seemed perpetually gloomy and even its greatest fans would not have described it as a classic racetrack.

The Boulevard was bleak even on a good day, and there was evidence the promoters had an often difficult relationship with the league people about who was supposed to do what at the stadium.

The city of Kingston-upon-Hull, which suffered more from wartime bombing damage than anywhere apart from London, is on the River Humber and historically it has been a major port. Nowadays it is best known for its Humber Bridge, which for a while after its completion in 1981 was the world's longest single span suspension bridge.

One big attraction was that Hull was an easy ride from Manchester along the M62, the main road route into and, just as importantly, out of the place.

And yet, just as we had done at Newcastle, that other example of northern exposure, we were received with great warmth and enthusiasm. The people of the East Riding are a law unto themselves, not like your traditional Yorkshiremen at all.

Ian Thomas had come a long way from being a struggling second half rider in 1963 to being one of England's most respected promoters who loved to put on a show. It made sense to respect Ian because he always was a bit of a conjurer, which was fitting, as his 'day job' and one he has worked at for many years was as a magician and entertainer.

No surprise then that he built a good portion of his reputation upon his ability to work the rule book to full advantage, and to use sleight of hand and the art of illusion to win speedway matches and unsettle opponents. He was the architect of several speedway innovations including the National League Fours and of course had as many critics as he did admirers. No wonder we hit it off.

He had talked Briggo into a comeback in 1976, no mean effort considering that BB was contemplating the easy life in California, was a tax exile limited to spending 90 days in Great Britain in any year, and was by this time on the wrong side of 40.

Barry enjoyed Ian's enthusiasm and entrepreneurial style and considers the season he spent with the Vikings as one of the most enjoyable of his life. I was mindful of that, but I never thought of going there as a transition to retirement.

As world champion, I felt I still had plenty to offer as a rider, and as long as I was there I wanted to be a force. I was also conscious of the fact my influence with the team, the composition of the side, the pairings, and attention to 101 little details which separate winners from the rest, could bring to Hull some of the ingredients they had been missing.

Any new challenge has to contain a variety of incentives and one which is always present is the need to demonstrate to any doubters – including myself – that I could not only meet expectations but hopefully surpass them by some distance.

So critics who figured that Exeter had had the best of me, that my use-by date was fast approaching, that my points contribution, commitment or ability to influence matters would all be on a downward spiral, were lining up with their negative predictions.

288 – Ivan Mauger

Circumstances like that have tended to fuel me up and make me want success all the more. It is true that missing out on that elusive league championship still rankles – after title wins at Newcastle, Wimbledon, Belle Vue and Exeter my appetite was still intact.

It was my long-term plan to continue riding in the British League for another two or three years and thereafter do international individual meetings in Europe, the World Pairs and the world long track championship for another few years and finish completely in 1985.

At the time of going to Hull, I had not decided exactly when that would be but talking it over with Raye and my advisers it was generally agreed that after I stopped riding in the UK I would then map out the remainder of my racing career one or two years in advance.

My original agreement with Ian Thomas was to ride for three years and then retire at the end of 1980, leaving him with a Belle Vue type of team.

Such a prospect would have been pretty attractive to the Hull people at the end of 1977, a season in which they lost five matches at home, won just two away and finished 14th in a 19-strong British League. They had a fairly ordinary team, in which young Joe Owen was the only ever-present.

I remembered Joe as a cheerful cheeky young kid who had rides after the meeting at Barrow when Wally Mawdsley, Peter Oakes and I opened there and was aware of his developing talents which really began to blossom at Newcastle a couple of years later.

There was potential for improvement from Phil Kynman, another 20-year-old, and from the more experienced trio of Bobby Beaton, Graham Drury and Frank Auffret. But we recognised that for the team to make a serious impression, there needed to be at least one significant new signing.

Kelly Moran turned out to be that signing. Travelling to the United States every year gave me the first look at virtually any new American and it didn't take any time at all to identify Kelly as a great talent. He was personality plus, great on the bike, and Ian was happy to take my word for it and sign him up.

As events turned out, both Joe and Kelly made a premature exit from the 1978 season because of serious injuries and young Kynman lasted only a couple of months before deciding his talents were better suited to the National League.

Fortunately because of the Newcastle connection Hull could call on Tom Owen, the best number eight going around, and with his help and a solid improvement from all the supporting cast, it was a much more convincing Hull team than it had been.

After struggling in early matches, the Vikings were unbeatable at home in the league, good enough to win four and draw a couple on their travels,

STREETS AHEAD – Hull were good value at home, seeing off all comers including 1978 British League champions Coventry

and finished a highly respectable third on the ladder. The only teams ahead of us were Coventry and Belle Vue, both of whom we absolutely smashed at The Boulevard.

In that respect it was easily the best season since Ian and Brian opened, and I ended up with nine maximums in 15 home meetings and the track record.

On a personal level though, I was a couple of race wins short of achieving a double-figure average for the first time since 1965. It was enough of a blip on the radar to provide my critics with ammunition to suggest that perhaps my talents really were on the wane. The only way to put that to bed was to come back stronger than ever in 1979 and that is exactly what happened.

After my first season with the Vikings, I was off to do the usual series of meetings in California and Ian asked me to look out for some more likely riders for Hull. I called him after a couple of meetings and said Dennis Sigalos was looking quite good. Ian told me what kind of a deal to offer him which I did and the result is that he rode for Hull in 1979 and again in 1980.

When we first went to America we would ask the riders what gear they had on and what were the ignition settings for the tiny tracks. Probably only

BACK TO THE BOULEVARD – parading the world championship trophy with the family prior to Hull v Halifax

Mike and Steve Bast and Bill Cody could tell us. The rest just said 'gee, my dad does that' or 'gee, my mechanic does that, I don't know'.

One of the conditions Dennis asked for when he came to Hull was that he could park his bike next to me so that he could see what I was up to and learn what I was doing between races. He wanted his mechanic Kevin Hart to be able to quiz Gordon Stobbs during the meeting about gear ratios, bike set-ups, tyre pressures and all the other small details which make a big difference.

One night Kevin asked what gear he was putting on and Gordon told him I did the gear ratio and gave instruction as to which sprocket to put on. Kevin said 'Oh I think I am going to put a taller gear on tonight for Dennis because he was a bit slow last week'. Gordon just had a laugh and had to walk away.

Whatever the technical details were, Dennis quickly showed some glimpses of genuine promise and his inclusion certainly boosted the side. As usual, there were a few teams who fancied their chances and got a few results. But the longer the season went, the more likely it became that in the end it would be all down to Coventry and ourselves.

The Will To Win – 291

Joe Owen and Kelly Moran came storming back stronger than ever, such was the optimism of young blokes who shrugged off their misfortunes of the previous season. Bobby Beaton upped his average by more than a point, and a nice early run of home matches lifted everybody's confidence.

I tended to be at my best in situations like that. I loved to lead and was repaid many times over by the fact the other riders began to feed off the confident mood which was developing. There were seven away wins, including a massive 49-29 at Sheffield and a record 52-26 at Wolverhampton, both in the last month of the season, and a couple of draws.

In every way we were legitimate championship material and on a personal note I relished being back in more familiar territory. A 10.53 average – with 10 maximums in 16 matches at home – put me second only to Scott Autrey who incidentally was one of only two visiting riders who achieved a full score at Hull (Bruce Penhall was the other).

There was much to celebrate, and none of us involved will forget the fantastic reception the Hull people turned on when I came back from Poland with the world title. Even that party seemed a fraction subdued compared to the World Team Cup victory a couple of weeks later, followed by my birthday at which so many of those associated with the family and my successes turned up to say nice things.

A British League title really would have put the icing on the cake, so to speak, but it was not to be. One little remembered (and forgettable) extra to that year was qualifying for the final of the Knockout Cup. Unfortunately we were blown away by Cradley Heath, who turned the knife by winning a re-run second leg 58-50 at Hull after taking a 16-point lead in the first leg.

Overall though, there was not much more anybody could have done. Ask any long-time Hull follower what was their all-time favourite year and virtually every single one would nominate 1979. They had the world No.1, the world No.4 in Kelly Moran, and witnessed the championship go to the wire.

On the face of it, there was no good reason why things should not have got better. But the hoped-for natural progression from third, to second, to first never gathered any momentum.

With continual rumours of a rift between the promoters and Hull Rugby League Club, and a few other distractions to contend with, the Vikings slipped down to 12th in the league and the impetus and adrenalin high of the previous season faded into a blurred and increasingly distant memory.

Although many of the basic ingredients were there, it was clear the side could do with further tinkering.

Kelly was proving a bit of a handful with his off-track exploits and in due course Ian sold him to Birmingham, having brought in Shawn, his younger brother, to replace him. He had seen Shawn in action at Ascot Park, liked the look of him, and brought him over to have what was supposed to be a secret try-out at The Boulevard before the end of the year. Shawn rode a couple of second halves under the assumed name 'David East' and looked almost a replica of his brother, with talent to burn.

It was a big ask to expect him to immediately replace the scoring capabilities of his brother, and Graham Drury was another member of the side who moved on and was not satisfactorily replaced. Graham decided he would do a season in Germany and in came John Cook, yet another American who never really got going.

I was sick, and far from good health in the opening weeks of the season during which time, as attempts were made to juggle the team to come within the 50 point limit, the unthinkable happened. We lost at home to Hackney and then Halifax, Sigalos missing both meetings.

Whatever calculations are used in the setting up of a side, a promoter and captain's dream is to have a team of riders, most if not all of whom are capable of improving their average and level of contribution from one year to the next.

The younger Moran looked a good signing but after a while Ian had to move him on to Sheffield. Both Morans were enormously talented and very popular with the crowd but took far too much looking after between meetings.

With Hull in 1980 the only person who didn't go backwards was Sigalos. Having the challenge of a rider who was as keen to be the top man as I was to retain that role is usually a positive thing. But Siggy, or maybe his advisers, spent a lot of that season in a less than positive frame of mind.

The better he got, the more he seemed to have to complain about. I missed a month because of illness but came back to score a maximum in a home win against Sheffield. Dennis got the lot, too.

Dennis' dad Tony had come over to help him at a couple of meetings and see the Northern Riders Championship Final at Owlerton the following evening.

As Ian Thomas tells it, Tony went to him after the Wednesday night league meeting against Sheffield and said 'Dennis should be the captain of the team because he scored more points than Ivan tonight. He is going to win the Northern Riders Championship and that will prove that he is a better rider.'

Ian called me the next morning to tell me all of this stuff and it didn't take long for me to react. I told him in no uncertain terms that Dennis and his party could forget about winning the meeting. The manner in which the suggestion was made could not have been better designed to fire me up and I was determined to put in a big effort at Sheffield.

The bottom line is I won the title with a 15 point maximum. Dennis scored 13 and he was tied with Kenny Carter.

Kenny asked me if he could borrow my bike for the run-off and I said 'yes, why not'. I told him how to make the start and what line to ride to keep Dennis behind him. I also advised him what to do if Dennis was leading.

Carter won the run-off and in the dressing room after the meeting, Dennis said he had not expected me to lend a bike to Kenny for a run-off against a rider in the same team.

I told Dennis what his father had said and how it had got to me. If his dad had not said those things Dennis very probably would have won the meeting because at that advanced stage of my career I was not obsessed with winning the likes of the Northern Riders Championship.

SIDE BY SIDE – Dennis Sigalos, on parade at The Boulevard, wanted to learn from Ivan

294 – Ivan Mauger

There were nights like this which reminded people – myself included – of the best of times. But at 40, I wasn't quite up to scoring maximums week after week. I think my contribution to the team was never questioned but the figures weren't great. For the first time since 1967 I averaged under nine points.

The biggest challenge for me was to front up for business as usual because from the start of the year and for more than 12 months after that I was a long way from my usual level of fitness.

We had gone to Perth in the first week of January and on arrival I had a hugely sore neck. Con Migro got a doctor and then a physiotherapist to see me and both said it had been caused by the long flight.

The physio made me a neck brace which I used in two meetings at Claremont, one at Bunbury, and then at Melbourne and Mildura on successive nights.

During the trip to Bunbury my left knee started to swell. On the way back we usually stopped for a swim but by then I could not walk over the sand to get to the beach. Con called in a second opinion from another doctor and physio but they had no immediate answer and meanwhile my right elbow began to swell.

On the way up to Mildura with Jack and Kath Walker a few days later, the fingers on both hands were swelling. I called Harry Croft, who had been our family doctor in Christchurch for years, and he suggested I was suffering from polyarthritis. His advice was to get there as soon as possible and he would book me in to hospital.

Before the Mildura meeting Jack had to cut my glove along the seams of the fingers so I could get them on, and taped them so they gave some protection. Immediately afterwards we did the six-hour trip back to Melbourne, jumped on a plane next morning and went from there to hospital.

As it turned out, I did not have any kind of arthritis. The hospital performed tests every day for a week and then told me I had a blood disorder, with too many white cells not mixing with the red. They did a lumbar puncture and a few days later another one.

I was hospitalised for a month, needed complete bed rest and was fed a diet of aspirins four times a day. After a week they took me down to a heated pool, put me in a sling and lowered me into the water so I could keep my legs working.

When we got back to England in February Raye took me to Monsall Hospital – where I had been in October 1963 with meningitis. They kept me in for a couple of days to do their own tests and yet another lumbar puncture.

After all that, they wanted to see me each week. So every Wednesday on the way to Hull, I left home early with Gordon to check in. That later turned into every second week and by August it was only once a month – but it wasn't the ideal build-up for meetings.

I was on pain-killing tablets the Monsall Hospital doctors prescribed. and continued to take them three times a day until the start of the following year.

That NRC must have left a sour taste in Siggy and his dad's mind and he went to Ipswich for the 1981 season. It was disappointing to see him go because like all Americans he was a good guy to have around and a very team oriented rider.

His career really took off at Ipswich and by 1982 he was third in the world, a position he might have improved upon but for later injuries. Dennis also collected World Team Cup and World Best Pairs gold.

I was anticipating seeing out my three-year deal with Hull and then retiring from British League at the end of the 1980 season. But halfway through the year Ian asked me if I would do another season.

He said that he didn't think that he would be able to run in 1982 and if I didn't ride another year he was going to have some problems with other riders who wanted to be riding in the same team. I was reluctant to carry on but got talked into riding again.

We had a discussion and eventually I agreed to do the 1981 season that would be very lucrative to me with the additional financial incentives that Ian offered. I also had a huge sponsorship from IVECO Trucks if I was involved in British League. I still had a deal with them for Europe but it was only about half the total amount involved.

John Cook was included supposedly as a makeweight in an exchange deal which took Sigalos to Foxhall Heath and brought Billy Sanders to Hull. At the time and on paper it looked a great transaction – for the Vikings.

As it turned out Ipswich got a tremendous deal as Siggy continued to improve at a rate of knots and 'Cowboy' Cook, formerly a struggling reserve, reinvented himself as a race-winning, wheelie-popping crowd pleaser who vied with Dennis for the top spot at Foxhall Heath.

Sanders had been around for several years after turning up as a 16-year-old at Foxhall Heath in 1973. Along with John Louis and Tony Davey, he was a big part of the success John Berry and Ipswich enjoyed over a number of seasons, and he was talented enough to twice finish on the rostrum in a World Final.*

Billy had a reputation for being an unpredictable character but he was another very good team man and genuinely interested in Hull having some

---

* The six-time Australian champion, World Final third placegetter in 1980 and runner-up in 1983, Billy died by his own hand in 1985, aged 29.

ANOTHER MAUGER – *Kym suits up for Newcastle Diamonds, 1981*

success. He also was surprisingly knowledgeable with bike set-ups for different tracks. He was really interesting to talk to on those subjects.

However he was one of number of 1970s and '80s riders who liked to smoke marijuana, reportedly took a variety of other drugs and was subject to huge mood swings. Through it all he was a consistent scorer and we were not as vulnerable at home as in the previous year, losing only to champions Cradley Heath who won 11 and drew one of their 15 matches on the road.

But we contrived to draw four at The Boulevard – somebody said Hull would have been almost a draw banker on the football pools – and lost every one on our travels. Our finishing position was again 12th.

Joe Owen began to show what he might achieve as a top-division heat leader and Danish youngster John Eskildsen came on loan from Birmingham and was a steady contributor. We didn't have a great spark about us, though.

With some reluctance I accepted my days as an 11-plus rider were over but even so there were plenty of enjoyable moments. Going to so many tracks for the last time gave me the chance to make my private farewells with a number of venues and opponents.

There might have been a few more opportunities to do that but for the BSPA getting on their high horse when I went to Germany instead of riding for the Vikings in an Inter-League KO Cup match at Boston.

The Will To Win – 297

I had already missed a couple of matches after suffering bruising and concussion when Birmingham's Hans Nielsen clattered into me in a League Cup match at The Boulevard.

But Boston on a Sunday was never going to happen. Hull had my continental dates well before the fixture list came out. As I held my own contract there was no way they would or the promoters could make me ride in that meeting. I sent the BSPA a telegram telling them I would retire from British speedway first rather than be coerced into riding in a match which was outside any existing agreement.

I came back from the weekend meeting to be told the promoters had decided I should not ride in England for 14 days, which robbed me of several meetings, hurt the team, hurt Hull and denied the supporters at the away tracks where we were due.

Fighting battles with the promoters association was not something I was bothered to engage in at this stage of the proceedings. I simply took a few days' break and came back refreshed for the start of the British League campaign.

Everything was going along smoothly enough until I broke my right ankle very badly in the world long track final in Yugoslavia. It meant missing the end of the season, cost me another half a dozen meetings, and was a disappointing way to sign off.

And it wasn't just exit Ivan Mauger, it was exit Hull Vikings, forced out of their home of 10 years when the rugby league showed the promoters the door.

SO THIS IS LA – riders enter the arena before the start of the 1982 World Fin...

Heat 16

ROAD TO THE COLISEUM

IN 30 years as a rider I appeared in around 4000-plus meetings, and won more than 1000 international events in 26 countries.

That was the easy part.

In 35 years I have promoted, co-promoted and organised something in the region of 300 meetings, taking in five continents, including a speedway World Final and a couple of World Long Track Grands Prix.

I always enjoyed being involved in the organisation of events, whether it was a pick-up game of rugby with school mates, or running the first world championship decider held in the mighty Los Angeles Coliseum in 1982.

That historic occasion stands out although there have been many other highlights, including the formation of the World Series troupe in the 1970s, providing the basis of an idea which eventually germinated into the modern Grand Prix concept.

As a competitor, no matter how influential you may be, it's very much a case of turning up as well prepared as you can be to deal with however circumstances turn out on any given day.

As a promoter, you have the opportunity to shape the circumstances, to frame the way an event is put together, how it is packaged and costed, what the race track will be like, how the spectators can be best accommodated and entertained.

It is an enormous responsibility, because every aspect of the show and everyone involved in it in any way, whether as a rider, official or fan will be affected by your decisions and your ability to plan and execute.

When I first became interested in speedway, and in the early part of my racing career, I was only vaguely aware of the role of the promoter. The more I got into the sport, the greater my interest and awareness of what it took to get the show on the road.

It's impossible not to form an opinion about promoters and I have ridden for a few. Some, like Charlie Dugard, Kym Bonython and Ted Price played an important part in encouraging my progress early in the piece. They were real enthusiasts and it was no coincidence that the considerate attitude they displayed towards me was reflected in the way they went about their business.

Then there were the hard-nosed professionals like Mike Parker, Wally Mawdsley and Ian Thomas for whom promoting was strictly business, and other very influential personalities such as Jack Fearnley and Charles Foot who crossed my career path.

300 – *Ivan Mauger*

Every one of them would have owed something to Johnnie Hoskins, the man credited with pioneering speedway. He was born in Christchurch, got the sport up and running in Australia, was a huge player in England and Scotland for years before and after the war and became a legend in his own lifetime.

But the Kiwi who made the greatest impression upon me, and with whom I had most dealings personally, was Trevor Redmond. Nobody waved the flag for New Zealand more vigorously or effectively than TR, manager of the famous 1979 World Team Cup-winning side. That day at White City was a fitting, fantastic reward for him.

Trevor was one of the first riders from Christchurch to go to England after the war when he went to Aldershot in 1950. The promoter there was Fred Jepcott and the first time TR rode practice laps round the track he was watched intently by Fred's then 15-year-old daughter Pat. Some years later Trevor married Pat and they settled in the west country.

Trevor had been a livewire in New Zealand where he had dipped his toe in the promoting waters and he got a lot of things moving once he made a name for himself in England. He was transferred to Wembley where he was a member of a team crammed with talented and diverse personalities, and twice qualified for a World Final. TR was the first Provincial League Riders champion in 1960 and would have won it again the following year but for a broken chain in his last ride.

But by this stage he was developing his interests as a promoter. He had been a prime mover in getting New Zealand international recognition and played a part in organising several series both in the UK and overseas during the 1950s.

Whenever a young rider came over from New Zealand he was invariably there with a helping hand. Trevor was pretty much the adopted father of all the Kiwis and sooner or later everyone went to him for some kind of help or advice. Almost all of them had stories to tell about his generosity and wisdom.

Ronnie, Briggo and I all benefited from his kindness. Although he rarely went back he was a proud Kiwi at heart. I remember him singing the New Zealand national anthem word perfect the first time I won the world championship at Gothenburg in 1968 and holding up the flag.

After his involvement in one-off events and then various series TR got a track of his own at St Austell in Cornwall in 1958 and ran bikes and, mostly, cars there for the rest of his life. He also promoted at Neath, Glasgow and, in 1970 and 1971, Wembley, the home of his beloved Lions.

I learned a lot from TR about promoting. He was prone to exaggerating or doing extraordinary things for publicity. Prior to a Scotland v New Zealand Test Match at the old Glasgow White City he introduced me as the son of a Maori chief in New Zealand, much to my mum's irritation when she found out about it.

His great talent was building up every rider and every occasion as something special. It didn't matter if he was introducing a second half event or a no-name reserve, after the big introduction from Trevor you would have thought it was the world championship decider coming up.

The World Team Cup bid in 1979 was tailor-made for him. After some of the disappointments of other years we needed all the motivation we could get and TR made it his personal mission to rev up everybody connected with the whole campaign.

I regard it as New Zealand's greatest speedway victory – including our individual championships – and we all wanted so much to win it for TR. It was his proudest day in speedway.

I got large photographs of the presentation framed, gave one each to Pat Redmond, Larry Ross, Roger Abel, Mitch Shirra, Cribby and Motor Cycling New Zealand and kept one for myself. It has pride of place on my office wall.

When all the other countries had riders trying to get into their teams we only had three genuine international performers and Cribby, who was a second string at Wolverhampton.

TR fiddled an international licence for Roger Abel and although Roger did not get a ride in any of the rounds, he was a valuable help in the background and contributed greatly to the win.

For riders to come halfway across the world to race was an adventure in itself but TR pushed the international boundaries from very early on. He organised trips to South Africa and Europe but America was one frontier which eluded him.

When I went over there to ride after the 1968 British League season, with Briggo following on a week later, the place was wide open. Jack Milne was especially keen to see speedway revive after its years of inaction, and Harry Oxley proved an increasingly willing participant.

They did not have a finger on the pulse of world speedway and were only too keen to pick our brains. From just a couple of us putting on a show, it developed quickly, with the emergence of Costa Mesa as the place to go for speedway racing in California.

We made introductions and set up arrangements for Bert Harkins to ride there in 1969, with Briggo and myself flying in a few days later after the BLRC. Then the following year in addition to Bert we had Jim Airey, Dave Gifford and Bernie Lagrosse – who had been riding for Berwick under the assumed name Roy Williams.

Bert was a great character and showman. Taking a leaf out of the TR manual of promotion, we billed him as Scotland's number one – which I guess he was – and convinced him to wear a set of tartan leathers.

Amusingly, and surprisingly for a full-blooded Scot, he couldn't play the bagpipes either but we told the crowd and media that he could, and had inadvertently left his pipes at home. It was quite a challenge for him when people came up and offered their bagpipes for him to play. For once Bertola was lost for words.

The Americans were starting to flex their muscles and one or two riders were coming through, so they loved the idea of testing themselves against the imported stars. Riders finishing up after a long season in the UK thought it was a great way to round off the year.

This grew into the first USA v Great Britain matches in 1971 when George Hunter and Jimmy McMillan were added to the list. The Americans beat us 2-1 despite the fact Briggo and I were good for double figures and more in each of the meetings, two at Costa Mesa and one at Ascot.

RIDE HIM COWBOY – Ivan takes off ahead of Chris Pusey at Costa Mesa

It was on these trips Barry and I began to plan to broaden the scope and started to nut out details as to how, where and when we could put together our own show. This was the start of the World Champions troupe, although it took another couple of years before all the scheming translated into the real deal.

America and California in particular always has such a buzz about it. It must have helped stimulate our thought processes although the basic ideas followed us as we went off in different directions.

After the October/November trips to the USA I usually went off on holiday with Raye and the kids and these too were times when there was a chance to let the imagination roam.

New year activity in Australia and New Zealand was mostly a succession of individual appearances, although the promoters Down Under also liked the idea of gathering together a number of 'name' riders for different big-ticket events. Since Barry and I were the most-decorated active riders running around, anything which included us was going to be a drawcard and we had the contacts to call upon a range of other international attractions.

My debut among the ranks of the paid-up entrepreneurs came in a location less exotic or obvious than might have been imagined. With Peter Oakes and Wally Mawdsley as co-promoters, I had my first experience of speedway promotion when we opened up Barrow in 1972. My racing schedule was such that my contribution was more as a sleeping partner than anything, but it was a start – albeit a not very productive one.

For many years there was a rule which prohibited active riders from being promoters but it was a regulation which never was going to stand the test of time. Provided there was no conflict of interest between riding and promoting responsibilities, why not encourage and involve people without whom there would be no show in the first place?

I tossed around the troupe idea with Peter and when Briggo had some unplanned down time after injuring himself at Wembley, he applied his thoughts to the possibilities, tapping in to other alert minds including Phil Rising and TR. We concluded the possibilities were limited only by our imagination – although it required a lot of financial gymnastics and it would not come together without some crucial support.

Most important was the goodwill and co-operation of the promoters to whom we wanted to bring a fully-packaged show. What we were offering was the biggest and best gathering of international talent ever put together for a series of meetings in the US, Australia, New Zealand and anywhere else in the world which wanted us. It was a GP series 20 years before the world championship Grand Prix started.

What we needed was a big sponsor to underwrite the venture but then, as now, such creatures did not grow on trees. Eventually we decided to bite

304 – Ivan Mauger

the bullet and backed ourselves by staging some meetings in New Zealand at the beginning of 1974.

There were strikes going on in Britain, travel and transport problems, riders coming in at all times of day and night from various locations. Bikes didn't arrive when they were scheduled. Welcome to the world of the speedway promoter. Just another day at the office, really.

As rookie promoters we figured we had an obligation to drum up as much publicity as possible and make ourselves available for newspapers, television, radio and anybody else. The effort paid off big time, thousands turned out, which put a smile on the local promoters who had come to the party, and convinced us this was a venture worth pursuing.

We billed our enterprise The World Series. The FIM, the sport's world governing body, were not happy about that so we registered a company in Guernsey, Channel Islands, called World Champions Speedway Series Limited. By some oversight the programmes and all the advertising forgot to mention the word 'Limited' so by default or design it became World Champions Speedway Series.

To ensure it wasn't perceived as simply a two-man vehicle we asked Ove Fundin and Ronnie Moore to ride. Both had made occasional appearances since retiring from racing on a regular basis. The short, sharp nature of a series over a few meetings appealed to them and they were in. Ole Olsen was keen as well which meant we had five world title winners.

It could have been six but the PZM were reluctant to let out Jerzy Szczakiel, the so-called 'accidental' world champion of 1973. Zenon Plech and Edward Jancarz were Poland's two gun riders of choice and the authorities agreed to let them come provided they were accompanied by a manager, Bernard Kowalski, who we called Twiggy because he was grossly overweight.

We were also able to call on Chris Pusey and Scott Autrey who were two of the world's most exciting young up-and-comers, plus outspoken Aussie Garry Middleton and the always good value Scot, Bert Harkins. Completing the dashing dozen who lined up for the first meeting was Graeme Stapleton, the local motocross star-turned-speedway rider.

Where better to start it all than in Christchurch where Russell Lang, who ran Templeton, was as excited about it all as we were. The start had to be delayed as ground staff tried to shoehorn in more and more people. They just kept coming. It was the biggest turnout for a speedway meeting in memory.

The story was similar at Wellington and Palmerston North, where once again enormous crowds materialised. And when we hopped across to do meetings at Newcastle and Liverpool, the Aussie fans were equally enthusiastic. It looked as if we were on to a winner.

WORLD FIRST – riders line up for the inaugural World Series meeting at Templeton in January 1974. Back row, left to right, Zenon Plech, Ove Fundin, Garry Middleton, Ole Olsen, Scott Autrey, Chris Pusey, Roger Wright, Bert Harkins, Edward Jancarz. Front, Barry Briggs, Ronnie Moore, Ivan Mauger and Graeme Stapleton

A side trip to put on a show at the Houston Astrodome was another huge test. If we could crack it in one of the world's iconic venues, things really would get interesting. We paired up with Harry Oxley and ran in conjunction with Pace Management to put on a speedway event on the third and final day of a Motorcycling Spectacular.

Briggo, Ove and Zenon Plech flew over with me from New Zealand and Ray Wilson, Terry Betts and Josef Angermüller came in from Europe to ride on a programme which also included five of the American boys. It was not easy moving in to a venue like this for the first time and there were plenty of logistical problems but 16,000 turned out which was a promising start.

Eastern European countries were paranoid about the possibility of having their sportsmen defect and the PZM allowed Zenon to come to America under my surety and on condition Eddie Jancarz stayed with Twiggy in New Zealand. Plech lapped up the freedom of the American lifestyle and on the way back we made a stopover in Honolulu. This included an impromptu surfboard lesson for Plechy and myself on Waikiki beach.

Zenon was less keen on doing anything physical when the riders came out to Rocking Horse Road during our down time in Christchurch. I had

JOIN THE CROWD – riding a 250cc Kawasaki in Houston Astrodome

trained on the sand hills ever since seeing newspaper stories and pictures of the great miler John Landy with his famous trainer Percy Cerutty training at the dunes in Melbourne. It didn't appeal to Plechy though.

It wasn't all sunshine and sand, either. We had a meeting in Stratford near New Plymouth which was rained off two nights in a row before we got lucky the third time. The local newspaper ran photographs and stories for several days in a row which upset the president of the Stratford Stock Car Club.

He came to our motel and told Briggo and me he didn't like all the coverage and photos of speedway bikes and riders because they had such a hard job getting anything in about their stock car events.

Come the Wednesday night and the stadium was absolutely full, cars were lined up on the main road and the police said we could not start until the congestion was cleared.

The place was jammed and you would have thought the car people would be happy for us, but apparently not – the club didn't want us back again after that. They were a stock car club and resented bikes filling the place.

Overall the Trans-Tasman leg went swimmingly, in spite of a few inevitable teething troubles, although we had hoped to fit in more events. It wasn't possible and we signed out with a New Zealand v Rest of the World series before returning to the States for three US-World matches on successive nights at Costa Mesa.

They were very well received too and the pattern of that first year was the template from which we worked for the next few series. We did four years in New Zealand and Australia, had six years in the USA, went to locations such as South Africa in 1975 and Israel in 1976, the year we also branched into Europe.

During that period we underwent most of the highs and lows associated with sport, never mind which side of the fence you are on.

As troupe promoters we had great days and bad days, meetings where everything ran like clockwork and some where whatever could go wrong did go wrong. Weather is always a factor nobody can control, and there was a fair share of that too – in 1978 we had four meetings in a row rained off in supposedly sunny California.

British promoters were nervous that we were plotting some sort of world domination but it never was our intention to interfere with the established domestic programme. Even so, we did take a certain amount of pleasure out of demonstrating that speedway riders had a brain and did have the ability to put on a show, something previously assumed to be the exclusive preserve of the suits and ties.

Big names like Anders Michanek, John Louis, Egon Müller and Tommy Jansson came on board – followed later by Peter Collins, Bruce Penhall, Jiří Štancl and others – and we rotated the personnel for the American meetings. We slicked up the organisation and presentation as we went, and the staging tracks almost invariably were happy because we kept pulling in big crowds.

Our worst time was when Ronnie was injured in a crash at Jerilderie Park, Newcastle, in February 1975. The red lights came on immediately and I was the first rider to get to where Ronnie was lying on the track. It was close to the worst nightmare and the first-aid people seemed to be frozen with indecision.

He had swallowed his tongue. A paramedic was trying to get it out of Ronnie's throat and had an oxygen tank with what looked like an attachment to put in the mouth to help breathing. The guy was struggling to free Ronnie's tongue, so I reached in his throat, pulled out his tongue and I administered the oxygen.

I had no formal medical training and Briggo and I have often discussed that situation – I could not do it again, but fortunately on the spur of the moment it seemed just a natural thing to do in those circumstances.

Ronnie had serious head injuries and was taken to the Newcastle Hospital. Barry and I abandoned our last rides at the meeting and went in the ambulance with him. Doctors drilled holes through the side of the head to relieve the pressure on his brain but held out little hope of his survival.

Several hours passed and at about midnight we were told to go to our hotel and we would be called if there was any change in his condition. Briggo, his wife Junie and Raye and I could not sleep so we were still up when the hospital telephoned at 2am. A matter-of-fact male voice said: 'If you guys want to see your mate alive you had better get here quick.'

We jumped in the car, ignored the red lights and arrived at the hospital in record time. The surgeon seemed quite gloomy about Ronnie's chances but I told him he was dealing with a special person and a fighter and suggested he got back to work to fix him up.

After a while he reappeared and said his only chance of survival was to go immediately to Sydney's Royal North Shore Hospital, 100 miles (160 kilometres) away. Briggo and I hit the phones trying to hire a helicopter but there was nothing doing at that time of night and the earliest one would be available was not until 7am.

The surgeon said an ambulance would take a couple of hours so it was decided to transport him that way on an air bed. We were all down at the Sydney hospital by 8am. The surgeon there said it was just as well we could not get the helicopter as Ronnie would have died because of his serious head injuries if he was over 500 feet (150 metres) in the air.

The specialists in Sydney did a great job. Ronnie remained unconscious for a month but slowly he recovered and after about a year he was back to something like full health. It was a frightening time, though. To see one of the great careers end in that fashion, and on our watch, was tough to take.

For the most part the meetings in Australia and New Zealand were great. We went back to old familiar places and did our bit in helping push

ALL ACTION – Ole Olsen, Anders Michanek, Ivan and Jiří Štancl wheel to wheel at Mystery Creek, Hamilton

some newer venues. Interest in solos (as the speedway bikes are called in New Zealand and Aussie) has fluctuated down the years but these were terrific times.

Less obviously, we went to South Africa because Barry knew Buddy Fuller from when he used to go there in the early 1950s. Buddy came to London and asked us to meet him at his hotel. We were quite keen as we were always interested in taking the troupe to new locations. The finances would only stretch to five riders, though.

He offered two air tickets for each rider on the Belgian airline Sabena and a nominal guarantee for each meeting. This sounded more like a holiday than a full-blown tour but that was fair enough so Ole Olsen, John Louis and Egon Müller agreed to go with us on those conditions. Ulla Olsen, Pat Louis and Krystal Müller all came too, together with Barry, June and myself.

The trip started after the British League Riders Final at Belle Vue. The only problem was we had a little miniature dachshund called Lisa who was due to have pups about the same time. Raye had to stay behind with Lisa and came out to join us later.

Buddy arranged meetings in South Africa and Rhodesia. We rode at the 'other' Wembley Stadium in Johannesburg, in Durban and then down in Cape Town where we travelled on an overnight sleeper train. Jo'burg was at very high altitude and we had to have our engines on 16 and 17 to one compression and the ignition right forward but the bikes still seemed like 350s.

Briggo and June, who honeymooned there in 1956, spent a lot of time staying out in the suburbs with old friends the Jankelowicz family. Raye and I were in the hotel in the centre of city essentially looking after the whole group.

South Africa in the middle of its isolated apartheid years was confronting in many ways. Theft from hotel rooms was a regular happening and I hated the way many of the whites treated the black population. Their behaviour was quite alien to anything we encountered elsewhere.

The Cape Town trip was very interesting and so much better than flying because we saw a huge amount of the country. It was deemed to be too dangerous to drive through some of those parts at that time. We got to go up to the top of Table Mountain and in Durban enjoyed the beaches and again played at being tourists.

In between times the drive up to Rhodesia was another memorable affair, with the possibility of being intercepted by unfriendly tribes ever present. We had to stay overnight at Pietersburg (now called Polokwane) and crossed the border at Beitbridge. That took an hour or so in extreme heat as we had to stand in the sun. The border guards would not let us stay in air-conditioned

310 – Ivan Mauger

cars. We had to troop out and fill in a visa form in what were surprisingly informal conditions.

We were in a convoy of rental cars Buddy had arranged. Much against our normal instincts we all had to observe a 50mph limit. There were police every few miles and they were thought to be generally lacking in humour. It was only 430-odd miles from Jo'burg to Bulawayo but took over 10 hours actual driving not to mention the overnight stop.

Some of the memories were out of this world. We saw so many wild animals, including hundreds of monkeys on the side of the road, wild pigs, buffalo and other creatures you don't normally encounter on the way to a speedway meeting. It was sensory overload in the end.

Before our first meeting the promoter told us he had an English guy who would be doing the announcing. We almost fell over with surprise when Ian Hoskins, son of Johnnie and a multi-track promoter in his own right, walked in on practice day complete with the long shorts, the khaki hunting jacket, long socks and hunter's hat looking like a replica of Stewart Granger in *King Solomon's Mines*.

Briggo and I laughed like mad because our usual impression of Hossie was someone with gum boots on and an umbrella standing at Old Meadowbank and telling us 'it is only a passing shower, boys, and it is quite dry underneath'.

After the second meeting, at Salisbury the next night, Raye and I, Barry and June, and John and Pat Louis chartered a small airplane to take us up to Victoria Falls and stay overnight. It was so spectacular and beautiful we all decided to stop for an extra few days which included a trip called the Sundowner Cruise on the Zambezi River.

It's a tragedy how badly things have gone in the country (now Zimbabwe) since we were there. We enjoyed the atmosphere and the people seemed much more tolerant and less abrasive than some of those we encountered in South Africa.

Doing something different in an environment much closer to home provided another high point. Successfully getting an indoor show into Wembley where for four years (1979–82) Briggo, Ian Thomas and I ran the Lada World Indoor was a big highlight.

We started a company in Guernsey called World Champions Speedway Series Indoor Limited and Lada were very happy to sponsor the show. ITV, big friends of speedway in those times, guaranteed 30 minutes of television and that was a key to it all.

The Indoor Arena at Wembley was configured to accommodate 8,000 people. We filled it the first year and went close to filling in the other three years.

All good things come to an end, though. And, when the telly people would not guarantee screening it on *World of Sport,* that significantly affected the Lada money – and thus the viability of the whole enterprise.

Coincidentally it was off the back of our first indoor promotion, in Houston Astrodome, that the opportunity came about to stage the 1982 World Final. Barry and I ran meetings in the Dome in '74 and '75 and initially the American Motorcycle Association (AMA) were very enthusiastic.

There was a highly complimentary piece in their magazine about how great it was Ivan Mauger and Barry Briggs had brought an international troupe to the USA. It wasn't the first time – we had been bringing riders to Southern California for a couple of years – but Costa Mesa was not an AMA track.

RIDER AND PROMOTER – Ivan and Jan Andersson in a Lada Indoor meeting at Wembley Arena

TIME TO RACE – even as a co-promoter of the meeting, Ivan still finds time to take out the 1979 Lada ice title, flanked by Jimmy McMillan and John Davis

Later the AMA changed their tune and suggested Mauger and Briggs were very bad for American Speedway because we had taken international riders to Houston who beat all the American riders. It was the start of a relationship which eventually went from bad to worse.

It came to a head when we were in Los Angeles preparing for another USA v The World series at Costa Mesa. Out of the blue the riders were told we would not be eligible for international competition if we rode on an unsanctioned track in the US.

Up to this point the Americans had given approval for World Series events but since Costa Mesa was not an AMA track that was sanctioned year round, they decided to demand that all the race meetings at the Orange County Showgrounds should come under their jurisdiction. Gene Wierwand, the AMA's FIM speedway rep, threatened to can the US-World matches unless that happened.

A short time later Harry Oxley went riding with a lawyer friend. It was another rainy day which put a damper on the plans so the two of them ended up sitting in the back of the van talking. Harry told him about the problem and filled him in on a few questions about the FIM's business in the US.

His legal opinion was the FIM had no idea of the power and seriousness of violating federal international trade laws. Their refusal to grant a sanction through the AMA and their threats concerning the international riders put them in a very tricky position. He felt we had an extremely strong case against the AMA and the FIM for international restraint of trade.

DIFFERENT WORLD – with Raye in Tokyo for the 1981 FIM congress

On the basis of that advice we sued AMA under the American Anti Trust Laws which meant in effect we were also taking action against the FIM. I was international riders' rep, knew the FIM Secretariat people quite well and discreetly enquired how much money the FIM had.

The legal processes ground along slowly. After several months and dozens of meetings with the attorneys, including depositions from Ed Youngblood, the director of the AMA, Gene Weirwand, legal counsel, and Bill Boyce, the AMA's local speedway representative, we decided to sue the AMA for more money than the FIM had in their coffers. It was a bit preposterous but that is how the American law works, with massive claims lodged but mostly later reduced by a court to a much lower figure.

You didn't need to be a legal genius to realise that the AMA and FIM would be very anxious to settle the matter. If the suit went to court and they lost, the penalties could have run into hundreds of thousands of dollars and they wisely did not want to take a chance of losing in the US court.

We were due to go to court somewhere in 1978. On the FIM international calendar, the World Final was scheduled to be held in Poland in 1982. Before the court case was due to be heard the AMA asked if we would compromise. We said we wanted to promote the World Final in America, preferably at the LA Coliseum, and some money as compensation.

The Poles were the meat in the sandwich but Wladyslaw Pietrzak, chairman of Polski Zwiazek Motorwy (PZM), and president of the CCP (the FIM track racing commission) was one of the most able and astute administrators. After a while the AMA in consultation with FIM and PZM and Mr Pietrzak agreed to give up Poland's right in 1982.

The offer was made to take care of our legal costs and grant sanctions for the world championship and the World Team Cup a couple of years after that. It was ground-breaking stuff because up to this point the World Final had never been allowed out of Europe.

It led to another first because we had to agree to run an international meeting at the LA Coliseum a year before the world championship. The granting of track approval by running a test event had never been done before. It was the first instance of a meeting of this kind being held on a one-time track laid over artificial turf.

By now we were a year out from the World Final and a promoting consortium titled World Class was set up with capital stock of $100,000. Jack Milne was the company secretary, Harry Oxley its president and Barry and I were the other two directors and shareholders.

Our 'trial run' was to run an American Championship meeting at The Coliseum to have the track passed. That was a monumentally expensive exercise and happened because the FIM and AMA decided to play hardball. The day after the meeting we had to demolish the racetrack.

314 – *Ivan Mauger*

It was years later when the Grand Prix started to build one-off circuits that the practice became widely accepted.

I was riding for Hull and somewhere in Europe every Sunday so there was not much opportunity for me to be hands-on in the process. Briggo was spending plenty of time in California and with Jack and Harry organised the laying of the track.

They did a perfect job and it was to be the same for the final. It was very wide in the corners, produced a lot of great racing and never cut up. It certainly was not slick as so many of today's specially-constructed GP tracks have tended to be.

We each had our particular jobs to do in the promotion. Jack Milne was the anchor man. Here was a guy who was 74 years of age, who had been world champion a lifetime ago, yet he still was bright, sharp, full of enthusiasm, and a very astute businessman. Harry was very good with the sponsorship deals and very well connected with people who mattered in California.

One of my responsibilities was to be on top of everything which was happening at the various qualifiers in Europe. Then I had to organise all the air tickets and freight arrangements for the 16 riders who made it through. One of the FIM conditions was that we had to provide four air tickets for each rider and transport two bikes and spare parts, tool boxes and other equipment.

The Inter Continental Final was in Vetlanda on Friday, July 23 and 11 places were up for grabs. The other five would be arrived at from the Continental Final in Leszno two days later.

As promoters we were pretty keen to see the best possible field assembled and for once, there was no guarantee of a home rider. All the odds favoured the Americans getting some big name qualifiers but there was no seeding – they had to deliver.

Briggo and Harry flew over to see the meetings and we breathed a collective sigh of satisfaction when Bruce Penhall, Dennis Sigalos and Kelly Moran, all Los Angeles boys, duly did the business.

There were some significant casualties as Ole, Erik Gundersen and Bo Petersen all missed out, leaving Hans Nielsen as the solitary Danish representative. Peter Collins beat British champion Andy Grahame and Petersen in a run-off for the 11th and final spot.

He was a big name we could sell but getting the Californian boys in was critical. If the worst had come about and none qualified, we feared running to a near-empty stadium.

Les Collins emerged from his big brother's shadow and won the meeting. He loved the big open spaces and suddenly identified himself as

TESTING TIME IN LOS ANGELES – laying a track from scratch for the first time at The Coliseum was a huge challenge for World Final co-promoters Ivan, Harry Oxley and Barry Briggs

someone who could go well at The Coliseum, where the circuit would favour his Jawa.

Taking off my promoting hat, I was pleased on a personal level to see Kenny Carter come in second. The kid had that hunger and an aura about him which suggested he too would be a real show, especially if he was remotely close to being fit after some bad injuries.

My job was to get all the qualifiers together, distribute the papers and freight arrangements to each of them and hand out the airline reservations. Afterwards Harry, Barry and I went back to the hotel where most of the guys were staying and we were up until the early hours of the morning.

A few hours later we flew from Jönköping to Hamburg and then on to Templehof airport in East Berlin. We had arranged to hire a Tatra, a massive Russian-built V8 – bigger than a Rolls Royce, and of course it was black.

We left Templehof to go towards Leszno and it was getting dark. Harry did not have great eyesight and didn't want to drive so Briggo volunteered. I was sitting in the passenger seat while Harry was having a snooze on the back seat.

Before we got to the Polish border Briggo was struggling. He was following the white line on the side of the road to such an extent that he drove into a lay-by and back out at the other end. At that point he asked if I might like to drive and in the circumstances I was more than happy to do so.

316 – Ivan Mauger

I couldn't be anything but pleased to see some old favourites get through from the Leszno meeting. Czech mate Jiří Štancl was different class to everybody that day, and it was good to have Václav Verner through for his debut, along with Germany's Georg Hack.

Mikhail Starostin was a Russian we could market well, and in one for the nostalgia buffs, Edward Jancarz was the lone Pole. For Steady Eddie, it was a mere 14 years after his first World Final in Gothenburg back in 1968.

After the racing we had them in a room and gave out their papers and necessary documentation. Then we jumped in the Tatra and set off for East Berlin. With a predictable hold-up on the border we didn't get to Templehof until three in the morning, too late to get a hotel as we had to check in at the airport at 5.30am.

So we did some sightseeing! We drove around for a while looking at the Berlin Wall and what an eerie sensation it was to see one of the most infamous expanses of brickwork of the 20th century. We had to turn right or left at different junctions and the wall went between apartment buildings. It was a spooky sidestep along the road to The Coliseum.

At last we got back to Heathrow and Harry came on with me to Woodford for a few days before he went back to Los Angeles. Life went on as normal for me because I was still racing my usual schedule. Fortunately the guys in LA had it all under control.

The Coliseum people were quite amenable, but given the cost of hiring the joint, so they should have been. The 93,000-capacity stadium, which hosted the 1928 Olympic Games and was to repeat that honour in 1984, always was the only place we wanted for a World Final.

Jack and Harry showed their mastery of organisation. Our task was to oversee security, pit marshals, starting line marshals and other staff, recruited mainly from Costa Mesa and the Southern Californian tracks.

The FIM and AMA nominated all the top officials, including the referee, clerk of course, track inspectors and many others. It seemed everyone connected with the FIM was there in some capacity or another but that was all included in the fee we had to pay for staging the event.

The Coliseum was very expensive, and trying to get people in there was a major cost. It was the oldest promoters' dilemma, we couldn't afford to spend the money and we couldn't afford not to.

American promoters were used to paying a substantial percentage of their anticipated take on advertising the event, but spending $250,000 on TV adverts in the last week before the Final seemed an enormous outlay. Even then we reached something like five per cent of the greater Los Angeles and Orange County viewers.

We lobbed out about that amount on radio to catch the attention of a similar number of listeners. Southern California had dozens of TV stations and hundreds of radio stations. You could be listening to a radio station going along the street but turn left or right and another station would come up on the same band.

We got about 35 or 36,000 spectators which was enough to pay all the bills and get our original investment paid off with a bit to spare. Part of the deal with FIM was we got the World Team Cup at Long Beach stadium and that made money, although we had to wait for three years for that to eventuate.

History records LA on August 28, 1982 as the second of Bruce Penhall's world championship victories, after which he made a very public farewell from the podium and rode off into the sunset to star in *Chips* and spend the next few years of his life on a very different stage.

Les Collins joined the ranks of 'nearly' men, locals Sigalos and Moran were third and fourth respectively. And this was the World Final I still contend Kenny Carter should have won.

WHEEL TO WHEEL – Kenny Carter outside Bruce Penhall moments before their controversial coming together

FUMING – Kenny Carter's world title dreams in tatters after the exclusion which followed his clash with Penhall

Four years earlier I was up at Newcastle for an inter-divisional four team tournament and after seeing and meeting the then 18-year-old for the first time I immediately took to him. We got on well together. It was at a time IVECO UK had offered me a lot of money if I could get an Englishman to become world champ and Kenny impressed me as someone who could have a real chance.

The son of former road racer Mal Carter, he was a true Yorkshireman, a real tough character, and a really talented rider. He was very determined, in the end perhaps too determined to be world champion. In due course I put in a lot of time to try to help him achieve that ambition and LA 1982 was the tipping point.

Kenny could comprehend compressions, ignition timings and gear ratios, clutch settings, fork springs rates, fork springs heights, wheel bases and tyre pressures. He could grasp almost instantly whatever he was told and understood exactly why we had to do certain things at different tracks.

Not only was he very good technically, he possessed the ability to ride the bike and had everything about him to win big meetings. We worked on a lot of aspects of his gating and riding techniques. Next to Ole Olsen he

The Will To Win – 319

probably was the most receptive rider I have encountered, and there have been a few world and Under-21 champions among those I've taught.

I showed Kenny how I kept my record books and diaries and encouraged him to be brutally honest with himself. He was such a true believer it may just have worked against him in the final analysis. Any summary of what he achieved and just how good he was cannot fail to be influenced by people's reaction to his tragic end.

I never knew the Kenny Carter who in 1986 killed his wife Pam and then shot himself. Neither Raye nor I saw the dark side and we had a lot to do with him during a two-year association as his manager, mentor and adviser from early 1981.

A long distance review of the Heat 14 clash with Penhall which defined Carter's frustration at The Coliseum depends on whose camp observers were in at the time. Bruce was behind but drew level just before Kenny had to bale out as both riders got too close to the fence.

I will always consider the most important factor was Tore Kittilsen, the referee who made the decision to exclude Kenny. It didn't surprise me because he had a reputation for not excluding home country riders and awarding vital decisions in several previous instances. The other most talked-about case was in the World Pairs Final at Vojens in 1979 when Denmark won a controversial victory.

Kenny was not bothered about past history, although he had a serious problem with the American riders whom he detested, and he always had a chip on his shoulder about the way the Collins boys so often seemed to him to be much more in favour than he was.

The fact Penhall won his first title on English soil only intensified the hostility between KC, Bruce and most of the other Americans who didn't care much for the tough all-action Carter's antics on or off the track. Kenny was too preoccupied with dishing out some payback for past incidents when he should have had a single focus, which was to win the title.

He could have been champion in 1981 at Wembley when he stopped in one race while leading – on my bike! To be fair, Erik Gundersen had a similar misfortune and the two of them might so easily have been in a three-way run-off with Bruce. The world championship is littered with 'what if' stories.

Carter's real hard luck story went all the way back to a difficult childhood. Raye and I did our best to be supportive and encouraging when he and Pam came on a tour to New Zealand in the early part of 1982. They were barely out of their teens, and looked younger.

Preparing for the LA meeting he had more than his own demons to deal with. He hadn't ridden in England for weeks because of punctured lungs and ribs following a crash. Nobody realised how badly injured he was.

320 – *Ivan Mauger*

Kenny and I went to California a couple of weeks in advance of the final and he was in really bad condition. We sat in my hot spa for three hours a day just talking and going over what needed to be done at The Coliseum.

There was never any doubt about Kenny's ambition. Sure he was many of the things that people have said about him, self-centred, determined, aggressive. He had everything needed to be a world champion including absolute faith in his own ability, and he didn't care a stuff for anyone who didn't like him.

That's normal for anybody who wants to be a winner but he could be his own worst enemy. He couldn't help himself, often speaking his mind when some reactions and thoughts were best left unsaid. He couldn't get his head around the fact that all his rivals were perfectly entitled to be just as determined and ambitious as he was.

The fact he was British to the core and made such a play of it was one of the factors which worked against him in Los Angeles. Using a Weslake engine, a Comet frame made in Yorkshire, and components including several I organised from many of my UK sponsors, was a statement of national pride.

But it cost him big time. At practice his father came into the pits with a stack of tyres the Dunlop factory had made specially for him for the LA final. The Dunlop was only 100mm wide and the American-manufactured Carlisle, at 110mm, put so much more rubber on the track and they were so obviously the best tyre for the job. Most of the riders were using them and Kenny had one on and was going like a rocket in practice.

Then his dad started on about how the Americans couldn't make decent tyres and told him to put on the Dunlop. Kenny, the kid who always wanted to do things his way, meekly obeyed and it was a decision which had huge ramifications. Back at the condo I urged him to stick with the Carlisles for the meeting but he wouldn't go against his father's wishes.

Kenny managed to win his first three races at The Coliseum and was leading at the interval. But the script unravelled when a no-holds-barred Heat 14 tussle with his arch-rival ended with the English warrior crashing under the fence.

There was a lot of noise from Kenny's camp about what they wanted to do to Bruce but I told them there was no point blaming him. If Mal Carter hadn't brought those Dunlop tyres and insisted on them being used Kenny would have been 30 yards in front of Bruce. He was a very good fast starter but on the Dunlop he had been giving everybody a 10-yard start in the first half lap and that's not the way to win a world title.

The incredible Penhall-Carter scrap has long since passed into World Final folklore. To my later embarrassment I showed my anger very visibly at referee Tore Kittilesen's decision to exclude Carter.

The Will To Win – 321

No doubt I was over the top in what I said to him but that was a boilover from all those earlier questionable decisions dating back over the years.

Tore wasn't the only person to receive the benefit of my opinions. I told Kenny and his father a few home truths and it was not until the next morning that the red mist cleared a little. Kenny and I were in the spa again and I said if his dad was going to continue to interfere our relationship simply would not work.

For all his single-mindedness he was often prone to be deflected by some outside influence, be it his dad, some small-time sponsor or hanger-on. And some of his obsessions and personal rivalries were not helpful. You have to put all that stuff out of sight and out of mind. There was always the possibility of something or someone distracting his focus and we went our separate ways a few months later.

Of course some of the critics had a field day and I copped a lot of flak because of my involvement with Kenny. Simply, it was a case of putting my knowledge and experience at the disposal of a youngster who was desperate to learn. It wasn't the first time and nor would it be the last.

Accusations of 'conflict of interest' flew thick and fast but I don't buy that. Nothing about my association with Kenny Carter had an adverse impact on any aspect of the 1982 World Final – unless you count arguing with the referee – and the meeting achieved a great deal in pointing speedway towards the future.

It took the world championship to the world's most sought-after market, put the event in one of the great stadiums, and demonstrated that a perfect track could be put in and taken out within a matter of a few days. It was a blueprint the Grand Prix organisers adopted in later years.

Along the way, LA showed that the promotion of the most important event on the speedway calendar could safely be entrusted to someone other than the office-bound suits and ties and self-proclaimed career administrators of old. Winning a few world championships between us hadn't been a negative after all.

CHEERS – a taste of French sponsorship at Ricard headquarters in Paris

Heat 17

SIX AND OUT

THE critics had been writing me off for years and victory in Poland in 1979, my sixth speedway world title, finally convinced most of them to stop.

The more people wanted to see the back of me, the more determined I became to keep going.

But after Katowice, I was 40 and already a grandfather. It was hard to motivate myself to do everything you have to do if you want to keep winning the title.

For more than 15 years my training routine and eating and sleeping pattern was all designed around world championship qualifying meetings and the World Final. The truth is I was not prepared to put in the effort needed to win again.

I was determined to have more fun out of racing than I had when all I wanted to do was win the World Final. I was still doing a fair job for Hull and even allowed myself to be tempted into doing one more year than our original three-season contract had stipulated.

The grand plan, the exit strategy from England, was to spend the next three or four seasons riding long track and to enjoy those Sundays and occasional midweek meetings in Europe where I was getting very good money to race and also having a lot of fun.

There were offers to appear in countries including Hungary, Romania, Yugoslavia and France where I had not ridden much earlier in my career because there were other priorities. There was much to appeal about riding in unusual places and not having to worry every day of the week about being world champion, with all that entailed.

Instead of dashing in and out, it was great to take time to visit areas such as the South of France and be able to enjoy them more. Raye came with me which she wasn't able to do when the kids were young and I was racing more competitively. We got to stay for a few days in different countries, ended up with holidays down in Dubrovnik and other previously uncharted territory and had a great time.

I didn't train every day of the week and if we went to a meeting in, say, Budapest, we would have dinner on the Danube which I never would have done in the 1960s and 1970s. For 20 years enjoyment had come second to winning – winning was the fun part and the rest of it was hard work. It was time to change the balance.

324 – Ivan Mauger

We were able to contemplate this because in individual terms there was little left to prove and a couple of weeks after that last victory in Katowice, I took part in another piece of history which deserves to be considered as one of New Zealand's finest moments in speedway.

My World Team Cup farewell half a dozen years later, while not memorable from a result or points-scoring perspective, did contribute to one more entry into the archives of the sport. In the Overseas Final at Bradford's Odsal Stadium in May 1985, both Kym and I proudly wore the Kiwi breastplate. It is the only time a father and son had appeared in the same international side.

Kym was by now 25, and riding for Berwick – his fourth club, having started at Newcastle and then trying his luck at Glasgow and Weymouth. It was a huge moment for him and no less of a thrill for me.

Certainly the last few years of racing was a change from having one person to worry about – me.

In the intervening period, I continued to put my hand up for duty in all four championships and between 1980 and 1985, my 52nd and last, rode in 10 world finals – five in the pairs and five on long track.

After re-writing the record books in individual speedway, as the defending champion I was seeded to the next year's Commonwealth Final at Wimbledon, got 12 points and finished third.

The Inter Continental Final at White City offered a World Final berth for the top 10 scorers but proved a bridge too far this time and I only scored five. Keeping me company among the non-qualifiers were Ole Olsen, Scott Autrey and John Louis, which gives a hint as to the difficulty of the meeting.

The Down Under portion of my 1981 bid was almost like the good old days.

In February I won the New Zealand final at Napier with a maximum and just over three weeks later won the Australasian Final on the infield track at Liverpool, again going undefeated and breaking the track record three times.

That was a victory every bit as sweet and satisfying as winning at the Sydney Showground had been four years earlier.

Once more the so-called experts in the Aussie media confidently predicted that Ivan Mauger was now far too old and would not be able to handle the tight corners of the Liverpool track.

Easy pickings? I don't think so.There were four places up for grabs in Sydney and the non-qualifiers included Phil Crump and Billy Sanders. So much for the 'experts'.

STILL A WINNER – Australasian champion 1981 with runner-up Danny Kennedy (left) and third placegetter Larry Ross

It was back down to earth in July, though. At a rainy Inter Continental final in Vojens I managed four points, my least productive world championship round for 18 years.

Bruce Penhall served notice that he was fired up for the big one by going through the card and it was great to see Larry Ross make the cut. Ole was the 11th qualifier and John Louis, Dennis Sigalos and Kelly Moran occupied the three bottom places.

There was one more attempt in me; 14 points got me second behind Larry in the 1982 New Zealand final at Wellington.

My final speedway world championship meeting was on July 4 – the Overseas Final at White City won by Dave Jessup where half a dozen points were a couple short of the Inter Continental qualifying mark.

Again it was in good company – it also was the end of the road that year for Shawn Moran, Alan Grahame, Billy Sanders, Chris Morton and Phil Collins. Bear in mind too I was about to turn 43, Phil Crump was five months past his 30th and the other 14 riders on parade were all in their 20s.

From a promoting perspective, an angle of some interest to me because of my involvement with the running of the World Final in Los Angeles, the progress made by Bruce Penhall, Dennis Sigalos and Kelly Moran was good news. Bruce, however, for once did his golden image a bit of damage when he not so discreetly finished behind three fellow-countrymen in his last ride. And to think we once believed 'team riding' in individual events was the exclusive preserve of the Poles and Russians!

New Zealand riding stocks had never quite recovered from the retirement of Briggo and Ronnie. But the World Best Pairs remained a competition in which the Kiwis could usually be relied upon for some kind of a show.

Between 1969 and 1985, I was one half of a New Zealand pair in 15 finals, qualified for another and did not compete in 1975. In addition to striking gold in the first two, I collected runners-up medals with Briggo in Rybnik 1971, Ronnie at Borås in 1972, third with Briggo at Belle Vue 1974, second with Larry at Chorzów in 1978, a result we repeated at the same venue in 1981, and a third with Mitch Shirra at Lonigo in 1984.

The return to Katowice in '81 was so close to providing another gold medal. American buddies Bruce Penhall and Bobby Schwartz pipped us by a single point, with Plech and Jancarz another point adrift in the most close-fought meeting in the running of the event.

SIMPLY RED – helping with the harvest at the Kolbl family grape mill near Radenci, Yugoslavia (now Slovenia) as Raye and Erika Kolbl look on

The Will To Win – 327

Larry was my partner for seven consecutive years*, and we qualified for the 1982 final which was set down for Liverpool a fortnight before Christmas. I had a dodgy ankle and it wasn't too convenient to be in Australia at that time of year so Mitch partnered him in that one.

Larry and I reunited for a 1983 semi-final in Wrocław which we won convincingly, but then we finished last in the final at Gothenburg.

Mitch stepped up the next year and produced one of his best performances at international level in Italy, where Chris Morton and PC won on 27, with Denmark – in the shape of Hans Nielsen and Erik Gundersen – and New Zealand on 25. He was the best choice to go into the run-off but Hans denied us the silver.

The Danes went one better in Rybnik the following year, Tommy Knudsen partnering Erik to a near-faultless display. In my last pairs final, Mitch and I were not really at the races that day, finishing ahead of Sweden, Australia and Poland but behind the Brits and Americans.

Our lack of depth was rather more cruelly exposed in the World Team Cup. After our unbelievable success of 1979, I rode in the first round of each of the next six years, and whoever we fielded, it was never good enough to get into the next stage. It was almost as if we sensed there could not possibly be another meeting like that one at White City.

That victory, however, did identify New Zealand's potential, and set the bar at a height for future riders to challenge. With the format of the event as it is, it is difficult to see anything remotely like it happening again, but you never know.

In half a dozen Overseas Final appearances, we more or less made up the numbers on four of those occasions, the exceptions being third place at Reading in 1983 and again at Bradford in 1985 – when Kym rode. At least there was a positive angle to that one.

After collecting my sixth individual speedway championship I still had ambitions of trying to take out the world long track title again. For several years I was always one of three or four favourites to win but never did.

Mariánské Lázně in 1979 was a case in point. It was a track with good memories for me, although it was quite a struggle to qualify this time. My qualifying round was in Gornja Radgona. And in spite of having trouble in one race I got through comfortably enough.

The semi-final was at Scheeßel and that was safely negotiated but neither the bikes nor I had the same energy on the day of the final. I battled to put together eight points and finished well down in 11th place.

---

* I rode in pairs finals with Briggo at Eskilstuna (1976) Larry Ross at Belle Vue (1977), Katowice (1978), Vojens (1979), Krško (1980), Katowice (1981) and Gothenburg (1983), Mitch Shirra at Lonigo (1984) and Rybnik (1985).

COMING TOGETHER – crashing with Josef Aigner in the 1981 world long track final in Gornja Radgona

It was tight at the top with German's Alois Wiesböck finishing on 21 points, just one ahead of Anders Michanek with Ole Olsen a further point adrift.

My 1980 qualifying round produced a win at Korskro, followed by a second in the semi-final at Jübek in North Germany. Once again though, the World Final at Scheeβel was a big disappointment and I ended up seventh although amazingly I was beaten on the day only by German riders.

They had things all their own way by claiming the first six places – a championship record. Karl Maier had five points to spare ahead of Egon Müller, and next came Josef Aigner, Christoph Betzl, Georg Hack and Wilhelm Duden.

There would have been yet another German on the honours list but Alois Wiesböck, placed third initially, was later disqualified when a machine examination showed his motor measured 502cc, just over the limit.

The following year was eventful but for the wrong reason. Fourth in a qualifying round at Harsewinkel was followed by third in the Pfarrkirchen semi-final. The final at Gornja Radgona was a disaster. In my third ride I crashed at almost 200 kilometres an hour with Josef Aigner three quarters of the way along the back straight.

Aigner was doing the typical German trick of weaving down the straight which a lot of his fellow countrymen did to fill in the riders coming behind

OVER AND OUT – a badly broken ankle brought Ivan's season to a premature end

them. I made a bad start, passed Jiří Štancl and PC around the first turn and was catching up to Aigner very quickly when he swerved to the left.

My right ankle and foot went between the back wheel and his left suspension leg and I went end over end with Aigner's bike for about 50 or 60 metres. My right heel was almost cut off by his chain but the surgeon at the hospital in Mureck stitched it back on again. Apart from the stitch marks it has been perfect ever since.

I broke the bottom of my right leg and the ankle in many places and a lot of bones in the front of my foot and all my toes were broken. I put up with the pain for a long time but had major correctional surgery performed by Terry Saxby in Brisbane in April 2009. I was in plaster for about three and a half months but it came up perfectly and I can now walk straight with no pain and no limp.

Carlo Biagi wanted to do exactly the same operation when I saw him at the start of the 1982 season. But I was still fired up to try to win another long track title. To have had the op at that stage would have ruined my chances for that season.

Instead I finished third at the Mühldorf qualifier, and got second in the semi-final at Vilshofen. Sixth place in the final at Korskro wasn't a bad effort, but again the Germans were close to irresistible with Karl Maier heading off the challenge of Alois Wiesböck and Egon Müller.

The competitive spirit was still burning and everybody knew it. After a third place in my 1983 qualifying round at Gornja Radgona the semi-final was at Scheeßel and I was the last person to qualify for the final.

Things seemed fine early on but after going from first to fourth in one race because the generator was misfiring I needed to make sure I finished in my last outing. Just one point would put me ahead of the Austrian Walter Grubmüller. We changed the coil, did a few practice starts in the car park and everything looked promising. I jumped out of the start and then the bike started missing badly and riders were flying past me.

On the last lap I noticed someone had pulled out and was sitting on the centre green so there still was a point on offer. Then my engine stopped completely, 700 metres from home. There was nothing for it but to leg it for three quarters of a lap It was an extremely hot day and I did not want to waste time taking off my steel shoe, goggles and gloves so I ran and pushed it as fast as I could.

Kai Niemi and several other riders came out to encourage me but without touching me because that would have meant disqualification.

LONG WALK – pushing home for three quarters of a lap at Scheeßel to clinch a world long track final qualification place, 1983

Michael Lee, who won the 1981 final I missed through injury, was standing next to Norrie Allan in the pits and said for that effort I deserved to get to the final. I crossed the line with about five seconds to spare.

There was no happy ending though. My fitness had paid off and got me to the final. But at Mariánské Lázně I again got 10 points and had to settle for ninth overall.

Someone somewhere might have been trying to send me a message suggesting it was time to give it away. My 1984 qualifying round was at Vilshofen which produced a second place. Negotiating the semi at Pffarrkirchen was a much tougher business.

I was leading my second ride and at the end of the back straight my Godden engine broke a con rod and I was thrown over the handlebars at 200 plus km an hour. The fly wheels came out the side of the crank cases and after I stopped rolling end over end I heard a thump when they went through the safety fence halfway around the corner.

The steward disqualified me as the cause of the stoppage and organisers had to repair the fence. When I got back to the pits the track doctor said he would not let me ride again. I had to prove everything was fine in a bizarre fitness test, jumping up and down waving my arms, and sprinting 30 metres backwards and forwards before he allowed me to continue.

I had won my third race and I collected another in my last outing which got me into the final at Herxheim. That meeting started with a bad third when my outside suspension leg broke at the end of the first lap. It was a struggle to keep the bike on the track.

I was leading my next race when the ignition coil come loose, started shorting out on the engine and I eventually finished third. I did not complete the next heat after the left suspension leg broke as a result of the strain it had in the first race so my five points got me 13th. A new name, that of Erik Gundersen, appeared at the top of the list.

And next year Simon Wigg started off on his sequence of titles, winning in Korskro. A qualifier in Gornja Radgona and a second spot in the semi-final at Vilshofen got me to my last championship final.

No storybook finish here, though. After a second in my first race I did not finish any other races so four points got me 15th overall, not quite the farewell flourish I would have liked.

Apart from overseas meetings I did not expect to be riding speedway again in England after Hull finished. There were approaches from time to time, nothing terribly serious, and to be honest the desire to be involved in league racing had been well and truly satisfied.

That situation did not change when Midland Sports, the company which owned and operated Coventry and also owned Leicester's venue, dropped a

THE LAST TIME – Ivan leading Hans Nielsen and Bobby Schwartz in his last world long track final at Korskro, 1985

bombshell by announcing they were selling the Blackbird Road stadium to Barratts for a massive housing development.

That information hit the fan a couple of weeks after the end of the 1983 season. One person it did interest greatly was my old manager and sometime promoting and business partner Peter Oakes. Together with a couple of businessmen in the south-west, he was keen to take Exeter back into the top division – a status they relinquished when Wally Mawdsley decided to switch from British League to New National League in 1980.

For a number of reasons Exeter had found it difficult to continue in the top flight and reportedly they lost a lot of money.

Peter had such fond memories of our successful years there, and even moved down to Dawlish where he and his wife Pam lived for several years. The fact he was by now London sports editor of the *Daily Star* didn't deter him from his dream of reviving the Falcons at the top level.

Entry into the British League didn't come cheap but Peter saw Leicester's misfortune as his perfect chance to acquire an existing first division licence and the framework of a ready-made team.

The Will To Win – 333

The Lions had been left with little or no time or opportunity to conjure up a replacement venue. A deal was quickly put together in time for the Falcons to present themselves at the BSPA annual conference as a paid-up member of the 1984 competition.

Where Peter and his backers miscalculated was in believing they would be able to tempt Leicester riders such as Les and Neil Collins to the County Ground. Like many others down the years, they considered one trip a year to Exeter to be the extent of their interest in heading to Devon.

Exeter had bought the benefit of the rider contracts and as such they were powerful bargaining chips in the transfer market even if the individuals concerned didn't fancy Exeter as their new home base. The second and third brothers in the Collins clan were quality performers around whom any British League track might begin to build a side.

But they lived in Lymm, just down the road from me, and reasonably enough calculated there were a dozen tracks closer to home and more likely to suit their relocation plans, not that they had any plans – both had been negotiating new multi-year contracts in the expectation Leicester would be running indefinitely.

I was back in Christchurch enjoying the New Zealand summer break when Peter Oakes phoned me to say he was having trouble in putting together a team. I said I would have a word to see if Larry Ross might be interested.

Larry had gone to Belle Vue from Wimbledon and in three years there was a very solid and consistent performer but he wasn't likely to be No.1 as long as Peter Collins and Chris Morton were on the scene.

However he was not keen so I tried Scott Autrey in Texas. Scotty had developed into a class act at Exeter, finished third in the world in 1978, and later did sterling service for Swindon before quitting at the end of 1982 when only 29. Despite a year away he would have been a perfect fit for the Falcons.

He gave it some thought for a couple of days before deciding to stay retired. He had other plans in mind, including a crack at NASCAR racing, so it was a question of 'thanks, but no thanks' from him as well.

The suggestions didn't stop there but other riders I approached were not interested either, Bobby Schwartz and Václav Verner among them, whereupon Peter threw me a curve ball and asked if I would come out of retirement.

He said he could involve different sponsors who could do a great deal for me and it got to the stage where a lot of money was being talked about. One problem though was Exeter rode on Monday nights.

Raye and I had got used to spending the best part of the week elsewhere in Europe and getting back to the County Ground for Monday nights would be much more of a problem than it ever had been in my 1973–77 stint with the Falcons.

One night, very much tongue-in-cheek, I said to Peter how it sounded great with all those sponsors and different things lined up. I still had my relationship with IVECO in Europe and they said they would help out if I rode again in the British League.

The fact of the matter is I didn't particularly want to ride in England but said if Peter could find a way whereby I only had to do home meetings they would seem like open events to me – especially if they were run on Friday nights.

It still amazes me and most promoters that I have spoken to about it but Peter went to the BSPA management committee and got what we wanted. He phoned from London to say he had been given permission to change from Mondays to Fridays and also that I was allowed to do home meetings only. I could hardly believe it.

It was a one-off decision and will never happen again. People like Briggo, Ole Olsen and Anders Michanek, all of whom had come to a stage at which they wanted to scale back but always hit a brick wall when they tried for such a dispensation, couldn't believe we got away with it.

It is an open-ended argument as to whether it was a decision made in the best interests of speedway. It got the new British League venture out of a huge hole, but the season didn't go well for the promotion and in company with several other tracks, they didn't front up for top-division action the following year. It certainly didn't benefit any of the other tracks who usually had their worst crowds of the year when Exeter were the visitors – unlike 1973–77 during which they were guaranteed crowd pullers.

That was not my concern, and I really enjoyed that extra season back at Exeter. There was no pressure on me to try to be the best rider in the league. We had Neil Street as team manager, there were a lot of young guys in the team – riders like Andy Campbell, Sean Wilmott, Louis Carr and Frank Andersen – and it was a good year working with them.

We brought in Leif Wahlmann from Sweden and Buddy Robinson from America and things seemed to be looking up after a scratchy start. Then Wahlmann was killed in the European Under-21 championship and in summary, it was probably Peter Oakes's toughest year in speedway.

I did him what I hoped was a favour and the opportunity to meet up with and race against all the old favourites as well as a few emerging newcomers was a surprise but entertaining experience for me. Like me, Exeter were not the force of old but we did have some fun.

The Will To Win – 335

Riders often have a problem in identifying exactly the right moment to give it away, and I didn't want to be one of them. During 1984 I put a lot of work into planning and organising a 30-Year Jubilee Series which would bring down the curtain on my racing career.

For a while promoters in Europe started to ask me when I planned to retire because they wanted to have a special meeting for me before I finished. That gave me the idea for the long goodbye.

An important component was staging a series of meetings in Australia which required the goodwill and co-operation of the governing body as well as the various tracks who expressed interested in taking the show.

One Friday, I raced at Exeter, rode in Germany on the Saturday and Sunday and left Frankfurt airport on Monday morning to go to Sydney where the Australasian Promoters Association conference was being held at the Showground.

It was very early on the Wednesday when I got to Sydney. Jim Airey picked me up and we went directly from the airport to the meeting which went on until about 5.30pm. It was a worthwhile exercise as we arranged the dates and schedules with the Aussie promoters.

Then we went back to Jimmy's house for an overnight stay. On Thursday morning I had to fly from Sydney to Melbourne to do a deal with Shell who with IVECO were to be the major sponsors of the series so Jimmy took me to the airport at 7am and picked me up again at about noon.

I had some negotiations to do with Champion and IVECO during the early afternoon. By half past five I was getting ready to board the plane back to London.

With the time difference, I got in to Heathrow at what should have felt like breakfast time. It was an opportunity to grab an hour or two of relaxation until Falcons teammate Andy Campbell and his mechanic picked me up to go to Exeter for the meeting that evening.

Later that night they dropped me back to the Post House Airport Hotel so I was on the spot to fly to Munich on the Saturday. I rode in Germany on Sunday, Italy on Monday and Austria on Tuesday, returned from Graz via Frankfurt and Heathrow and got back to Manchester airport at about 11.30am on Wednesday.

That afternoon I was knackered and lying on the lawn asleep. My granddaughter Josie, who was four and a half, woke me up and asked: 'Granddad, haven't you got a proper job?'

She obviously thought everyone else went to work at eight o'clock and came home at five in the afternoon but I didn't have the luxury of a routine like that. Sometimes I was home for two or three days in a row but other

336 – *Ivan Mauger*

times could be away for four or five – or in this case 12, with a series of flights and 25,000 miles on the frequent flyer card.

The Farewell to Australia tour schedule took in a number of old familiar places and quite a few new ones some of which were unlike anything I had encountered in my career. We arranged more than a dozen meetings and a number of outstanding riders and good friends were full of enthusiasm for the whole thing, which started on Boxing Day and ran into the second week of February.

It was quite a galaxy of international stars, with world champions and national champions – we had Hans Nielsen from Denmark, Simon Wigg, Peter Collins and Kelvin Tatum from England, Germany's Karl Maier, Zoltán Adorján (Hungary), Václav Verner (Czechoslovakia), Armando Castagna from Italy, Dutchman Henny Kroeze, Kai Niemi and Olli Tyrväinen of Finland.

One champion who couldn't make it was Erik Gundersen. He had agreed to come but then after winning his first world title in Gothenburg in September 1984, followed immediately by the long track title, he had so many commitments back in Denmark he became a non-starter.

That opened the door for Hans Nielsen, who hadn't embarked upon his spree of title wins but clearly was putting together the results which made him a certain champion of the near future. It turned out to be a good break for Hans because he won the series, and Raye and I formed quite a friendship with him and his wife Suzanne which later translated into a business arrangement in the 1986 season.

We raced at places like Mildura and Liverpool, as well as featuring in the first meeting at Melbourne Showground. A few meetings fell by the wayside for different reasons but everyone had a great time. I did enough to finish third in the points (Wiggy was second) and had some days when I wished it could go on indefinitely, and others when I was relieved the time was approaching when I could put my feet up.

Speedway's greatest road trip kicked off at Claremont in Perth after which we headed to the mining community of Tom Price, about 1400 miles (2250 kilometres) to the north-east in the middle of Western Australia. The trip was sponsored by Hamersley Iron, a mega-rich iron ore company.

They used to take singers and comedians up there to entertain the very small community at the mines which were about 500 miles (800 kilometres) from anywhere. We were placed in the same category to entertain the mine workers and it paid well for me and all the boys.

Tom Price was 105 degrees in the shade all day every day and half way through the meeting the manager of Hamersley Iron came to me and asked if we could do another show the following night. I said there wouldn't be any time to advertise a second meeting, but apparently this was no problem.

HAPPY SNAPPER – Debbie was official photographer for the farewell meetings in Australia, New Zealand, Poland, Germany and the UK

All it required was a message on the notice board because everyone in town worked at the mines. By all accounts there were a few hundred guys working down the mines who could not get to see the first show and he didn't want them to miss out.

He said he would pay exactly the same guarantee so I said OK, went to tell the boys and they all agreed. So we left the bikes in the pits and put our leathers over the handlebars because they were wringing wet with sweat. Then we went back and did the same thing all over again.

A couple of days later we set off for Port Hedland which is just over 500 miles to the north-west. It was on the coast and cooler there, only about 100 degrees. The mining company put on a big bus for us and a large covered truck to take all the bikes, kit bags, tool boxes and other gear and supplied drivers and fuel on top of the sponsorship.

After another outback gig at Mount Newman, we headed down the coast road to Perth to fly to Adelaide which promised to be a little bit cooler and with a bit more to see.

338 – Ivan Mauger

The mining company also provided the big truck to cross the infamous Nullarbor Plain. It had to negotiate 2000 miles of the hottest most arid road in the history of mankind including three different time zones.

Closer to civilisation, we stopped off to a meeting at Broken Hill when Brian (Hollywood) Parsons – father of Scunthorpe's Joel – got the local club to join the tour. We were getting to see places few if any of us had ever visited and the locals turned out in force to watch the travelling circus.

It was more than a speedway tour, it was a shared experience all the better for the fact Raye, Kym and Debbie were involved. Kym and I rode in the meetings, Raye was the social director as usual and Debbie the series photographer.

Debbie also took all the official photographs in Europe, Australia and New Zealand over the next few months. It turned out to be a very wide-ranging portfolio as we did two farewell meetings in Poland, three in Germany, one in Scotland and another in England before heading back for the 1985–86 New Zealand series.

A long-time friendship with Wladislaw Pietrzak who was President of the CCP (Track Racing Commission of the FIM) as well as being President of Polzki Zwiazek Motorowy (PZM) opened the door for the meetings there.

Unlike the last 10 years or so in which riders have routinely gone to Poland each weekend, between 1965–85 my only trips there were for world championship meetings and official Test match appearances.

A lot of them included some of my most memorable moments and I got to know a lot of guys in Polish speedway.

Mr Pietrzak arranged for farewell meetings at Gniezno – where they gave me the Freedom of the City before the racing started – and at Leszno the next day. The organisers paid me a lot of Polish zlotys which in the fashion of the time all the boys had to spend while we were there.

They also provided a plane that held about 120 people and had room for all the western riders we took over, their bikes and equipment. The hotels for everyone were included, as well as bus transfers from the airport to the hotel in Gniezno, on to Leszno and back to the airport.

In addition to the riders I invited family members, about 30 or 40 other special guests, and then sold all the other tickets to supporters. Everybody had a blast although not everything went to plan. I crashed in my first race in Gniezno, collecting a cut above my right eye and some damage to my right foot. That was the end of my active participation in the back-to-back meetings.

As I wasn't riding in British League there was a bit more time in which to plan for the New Zealand series which was to be the final signature. As with the Australian tour, that required a flying visit Down Under to set up and fine-tune arrangements.

I rode in the World Pairs final at Rybnik with Mitch Shirra and travelled in the transporter overnight with Norrie Allan. He dropped me at Frankfurt airport on the Monday and I flew from Frankfurt to Auckland and then on to Wellington for the New Zealand Speedway Promoters Association conference.

Terry Lock, a mate and longtime neighbour from Woolston, came up to Wellington to meet me. He and his wife Shirley looked after our affairs in New Zealand from the early 1970s. At the conference we arranged 13 or 14 Farewell to New Zealand meetings. In the end we were to do several more.

Back in the UK the British promoters, many of whom had recognised after all the years that I wasn't such a bad bloke, gave permission for a Farewell to Scotland at Powderhall in Edinburgh (which Peter Collins won) and the Ivan Mauger Farewell to England at Belle Vue.

GOODBYE POLAND – on parade at Gniezno before receiving the freedom of the city in 1985

SITTING OUT – with Josie, out of the Leszno meeting because of injury

THANKS GUYS – lining up for the Farewell to England at Belle Vue, left to right, Neil Evitts, Erik Gundersen, Peter Collins, Phil Collins, Carl Blackbird, Jan O Pedersen, Andy Smith, Chris Morton, Larry Ross, Kai Niemi, Hans Nielsen, Les Collins, John Cook, Stephen Collins, Neil Collins, Preben Eriksen, Tommy Knudsen, Simon Wigg.

It felt right to do my last meeting at Hyde Road. Of all the tracks this was the one where I had as much success and enjoyment as anywhere. The hours of having the place to myself for solitary practice sessions meant as much to me as winning league titles or the BLRC.

I did a deal with Stuart Bamforth who owned the place in its last few years. Bammy was a bit of a rough diamond but he was a very successful and astute businessman and we both earned a quid from the meeting which I promoted myself.

We had more than 20,000 people, and it was the first time I knew accurately what sort of numbers attended big events at 'the zoo'. From that crowd we gauged there had been around 15,000 most nights when I was racing for the Aces, and over 20,000 for the BLRC.

Erik Gundersen, who had just collected his second successive speedway world title, won the meeting and John Cook went past Hans Nielsen on the last corner to claim second place on the night.

Now it was time for the last, extended goodbye in New Zealand. Julie stayed in Woodford to look after our little dog and Raye, Kym and I boarded the flight to Christchurch with a confused set of emotions. There was pleasure after the European meetings went so well, sadness at leaving so many old friends and acquaintances, and excitement and anticipation as to what the final leg would bring.

The line-up for New Zealand included some of the guys who had done Australia and a number of different ones. Simon Wigg – a genuine world champion by now – Kai Niemi and Olli Tyvainen were back. Newcomers included Bobby Schwartz and John Cook (USA) and Neil Evitts who went on to win the British title a few months later.

Then there were young Poles Grzegorz Dzikowski and Ryszard Francyszyn, Finland's Juha Moksunen, Einar Kyllingstad (Norway) and Manchester lad Barry Ayres (who was a mate of Kym's). And we built in a strong Kiwi component with Larry Ross, Mitch Shirra and David Bargh.

While we were getting ourselves sorted out there was the added distraction – a pleasant one – of filming *Circuits of Gold* which was and remains one of the best glimpses into my career. The first approach came from Jonathon Anyon of the New Zealand National Film Unit.

Jonathan was the producer and he and the crew followed us around for a few weeks, taking in the series and finishing off at Alexandra Park in Auckland. What made it extra special was setting a world long track speed record of 144.66 kilometres an hour round the trotting track.

The record still stands, something which gives me great pride. A few have got close to it over the past few years with mono shock bikes that keep the rear wheel on the ground, laydown engines, leading link forks, bikes that weigh 84kg and most importantly, softer compound rear tyres.

I rode a Hagon sand racer with a Hans Zierk-tuned Godden engine. My bike was 89kg. It had twin rear shocks that let the rear wheel bounce around and 15 horsepower less than the modern riders.

It made for a very different and attention-grabbing introduction to the film which eventually screened around April of that year, had numerous re-runs and after it went out on general release in VHS format sold a stack of copies around the world.

The farewell series eventually turned out to be 16 meetings and John Cook topped the score charts with 150 points, followed by Larry Ross on 113 and I was third on 101. In spite of being so bound up with the operation and smooth running of the whole show, the old guy could still ride a bike.

It was a great trip, Hertz provided six mini buses and a big enclosed truck for the series and a reasonable amount of money. Champion were the main naming rights sponsor and there were other good sponsorships from Shell, Suzuki and IVECO NZ.

PULL THE OTHER ONE – during the filming of Circuits of Gold

It was never going to be a case of all work and no play and Cookie was in the lead mini bus with a couple of jetskis on the trailer.

We did the South Island first with meetings at Templeton in Christchurch and the Dunedin stock car track near the beach and at Riverview Speedway in Invercargill.

The Cromwell club didn't want a round at first but after seeing the Dunedin show wanted to fit one in over the Christmas holiday before we headed off to Nelson. We changed our plans and Raye got us some cabins beside the lake at Queenstown.

Riders, mechanics, wives and girlfriends had a few days there before doing Cromwell and then rushing back up to Nelson. Cookie and Schwartzy were in charge of the jetskis and all the boys and a lot of the girls had a great time on the lake – including Debbie, Kym and me. Raye only liked to go slow on the jetskis despite everyone encouraging her to go flat out.

Dzikowski, who was a reserve for the 1985 World Final, earned himself the nickname of 'Felloffajetski' because of his inability to stay on a ski for more that a few moments.

We kicked off the series at Templeton on Boxing Day. In the new year we moved on to the North Island leg where we rode places such as Stratford, Rotorua, Gisborne, Napier and Palmerston North. One or two of the tracks were hesitant at first but once the word spread that all the meetings were pulling in big crowds, they immediately wanted us to fit them in too.

On the first weekend of February there was a break in the schedule and I took advantage by nipping across to Adelaide for the South Australia 150-year anniversary celebration, my last meeting in Australia.

It was quite a significant occasion because the venue was Wayville Showgrounds, where SA notables Jack Young, Bob Leverenz and Merv Harding all started. It was the first meeting there for 40 years.

Even better, Youngie and Kym Bonython were there for the occasion. John Cook flew across with me and the line-up included Shawn Moran, Phil Crump and Rick Miller. Moran topped the qualifying scorers but in the eight-rider, six-lap final I signed off with a victory. Shawn broke a chain when lying second on the final lap. Crumpie and Cookie took the minor placings.

To receive the trophy from Youngie and have Kym Bonython on hand was very fitting, given the huge influence both of them had my early years and subsequent success. It had been a long haul since the Rowley Park days, even longer since my debut at Aranui.

GOING OUT A WINNER – Ivan racing towards victory in his last meeting in Australia, at Wayville Showgrounds

344 – *Ivan Mauger*

Back in New Zealand, the last meeting in the series, and my last competitive appearance, was at Waikaraka Park, Auckland.

The preferred scenario was to sign off at Western Springs, where I'd had many good memories and got on well with Harley Arthur and Reece Facoory who ran the place down the years. As it happened the stadium was not available until two weeks later – by which time virtually all the overseas riders would have gone.

Harley said he would put on the meeting at Waikaraka Park which normally housed stock cars. He was an expert at putting down a track to suit the bikes and we practised on the 460-metre stock car circuit with all the TV stations and newspapers in attendance. It was perfect.

But when I asked for a permit from the New Zealand Speedway Control Board – a commission appointed by the Auto Cycle Union – they told me Western Springs had the speedway licence for the greater Auckland area and they would have to ask George Tervitt, the promoter, if he would agree. Tervitt, who according to Harley was upset he could not have my final meeting at Western Springs, refused permission.

There always is a way to do something if at first you don't succeed and Harley found an answer. He said the ACU controlled speedways which measured from 285 metres up to 500 metres, so why not make the track 280 metres and put an injunction on the NZACU which would protect the rider's licences. We got a permit through the Onehunga Motor Cycle Club for the riders' insurance purposes and officials from the club confirmed the track length on the documents they sent to the NZACU.

At about midnight on the Thursday – less than 48 hours before the meeting – Harley bulldozed through the centre green, created a new first and second corner, and made a new track of 284 metres, more out of devilment than anything else. The following afternoon Graeme Halse, of Reece Facoory's Auckland law firm Foy and Halse, filed a High Court injunction on our behalf – late enough for us to go ahead with the meeting, too late for the ACU to put in a counter injunction.

Graeme said the riders would be fine with their FIM international licences under the terms of the injunction and as an added precaution on race night, I had police on all the gates with photos of the SCB and NZACU people from their handbook and instructed them to refuse entry to any of those personnel.

As to the meeting itself, 10,000 people turned up, a good time was had by all and everything was set for a 10-man, 10-lap grand finale. Mitch Shirra, who wasn't part of the troupe, rode a GM which was not an approved manufacturer for the series, and won the decider from John Cook and Neil Evitts, followed by Larry Ross and myself.

It would have been nice to sign off with a victory, but in the final analysis, one less or one more, it didn't matter. I should recount just what my feelings were as I completed the last lap of my final race, but to be honest, it passed in a blur.

The first emotion to hit me after receiving the chequered flag was one of relief – for the first time in 30 years I didn't have to go to the gym to train my backside off the following day! I knew I would be putting on the leathers again in the future, but strictly for fun.

I even got to ride again at Western Springs later in the month, doing some match races with Neil Evitts for television and also receiving an official send-off from Prime Minister David Lange, who honoured me with his presence. He spoke some very kind words in the parade, there were brass bands and all the bells and whistles.

And then, suddenly, it really was all over.

HONOUR – farewelled by Prime Minister David Lange at Western Springs

Heat 18

ON GOLDEN POND

RAYE and I had such good associations with and memories of Australia, perhaps it was inevitable we should settle there when the racing had to stop. We have called the Gold Coast home for almost 25 years.

The Gold Coast is one of the most attractive places on earth, with more than 30 miles (50 kilometres) of unbroken sand fronting the Pacific Ocean, inland waterways, a boating paradise, great weather all year round, and a terrific lifestyle.

It is Australia's playground, home to theme parks and tourist attractions, and an exciting, fast-paced, fast-growing area of south-east Queensland less than an hour south of Brisbane, the state capital.

We always had great times in Australia, and had many friends there so it was a natural fit. It was where everyone wanted to be. Barry Sheene, the former world motorcycling champion, had come to the Gold Coast in 1985 from England, and Jim Airey, a longtime speedway friend and rival, sold his motorcycle business and moved up from Sydney the following year.

New Zealanders have right of abode and access to all the perks and privileges Aussies enjoy, so it was an easy transition.

Yet we didn't see it coming.

It always was our intention to settle back in Christchurch when I stopped racing all over the world. And that is what happened – for a few weeks.

Usually at the end of February we waved goodbye to our friends in New Zealand, got on the plane and went to California for a week or so, occasionally to Daytona, and then back to England.

But after my final meeting, we farewelled all the international riders and their mechanics, wives and so on at Auckland airport and went back to Rocking Horse Road. We had it tenanted for some time and in later years kept it as a perfect place to which to bolt when we were back in town.

My mum Rita and Raye's mother Nan were still in Christchurch and so too were relatives and friends from the old days.

Rita had somewhat reluctantly moved out of 50 Isis Street and was living round the corner at Clydesdale Street in Woolston.

The Isis Street house had needed a lot of work. Colin Tucker, whom we met in Auckland in 1965 and later built Crewe, Barrow, Hull and a few other speedway tracks in England, flew down and made a list of everything. It

RETIREMENT STATEMENT – two days after his final appearance at Alexandra Park, Ivan and granddaughters Sadie and Josie celebrate landing a 107kg marlin at the Bay of Islands

348 – Ivan Mauger

worked out to be a costly exercise and after doing all those repairs it would still be an old house.

Raye and I wanted to buy Mum somewhere new but she was very fixed in her ways and said she didn't want to move because 'all my friends know where I live and they know my phone number'.

Unbeknown to her, we looked at properties for two or three weeks. When we found the right place which was close enough so she could keep her phone number, and took her to have a look at it, she was as keen as could be and decided she was happy to move.

It was quite a new place with a sunny outlook and from the kitchen window Mum could see the Port hills, which she loved to look from the verandah at Isis Street. Better still, from the lounge and out the back door she had a great all-round view of the Southern Alps which looked majestic in the winter with snow on them.*

Bernie Lagrosse was another good rider/carpenter and a friend since school days who bought and sold several houses in and around Christchurch. He would buy old ones, do them up and then sell them for a profit. He happily bought Isis Street and did the same there.

Our intention was to buy a really big house on Cashmere Hills with views to the Canterbury Plains and also looking out to the mountains. But that didn't happen.

We thought when we planned to live in Christchurch we could have meals with all our old friends and pick up the social threads. I could play golf, get out the jetski and generally live the life of a retired gentleman.

In the event many of our old friends who got married much later than we did had children who were maybe seven to 10 years old and could not go out with us on Friday nights or Saturday nights to restaurants or functions.

In the first few days back there I started playing golf with Bernie Lagrosse and some of my other mates. By halfway through March it began raining and for much of the time the golf courses were closed because of puddles on the fairways.

The real shock to the system was how cold it got midway through March. For 30 years we had only ever known Christchurch in January and February when invariably it was nice and summery.

The Gold Coast was entering a big growth phase with development and a huge push to consolidate its position as Australia's premier tourist

---

* My niece Jacqui used to stay at Clydesdale Street at the weekends and came to love the house. After Mum died in 2003 she bought it from us, so it's still in the family. Raye's mother passed away in 1988.

destination. The waterways were magic and because of the temperate year-round weather it was a magnet for interstate and overseas tourists.

It was very warm there so from the middle of April we started doing trips to the so-called sunshine strip, where on a typical winter day the temperature would be between 21–28 degrees with hardly a cloud to be seen.

Raye and I hopped across the Tasman so often and caught up with a lot of mates including Ronda and Jim Airey and New Zealand motocrosser Graham Sword and his wife Sarah.

We enjoyed ourselves so much it got to the stage where we thought we should buy a small place on the Gold Coast to spend the winters there, and then buy another house on the hill in Christchurch.

Back in England, Julie was married and already had Josie and Sadie, while Kym and Debbie were still single. But from when we went to New Zealand in November 1985, and frequently during telephone conversations, the kids said they planned to wait before coming over to make sure where we were settled as they all wanted to live close to Mum and Dad.

Even though we were certain about wanting to return to the southern hemisphere, equally certain was that we wouldn't completely cut our ties with the European racing scene which had been so much a part of our lifestyle for years.

There were plenty of opportunities to continue with some involvement in the sport and hooking up with Hans Nielsen in a consultancy and management role, to be followed later by a similar arrangement with Simon Wigg, kept me close to things.

But I think the kids must have known we were going to end up on the Gold Coast. It did happen at last on one of those trips in the southern winter of 1987 when we saw a house in Runaway Bay that was partially built and faced north to water.

It was property boom time, the Coast was going a hundred miles an hour and people were building houses flat out. On the spot we made the builder an offer although only part of the downstairs framework was completed.

Without so much as looking round he said if he didn't get the price he wanted by the end of the week, he was going to take it off the market, semi-complete it in the next six weeks and then put it back on sale at about $50,000 more than the price as it stood. Raye and I definitely wanted it so we agreed the price on the spot.

The builder was Les Nichols, a good old craftsman from Tasmania – and everything was an extra. We went out next to the canal and he told us of his plan to put in a kidney shaped swimming pool. We said to him we wanted a long pool so we could swim laps. That would be an extra, he said. We soon learned that everything with Les was an extra.

350 – Ivan Mauger

Most Fridays for the next couple of months I would visit him and pay for all those extras. Whenever we asked for anything such as door handles, bathroom taps, or sliding doors to the patio, they were all extras. Les said he was going to build a double garage I told him we wanted a triple garage. You guessed it … that was also an extra and more to find on Friday.

There were several other houses on the island or near us and I wanted him to build me a boat shed. Les said he hadn't time to build boat sheds as he had houses to build which earned him a lot more money.

So I got a front end loader to scoop out my boat shed, Bernie Lagrosse came over to do the block work, and Jim Airey was around pretty much every second day looking at the progress.

During the building of the boat shed we had to be a couple of metres back from the canal and a certain height. The same Gold Coast City Council inspector came round to inspect the slab and the back wall. It was lucky Jim was there because he recognised him from the Sydney Showground days.

That worked perfectly because when Jim said Ivan wanted the boat shed a little bit taller than was allowed. The inspector said we could make it a couple of building blocks higher and he would pass it.

We sold the house in Woodford in December 1987 and moved into Limetree Parade a week or so before Christmas. It wasn't finished then but had white carpets throughout. Julie came over to spend the holiday with us and brought Josie and Sadie.

There was sand all around and we had builders' planks to walk on. That meant we needed to have a foot bath by the front door and the three patio doors with an old towel to wash our feet before we came inside.

After I finished racing Debbie was working in Auckland for Global Sports and Promotions, the people who set up the original World Super Bike series. She also had a house on the shore at Takapuna, but once we were headed for Runaway Bay she decided the Gold Coast was the place for her.

Julie, Josie and Sadie went back to England in the new year. A little while later they came back permanently with Mike Shawcross, who was Julie's husband at the time.

I flew to England to oversee the packing and dispatch of mountains of possessions from Chester Road. Kym, Norrie and I loaded up four 20-foot containers with furniture, workshop tools and all sorts of other gear. But we couldn't bring everything.

There was a 40-foot container at the back of the property which Gordon and I used as a store shed. When we used to get new Jawas from the factory we would take off the original handlebars, steel guards, steel tanks, clutches and many other pieces and put them into tea chests.

SIZZLING PROSPECT – Jim Airey and his wife Ronda quickly convinced Ivan and Raye of the merits of the Australian lifestyle

Much to the later disgust of Peter Collins, we took all that stuff to the dump at Wythenshawe and threw it away. Since then PC has been restoring Jawas back to their original condition and is always looking for the long banana seats, steel guards, original Jawa tanks and all that gear.

We had professional packers Pickfords to pack all the crystal vases and my trophies. They all went into one of the containers and when it arrived we only unpacked the vases. The rest in almost 50 tea chests went to a store on the Gold Coast and has not been opened since.

We have been so busy in retirement it is a source of amazement to Raye and myself how we ever had the time to do things before. To our great delight, having family around us explains at least a part of why our lifestyle is so full-on. All three kids moved permanently to Australia within a year of us deciding we would settle there.

Julie and Mike had a third child, Edward, born on the Gold Coast in 1990, and Kym, who came out at the time Expo was on in Brisbane in 1988 and has been with his partner Cheryl Hillier since 1990, had a daughter, Zasha, the following year.

Kym had a building diploma in England and has used his skills in a variety of enterprises. He has been involved in movies and television series, building film sets at Movieworld, a Warner Brothers theme park on the Gold Coast, and overseas.

These include the 1994 release *Streetfighter* with Jean Claude van Damme and Kylie Minogue, *Anna and the King* (1999) starring Jodie Foster, and, most recently, *The Chronicles of Narnia: The Voyage of the Dawn Treader* (2010).

Kym was involved in the building of the Movieworld at Düsseldorf in the mid 1990s and worked on *Anna and the King* in Kuala Lumpur for several months in 1999. Cheryl and Zasha went on both trips.

He and Cheryl – who operates a hairdressing business – live in Helensvale, a northern Gold Coast suburb about 10 minutes from us, in a house Kym built.

Debbie went back to Cheshire on a holiday and came back to Australia with Ian Pritchard, a financial manager who she married in 1990. In 2001 they had a daughter, Skye Raye who is the apple of their eye.

Ian is now general manager of the Wesley Research Institute in Brisbane and they live at Monterey Keys, the suburb between Helensvale and Hope Island.

For 10 years Debbie worked for Integrated Memory Systems, a company owned by one-time Bruce Penhall associate Pete Rovazzini, which operated out of the Bond University campus on the southern Gold Coast.

Phil Collins, the third of the Lymm brothers, worked there for a while and so did Martin Hignett, who had been a spannerman for Peter Collins and Michael Lee and later formed his own company in the UK.

PLAYTIME – *away from it all, enjoying a day on the water*

The Will To Win – 353

Julie was also busily involved in the workforce from the moment she arrived back, being involved with the launch of Sanctuary Cove – Frank Sinatra and Whitney Houston were the stars at the opening of Australia's first integrated residential resort.

She had positions at the Hyatt Regency, the Radisson at Palm Meadows, was special events manager for Warner Brothers Australia, corporate relations manager for Diabetes Australia and state manager of Guide Dogs Queensland.

In 2007 she married David White, a longtime name in the Australian music industry, and they co-produced the nationwide tour of *Buddy The Musical*, which tells the story of Buddy Holly, one of the brightest stars in popular music whose songs remain as popular today as they were when he lost his life in a plane crash more than half a century ago.

Julie and David's latest ventures are into theatre and movie production. They live just round the corner in Runaway Bay – even closer to us than Kym or Debbie.

Zasha and Edward are at university nearby, Josie, an accountant, works locally and lives with Tommy, her Irish partner for many years. Sadie spends half the year in Queensland and the other six months in Majorca with Jordi, her partner who is Spanish. When she is back in Australia, she and Jordi live with us. Skye is at school, so we take a keen interest in what they are all doing and delight in the time they spend with us.

With so many family members gathered around, we always looked forward to spending more time with all of them. During the height of my racing career there were plenty of absences, some quite lengthy, although the upside was all the kids had opportunities to travel and to see people and places round the world.

The retirement dream also involved a lot of sport and recreation, a big priority for anybody living on the water. Top of the shopping list was a boat. Jim Airey was sales manager for a local firm and through him we bought a Fairways 36 which we named *Aranui* because without Aranui all those years before, there never would have been a boat, never mind a 36-foot motor cruiser.

It was like having a house built. I was at the Fairways factory two or three times a week and every time we wanted different taps, showers, toilets and the rest, they told us to go away, get the items and they would fit them.

We had her moored at the jetty for 15 years and made many a trip out on to the Broadwater and beyond for social and fishing expeditions. In 2006 we traded the boat for a 22-foot Southwind called *Aranui 2,* which has a 225 horsepower four-stroke V6 Yamaha outboard motor – a more fitting vessel for a couple of pensioners!

354 – Ivan Mauger

The Gold Coast was the ideal place to give full rein to my passion for jetskis. This was sparked on a visit to Western Australia at the start of 1974 when I first saw a couple of them flying down the Swan River. They had only just appeared in the country, looked to be a fantastic fun machine and of course I had to have one.

The following week we were in Melbourne with old friends Jack and Kath Walker and I was telling him about what I had seen. Jack, who was a handy sidecar specialist in his day, said his son Ken, later Victorian and Australian sidecar champion, was sponsored by Kawasaki who had a couple of jetskis in their local showroom.

Ken made a call to Japan and was told I could have one at half price. We hooked up the trailer and went straight down to do the deal. Customs in Christchurch told me as a non-resident I couldn't bring it into New Zealand so my Kiwi mate Bob Thomson brought it back as personal property. When we moved to Runaway Bay all those years later my boat shed wouldn't have been complete without a couple of jetskis.

Simon Wigg, who rode in my series in Australia and New Zealand as well as the UK meetings, had a house nearby at Paradise Point. He was always a willing playmate and often kept his ski on my boat ramp or in the boat shed. We had so much fun racing each other, jumping over waves, and making the most of being off duty.

Lots of other neighbours, speedway names including Mike Farrell, Troy Butler and Mark Carlson and some of the Aussie motocross guys, were regulars too, having a great time out on the Broadwater.

Yamaha sponsored me in jetski 100-mile enduros from the early 1990s. At one time there were up to 140 entrants in a race. My best finish was a fifth placing behind guys who were at least half my age in most cases.

The Gold Coast is a haven for golfers, with more than 40 courses including some which have staged big championships. For reasons completely unconnected with my ability to play the game, since the mid 1980s I have been sponsored with everything to do with golf equipment and clothing by PGF in Aranui.

They supply clubs, bags and clothing to golf shops in New Zealand, Australia, USA and England. They also support a lot of professional players in England, New Zealand, Aussie and California. My more modest claim to fame is I have played in corporate golf days in all of those places.

You have to look the part and a few years ago PGF made me a pro bag the same as they supply to their professional contracted players in my red, black and white colours and put the New Zealand flag on the side. I haven't played much golf in recent times because of my ankle operation but have every intention of getting back into it.

FLYING THE FLAG – Ivan, sports ambassador for New Zealand, and Mike Moore, Minister of Sport, later PM, and now ambassador to the USA

Living on the water, though, there always is so much temptation lapping at your back door. If we weren't messing about in the boat, it never required a second invitation to get out on the jetskis and, when my relationship with Wiggy developed, quite a lot of our consultations coincided with those early morning excursions.

We would ride out and sit on one of the little bays or beaches and talk about anything and everything possible for the improvement of speedway and long track, bikes, equipment and the following season's world championship rounds.

We often made decisions at these times that we would carry out to the letter seven or eight months later at some long track in Europe. Often we became so engrossed we might sit there for hours because the conversations were timeless.

Even with so much emphasis on a leisurely good life, there was no way I was going to escape from connections with racing just because we had settled on the Gold Coast. In fact, there have been a number of pleasant reminders of the old days.

A year after my farewell tour the FIM awarded me their Medaille d'Or (gold medal) – their top honour. We had to go to Paris for the presentation,

MILLENNIUM MAN – Ivan and Raye with Millennium Man presentation night hosts Peter Lipscombe and John Chaplin at Beaulieu Motor Museum

made by Guy Maitre, secretary general of the governing body of international motorcycle sport.

During my time racing I had received the MBE from Her Majesty the Queen at Buckingham Palace on July 28, 1976, and in 1985 Mike Moore, the Minister of Sport, appointed me a sporting ambassador for New Zealand.

After retirement I was awarded an OBE, presented by Sir Paul Reeves, her Majesty's Governor-General to New Zealand at Government House, Wellington on May 19, 1989.

The following year I was inducted into the New Zealand Sports Hall of Fame by John Banks, the Minister of Recreation and Sport. In 2004 I was admitted to the New Zealand Motorcycling Hall of Fame, a year later came induction into the New Zealand Speedway Hall of Fame and in 2007 I was inducted into the Australian Motorcycling Hall of Fame.

Also in 2007 I was awarded the freedom of my home city of Christchurch. This came about when I was there setting up the arrangements for an exhibition at the Canterbury Museum at which many of my souvenirs and trophies, including the gold bike, were to be put on display. When the then Mayor Garry Moore heard I was in town, he invited me to have a yarn with him at a coffee shop in Cathedral Square.

Even before the waiter brought our coffees Garry said he would like to offer me the freedom of the city. He would liaise with Anthony Wright, director of the museum, and invite all the guests to the freedom ceremony and then lay on transport to take everyone to the exhibition that was opening later in the evening.

The Will To Win – 357

During the conversation I suggested Ronnie Moore and Barry Briggs would be equally deserving recipients of the honour as both won world championships and had been great ambassadors for Christchurch all over the world. He readily agreed and it was following that discussion that they also received the freedom of the city.

I was a bit annoyed when Briggo wrote to the mayor suggesting Ronnie did not get the credit he deserved when I was around. I have said many times if there was no Ronnie Moore in speedway there would very likely have been no Briggo or Ivan. I have always said Ronnie was the main reason both of us started.

The mayor called me when he received Briggo's letter and wondered why he should have written it. He said he was not going to read it out but I told him to read it out anyway as Ronnie and all my friends in New Zealand know how I feel about Ronnie. At the time I wished I had never recommended Briggo for the honour.

One standout moment for me was to be voted Man of the Millennium by readers of *Speedway Star* and *Vintage Speedway* magazines. Although I got a great reception in most countries, I wasn't always top of the popularity parade in the UK yet here I was being feted by everybody.

Had I realised how popular I was to become after retiring from racing I might have considered giving it away much sooner than I did!! But funnily enough, nobody boos me these days. Attending the ceremony at the Beaulieu Motor Sport Museum in 2000, with John Chaplin and Peter Lipsombe presiding over the show, was a memorable occasion.

We continue to keep in touch with old and not so old racing friends by making regular trips to the UK, the USA and New Zealand. In the past few years I have been president of the World Veteran Riders Association, the Australian Veterans Association and also the New Zealand veterans, and we frequently attend functions and social gatherings in different countries.

This probably reads like a non-stop round of self-indulgent hand-shaking and back-slapping but the 'retirement' years have not been all sunshine and light. The grand plan certainly did not include being caught up in the financial drama which pursued Lloyds of London for several years.

Riding in the fast lane for a number of years had brought its own rewards. There is no telling how long a sporting career will last and I was always determined to make the future secure for Raye and the family. Seeing great champions like Ronnie and Youngie in circumstances which did not reflect their status was a huge motivator for me.

When people earn decent money they give themselves choices. For some, it is an opportunity to radically change their lifestyle, not always responsibly. For me it was about ensuring I was adequately compensated for putting my neck on the line and helping to draw big crowds through a promoter's turnstiles.

Lloyds then and now was regarded as the world's leading insurance market. Its origins were in shipping but it expanded into every area. Membership was limited to investors who were well known, famous for sport or some other area of achievement, or extremely wealthy.

That zealous tax official from Walsall was not the only person who became interested in my personal circumstances in the 1970s. When an invitation to join Lloyds came my way, I viewed it that membership was on the basis that being associated with one of the most famous institutions in the world of finance allowed investors to have money in a safe place with every expectation it would generate some significant dividend over time.

I became a 'name' which required investors to declare everything they owned anywhere in the world, including major bank accounts, because effectively they became a reinsurance agent. A prospective newcomer had to be nominated by three people who were already members of Lloyds.

If accepted it meant going to the Lloyds House in London to be interviewed. Provided the interview was satisfactory a letter would follow indicating acceptance and then you had to go back to be sworn in. In front of all members of the board a newcomer has to place his or her hand on the Bible and swear that everything you have declared you own personally.

From that day it took three years before being accepted as a full Lloyd's member because most insurance claims for natural disasters take up to three years to complete. Similarly whenever you resigned from Lloyds you were still committed for a further three years. It was compulsory to be in aviation, fire and general accidents. Most people do not realise 75 per cent of insurance claims are from household-related accidents.

Lloyds was set up in 1688, although its constitution was not adopted until 1811. There had been only a handful of occasions when they didn't pay their investors a big dividend and their reputation was cemented in 1906 when they paid out millions following the San Francisco earthquake.

That was the history and it was widely considered to be as safe a place to invest as any. That was until the late 1980s and early 1990s when it was decimated by a combination of factors. There was a certain amount of bad luck, a series of costly natural disasters in quick succession and a component of mismanagement. The bottom line is it was one of the biggest financial crashes in history.

When things started to go bad at Lloyds I was among dozens who resigned immediately. It did not prevent us from losing money but the losses in the first three years were contained up to a point because I was in nine syndicates and eight of them made a small profit each year.

However I was in syndicate 305 which had asbestos claims going back to 1952. I hired a high-priced London lawyer to fight my case when I found out about that date. My argument was that had I known about them before I joined Lloyds or accepted syndicate 305 I would not have signed up. But there were pages of small print and every syndicate's terms included an undertaking to agree all of Lloyd's demands.

Following the publicity attached to the whole affair and the number of people who had been badly burned, the British Government in association with Lloyds started a reinsurance company called Equitas Holdings Limited. It meant if they had sufficient money available Lloyds 'names' could buy themselves out, at least nominally.

We had enough money in different parts of the world and were able to do that but it was also a long process. Having paid Equitas what they wanted, a considerable sum by any standard, we then had to endure three more years of losses on the 305 syndicate.

All up, we were involved in worrying and lengthy proceedings over the best part of 10 years which cost us a huge amount of money. Even after that, other 'names' and I will never be completely out.

The British Government tipped in billions of pounds but it would never be sufficient if two or three huge natural disasters were to happen in the world within the same year. And a clause in the Equitas agreement stated if (and it is a very big 'if') Equitas should ever have insufficient money to meet claims the 'names' must pay.

There was a time when I used to look at the news and see earthquakes, hurricanes and other natural disasters and wondered how much it was going to cost me. These were unworthy thoughts because many people died in those disasters. Now I look at all the shocking happenings around the world and have more compassion for the people involved.

Many others were far less fortunate than we were, some losing their entire savings. This was a time during which something in the region of 35-plus 'names'committed suicide. My friends in England would often send newspaper cuttings and video reports and television documentaries about Lloyds. There were so many stories, especially when high-profile sportspeople including Henry Cooper, the boxer, and Wimbledon tennis champion Virginia Wade lost thousands.

One consequence for us was that instead of getting into a number of intended investments in Australia, especially in commercial and residential property, we had to look at other ways of bringing in some income. This, as much as any other single reason, was why we continued to promote speedway tours and meetings around Australia and New Zealand for the best part of 20 years.

360 – Ivan Mauger

The ongoing involvement was enjoyable and kept us in touch with many people with whom we had been associated, but possibly would never have happened – certainly not on the scale into which it developed – but for the Lloyds business.

That is not to say we went into those promoting ventures with anything less than our usual enthusiasm and determination to do things properly. However, there were times when I was reminded of different promoters in England who had often said 'there are many easier ways of earning a quid than running speedway'.

As a rider, I concentrated on what I could do best and knew best. There was plenty of opportunity to see at first hand how different promoters went about their business. Some provided the example of 'how not to' and others lived up to the title by pouring in all their energies to run a show that was both exciting and profitable.

A lot of Continental promoters, who ran maybe just the one big meeting each year, knew how to put on a show and I had wanted to run a long track in Australia or New Zealand as they did in Europe. There were bands playing, riders from all sorts of nations, the mayor welcoming everybody and a carnival atmosphere.

I was at a Sydney Showground reunion in the early part of 1989 and former rider Kevin McDonald asked what I was doing since I retired from racing. When the long track idea cropped up in the conversation, Kevin said there was a good track at Bathurst which might be ideal.

Raye and I planned to drive back to the Gold Coast the following day but in the event we went up for a few days' stay in the Blue Mountains, and then went in to Bathurst, a regional city 200 kilometres west of Sydney and best known for its Mount Panorama motor racing circuit.

The people I spoke to at Bathurst Showgrounds were keen on the idea of hosting a big event and a few months later the Australian Long Track Grand Prix was born. We were to take it to several horse trotting stadiums. The huge size of the trotting tracks, many situated in country areas, gave thousands of fans the opportunity to see the world's best in action on some of the fastest dirt tracks in the land.

The event ran until 2004 and we regularly had between 15 and 25 international competitors every year. I had a contract with Continental Airlines. Taking a leaf out of Trevor Redmond's book, part of the deal was that any rider who was a world champion travelled free in business or first class. A national champion would also go free but in economy class with an upgrade to business class in their booking reference.

There were a few genuine world champions like Simon Wigg, Egon Müller, Karl Maier, Marcel Gerhard, as well as Kelvin Tatum and Mark Loram who were to win titles. But any riders who had been part of a World

Pairs championship or a World Team Cup-winning side were labelled world champions so they were travelled free up in business or first class.

The others I told Continental Airlines were national champions of whatever country, be it on speedway, long track or grass.

There were guys from England, Germany, Canada, Czechoslovakia, New Zealand, USA, Switzerland, France, East Germany, South Africa, Sweden, Norway, Russia, Poland, Holland, Scotland and Ukraine.

Mark Loram

I only had to pay for the odd rider who was not a national champion, which helped no end with the promoting bottom line.

I learned a lot from Ronnie Greene and Kym Bonython about how speedway should be promoted and incorporated most of that into my long track promotions. The Aussie riders and officials were not ready for all that discipline but they had to accept it.

That's why I fell out with Motor Cycling Australia and most of their officials when I promoted the first meeting at Bathurst. The relationship had its ups and downs for many years, more downs than ups.

Some of the places we went were a challenge, too. We ran at Bathurst for three years and it was usually a juggling act to please three landlords – the Showground Society, the Bathurst Agricultural Horticultural and Pastoral Association and Harness Racing Club. All were responsible for different aspects of the venue and some groups wanted us there very much more than others.

From 1992–95 we switched the Australian Long Track Grand Prix to the Canberra Exhibition Centre, and then Tamworth Showgrounds until 2002. We also took the show to new places including Dubbo, Parklands on the Gold Coast (just four kilometres from our house), Bankstown in Sydney and Redcliffe, just north of Brisbane. Most of those places were tremendously welcoming, but not everybody wanted a race meeting in their back yard.

One of the biggest successes was in 1991, with a Wednesday night meeting at Albion Park, a trotting track right in the centre of Brisbane. Everything was agreed with Damian Raedler who was in charge of the complex and the Brisbane media helped drum up massive interest, so much so that local residents were threatening an injunction because of the numbers expected.

The gates opened at four o'clock and an hour later there were only a couple of hundred people in and we thought it was going to be a fizzer. Then they started coming in their thousands after work finished. The police came to tell us we had to direct the traffic away because it was blocking up the city.

As a promoter of course I ignored the police warnings because there were people queued up a dozen deep at the turnstiles. Our operations manager went through the crowd telling people who had the correct change to go through the double gates to the pits.

My two sons-in-law and I were there taking the cash, and when our pockets were full we had to start stashing it down our shirts. Eventually I managed to call over a trusted friend with a bin liner in which to dump the cash which he locked in the boot of his car, while we were still taking money.

The meeting was scheduled to start at 7.30pm and Damian came down to me in a panic at about 7.05 and said the residents were in the process of getting an injunction served. I told the pit managers to get the riders ready for the first three heats. A big brass marching band had to be immediately directed on to the infield.

Bob Gibbs MP, the Minister of Tourism, Sport and Racing, was at the start ready to officially open the event so I briefed him, told him to keep his welcome short and sweet, and to declare the Australian Long Track Grand Prix open, which he promptly did.

As he and I walked off the track the riders came out for the first couple of races which instantly had the huge crowd on its feet, roaring with approval. As I walked up the steps on the outside of the track with Bob Gibbs a police sergeant came down and said he had an injunction to stop the meeting.

I told him if he had big enough balls to go out and make the announcement with the third race coming up to the tapes, he could be my guest. While he was thinking that over, I kept walking, disappeared into the crowd and made myself scarce for the next hour or so.

The whole show was an enormous hit, with one exception. During the previous week Damian and I met with the catering manager and explained there would be a huge crowd, unlike the handful which attended the trotting races, and he should order more beer, hamburgers, Coca-Cola and the usual spectator favourites.

He couldn't have been used to taking advice because he angrily told us he ran the catering, had it all under control and didn't need anybody telling him what to order. The meeting hadn't been going 20 minutes when

SIX OF THE BEST – world champions all, Egon Müller, Ivan, Ronnie Moore, Briggo, Gerd Riss and Shawn Moran at Addington, Christchurch, for the 1991 New Zealand Long Track Grand Prix

they ran out of beer and food and all people could get to drink was warm soda water.

Damian and the Albion Park committee sacked the guy the day after the meeting. It was a full house with 12,000-odd paying but sadly, we never got to do it a second time.

Incredibly, we doubled that number three weeks later when I promoted the first New Zealand Long Track Grand Prix at Addington Raceway in Christchurch.

People couldn't do enough to welcome us and help.

The Christchurch City Council paid for all the radio advertisements and Smokefree paid for the TV ads. Many very good sponsors included Shell who not only put in money but also let us use their garages to sell tickets in advance.

We sold 18,000 advance tickets and 6,000 on the night. I had about 1,200 relations, old mates from Christchurch and sponsors in a huge VIP area up at the top of the steward's room. The sponsorship from the local brewery included picking up the tab for all the drinks and food in the VIP room.

In 1992 we ran again on one of the coldest and wettest days in Christchurch for over 40 years and still got approaching 9,000 spectators. Addington was not available for the next few years and in 1994 we ran at Claudelands Trotting Track in Hamilton. We were back there in 1995 and that was when Kym won the New Zealand long track championship, one of the high points of his on-off racing career.

In 1996 we were back at Addington Raceway on a hot Sunday afternoon and had enough paying spectators to pay all the bills and the expenses for the international riders. Sponsorships added to the profit. It was tougher going at Wellington's Hutt Park the following Saturday night, very wet and cold. The gate was not enough to pay all the bills but the sponsorship money meant there was some profit.

Raye helped organise all these meetings and continued to do so. At the long tracks she was responsible for the ticket sellers and the gates, ably assisted by old friends Kath Walker and Colleen Thomson.

CHIP OFF THE OLD BLOCK – Kym Mauger, New Zealand long track championship winner at Hamilton, 1995

For much of the time these meetings were running in Australia and New Zealand, Simon Wigg was a headline act. He was virtually an ever-present up to the time David Tapp unveiled his speedway series in 1994.

The son of legendary horse racing caller Johnny Tapp, he had many connections with television and was able to obtain very good sponsorship for his series.

Tappy used to call me quite regularly to seek advice and phone numbers of different riders. It was during one of the conversations I told him he really needed an outstanding English rider because of the huge expat population in Australia.

I cited Wiggy as the perfect example – a great personality, a class rider, an entertainer and one who could speak very eloquently on television interviews, on radio and to newspaper reporters.

A short time later Simon called me from England to tell me David Tapp had rung him and was offering him a lot more money than I could ever pay him to do my long tracks. It was a measure of Wiggy's loyalty that he was still prepared to do my meetings and turn down Tappy.

But I was very impressed with the series David was putting together, and thought it would be good for the Australian speedway scene. I told Simon to take the money on offer and meanwhile I would bring over Egon Müller or Gerd Riss instead.

He did ride for me again later on and as always, with that great big smile and winning way of his, continued to be the identikit promoter's dream. Few riders have better appreciated how important it is to put on a show.

It's not like racing, but the buzz involved with organising and promoting big events can be considerable. Some of the excitement can be lost if the financial returns fail to add up. It was some years before I was involved in another meeting in New Zealand and then it was as an agent for the promoting group at the Ascot Park Raceway in Invercargill in 2003.*

They wanted my international riders and put on their meeting a week after my Australian Long Track Grand Prix. I took across 14 international riders and was paid for providing the stars for their show, but a repeat performance the following year was a financial train wreck because even by Invercargill standards it was a cold, wet day and not too many people turned up. I'm still out of pocket on that one.

That experience, and the loss of major sponsor Jack Daniel's from my Aussie meetings, should have curbed my enthusiasm. But I'm a sucker for getting involved in anything new and exciting. My role in bringing the World Long Track Grand Prix to New Zealand in 2003 and 2004 certainly meant signing off there on a high note.

* Jack Daniel's paid me to do match races with Phil Crump at Redcliffe and Invercargill.

366 – Ivan Mauger

The FIM had seen speedway extend its influence as far as Sydney when a Grand Prix was held there in 2002. They were openly receptive to the idea of staging a long track in Australia or New Zealand – or both. In the end nothing came of our enquiries in Aussie, but I ran the final round of the long track GP at Pukekura Raceway in New Plymouth in successive years.

More than 20 years had elapsed since my participation in the 1982 speedway World Final in Los Angeles. This time I was pretty much on my own and it was a huge thrill to bring an event of such stature to the country of my birth.

It could not have happened but for huge sponsorship from the New Zealand Government and the New Plymouth District Council where Mayor Peter Tennant was a highly committed supporter.

He even helped provide an introduction to his father-in-law Noel Yarrow of Yarrows The Bakers who became naming rights sponsors.

There were all the regular sponsorships from Shell and Smokefree, Hewlett Packard, Makita, Stihl and there were many other smaller backers who tipped in support in various ways.

Through the influence of John Knowles, who I met when he was head of sport and special events for Television New Zealand and later went to Tokyo in Japan to be head of Sky Television Sport, the TV coverage reached 166 countries and a total audience of over 490 million viewers. All the regional stations, radio and newspapers gave terrific coverage before, during and after, too.

We went to a lot of trouble to ensure the meetings had loads of pomp and ceremony. The council put on a reception both years in the main chambers at which Peter Tennant presented competitors, team managers and FIM officials with mementos of New Plymouth and the Province of Taranaki. FIM president Renzo Giannini of Italy and I distributed the official riding vests in draw order.

Maori groups came along to sing and perform traditional dances, and we maintained the theme on race night with as much colour and spectacle as we could muster. The locals and motorcycle enthusiasts from all over New Zealand turned out in good numbers and everybody had a great time.

Germany's Robert Barth came to the 2003 event holding a decent lead, and although Kelvin Tatum and Gerd Riss pushed him back to third on the day, he had enough points in hand to claim the title.

Riss, statistically the most successful performer the 1000-metre discipline has seen, returned the following year, winning the meeting and his fifth championship.*

* Riss also won the championship in 2007, 2008 and 2009.

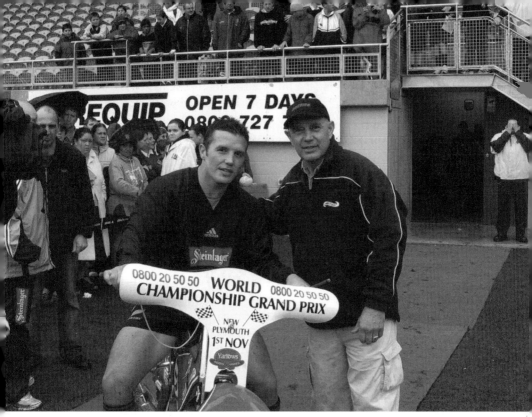

THANKS, MATE – All Blacks rugby star Aaron Mauger with Ivan at New Plymouth, venue for the World Long Track Championship Grand Prix

Possibly the biggest impact though was provided by Jason Crump, who was a wild card just a few weeks after clinching his first world speedway title. He conducted himself brilliantly on and off the track and but for a broken front chain when leading in his first race would have gone close to winning the round.

Unfortunately the following year there were changes in the New Zealand Government and the very significant backing dried up. Without the Government money which had underwritten the cost of bringing riders, equipment and officials halfway round the world, it was impossible to run. But we had a ball in those two years.

Kiwi officials generally have been much more in tune with the protocols required for running major events. Years earlier I brought in an official speedway USA Test team ratified by the American Motorcycle Association and a New Zealand Test team which was granted official status by Motorcycling New Zealand.

When we first ran the NZ Long Track GP at Addington, Motor Cycling New Zealand were happy to comply with every official requirement and had no difficulty dotting the Is and crossing the Ts.

368 – *Ivan Mauger*

In many ways Kiwis are closer in their attitude to the UK than the Aussies, most of whom have a bit of a rebellious streak in them which can be attractive at times and a real pain on other occasions.

Overseas riders used to the strait-laced attitudes and hard and fast regulations in Europe liked to come to Aussie and New Zealand because usually things were a bit more laid back. This did make it a bit easier on promoters who wanted to bring in some of the speedway boys on a casual basis.

The first year we were in Australia I got a Russian team to come. The following summer we put on a World Series with Wiggy, Sam Ermolenko, Shawn Moran and some Aussie guys riding along with eight imported riders from Poland, Russia, Germany and Norway.

After the success of the Australian Long Track Grand Prix meetings a couple of my mates in Sydney suggested starting another World Series troupe. I didn't do much about it at the time. But when we were in England and Europe during the 1992 season Václav Verner and others approached me about doing a speedway series after the long tracks.

Memories of those Golden Helmet series Phil Bishop used to organise in Holland gave me the idea of doing something similar in Australia. So many riders were keen to participate. I had plenty of Golden Helmets and only needed to get a stand for one of them. It took another year to get started, Toshiba enthusiastically came on board as major sponsors, and suddenly we had a series on our hands.

The format we used was the 12-rider set-up Briggo, Phil Rising and I worked out in the old *Speedway Star* office in London before the start of the World Series in 1974. That involved 12 heats, two semis, a consolation final and the Golden Helmet final with points accumulated through the tour.

I was an agent for the speedway clubs in Australia, my role being to tee up the international riders, and when the package was complete we sold the whole show to each of the clubs. Dozens of riders wanted to come and the selection criteria included their publicity value, how they would perform on Australian tracks, and the costs involved in transporting them and their bikes.

We brought riders from all over the world, including veterans like Bobby Schwartz (USA) and John Jørgensen (Denmark) and a few Russians but mostly young riders seeking to broaden their experience and bolster their international reputation. We used to ring the changes each year to ensure variety.

Series winners who became Grand Prix riders included Rune Holta of Norway (1994), Gregorzsz Walsaszek (Poland), his compatriot Krzysztof Cegielski (2000) and the Czech brothers Aleš (2001) and Lukáš Dryml (2002). Other GP guys included Lee Richardson, Andreas Jonsson and Jarek Hampel.

Each of the riders' financial demands were different but there was sufficient profit margin built in so for several years all the tracks paid the same money. With most of them and club presidents I knew it was case of presenting an invoice and being paid on the night. Some I didn't know too well and also learned were a little bit dodgy in paying. They had to pay 50 per cent up front two months in advance before the riders had left their European bases.

From 1993 the International Golden Helmet Series appeared at Darwin, Katherine, Gove (Nhulunbuy), Tennant Creek, Alice Springs, Mount Isa, Cairns (at two different venues), Townsville (two venues), Ayr, Mackay (three different venues), Rockhampton, Gladstone, Bundaberg, Maryborough, Yandina, Archerfield, Brisbane Exhibition Ground, Gold Coast, Lismore, Grafton, Gosford, Sydney Showground, Adelaide, Gillman and Mildura.

Václav Verner

Václav Verner was a regular competitor in the early years and increasingly helped with the administration and management. He had a very bad accident at the Bohle track in Townsville, where he suffered a broken right arm and shoulder and did not ride after that. But I still brought him back each year because he was invaluable in looking after the riders during the week.

Brian (Hollywood) Parsons was another key part of the whole operation. He and Václav stayed at the motels with the riders, and drove them everywhere in our two Toyota Hi Ace mini buses with an extended roof for the airconditioning

We had a contract with Comet Transport who took the bikes from one track to the other. Mainly we used the Comet freight depots which had pressure washing machines and air compressors to clean off the bikes. Part of the deal for every club was for them to take the bikes from the Comet depot to the track and back again.

Riders were required to clean their bikes on Sunday mornings and do any repairs necessary so they were ready for the press and television day at the next venue. We had a media call on the Thursday before each meeting and got very good local television news coverage and reports and pictures in the local papers.

The International Golden Helmet Series consistently drew the highest crowds to all those tracks each season. All the international boys were great, they knew what they had to do, did it very well and I was proud of each and every one of them.

The series ran until 2007 after which Motorcycling Australia decided they would demand very high FIM permit fees. They also came up with a series fee. There were some spirited discussions with MA officials but there was no shifting them. None of the clubs wanted their costs jacked up and I couldn't see any justification for change so for the next couple of years we had a domestic series involving Australian riders.

It is a shame things went that way, because the goodwill of the clubs and the potential for Australian speedway is still there. But it's always been a bit of a battle for the solos, as bikes are called in Aussie. Australian 'speedway' is and always has been about several categories including cars, sidecars and other events.

In the current climate it is difficult to predict where the solos are headed. In recent years there have been a lot of very good Aussie riders on the world stage such as Jason Crump, Leigh Adams and Ryan Sullivan, and there are some decent ones coming through including Chris Holder and Darcy Ward.

With training centres which have produced good talent in Adelaide, Mildura and the Gold Coast and a keen appreciation of the development needs of young riders, Australia keeps producing kids who have some talent. Great Britain and UK promoters seem to be the biggest beneficiaries, though.

The vast distances between centres and the difficulty finding suitable venues is a fact of life which inhibits domestic speedway in Australia. The major centres of old such as the Sydney Showground, Claremont in Perth, Rowley Park in Adelaide and Brisbane's Ekka no longer run speedway, and the problem is not going to go away.

Nevertheless, I think Australia could successfully stage a Grand Prix, learning from the lessons of 2002 when a one-off was held in Sydney which finished the schedule for that year. The trick will be to find the right stadium and the correct scheduling and it can be done.

Instead of an end-of-year GP when the title is run and won and most of the boys are in holiday mode, it should be at the start of the year. Logistically, it ought to be possible to stage an Australian and New Zealand GP in early March.

That idea might come even closer to fruition if Malaysia were to be involved. There is a lot of interest there in Formula One and road racing and I'm one of the few Westerners to have first-hand knowledge of what potential there might be for speedway in this highly-populated nation.

Towards the end of 2006 the Malaysia Motorsports Organisation and Competitors Association (MMOCA) approached me because they wanted to get speedway up and running there. From April until November 2007 I spent seven to 10 days a month in Malaysia helping to identify riders and get some structure into position.

I taught the youngsters the basic skills of speedway on a makeshift track on the outskirts of Kuala Lumpur prior to the building of a circuit I designed for them at Family Park, almost in the centre of the capital. Linden Warner who rode for Ipswich and Hackney in the 1980s was living in Kuala Lumpur and read in the newspapers about speedway starting. He introduced himself and later became my assistant trainer.

I had to do several demonstration rides during the practice sessions. At first their guys had no speedway clothing or equipment but they soon got themselves organised. The locally-produced 112cc bikes were fine for the Malaysian kids many of whom were extremely light but those little bikes were not built for my 70kg. So the Malaysians asked me to get some 500cc bikes which I had sent over from Australia. A dozen from the Jawa factory followed later in the year.

Officials told me their ambition was to have an international meeting at the end of October and they wanted a suitable safety fence. My FIM standard safety fence, warning lights and referee's panel were stored in a couple of containers in New Plymouth and of no further use to me. A price was agreed and the equipment was shipped to Port Klang, about 50 kilometres from KL.

Hanifa Yoong Yin Fah, director of the Shah Alam road racing circuit for 10 years, was the man in charge of the whole project and he assembled a

THE BIG DAY – lining up for the FIM Malaysian International Gold Cup in October 2007, left to right: Nazrie, Azizi, Ariff, Haniff, Abdussobur, Helmy, Roda, Hideaki Ota, Linden Warner, Sam Taylor, Ricky Wells. At back: Ivan Mauger, Hanifah Yoong

372 – Ivan Mauger

great team around him. The Malaysians are very industrious people. The next time I went back the fence and lights were up in the correct places, there was a referee's tower and my FIM referee's panel was already installed.

Domestic meetings in a six-team league were taking place on a regular basis and some of the riders showed distinct promise. For the international meeting, the deal was there had to be four locals and four imported riders. Matthias Rohde, an FIM referee in Germany who was also living in KL, volunteered to be the referee.

Linden coached the Malaysians twice a week during the time I was not in Malaysia and the top four chosen for the big event were Rody Sofian Buang, Muhammad Helmey Hamsa, Mohd Haniff Borham and Mohd Abdussobor Turino. The Malaysians always shortened the names so they became Rody, Helmey, Haniff and Sobur – much easier for the announcers.

I ended up taking New Zealand-born, California-based Ricky Wells, Sam Taylor from Christchurch, and Hideaki Ohta, a Japanese long track rider I met in 2001 when he was riding in California and had at the 2003 Australian Long Track Grand Prix and New Zealand Long Track Grand Prix. Linden Warner completed the international quartet.

The big event went off smoothly and everybody seemed very enthusiastic. But the following year a new Minister for Youth came in with ideas of his own and the Government funding, supposedly for three years, suddenly was withdrawn.

Without that financial assistance the grand plan to popularise speedway in Malaysia went on the back burner. Even so, their officials have remained in regular contact and plans are afoot to try again very shortly.

With or without a regional or national competition, the possibility of a GP there remains good. An Asia-Pacific leg of three in four weeks, not impacting upon the European scene at all, would be even better. Imagine Kuala Lumpur, New Zealand and Australia staging a GP in March to kick off the year.

It's unavoidable to think globally on a sport which crosses so many boundaries, and Raye and I consider ourselves fortunate to still be able to travel round the world and meet up with old friends and new. We love going back to Europe or America, and pop across to New Zealand a few times each year. But as the Frank Sinatra song goes, it's very nice to go travelling, but oh so nice to come home.

One of our most memorable gatherings was in February 2007 when more than 100 people helped us celebrate our 50th wedding anniversary at Chancellor Resort, Hope Island.*

---

* As if one anniversary do was not enough, we had get-togethers with more old friends in Scotland and California in February and March of 2007.

The Will To Win – 373

All the kids and grandkids attended. Raye, who has been singing since she was very young, brought the house down with her favourite *Hey Big Spender* and Josie and Sadie sang *You're Still the One*, the Shania Twain song Kym's partner Cheryl and daughter Zasha Mary always say was written for Raye and me.

Some of the people there had been around for the best part of half a century or more: Nigel and Cynthia Boocock, Jim and Ronda Airey, Val Andrews, Jack and Kath Walker (Jack and I met when he was grading the track before the 1961 Victorian Championship), Mike and Maureen Farrell, former Western Springs promoter Reece Facoory and his wife Dorothy, Martin and Lin Rogers, Vic and Daphne Paivinen, Greg and Claire Kentwell, Bobby and Colleen Thomson.

We came across Bobby in the early 1970s at Palmerston North and he said he wanted to go to England to ride. I told him he wasn't ready and he should go to North Queensland where there was a meeting every week during the winter. He ended up in Sydney, met Colleen and never went to England until March 2001 when he came with me to the Veteran Riders Dinner and we had a trip around the country for about a month.

We have been so blessed in so many ways and it is too easy to forget or to take the good things for granted. The way Raye and I see it is that for most of our life together we have been extremely fortunate to be rewarded directly or indirectly for my ability to ride a motorcycle.

It's something I would happily have done for nothing, after all.

IT'S GOODBYE FROM HIM – at Ole Olsen's farewell at Coventry in 1983

AND IT'S GOODBYE FROM ME – Mauger v Olsen one last time, Vojens, 1999, with future champion Jason Crump in pursuit

Heat 19

THE WAY WE WERE

WORLD championship silver medals provide all the motivation you need to win. Many people don't know or even care less that I have 10 silvers and five bronze medals from world championships.

One obvious conclusion to be drawn is that while I enjoyed a lot of success for quite a few years, there never was any shortage of outstanding contenders capable of winning the big prizes. There were guys who had been up there and were desperately keen to do it again. There were others whose ambition was to join the elite band.

To get there then, as now, required great determination, especially when there were the inevitable setbacks. Then came the greatest test, to constantly prove yourself as being worthy of the title and strong enough to withstand the pressure of having every other rider fired up to knock you off that top position.

For years speedway folk talked about whether a newly-crowned top man had what it took to be a 'good world champion'. Winning was one thing, but it came with extra responsibilities, an understanding of the traditions of the sport for which the world champion became an instant ambassador and standard bearer.

I'm not convinced ambitious young riders see it quite in those terms. Too many just want to show that they are 'the man' and to increase their earning power and marketability.

Anybody with these ambitions has to serve an apprenticeship, consolidate the learning curve for a few years and get the mind power and visualisation techniques working for them.

If you can't get your head around it, you will never become world champion by accident. You need to prepare physically and mentally and then you need to ride 25 per cent harder than at any time in your life.

Finally you need to accept that most of your hardest rivals will be doing the same thing as you in their preparation. I raced against half of the other 30 guys who have been world speedway champion, and for years it was them or me. In my 14 World Finals, there were half a dozen others who won the title so there always was plenty of serious opposition.

The reality is almost anybody can beat anybody else on a given day. But a handful are just so much more consistent than others and most of that comes down to desire and the right temperament at the big moments. You have to want it more than the others, and do whatever it takes to give yourself the best possible chance.

Only the few who have what I call 'the complete package' win world championships in any sport. I learned that from the great champions who helped point the direction for me.

Most sportsmen claim not to take much notice of the record books. Don't believe them. Results are the yardstick by which history judges us all.

People can and will argue indefinitely about whether Ole Olsen was a better rider than Hans Nielsen, whether Briggo or Peter Craven or Peter Collins was the most spectacular, or if Tony Rickardsson was a superior technician to Ove Fundin.

All of us can point to titles that got away. It's just talk in the end.

Forget all the debate; it was an enormous thrill to go past Fundin's five world titles. There was a sense of fulfilment for me when I did that, and I reckoned it was unlikely anybody would go close to winning six for a long time.

It was 26 years before Rickardsson matched that mark and for five of them he had the luxury of a Grand Prix series. There is no telling whether Jason Crump or Nicki Pedersen of the current crop might also get to that point but they will be pretty tired if they do.

Now they have Emil Sayfutdinov to contend with, and these are the only contemporary riders who seem to me to want it enough. With the old World Finals there were plenty of guys who went in thinking they could win it.

Money has never been the motivation needed to be world champion. It's all about ambition and that 'will to win'. You have to want it 24 hours a day for years before you get there, and for a handful, that desire is fuelled by the taste of success.

Tony, Ove and I all had 11 years between our first and last win. In sporting and racing terms, that's a long time to be there or thereabouts. As far as durability goes, Hans and Briggo were on the world championship scene for longer but even their four wins spanned only nine years from the first to last.

It is as difficult for me as a former competitor as it is for any observer to try to separate one great from another. I had the greatest respect for all of them but patriotism and mateship demand that any such comparison starts with Ronnie Moore and Barry Briggs.

Ronnie was the original, the inspiration. He had enormous natural talent. He was and still is my hero.

A very modest man, Ronnie has never fully grasped just what an influence he had on my career. New Zealand had never had a sportsman like him. All the kids in Christchurch, and especially in my district, absolutely idolised him. It's fantastic even now to see the respect and awe in which he is held by today's generation of young riders and their parents.

GOLDEN GREATS – Ove Fundin with Ronnie Moore and Peter Craven after their run-off at the 1960 World Final

Even the supremely gifted and natural talents have to work at it. Ronnie had the ability to make it all look so easy, he was uncannily comfortable and controlled on a bike and he had a racing brain as flexible as any computer. He could win races from the back just for fun and Wimbledon fans will tell you there never has been a better team rider.

Partnering him to World Best Pairs success in 1970 was an unimaginable thrill which remains right up there among my most cherished speedway moments. Only Raye could understand my emotions standing on the winner's podium with my all-time hero while the New Zealand national anthem was being played.

This, remember, was 20 years after Ronnie first qualified for an individual World Final. It will remain a topic for argument as to whether he could and should have achieved even more. Two world titles do not begin to tell the story of how good and how influential he was.

When he won the first of them, scoring a maximum in spite of a broken leg, he was the youngest world champion to that point. (When riders carry injuries into a World Final it inspires them to try harder as happened to me in the long track at Mühldorf and at Wembley in 1972.) When he won his second it was after taking a year and a half out of the sport because he wanted to race cars.

Sweden in 1971 was his 14th World Final appearance and yet he missed the equivalent of seven British seasons. That he could flit in and out of racing at the highest level barely missing a beat was a measure of how special he was. Even on the last of his several comebacks he still was a rider to be reckoned with.

He helped to change the face of racing when as a 17-year-old he started scattering the old soldiers, not with bravado and brute force, but with style, skill and sophistication.

This was on the Japs, remember, with their 22-inch rear wheel and spindly frames that were hard to ride and flexed every lap on tracks that had deep surfaces – not the 19-inch version adopted later. This was a motorcycle which behaved and responded quite differently to the Jawa on which he rode in the twilight of his career.

On the Czech machines, most people could look smooth. Ronnie had the artistry and technique to do so on equipment which was much more difficult to ride. Maybe he accomplished so much so soon that he grew a

NOT QUITE – Ivan consoles Briggo after their second place in the 1971 World Best Pairs Final in Rybnik

little jaded, perhaps he was more of a homebody than people realised and certainly he never sought or basked in the spotlight.

It is easy to overlook the fact that child prodigies, whether they ride a bike, swing a golf club or wield a tennis racket, can fall out of love with the demands of elite sport. It all appears so glamorous but when you come right down to it, it's not your run-of-the-mill nine to five job. When you're in it, you are in it 24/7. The only escape is to get out while the going is good.

Sadly, Ronnie got out, came back, got out again, came back again, got out again – and then suffered those life-threatening injuries at 42, riding for the World Series troupe in Newcastle. It was a year before he was healthy again. Like Briggo, he also had to contend with deeply personal tragedy, prematurely losing his wife Jill to cancer – June Briggs died in 2003, another good one taken much too soon.

It is a measure of Ronnie's character that he was one of the few world champions everybody genuinely liked. His attitude and performances commanded respect, he was even-natured and assured when thrust into a man's world, and he has changed little. It didn't matter if he was mixing it on World Final night or on Sunday mornings instructing a handful of wide-eyed and attentive kids at Moore Park – the track outside Christchurch dedicated to him – the same old Ronnie would be in evidence.

He is a steadfast ally, a dry humorist whose wit and understatement sits comfortably in any company. Maybe that is why he rarely seemed fazed at championship events. If he was having a good night or, occasionally, a bad one by his standards, it was difficult to detect any change of demeanour.

From his teens until the injury which cut short his 1963 season he was for year after year one of the favourites for the world title, with successive finishing positions of 4-4-6-1-2-2-6-1-2-6-5. One of those silver medals came in 1960 when he was placed between Fundin and Craven in the first three-way decider in history after they had each scored 14 points.*

So when talking about riders who could have finished up with more titles, Ronnie came closer than most. Not for nothing was he regarded as one of the 'big five' who ruled the roost during the period when I was coming up with my career Plan B in Australia.

Barry, like Ronnie, was usually there or thereabouts. His record of consistency was even more impressive, 17 finals on the trot, 10 times on the rostrum. He made himself a contender by force of personality and a willingness to charge at anything and any situation. His sheer physical presence made him a force to reckon with and he wore the motto 'if in doubt, flat out' like a badge of honour.

---

* The only other three-man run-off for the title was at Bradford in 1985 when Erik Gundersen (13) relegated Hans Nielsen and Sam Ermolenko to the minor placings.

380 – Ivan Mauger

Ronnie flitted on and off the scene as the mood took him; Peter Craven was brilliant before his untimely death, Björn Knutsson a big player who retired prematurely. Ove had a greater hunger for longer.

Briggo, though, rode as if his life depended upon it for year after year after year. He loved the scent of competition and the buzz of racing around the world. I can identify with that.

He had a reputation for being disorganised and the scrapes and panics involving Barry are legendary. He did not discourage that image and his bikes never were the prettiest to look at but that was part of his act – he always had fast engines.

Although he was the Jawa agent he always seemed to be borrowing spares from me that put my routine at big meetings out of whack. In the end Gordon and Wilfried kept a box with BB on it in my transporter which contained parts he had got from me. It was not until the veteran riders' dinner in 2007 they both told him.

When it came right down to it he was a tough, uncompromising racer, not the sort of rider I could ever be but always one of the most difficult to beat.

Briggo was at his best measuring himself against the best. I'm sure he found an extra gear when Fundin was alongside him although the association with Ronnie was a big part of his early development. Following Ronnie to Wimbledon, accompanying him on various trips, he had a ready-made role model and guiding light all rolled into one.

After that he usually was at his sharpest if there was someone outstanding in the same team, the best example being when he and Björn Knutsson rode together for Southampton. Their friendship was tight and yet their rivalry was immense as might be expected when both were as good as anybody in the world.

It's been a bit like that with me and Barry. For most of the time since I arrived at Plough Lane in April 1957 we have been on good terms, although he and others thought I was a bit of a young upstart and to be honest, I was at that time.

But anyone in any sport who has ambition tends to be like that and Briggo from all accounts was exactly like it in his early days at Wimbledon. There probably never has been a world champ who did not start out that way.

After a while we got on great but in a lifetime of close association of course there also have been times when it wasn't quite like that. Briggo disagreed with some of the things I said and did and it was very much vice versa. Many's the time we agreed to disagree.

WE THREE KINGS – *Christchurch boys Ivan, Briggo and Ronnie*

When highly motivated and ambitious people are going for the same target, the competitive juices come to the fore and while similar in that respect, we are quite different people. I had my methods of pursuing success and Barry had his and in the final countdown, we both proved to our own satisfaction that whatever works, works.

My approach was quite studious whereas Briggo had a more bull at a gate type of style. If a challenge or a problem presented itself he usually had an instinctive way of dealing with it. You got the impression he didn't spend months or weeks thinking about big meetings whereas I soaked up information and had plans formulating often years in advance.

That's not to say he wasn't a thinker. He was always trying different ideas when he was racing and his search for innovation has not slowed in his retirement years. He has come up with plenty of schemes out of left field, often going to great lengths to disguise his intentions until the master plan has been refined.

Between us we spent hours talking speedway and dreaming up schemes, the most productive of which would have been our World Series adventures. If our interest in speedway and similarities in our background meant we always would have plenty in common, the friendship between Raye and June was the glue that kept it together.

382 – Ivan Mauger

Speedway wives, especially those who develop the kind of close friendship those two did, have a different angle on everything. If Briggo and I ever got our wires crossed, over racing, business or anything else, those two were always smart enough to defuse the situation and pull us back into line. Their connection went way back to when Barry and June and her mum Queenie were so helpful to Raye when Julie was born.

Briggo could be ferocious on track and a laugh a minute off it. He enjoyed handing out nicknames to riders. It's because of him Ronnie became Mirac – short for Miracle Man.

My long-time nickname of Sprouts was his creation too. He reckoned my handlebars were so low in 1957 they were a ringer for Sprouts Elder, a famous American rider in the sport's pioneering days.

Only a few people around the world call me Sprouts – and even fewer call Raye by her given name of Sarah. Briggo was responsible for that one as well after hearing a nurse in St Stephens Hospital call her by her correct name when Julie was born.

People have assumed Ronnie and Barry were the people who advised me and taught me what I needed to know. That never was the case and neither gave me any particular help when I needed it the most as a kid at Wimbledon. Of course their example and achievements influenced me, they set the bar high and I was keen to get to a similar standard.

They were established as superstars and preoccupied with their own stuff while I was still a kid. Our paths crossed and the two of them were never less than encouraging but it probably wasn't until 1966, the year he won his last world title that Briggo and I were in the same ball park. With Ronnie, it was even later, when he had his third and last crack as a full-time rider.

In the first few years of my career, though, we raced with or against one another very infrequently. It was the exception rather than the rule. My early battlefields, Eastbourne, Rowley Park, and Newcastle were a million miles from Wimbledon or Wembley.

As a second-halfer I did learn a lot from them travelling to away meetings. But even at the Tuesday morning practices at Wimbledon they didn't say I should ride inside or the outside or use more or less throttle on the starts. There was no advice about the mysteries of changing gear, ignition settings or the compression.

They never talked to me about such things until we became international colleagues in Test matches, World Team Cups and World Best Pairs. By that time I had accumulated some knowledge of my own and the discussions were between equals.

Present and past champions have no obligation to pass on the secrets of their success, especially to potential rivals. It is a hard slog to the top and very few people hand out favours. When my track record and opinion

MASTER CLASS – Jack Young had so much knowledge to impart

was worth listening to, I was selective about what I wanted to share, and with whom.

It's a different thing if there is a generation gap. It was my good fortune that Jack Young, another great champion, was generous with his advice and guidance when I was at my most receptive. From first going to England thinking I knew plenty, to coming back realising I knew very little, was an education in itself. That was a point at which a sympathetic and worldly-wise mentor was a godsend.

Youngie had won his two world titles years earlier, he was winding down and devoid of further ambition yet sufficiently dialled in to recognise when he had a willing audience.

No man had a greater impact upon my mindset and the way in which my second shot at the big time panned out.

Money was not the main motivation, success was, but nevertheless I was dazzled with tales of the meetings he rode and the sums he earned in his heyday. Riders could race up to six nights a week in the early 1950s and never go outside of London and they were earning up to £500 a night – a bit different to when I came back to Christchurch in 1958.

Jack taught me the most about riding techniques, throttle control and many other aspects of speedway. He was wise in so many ways. I watched everything he did on and off the track. And he allowed me a grandstand seat because he said I could ride as close to him as I wanted when we met on track as he didn't get crossed up or out of shape.

384 – Ivan Mauger

Many times I was able to put my front wheel almost against his clutch going into the turns and then riding an inch or so from him down the straights. That helped me when I got to European and world championship finals because everyone rides hard particularly in the first and last turns in those meetings.

The pit gate was just by the exit of the fourth turn at Rowley Park and one night Youngie watched me ride, and then told me I had been spinning coming out of the corner. He looked at my back tyre and indicated the scuff marks on it. I turned the tyre round and had a new edge for the next race and did what he told me to do with the throttle.

Jack gave me a pass mark after watching my next ride to see if I was following his instructions. He again looked at the scuff marks and complimented me for having used much better throttle control with my wheels in line coming out of the turn.

Youngie had no hang-ups about my improvement and possessed a great sense of humour. We came back from Maribyrnong after I beat him in the Victorian titles. At breakfast, his wife Joan asked how he went and he said 'last night I rode better than at any time in my life' and put the trophy on the outside table.

After a while I had to leave and picked up my trophy. Joan was taken aback and asked me if I had won it. When I said I had, she turned to Jack and said 'I thought you said you rode the best in your life last night'. Youngie told her that was exactly right but admitted he was not going well enough to stop me.

One of his pearls of wisdom was that riders didn't get any credit for doing the fastest time in World Finals but if you were the top scorer at the end of the night then you were the champ and times did not come into it.

That framed my philosophy. I went as fast as was necessary to win races and always conserved my machinery as he had advised. I have held a lot of track records but rarely set out to break them. The most likely setting for doing that was at away tracks where the fans had given me the bird. I took pleasure in breaking the record in the first race next time I was there, just to annoy them.

Another nugget from Youngie's fund of advice before I came back to join Newcastle was he taught me to take deep breaths going to the start line. It puts oxygen in the blood and brain and makes you think clearer just before the tapes go up.

He also advised me to remember to take big breaths along the straights to increase the level. That was the key to passing guys on the last half lap when they got tired and lost concentration.

Another tip was to have the same ritual going into a World Final. In February 1963 I was a million miles away from qualifying for a World Final

The Will To Win – 385

but the fact Jack spoke as if it was inevitable certainly helped my confidence in eventually achieving it. He was one of the first people I called after the 1966 European Final to tell him I was on my way to Gothenburg.

Many times during my racing years I was able to think back and use what Youngie had taught me as a reference point. Those lunchtime yarns in Adelaide, or the lengthy question and answer sessions and tutorials when we shared cross-country trips to Melbourne and Sydney, imparted a treasure trove of information and sound advice.

Watching Peter Craven at Rowley Park in the 1960–61 season, it was easy to see why he was so highly rated and popular with fans. He was the opposite to Youngie or Ronnie, who appeared to be so casual and unhurried whereas Peter, a tiny little guy, was all action and excitement.

By all accounts when he first rode at Liverpool as a kid he fell off so often Gordon Parkins and almost everybody else associated with the promotion despaired of him ever becoming a rider. Yet he got the hang of it all so quickly, he was world champion by the time he was 21.

Big tracks or little ones, they all came the same to him. He was fast and brave, had super balance and reputations didn't bother him. Although Peter's two titles were separated by seven years he was in the mix every time with a couple of bronze medals to show for it. He still is England's only dual winner.

I rode against him only a handful of times in Australia and England and beating him was a huge occasion for me. Belle Vue wanted me from the moment I headed Peter around Hyde Road in 1963 but it was to be six years before they finally signed me.

By then Peter's spectacular performances were only a memory – but what a memory. His death at 29 was a tragedy in every sense and I am sure he had another world championship in him.

Ove Fundin had an insatiable appetite for winning. He was pretty much winding down his racing by the time I was joining the ranks of title challengers but we quickly developed a healthy respect for one another. Ove was a completely different kettle of fish from Briggo who was his greatest rival over a sustained period of time.

In many ways we had a similar approach. The stories go that he was very casual until the time came to go and race. Legend has it he never picked up a spanner and all he wanted to do was to be given a bike to race and then left to his own devices. I don't believe he could have been as good as he was for as long as he was without having a lot more about him than that.

On the big meetings Ove kept himself to himself, parked himself in a favourite corner of the pits, and not many people were game to approach him when he was in his trance-like state (much as I was in World Finals).

My guess is he was strongly into the mental preparation and attention to detail which served me well.

He missed very little, learned from every meeting and each venue, and studied tracks a year in advance. At his peak, in 11 finals from 1956–67 he amassed a remarkable 145 points and was never out of the top three (apart from 1966 when he failed to qualify for Gothenburg) with five gold, three silver and three bronze medals. Ove also won five European championships and when he retired could reasonably claim to be the world's most successful rider.

The Briggo fans would argue that one until the cows come home. For years before I came on the scene the pair of them wanted the same thing and their rivalry polarised opinions. Fundin wasn't everybody's cup of tea and neither was I but I always got on with him OK. He was the best inside rider ever, a good reflex starter, tremendously consistent.

Once it was all about the Swedes but Ole Olsen changed that. The Danes had nobody before him, and a string that followed after he had set the example. The story about how I helped get him a British League opportunity and the closeness of our relationship has been told many times, as has the chronicle of our rivalry during the 1970s.

He won the world title in 1971, 1975 and 1978 and at just about every major championship during that decade, he was the man to beat. We shared the same determination to be world champion although we had different ways of going about it and very different values in life.

Ole parked next to me, lived with me, and travelled with me in his first two years at Newcastle and was as much of a sponge and accumulator of information as I had been with Jack Young. All of that became common knowledge. In fact he learned very well, and reasonably enough couldn't wait to be his own man.

When I moved on Ole captained Newcastle and later Wolverhampton and Coventry, and always had input and influence into the teams for whom he rode. He also became a very good world champion and I have always been proud to have played a part in helping him achieve his racing success.

He would have done it anyway sooner or later. My help probably brought success much sooner and for sure cost me at world championship level in 1971. For a large part of our respective careers the common denominator was our obsession with the championship each year and the unspoken fear that we would fail to win it. That fear was one of the ingredients which drove us and made us successful. If anything we both had too much pride in our own performances.

After becoming a works rider I recommended Ole to Jawa in 1970, and although we were no longer teammates, we continued to travel together to meetings around the world in various forms of transport and to an assortment of venues.

But whenever we met we went to extraordinary lengths to beat each other. Whoever won, the other was angry with their own performance – not with either one of us for winning. During all this we had a mutual trust and this created a bond of friendship and respect for each other's ambitions that still exists.

His success inspired a generation of Danish riders and the likes of Erik Gundersen, Hans Nielsen and Jan O Pedersen followed his lead so assiduously they all became world champion. Denmark also enjoyed success at team level that would have been unimaginable before Ole, who was immensely passionate about his heritage. Latterly it has been Nicki Pedersen who picked up the baton.

It soon emerged an easy way to wind up Ole, who did not like Germans at all, was to point out that but for chance he could easily have been born a German – his home in Haderslev is close to the border. To gee him up I used to tell him if he had been born a bit south he would be a German. It took Ole a lot of years to get back at me.

Many years later he was on the World Series and after a Saturday night at Christchurch, we drove all night to race at Invercargill, which is about as

TITLED TRIO – Jack Milne, 1937 world champion, with Ole Olsen (1971, 1975, 1978) and Ivan before the Golden Jubilee World Final at Wembley

FLAMBOYANT CELEBRATION – Egon Müller, excellent on long track, one world speedway title to his name at Norden in 1983

far south as you can get in New Zealand, and raced the hell out of each other next day.

It was traditional afterwards to have a dance at the St Mary's club, where there were loads of local oysters and whitebait. We were rock and rolling until the early hours of the morning when Ole came over to me and said 'Sprouts, if you were born any further south you would have been an Eskimo.'

There were a couple of instances when we came close to falling out. He had his partner and manager from Vojens call and ask me to do a match race series with Ole in his British Farewell meeting at Coventry in 1983. When I asked why he had not rung me himself, he replied that Ole was too busy.

Ole was never too busy to phone me and ask my advice on 100 different subjects when he was riding. I told his manager I would be pleased to do the match races with him but he needed to give me a call. The call never came and I was at home on the day of his farewell.

It was getting close to start time before he realised I wasn't there. When he came on the line in a flap I told him that I would come down but in the future I didn't want one of his flunkeys to call me. When I wanted Ole to do a meeting with me in any one of a dozen countries I always did the job myself, and in proper time.

I said it would take me an hour and a half from Woodford and he would have to let me ride one of his bikes. That was fine as from day one, Ole had everything on his bike set up exactly the same as mine, even down to how I had the Elastoplast tape on the handlebars, although later on he had his right bar higher than mine.

I threw a pair of my bars 'n the boot and took off for Coventry. We didn't need to practise exhibition match races as we had done them dozens of times. We could usually pass each other a couple of times on each corner. Whoever was on the inside down the straight would go past the corner and the other would turn back and go past and then drift out wide coming out of the turn. We would pass each other again coming out of the turns and then rub elbows down the straight.

Just as Youngie encouraged me to ride close to him as part of my learning curve, Ole and I choreographed that routine on the second day of the Belle Vue training school in 1967 and over the years could pretty well do it blindfolded. A while ago we rolled back the years, got our gear on again and had a great match race at Vojens that was fantastic fun. I told Ole those four laps were more fun than I have on my jetskis all year.

When both of us were at our peak it was a matter of some concern to him if I was paid more than he was to appear at European long track and grass track meetings. His English manager Peter Adams was economical with the truth one time in 1981 when he spoke to the Cloppenburg club and arranged for Ole to go there instead of me for a big guarantee.

Bottom line is I didn't do the meeting for which they had contracted me and which was scheduled to earn me a lot of money – much more that I would normally get in Europe – and there were threats of legal action flying about. By way of compensation Peter had to part with a substantial sum to get me to do a meeting he was organising in Ballymena, Northern Ireland.

The irony is that Cloppenburg approached me because they fancied my chances of beating Egon Müller, absolutely the best grass tracker in the world and one of the best long track riders there has been. Müller, who won the 1983 speedway World Final in Norden, was not everybody's favourite and the local promoter wanted his colours lowered.

Egon was not so difficult to beat on speedway, a difficult opponent on long track and nearly impossible to overcome on the grass. I was never going to beat him at Cloppenburg so I thought it poetic justice Ole was going to get his ass kicked by Egon who he did not like at all.

Each had a healthy suspicion of the other for years. Then they had a big falling out at Cape Town when the World Series troupe went to South Africa in 1975. Their fragile relationship never quite recovered from that spat.

It's easy enough to fall out with a rival but as far as Ole and I were concerned, we had many tremendous battles all over the world on speedway and long track and somehow we remain best of friends.

In our case the animosity and rivalry existed mostly between Gordon and Henry Bork, our mechanics. They always were pretty guarded with one another.

Henry liked to tease Gordon about Ole's ability to beat me in the Golden Helmet in Pardubice, which he did more times than I care to remember. Gordon would get back at Henry every time I won a world championship on speedway or long track.

Everybody rightly respects the role Ole had in getting the Grand Prix into shape from 1995. While some of the things he has said and done haven't met with universal approval, no one doubts he always tried to act in the best interests of the sport and its long-term future.

Usually it was easy to predict where the big challengers were coming from but for many speedway followers, Jerzy Szczakiel's 1973 world title victory was the biggest upset in the history of the sport.

All I can say to that is had anybody seen him in the World Best Pairs in Rybnik a couple of years earlier, when he and Andrzej Wyglenda were unstoppable, they would not have been quite so shell-shocked.

History does not remember Szczakiel kindly and many observers put down his individual and pairs victories as a freak. His inability to travel well, and especially a couple of horribly disappointing trips to England, obscured the fact he could ride. Of course the Grand Prix series would have found him out but in those times you had to do the business on the day and he proved he could do that.

If his win was an upset, it was a surprise to many that Anders Michanek took until 1974 to win a world title, and then did not repeat it. Anders was a very consistent rider from the first time he appeared in the British League, arguably Sweden's best after Fundin.

In major meetings he frequently looked the part and the previous year won the British-Nordic Final and the European Final.

When he scored a terrific maximum in Gothenburg it was one of the most comprehensive World Final wins. He was half the length of the straight ahead of everybody after the first lap. It was a case of the other 15 trying to get second which I did by beating Sören Sjösten in a run-off.

The truth is Anders was in a league his own that night and yet when he trailed in third in his first race at Wembley in 1975 he seemed relieved. He peeled off four wins and finished second to Olsen and later told me he was happy because he didn't want to be world champion again.

His take on it was that when you climb to the top of the mountain you don't want to do it again.

It's a point of view, not one to which I subscribe, but the relentless pressure and expectation that accompanies being world champion is not for everyone. Anders often considered the commuting back and forth and the pull on his loyalties in Sweden and England to be a big price to pay. In 1974 the Swedes were banned from England and that helped rather than hindered him in his one title-winning year.

Peter Collins, who delighted so many fans when he lifted the crown in 1976, had the talent, the excitement factor and widespread appeal the British had been waiting for since Peter Craven's death.

TRADING PLACES – Peter Collins gets his hand on the 1976 world title, the one Ivan regards as his greatest lost opportunity

392 – *Ivan Mauger*

I never hid my regard for his ability and was instrumental in pushing his early career at Belle Vue. He had an easy manner, plenty of confidence which stemmed from having ridden on grass with a great deal of success, and at that stage he was quick and fearless.

Temperament seemed to be his strong suit. He had epic battles with Michanek in the Daily Mirror International tournament final at Wembley as a 19-year-old, and famously in the Speedway Star KO Cup final run-off at Hyde Road at the end of the same year.

In '74 he headed me and Ole in a European Final run-off which raised the rafters at Wembley. There is no doubt he was destined to be a champion and he might have achieved it a year earlier but for the fiasco on World Final night in 1975 before getting it all together in Poland.

It definitely was a sore point when the press virtually ignored my unlucky near miss in Katowice, preferring to concentrate on celebrating the fact PC had won and Malcolm Simmons was runner-up. Peter was on his Dave Nourish-tuned engine and both had special cams made for that track and twin carburettors which the FIM later banned.

There was little or no recognition that I had their measure even as the only rider on a two-valver and my race breakdown was conveniently ignored. Of course a miss is as good as a mile and the world of sport is littered with 'might have been' moments, but it grated with me.

I could hardly wait to take some serious revenge when the next chance presented itself.

Lady Luck moves in mysterious ways. Peter was a big favourite to win again but suffered a nasty shin injury days before Gothenburg, where I was to collect my fifth title. Fully fit, maybe he would have done it again. Less than fit on a night which tested the nerve and health of everyone, he had to settle for second and never again was he a title contender.

He had a shocker and failed to qualify in 1978 and the following year another injury on a wet night at Cradley knocked some of the bounce out of him. PC was a more careful rider in the 1980s, still very good, sometimes brilliant but not quite the meteoric presence of his first few years.

His legacy is a solid one, he and his wife Angela have been longtime friends of ours and for some years were our neighbours in Cheshire. He is one of the most fondly-remembered of stars. He was a special talent but like some others so blessed, he wasn't convinced of the need to work harder and cultivate more of a cutting edge.

Peter loved the ride when he was a star on the rise but in the final analysis probably achieved less than he should have done. He was and is a tremendously engaging personality and rightly regarded as one of the best England riders. Some claim him as the best.

He flew the flag with great distinction as he featured in five World Team Cup-winning sides and picked up World Best Pairs gold with four different partners. Twice British League Riders' champion, he was a good tourist and ambassador and a great addition to our World Series troupe.

Peter always has had a solid respect for speedway and its traditions. He allied himself with the bid to keep Belle Vue going after Bammy sold Hyde Road and has kept in touch with the sport. For several years he has been the busiest and most enthusiastic collector and restorer of old machines.

I never could bring myself to have remotely the same regard for Michael Lee, who like PC burned like a shining star for a while, winning the world title in 1980 and the long track crown in 1981.

Michael won two British Finals in a row while still in his teens and was a natural-born racer. He had the world at his feet but all too early got into some bad ways, received poor advice and as a consequence never properly fulfilled his enormous potential.

It is enjoyable seeing how experience comes out against emerging youth and we had some good races as his career was taking off and mine was approaching its later stages. When it became obvious Michael was leading a lifestyle which suggested he was likely to be around for a good time rather than a long time, my reaction, and that of most others, was that meant there was one less dangerous rival to contend with.

Seeing great ability wasted is something which happens in sport. At the same time, the Moran brothers identified themselves as two of the most brilliant talents ever to step on a bike, great guys and terrific entertainers, but they also could have done so much better. They were extreme versions of the laidback Californian party boy crowd and made their own choices.

Bruce Penhall learned his speedway in a similar environment but he had the focus and the discipline to keep everything in perspective. When he rode against us and then with us on the World Series it was clear he was destined to go all the way to the top.

Bruce listened to the advice Briggo and I gave him during the World Series tours and was a smart boy. While he was very image-conscious and found time for fun, when it came to the racing he was strictly business.

Many speedway folk tended to write off Egon Müller's 1983 victory as a fluke, much as they did with Jerzy Szczakiel. That undervalued the ability of the rider and overlooked the quality of opposition that had to be dealt with on the day.

The next two world champions, though, were riders of the highest quality when measured alongside the all-time greats. Erik Gundersen and Hans Nielsen were products of the wave of enthusiasm which enveloped Denmark once Ole started to feature in the big time.

394 – Ivan Mauger

Erik was a cheery, outgoing character, very energetic and all over the bike. He was an immensely popular personality who always was going to be top man sooner or later.

As events turned out, he won the speedway championship three times, the long track once, and was a big part of the Danish surge in the 1980s. It didn't hurt his cause at all to have Ole in his corner and for a long while he was the favoured one while Hans and Ole had a very distant and cool relationship.

Until the shocking accident which almost cost him his life, Gundersen was an entertainer and enterprising with it. Nielsen was much more stylish, studied and methodical.

If the GP system had been brought in earlier, Hans almost certainly would have won even more. In the early 1990s he was the most consistent rider for several years in a row, but his failure to win all-important races cost him at least three of the last few one-off World Finals. In a GP format they would not have mattered.

Nevertheless I think Hans would agree I helped him finally crack his world championship hoodoo as his adviser in 1986. He was desperate to learn how to win after having finished as runner-up to Erik in the previous two finals.

I got to know Hans and his wife Suzanne very well when he came on my retirement tour in Australia, ironically as a replacement for Gundersen. Because most of the guys were single they would be doing their own thing while Raye and I would stay in the hotel with the Nielsens. We regularly ate meals together and sat around the swimming pools over a two-month period.

After the tour, Raye and I were chilling out at our condo in California when Peter Oakes called to say Hans was asking if he could contact me to see if I would help him. Later Hans phoned and when we talked about a financial arrangement I hit him with a figure which admittedly was quite a lot for those days.

There was silence on the other end of the phone until I said I only wanted the money if he won the world championship. If he finished second or third I didn't want a penny other than my expenses. I pointed out I had more to lose than he did, unless he won it.

There was good chemistry between us. We made many small but important changes to his set-up, analysed tracks and riders and achieved a happy outcome as Hans won convincingly in Katowice, and backed up by winning the two-day final in Amsterdam the next year.

Erik hit back in 1988 when Hans went against my advice over the choice of tyres (Kenny Carter all over again) but our partnership continued into 1989 before coming to an end a few weeks before Munich.

When it came to firming up our arrangement for '89 late in the piece Hans said he didn't want to continue as he thought he could win again without paying me all that money. It was annoying because I had been advising him all the way through the year and a lot of things he did at the final were following our discussions.

Possibly he considered there was a conflict of interest as I was also helping Simon Wigg, primarily with the long tracks. To be fair, Simon was also going well enough that year to finish second in the speedway World Final. Hans won on his own merits, we didn't fall out and remain good friends, but you have to wonder why he won only one more individual title after that.

More than tennis players or golfers who also have coaches or technical advisers, speedway guys are usually macho types who want everyone to believe they do it by themselves. No world speedway champion ever does it by himself. But I think Hans felt he had learned as much as he could from me and needed to make his own decisions.

After our tie-up was announced, Briggo phoned me and said 'Sprouts, what can you tell Hans Nielsen that he doesn't already know? He has been second in the world for the past two years.'

But that was the whole point. I told Briggo that if he didn't get help from outside he was going to keep being second. His win in '86 broke the ice and cracked the mental hold Erik and Ole had over him.

AFTER OLE – Erik Gundersen leading Hans Nielsen in the 1989 World Final in Munich, the last in which these great Danish rivals clashed

VICTORIOUS – Ivan on hand as Hans Nielsen tastes world championship success at last, Katowice 1986

Theirs was a partnership which worked very effectively and for a long time there was something of a Cold War atmosphere – most of it, I believe, generated by Ole who never got on with Hans from the start.

Hans could beat Ole very soon after he first came to England and I think Ole saw his Danish No.1 position threatened for the first time. On Sunday mornings flying with me to Europe, Ole regularly complained about Hans's tactics at various meetings.

Hans had ridden for Birmingham, Wolverhampton and Oxford, all little tracks where he tended to go very fast into the corner, come to a bit of a halt in the middle of the turn and accelerate out of it. He needed to come to grips with the bigger tracks and above all he had to believe he could win when the chips were down.

To give him his due, he was receptive when I told him what he needed to do to square off the tracks like Katowice. There are four different scenarios on how to ride a lap on the large Chorzów circuit. Our detailed planning paid off in rich dividends when Hans blocked fellow countryman Tommy Knudsen when he attempted to go under him off turn four in a crucial and highly controversial crash.

Knudsen complained that he had been a victim of foul riding and the exclusion cost him dearly. It was one of those 50-50 decisions, some you win, some you lose. Hans did the same thing to Sam Ermolenko in the 1993 World Final and was disqualified so it was probably tit for tat.

We worked together all through 1987 and although Gundersen was leading after the Saturday night in Amsterdam, I told Hans if he stayed steady and kept his resolve he would win it overall. He had a sponsorship from Barum tyres and used them on the Saturday night and planned to use them on Sunday.

But Dunlops were by far the better option and I told him to put the Barums out of sight or I wasn't going to be around on the Sunday. He did that, outscored everyone on the Sunday afternoon leg and ended up as champion again.

The tyre debate came back to haunt us in Vojens when Hans had the chance to equal my record of three wins in a row. It so often rains there and the idea of using Barums was still a bad idea. Hans did not agree and claimed they were good in the wet from the start. He fitted one in his first race but lost it to Erik.

There was no disgrace getting beaten by Erik in a world championship but there was no sense dropping a point to your main rival without good reason. Hans changed to Dunlops, won his next four races and got himself into a run-off for the title when Gundersen failed to win his last ride.

Out of the blue, Hans decided to switch back to the Barum tyre for the decider. His reasoning was he felt it was better suited to the deep, wet conditions off the inside grid. Deep down I was sure it would spin and cost him and of course that's just what happened.

To this day Hans probably feels he made the right choice but if he had started on the Dunlop he probably wouldn't have been in a position to have needed to do an extra race.

After finishing my association with Hans, I continued to have a lot to do with Wiggy and I think both us felt it was a worthwhile working arrangement, quite apart from the fact we got on so well socially.

Our contract was aimed towards the long track and almost identical to the one with Hans although we also had a sliding scale for speedway. Pretty well everything we did as far as mental and physical preparation, nutrition, mind power, relaxation and visualisation were concerned applied to both disciplines.

The long track world championship has never recovered from the loss of Wiggy. For 20 years from 1970 most of the top dozen or so speedway riders rode in it as well as loads of world quality long trackers such as Egon Müller, Karl Maier, Marcel Gerhard, Alois Wiesböck and of course Simon.

398 – Ivan Mauger

His departure from the scene coincided with Egon and Karl retiring. All were personalities and showmen in their own right but Wiggy had their measure and was such a dominating character.

Gerd Riss took over the mantle in later years but when it came to personality, Simon was a one-off. His illness and death from a brain tumour at the age of 40 was a huge loss.

I knew Simon's brother Julian quite well from grass tracks in England and Europe in the 1970s. Wiggy started coming over to the continental grass tracks when he was about 17 and we struck up a friendship almost immediately.

I raced against him many times during the last five or six years of my career and he often travelled to European meetings in my transporter. Most Fridays Norrie would take the transporter from our base in Cheshire to the Continent and if Simon was in the same meeting they usually teamed up and travelled together.

Later he became a high-standard speedway racer but it was on the long tracks and grass that he was an out and out superstar. At one stage he was having an unusually lean spell and asked me if I would help him.

Much like Ole and Kenny Carter, he was always receptive. In a three-year period he won the long track back-to-back and was second in the speedway World Final in Munich. I was proud of that association and Simon's complete trust in following out our game plans.

Simon didn't question things. We agreed I would always be the last one to speak before he went to the tapes. I would have five seconds to relay final instructions or reprise what we had planned. He always kept to that and would do everything I told him.

It's not the same as winning it yourself, but it is immensely satisfying and pleasing when a rider follows a strategy which has been formulated and goes out and wins a world championship. In the end of course it's up to the rider and the record shows Wiggy had the ability to deliver.

He won twice more after our business arrangement had ended, but it was not the finish of our relationship, or even of our in-depth discussions about various aspects of the sport.

Simon was a natural, a larger than life personality whose vibrant zest for life touched everybody. I'm proud to have known him as a rival racer. I knew him as a travelling companion, as his manager and motivator, then as a promoter.

I had known him as a neighbour when he finally achieved his great ambition of moving to Australia as a permanent resident for what turned out to be such a tragically short time, and most of all, I had known him as a friend.

WHEELIE WONDER – Simon Wigg, five times world long track champion, putting on the style at Brisbane's Albion Park

After he had to finish riding, he bought another home on the water at Paradise Point, a couple of miles from our house. By this time he was not allowed to drive. I told him I had a pushbike he could borrow and Simon said he would walk over.

Time went by and I was worried something had happened to him. Then this nose and great big grin came through the gate and there was Simon – looking like someone straight out of the Tour de France.

He had everything, the cycling shorts, the cycling shirt, the special shoes, the helmet and the sunglasses! He had the lot, including the bike. It turned out halfway between our houses there was a bicycle shop where he stopped and bought not only a racing bike but everything to go with it.

That was so typical of him and it is an abiding memory. Another was the last time I saw him, his health deteriorating fast and obviously a very sick man in a hospice in England where he returned for what proved to be the final time in 2000.

After we had left him for the last time and were about to leave, Raye said 'I think Simon would like to see you on your own, Ivan, why don't you go back'.

I went in by myself, gave him a big hug and told him 'I've always loved you, Wiggy'. As clear as a bell he said 'I know that' and put both his arms around me in a big cuddle. In that instant he wasn't like how we had seen him for the months before, it was like the old irrepressible Wiggy.

A few months after Wiggy's funeral his wife Charlie and brother Julian and their families came to the Gold Coast to have a memorial service. They knew better than most how close we had been, and how many happy hours we had spent on the water.

They had decided Simon's ashes would be spread on the water and after quite a function around at Wiggy's house, I was asked if I would perform the ceremony. I was so touched and we went down to the end of the jetty and I sprinkled them onto the water, just as the tide was just coming in.

So many images live on. In the first Australian Long Track Grand Prix at Bathurst the TV cameras were there and Wiggy was the star of the show. He did a beautiful wheelie all the way along the front straight and we used that action shot in our television commercials for the long tracks from then on.

MODERN HERO – Jason Crump, one of the best of this or any era

I'm sure it is the way Simon would like to be remembered, entertaining the crowd and giving his all.

Mentoring riders is something I have always enjoyed, whether it's at a training school for youngsters or working with experienced stars who felt they wanted something extra to give them a push into the winner's circle.

After working with Hans and then Wiggy, I took pretty much a back seat. With the odd exception, I've viewed riders over the past few years just like any other observer – well perhaps not quite like that, but you'll know what I mean.

My path barely brushed that of Sam Ermolenko or Per Jonsson and I didn't race competitively against Jan O Pedersen, Gary Havelock, or Tony Rickardsson, who took their turn in winning over the first half of the 1990s. But I have had some connection with a few of the guys who have won since the Grand Prix era started in 1995.

Billy Hamill came to a training school at the South Bay Stadium in Gardena, California, when he was just 15. Justice Brothers had given me a load of T-shirts numbered 1 to 30. Billy wanted the No.1 and as he was the youngest I gave it to him.

He was very attentive during the school and even then was called Billy the Bullet because of his hard-charging style of riding. I told him afterwards I would send him a photo when he became world champion and did just that when he won in 1996.

In 2000 I had quite a few conversations with Mark Loram who won the title that year. The connection there was via Norrie Allan who became Mark's mechanic, manager and adviser. Mark rode in a few of my Australian meetings and, just as he did in Europe, gave tremendous value – one of the most spectacular racers of recent times.

My contribution in the early days was to give Norrie some advice in matters such as contract negotiations, and, during that year to talk to Mark in the lead-up before the Grand Prix meetings and put it into his head that he could win.

Nothing has provided me with greater pleasure than to see Jason Crump establish himself as one of the great performers. Three world titles say all that needs to be said although it is worth noting he has a remarkable record of consistency going back over many years, including five silver medals and one bronze during the same period.

I have known Jason since he was riding junior speedway on 125cc bikes at Mildura. Phil Crump has been a close friend, racing colleague and rival, and it was inevitable I would take more of an interest in Jason than other kids – and he was worth it. In a relationship based on mutual respect and trust he is the modern-day rider whose success gives me the biggest kick.

SIX PACK – Sweden's Tony Rickardsson, the only other person to know what it takes to have won six speedway world titles

I was the first promoter to pay Jason a minimum guarantee when he rode in my 1993 Australian Long Track Grand Prix at Exhibition Park, Canberra. I told him I would pay him what he wanted only because he was Phil's son.

Ten years later I paid Phil to do match races with me at Redcliffe near Brisbane and at Invercargill the following week. We had a laugh about it when Jason called and said I was only paying Crumpie because he was Jason's dad.

Not everybody in modern speedway thinks Jason has a sense of humour but that is solely because when he is at work he is a man on a mission. He loves to race and he races to win. He has shown great strength of character, has always listened to and respected any advice I have offered him, and his appetite is as sharp as ever.

I haven't had anything much to do with riders like Tony Rickardsson, Nicki Pedersen, Greg Hancock or Tomasz Gollob, so my observations on them are based on what I have seen in person or on television or what people whose opinion I respect and are closer to the action have told me.

Hancock has been terrific, very steady, very consistent and a great ambassador. Gollob is usually worth the price of admission alone yet never quite found a way to win under the GP system. But his brilliance, especially at Bydgoszcz and Leszno, would have won him a one-off title at either of those tracks.

Emil Sayfutdinov brought a complete new dimension to the GP in 2009. Winning three of them at 19 years of age and getting on the rostrum at the first attempt suggests there could be a Russian winner in the not too distant future. That has to be an attractive prospect for the GP organisers because the same guys have been up there for a long time.

Three of them have shared the last nine titles. Pedersen is another excitement machine, sometimes too exciting for his own good. One title you can fluke, getting another has been beyond plenty of good riders and three championships is a pretty solid body of work.

Rickardsson obviously was out of the ordinary. He was a classy rider, strong and tactically organised. He had an aura about him, a certainty and self-confidence which defined him as the man to beat for several years.

Tony did things differently, he was not afraid to be an innovator and he used modern technology very effectively. Was he as good as, or better than me, or Fundin? That's not a question for me to answer.

All I can say is nobody is better placed than I am to appreciate how much effort he would have had to put in to win six titles. I hope he's enjoying life after speedway as much as I am.

THE TWO OF US – celebrating after Ivan's world long track championship win at Mariánské Lázně in 1976

Heat 20

THE LAST WORD

Ivan, the husband, father and grandfather

EVERYBODY has their own idea about the identity of the 'real' Ivan Mauger.

One book on a person's life can only give part of the bigger picture because collectively the memories are too long to fully capture on paper.

Many things help shape the person. However, there is a centre within us all that produces the true essence.

Along with our children, I am proud to have been among those who helped shape Ivan's life. And in writing some of my memories I hope to give a semblance of the nature of the man.

Ivan was 17 and I was 16 when we married. Speedway has ruled our life for over 50 years and neither of us has regretted it.

We are grateful for the life it provided. The children and I are just as aware that we have given most of our life to speedway.

Any teenager will have a hard time understanding where we came from and the hardships we had to endure for Ivan to eventually realise his ambition of winning the world championship.

by **Raye (Sarah) Mauger**

I was born in Carlisle, not so far from Newcastle upon Tyne where later Ivan rode for the Newcastle Diamonds. I was the 13th child from Scottish parents and along with my brother Matthew the only 'Anglo' in the family. My father was an aero technician.

We moved to New Zealand in January 1950, the country's centenary year, and arrived to a festival atmosphere. My parents paid the full fare and sold everything they owned in the UK, missing out on the scheme under which it cost only £10 to emigrate.

Christchurch is a small dot on the planet, and it was even smaller when Ivan and I met. We were still at school and riding pushbikes. The Telfers lived in New Brighton, a seaside town, and the Maugers in Woolston, about three and a half miles away.

It seems amazing that in addition to our first home in New Zealand, Ivan and I lived at Fulham, Wimbledon, Whalley Range, Denton, Bramhall and

TRUE BELIEVER – Raye never doubted Ivan's ability to win speedway's most coveted trophy

Woodford in England, had a home in California and for the past 23 years have been at Runaway Bay in Australia.

When Ivan was racing we travelled round the world so many times, I lost count. How many people have had what we have?

We've so much to be grateful for. Our children had the worldly experiences with us, and they too have a lot to be grateful for.

We are a close-knit family. Julie, Kym and Debbie and their families live within 10 minutes of us on the Gold Coast. I like to think we grew up together and that is what we are still doing even now, growing up together and unlike so many less fortunate families, we are friends.

We love our lifestyle and like the fact we are one jump away from New Zealand where Ivan and I still spend some of the year.

After travelling a great deal, I find it the most beautiful country in the world. Visitors leave talking of the breathtaking scenery. We travel by road as much as we can when we are in New Zealand and every bend brings a new and eye-catching scene.

Christchurch is in the South Island of New Zealand and with hills on one side and a view of the Southern Alps on the other it is very picturesque.

But Ivan always had ambition to conquer new frontiers and his ability to ride a motorcycle was our passport.

My first trip on a motorbike with Ivan was memorable. Ivan was 14 and came to take me out on his brother Trevor's bike. He picked me up from home, intending to take me for a short trip. It ended up being just that.

I was not allowed to wear slacks as my parents said they were for boys, and in those days 'it was not becoming for a young lady.'

I tucked in my skirt as best I could and put my hands on Ivan's waist. It was not the most comfortable sitting pillion so maybe it was just as well the ride was so short-lived. As we rode over a bridge, half a mile from my home, a car ran into us and I landed on the bonnet with Ivan on the other side of the car.

The driver was visibly upset, most concerned and profusely sorry. We assured him we were not hurt and the bike was all right. As he drove off, we breathed a sigh of relief, as there had been no question of insurance or exchanging of addresses, never mind a licence.

As a child I daydreamed about becoming a singer. Ivan's dream was to go to England and race but as we did not have enough money for me to go with him, we decided to become engaged. I was only 15.

Without consulting anyone we bought a little heart-shaped ring from a jeweller's in New Brighton, the only place in Christchurch where the shops were open on Saturday.

By Sunday, I had picked up enough courage to tell my parents. My mother in her broad Scottish accent told me in no uncertain terms what I had to do with the ring.

'You are still a bairn,' she said.

'You have no idea what you are thinking about. Just you take that to the shop you bought it from and get the money back, and you can tell Ivan you are both too young.'

My father agreed with my mother but I was not perturbed as I felt they would come around to my way of thinking.

Next day I went off to work as usual and suddenly realised I had left the ring at home. I worried for the rest of the day, thinking my mother would have found it and what she would do with it.

Riding home I nearly had an accident with a car. I stopped on the side of the road and took a few deep breaths to calm myself down and said a quiet prayer. (When I was young, I asked God for help quite often!)

As soon as I got home I ran to the bathroom but the ring was not there. Then I dashed to the end of the hall into Mum and Dad's room, went straight to the five-drawer tallboy and opened the middle drawer.

When I put my hand in the left hand corner there was a little box containing my ring.

My mother said she did not know where the ring was, and looked at me in disbelief when I produced it. Mum didn't speak about it again until my father came home at 9.30pm after working late.

After his supper Mum told him what had happened. I can still hear them talking in that lovely Scottish accent, Mum telling Dad what I had done and my father saying: 'Well Nan, it is the will of God and as young as they are we cannot change that.'

Ears glued to the door in the hallway, I tiptoed away with the greatest smile on my face, giving thanks for the help I had received. I'm sure this all happened to help us in what was to follow when I became pregnant.

Young love is quite ignorant of nature. If anyone had asked us if we would marry we would have said yes. 'When' was a different answer.

We spent as much time as possible with each other and my eldest brother David's wife Hetty warned my mother as well as me.

'What do you two think you're doing, always cuddling and canoodling?' she said.

'This has got to stop.'

Hetty and David had not long arrived from Hawick in Scotland and were living with us while they were waiting on their house. Ivan got on well with them both as he did and still does with the rest of my family.

It was frightening when I found out I was pregnant and I hardly slept all night. My mind worked overtime. We did not know if our parents would allow us to get married, or even if they would make us give away our baby.

I wasted my energy worrying as Dad and Mum, having already decided it was the will of God when we became engaged, now accepted we should be married. When Ivan came over and we told them, Mum was upset but Dad just said they would talk it through and asked him to bring his mother and father to discuss things further.

My mother and Ivan's mother were chalk and cheese. Ivan's mother Rita was an extrovert and mine was much more introverted and came across as a 'lady'. Rita on the other hand said what she thought and damn the consequences. I loved them both.

Dad Mauger was not in the best of health and was unable to drive over to our home. Ivan's mother arrived on her pushbike, on what was a very hot day. Ignoring the front door, she left her bike at the back door, entering the family room through the scullery and kitchen and swearing about it being so hot.

After the introductions, it did not take long to decide that we were to be married. Everything was going to be all right after all.

'Well, they will be getting married in a church,' said Rita, to which my father and mother replied: 'Of course.'

My father was a lay preacher at his church and rather a religious fanatic in my eyes. I expected him to say more on the subject, but he was diplomatic and kept his thoughts to himself.

'What a woman,' said my mother when Rita disappeared down the drive.

'Used the back door, did not knock, and swore her way into the house. Mind you, she rode that bike from across the other side of Christchurch. She has got some spunk to do that.'

My father agreed.

FOR THE LADIES – Ivan's mum Rita and Raye toast the 1977 champion

Rita sure did have a lot of spunk and later in life rode a motorbike from Christchurch to Invercargill to raise money for the Commonwealth Games. She was given a motorbike to ride by Craig Jones who had ridden speedway and owned a motorbike shop. Not only was he to sponsor her, he also had to teach her to ride a bike. No one knew it, but she never did have a motorbike licence.

Mum Mauger raised more money towards the Commonwealth Games than any other individual in New Zealand.

In next to no time, my family learned to love her and Dad Mauger as I did, and it was comforting to know they loved me from the start.

Ivan and I chose the Methodist church to be married in as we both thought there was one God and the nearest church would do fine. Neither of us were or are especially religious in any way but I do feel a superior being helped me find the ring and convince my father it was the will of God.

When we had our children, we decided that they could make there own choice about religion and we never had them christened or baptised. They all grew up with good morals and decent principles. We are extremely proud of them, especially as we had the three of them before I was 21. They are all very humane in their approach to life and respectable citizens.

Both Ivan and I learnt many of life's lessons in our early years. From 12 years old until he left school, Ivan worked doing deliveries. From 13 I was paid £5 to work Saturday and Sunday in a restaurant/milk bar, and I baby sat occasionally for two women who worked in the restaurants, making another £5 from them.

I was a pleasant outgoing teenager and as young as I was a Jack of all trades, clearing or serving at tables, serving in the milk bar, weighing vegetables or fruit and making the ice-cream. There was a jukebox in the milk bar and I learnt the songs easily.

I had quite a good voice and sang a lot.

When I left school to work as an office junior I was only getting £2-10-0 a week, less than I was getting in the restaurant. Unfortunately after only working for a few months I had an operation on my right leg – I had polio when I was three.

After the operation, I was using crutches for some months and this meant I had to give my permanent job away as it was up three flights of stairs. I found another job in a clothes factory sewing. Ivan was working in a subsidiary of the same firm.

I still worked most weekends in the restaurant and just occasionally managed to go to the speedway at Aranui when Ivan started to race. Saving up was the big thing, so he could go to England. We desperately wanted to go together but it didn't seem especially likely at that stage.

Even so, we watched every penny, going without ice cream and milkshakes which normally would be a teenager's staple diet. We went to garage cinemas in people's homes paying sixpence each instead of going to the normal movies and paying one shilling and six pence.

It was the bare necessities for us, no fancy clothes and no treats and we were to continue this for many years. It was to be a long time before we could kick what became a habit and relax into the finer things of life.

Because we were under age, a magistrate had to give permission allowing us to be married. Deciding we would marry in the Methodist church, Ivan and I had then to speak to the minister who explained he did not have to marry us. After we told him a bit about our lives and met his young son, who had some sort of illness, and who took a liking to me, all was OK and we were to be married.

I went to bed that night and thanked God for once again taking care of us.

Ivan went and measured up for a hired suit and my mother took me to have my dress made.

OFF TO SEE THE WORLD – leaving New Zealand for London was such an adventure for the kids from Christchurch

I did not choose white as white was for purity – I tried not to be a hypocrite.

Instead I chose the colours I liked and made me feel good, pastel blue for myself and pastel green for my bridesmaid Beverly, my brother Kenneth's girlfriend and later his wife.

Audrey Flower, one of my girlfriends, made our cake and I have not seen a cake to match it. With its very intricate white icing in a three-looped fence and beautiful pillars, it was the nearest I have seen to filigree in icing.

We ended up with around 70 guests, mostly relations and Rita's and our speedway friends. Mum and Dad could not afford a larger invite. Ivan, who in later years was so particular about how he appeared in public, had to have his wedding suit pinned on to him by my sister Margaret as the hire firm had muddled things when he picked it up.

After the wedding, we stood at the entrance to our reception greeting our guests. I remember everyone gave me a kiss and some of the riders including the old ones going to the back of the queue and coming back for another kiss. Ivan ended up joining them. It makes me smile to remember it.

We had a sit-down wedding breakfast and speeches, and then left to change our clothes for the trip to the North Island. There were all the usual goodbyes before we set off to catch the ferry for the beginning of our honeymoon.

And after that, the trip to England lay ahead. Our savings stretched to a second fare and Fate had decided we would go together after all.

We spent our first days as a married couple at my cousin Leslie's two-storey home at Karori near Wellington. It had great views over the bush and down to the sea. Leslie and her husband Ralph worked at the telephone exchange, monitoring overseas calls.

Ivan and I travelled into Wellington to pick up my passport.

THAT'S MY MAN – Raye makes sure Ivan looks the part, Wimbledon practice day 1957

We returned tired out, as we had to walk up and down quite a few hilly streets. But several weeks on the *Rangitoto* gave us every opportunity to recover.

Having separate cabins was a letdown, but we sat on the top deck at night, away from the other passengers as we could not afford to buy soft drinks for every penny counted.

As we preferred to eat early, we chose first sitting in the dining room. At our table, we introduced ourselves to the six people with whom we shared a table. There were two single men, a married couple and two single women, all of them very amicable.

One can only imagine what they thought of the two kids venturing out into the unknown.

Sitting in the restaurant, we surveyed the cutlery, not knowing which pieces to use and in what order. We waited to see what the others did. The two girls told me later they were doing the same.

On the first couple of days we found our way around the ship, especially where to do washing as I had only four changes of clothing. We made friends with people and played games on the decks. One day a young girl asked me if I would introduce my 'brother' to her. She was so shocked to find out Ivan was my husband, I never saw her again on the trip.

Because of our age Ivan and I had no fear. We were afraid of nothing. When we arrived in England, on our own and facing the outside world, we soon found out there was a lot to be scared of. But we managed to accept this as life and even though we were so young, were determined to get along whatever came our way.

In our first month, we went from a guest house, to a very basic bedsit in Fulham Road, and then found a place in Hayden Park Road, Wimbledon. Even at this stage, I knew I would have to go to work as soon as the baby was born.

I also knew if we had to find the money to return to New Zealand we could not save enough even with me having a job. I put a deposit on a layette for the baby, how I was to get a pram I would think about later though I knew it would have to be second-hand.

About this time, we went to a track with one of the riders and his lady. I noticed she had no wedding ring on and told her 'I thought you were married?' She promptly produced a gold ring from her purse telling me she was allergic to gold! They were a nice couple who were very kind to us. I soon found out they were in a de facto relationship.

Over the years, I met a few more girls without rings on, not all of them a de facto.

We took most things in our stride but the birth of Julie was not without drama. Ivan was riding in the second half at Wimbledon on the Monday night and as our first-born was almost due I had decided not to go.

When he did not come home on time, my mind started to race.

Then Barry and Junie Briggs came to the door and said Ivan was in the hospital under observation as he may have had concussion after taking a fall. They told me they would be back first thing in the morning to take me to pick him up.

As they left and I got ready for bed, the shock of it all was too much and I could not sleep. I walked the floor with my mind in a turmoil. I felt that Barry was telling the truth and Ivan would be OK; but hours later, I was imagining all sorts and my mind began to fabricate endless possibilities.

As it turned out, I had more to concern myself with the next day when it was time for me to go into hospital to have the baby.

Of course he was all right, if a bit the worse for wear, as I saw for myself when they brought him to see me and our new baby on the Wednesday. This taught me a lesson and I never allowed this to happen again. Whenever Ivan had an accident, I always remained controlled and positive.

When Julie was six weeks old, I started a job. I had to lie about having a child, as in those days women were treated like second-class citizens. They had not burnt the bra yet – I was privy to this in the 1960s. Just as well, as I was feeding Julie!

Sid and Renee Hone helped by looking after the baby, as did Mrs Walker, a Salvation Army lady who lived across the road. Finally my doctor found a woman to look after Julie in a child-minding centre. It was hard though as every time Julie cut teeth she would get ill and the child-minding centre could not look after a sick baby.

We were broke and could not make ends meet. When I returned to New Zealand at the start of the 1958 season I wondered how our marriage could last. Things were not how we had dreamed they would be and I had to borrow some money from our parents to help me get home.

On my return, I stayed with my parents and my mother looked after Julie while I found work to pay back the money and save for Ivan's return home at the end of the season.

When he got back, it looked very much as if his dream of speedway stardom was going to have to be put to one side. But at least there was the prospect of having a 'normal' life and thankfully, we were together again.

Our next target was to save sufficient money to buy our own place. By going without any luxuries we built up enough to afford a little wooden bungalow at South Shore. As we were under age, we had to get a court order to buy the house.

I had to give my job up in 1959 when I was pregnant with our son Kym. Then Ivan had to take a second job for a few hours four nights a week.

It was work, work and more work. When Ivan received an invitation to ride at Rowley Park in Adelaide, it was a blessing.

We rented out our house and this paid the mortgage. Ivan went to Adelaide and I followed three weeks later. Our son Kym was born in Burwood Hospital, Christchurch, and at the age of 10 days he, Julie (who was then two and a half) and I left New Zealand on a ship bound for Australia.

We stayed in a guest house, apart from a couple of months in a flat, and the weather was hotter than anything I had experienced. Kym, in particular, did not appreciate the heat. I bought a fan and had it going non-stop near his cot. Julie was often put in the bath to cool her down.

Before we returned to New Zealand, we decided if we were to come back the following season we had to find something at the beach where it would be a lot cooler. And that is what happened. We ended up doing four summers in Adelaide. Our daughter Debbie was born at Princess Margaret Hospital there in 1961.

When the other children were born, Ivan was spared the ordeal but this time was different.

We now had three children and I was only 20 years old. When the

FAMILY UNIT – Raye and the kids in Rockhampton, before preparing to swap the Australian sunshine for the delights of England

birth control pill arrived on the scene we decided three was definitely enough.

They were great times, but still hard times and we had no money to spare. But in addition to racing, Ivan always managed to find a job and we made ends meet.

We did one season up in Rockhampton where Ted Price, the promoter, would bring us boxes of pineapples and his wife showed me how to cook them. Every day was something new and life was good to us. We discovered there were a few different types of pineapple and we loved the spiky rough leaf variety that was sweet.

We ate so much of it one day we all had sore mouths.

Money was not the object in our life. Here we were experiencing another way of life and meeting some of the people who helped settle this great country. Ivan and I found the people very friendly, asking us out for breakfast, picnics and dinners.

Because it was tropical and it was the beef capital of Australia, most people had a cooked breakfast and a snack at lunch. I was never a big meat eater and was amazed at the large steaks people ate along with bacon and eggs for breakfast. There was always a huge bowl of tropical fruit salad.

Probably the biggest influence on Ivan in these years was Jack Young in Adelaide. He was a terrific person, and a great help who passed on a tremendous amount. The people from Adelaide had watched while Ivan raced with Jack, to begin with from behind where he observed Jack's every move and then later they saw him taking over the lead.

Our friends knew Ivan had the potential to do even better and encouraged him to go back to the UK. It was time.

Ivan Crozier, who came from Christchurch, seemed to be a catalyst for Ivan as he helped to get us accommodation in Adelaide, and had spoken well of him to the promoter, Kym Bonython.

When my Ivan was writing to clubs in England, Ivan Crozier – who had not long gone there – said he should write to Mike Parker at Newcastle. He had told Mike that Ivan was too good not to bring over. As has been well documented, Mike Parker agreed to pay for us all to go and in February 1963 another chapter of our life began.

We set off on the train to Melbourne to catch the ship which stopped in Auckland on the way. Our relations and friends came up from Christchurch to see us off. My lingering memory of the time spent at the Auckland terminal is of my father. Dad had a weak heart and my mother told me to go and sit with him, which I did.

What I did not know was my mother had told Ivan there was a chance we may never see my father again, which turned out to be correct as he died just before his birthday in 1965. It was only then Ivan told me what my mother had said to him, as he had not wanted me to worry.

Arriving in England at Southampton, we met up with Barry and Junie Briggs who lived close by.

It was Easter and when we arrived at their home Junie's mother Queenie was there and promptly told Junie to give her Easter eggs to our children as 'the poor little things have to have something for Easter and we must share'.

Junie shared her eggs with our children, a memory to treasure, and for weeks to come it was to be the nicest thing that happened to us. Mike Parker sent Eddie Glennon, his manager, to pick us up and take us north to Upper Chorlton Road, in Whalley Range, with our friend Rolf von dor Borch who had travelled over from Adelaide with us.

We were dismayed on entering the upstairs apartment, the accommodation we had been promised. The carpet up the stairs was filthy with dog hairs. Entering the lounge, you could smell the chimney smoke.

The thick-crusted ash in the grate of the fireplace would have to be chiselled off. The kitchen was filthy and the stove was rank. There weren't even any beds.

As there was no cot and Debbie, who was only 18 months, needed a nap, she had to stay in her pushchair. I was devastated and put my head in my hands. It was cold and there was no heat. I felt very despondent. I found it hard to believe that Mike Parker, a married man did not seem to care two hoots for us, after we had arrived from the other side of the world. It was incomprehensible to me and I never had any respect for him from then on.

I stayed with the children and Ivan and Rolf went along to find out from Eddie Glennon how we could possibly get things sorted out. Mike's wife sent round a clean cot, mattresses and beds arrived later in the day and I made a list of cleaning utensils. After going to the local shops to buy them plus cutlery and some food, Rolf and I proceeded to clean the flat.

It had been an eventful first day. Kym and Julie fell asleep on the couch with Debbie in her pushchair. I remember looking at them in relief that they were able to sleep, and as I turned away into the kitchen, how I wished we were back home in New Zealand with our families and friends where everything was orderly, safe and clean.

I knew there were cleaner and nicer places to be found in Manchester and nicer people.

We met some of those very nice people later who are still our friends to this day. But to me Mike Parker showed his colours and Ivan was only a means for him to make money.

Now when I look back I realise it takes all types to make a world. Now that I am older, and wiser I accept that this is so without grudge to anyone.

If it had not been for Mike Parker taking a chance on Ivan he may never have been world champion so we have to be thankful to him for that. It was a big chance and it paid off. Brough Park Stadium at Newcastle was always packed. Mike Parker had backed a winner.

From the time he resumed racing in Britain, Ivan never looked back. The history books prove that he was the greatest rider ever. In his second meeting at Newcastle, he broke the track record, in his third meeting he got maximum points followed by many more at home and away. He was top of the averages and won numerous individual events including the Provincial League Riders Championship

I never doubted that he had the capability to achieve what he did and as our children grew; they knew the same as I did. Ivan was an achiever. When I first met him, I knew that he was ambitious and I backed him then and right through his career, as did our children as

GREY SKIES – another family outing, this time to a grass track at Buxton on the Derbyshire moors in 1966

they grew. We were always there for him through thick and thin.

During the winter, we went tobogganing with the children. They all loved the snow and Ivan would help make the snowman.

In summertime, we took the children swimming when we could and had picnics in the parks up in the hills.

Our house always accommodated Kiwis and Aussies in Britain and Europeans in New Zealand and Australia. In our younger days there were times when our spare bedrooms overflowed into our lounge. The riders did not have much money, we all helped one another out, and at meal times there were plenty of hands to do the cooking and we all had a lot of fun doing so.

We had parties to celebrate the end of the season when riders and their wives would come from as far as Scotland, northern England, the Midlands, Wales, and from our nearest track Belle Vue. We had mechanics and team managers plus friends, too. Even if no one had much money, we all knew how to enjoy ourselves.

The first time Ivan rode at Wembley and the first time he earned any significant amount was when he won the 1966 European Championship. The £1000 prize money he received we put straight into a building society. This was to be of great benefit to us as later we were able to obtain a mortgage from the building society to buy our first house in England.

The Will To Win – 419

When Ivan started riding for the Belle Vue team, they had to supply us with a house and that was in Denton, Manchester. We were there for four months before buying our first house in England at Bramhall and then finally our house in Woodford, Cheshire where we lived for 17 years.

Coming home from the away speedway tracks, we would stop to have supper at motorway restaurants or truck stops. There was a post-mortem of the meeting as we ate. This was a time to share no matter that you rode for opposing teams. It was a bonding exercise and the riders looked forward to it on their way home. It was also good for the wives to get to know one another.

Some of the wives were very much a fan of their husband when he was racing. One such person is my very good friend Cynthia Boocock. One night at Sheffield, we were watching when Nigel came off and Cynthia, who was sitting next to me in the restaurant, turned to me most irate and said 'That Mauger knocked him off and he should be disqualified.'

She said a few more things besides and I replied by offering, to buy her a drink. That was the beginning of our long friendship. Nigel told her later that Mauger was not the cause. Cynthia often repeats the story and we still laugh over it.

I knew when they were racing the riders had their own technique and they can become over enthusiastic, but they had a great respect for each other. In Ivan's racing career, they regularly loaned their bikes to other riders.

Everyone helped the other guy even if they rode for the opposing team.

As his career developed, Ivan had a huge fan club run by Kathleen Nixon whose husband Alf was a photographer. Pictures had to be signed personally and Ivan had to attend meetings. Kathleen was very good at her job and the club gained thousands of members. It overstepped into Ivan's life and became a burden to me somewhat as I had to buffer the phone calls every day and help Kathleen as much as I could.

Kathleen, Alf and I put together a display of Ivan's trophies in a hired hall at Belle Vue and, with the help of a few fans, we opened the doors at 7pm. The proceeds went to the Speedway Riders Benevolent Fund.

It was an amazing night as several thousand people lined up along Hyde Road, and we had to get them through the exhibition.

It had been a huge project and Ivan had to oversee the final preparation, as he wanted everything to be the best it could.

The nature of Ivan, which is the theme of his life, is that he never leaves anything to chance. It was not that he did not trust us to produce the best results, it was and is his nature.

As time went by, we owned our large house at Woodford, two condominiums in America, two blocks of apartments and two houses in New Zealand and a large block of land in Australia. Our lifestyle had definitely changed from what we once knew.

We travelled back and forth to the European continent during the summer months and over to Aussie and New Zealand during the northern winter. We made several trips by sea, to Britain or New Zealand, and when air travel became easier started our annual trips by aeroplane.

In the early days the planes were DC-8s and DC-10s and we had several stops en route. It was a doddle after our five and six-week trips by sea. A few years later when the big jumbos began flying, it was so much easier again. California became part of our annual trips when Ivan started riding there and we were able to take the children with us.

The children and I made friends everywhere we went. Often we took other children with us to the speedway meetings and sometimes we took their friends on holiday with us. Our children travelled round the world with us extensively.

There were times as they grew older that we would leave them with Ivan's mother or my niece Peggy for four or five weeks in January and February in the English winter. This was when Ivan was racing in Australia and New Zealand.

During these times, I pined for them and ended up with pains in my stomach. It was always a relief to get home to our family.

Over the years, there were many sporting awards and dinners Ivan was invited to. I often felt shut out especially when it happened several times in one year. In 1969, Ivan won the Vat 69 Scotch whisky award, as he was the top speedway rider in Britain. Vat 69 gave the highest achiever in each sporting category in Britain two special decanters and 69 magnums of their whisky.

Belle Vue had organised a dinner at which Ivan was to receive the award after a meeting and no women were invited. I told Ivan I was disappointed to be ignored. He promptly told Jack Fearnley, the promoter, who arranged for his wife and the manager Dent Oliver's wife to attend and extended an invitation to me.

It wasn't always like that. Over the years, we met quite a few of the royal family and some very famous people.

In May 1975, we attended a dinner of the Variety Club of Great Britain at which HRH Prince Philip was guest of honour.

Ivan was introduced to him and then the prince had stepped forward and offered me his hand, saying as he did so 'And this is your good lady!' I was delighted.

HONOURED BY THE PRESS – voted SWAPA man of the year for 1979, Ivan's second win in three years

Later it occurred to me Prince Philip would have known what it is like to walk a few steps behind.

I wrote on the back of the security pass that I sent to my mother, 'I thought you would like this. I will send you a photo when I get one. It was very pleasing to have had the opportunity of meeting Prince Philip who stood talking to Ivan for several minutes. He had the courtesy to acknowledge me. (I had to stand a few steps behind Ivan, as I was not on the list to meet the Prince.) What a humane face he has, it is so full of character!'

Attending all sorts of functions, we mixed with aristocracy, met Prime Ministers, film and TV stars, great sporting heroes and famous reporters.

In 1976 we attended Buckingham Palace where Ivan was awarded the MBE by Her Majesty Queen Elizabeth who chatted to him for a few minutes about New Zealand and speedway.

We were amazed at how the Queen stood for so many hours

CELEBRITY SPOTTING – household names at a weekend shooting party at Chester in 1982. Can you spot Jackie Charlton, Ted Edgar, Allan Wells, Lord Montagu of Beaulieu, Ivan, Andy Irvine, Gerald Harper, Bernard Cribbins, Barry Gibb, HRH Duke of Kent, Ed Stewart, David Hamilton, Angus Ogilvy, Mark Phillips, The Duke of Wesminster, Tony Jacklin, David Broome, Steve Cauthen, Henry Cecil, Jackie Stewart, Lord Lichfield and Gareth Edwards

and how knowledgeable she was about everyone presented to her.

In 1989 Ivan was bestowed the honour of OBE in New Zealand by the Queen's representative the Governor-General of New Zealand, Sir Paul Reeves, at Government House.

Meeting such people illustrates just how much our life had changed. Our travels round the world taught us it was better to have an open mind as we had seen so much brainwashing. Religion and politics we decided were what divided the world. This I am sure helped us when we went behind the Iron Curtain where we were always treated with dignity.

There were many trips to Eastern Europe and one could feel desolation in most places we went. There were always the people at the top who fed off the underdog. Those who had a city house and a holiday home were definitely in control of something or belonging to the Communist Party.

We found the presence of many soldiers in uniforms with guns on the roads and streets quite intimidating. It seemed that all the men were in the army. To get anywhere in these countries you had to join the party. There was a regulated control and in some places an officiousness beyond comprehension.

One time I drove with Ivan in his transporter when he went to the Jawa factory in Czechoslovakia to pick up his new bikes. Many of the roads were cobbled and by the time we got back to Checkpoint Charlie at the border I had slipped a disc in my back. The police made me climb out of the vehicle while they looked through it. I had perspiration pouring out of me and was nearly passing out with pain.

When we were in the communist countries, the huge menus in the restaurants which displayed over 50 choices usually had only four which were available. The menu looked good though. If we asked for steak and vegetables, the waiter would say 'Sorry this is not on today.'

After trying several alternatives, the waiter would then point to the items that constituted the real menu.

Not all of the places were so forbidding. In Radenci, part of Yugoslavia in those days, we had great times. It is now Slovenia and was, and still is, a spa resort. After visiting other communist countries, we found it was rather more upmarket than most of the places we had seen and there seemed to be more freedom of thought.

Our friends in Radenci would invite all the speedway riders, and their mechanics, to their old family wine cellar. These trips were at the end of the speedway season in England and were always a barrel of fun in more ways than one as the wine flowed.

Another of our favourite places was Mariánské Lázně in Czechoslovakia. It too was a spa area and steeped in history. The buildings and the hotels once held kings and queens of Europe who holidayed there.

The height and size of the hotel rooms and the magnificent chandeliers made you realise the opulence of days gone by.

But when we were there the furniture was rather meagre, the huge taps clanged and if we did get water, it was brown. Still it was a fairytale place to visit and the people were helpful and friendly. Today they have repaired the monuments and old buildings and the spa area is again 'European'.

I encouraged Ivan to retire from racing after the severe accident at Gornja Radgona in 1981 where he nearly lost his foot. It was then I lost interest in his

FANCY SEEING YOU – meeting Sweeney actor John Thaw at White City after receiving the MBE

career. When I was young, I never worried if he was to hurt himself but now I was afraid.

One of the characteristics of Ivan was that he never left anything to chance and sometimes he would get on people's nerves checking things out. The mechanics and secretaries he had were all 'true blues' and he could trust them to the end of the earth.

Sometimes I thought Ivan was quite pedantic with his rules and this was rather ironic, as everyone around him knew he did not conform to standard.

Peter Oakes who was a Fleet Street journalist and a close friend became Ivan's press agent. Prior to world championships, our office phone would ring non-stop with calls from newspapers; magazines; radio and TV.

Margaret Stobbs, who was then Ivan's secretary, and I would answer and refer them to Peter who would set up a time for interviews and give them press releases.

Ivan was and still is a phone-aholic so at those times we warned him he was not to answer the

HAPPY COUPLES – Barry and June Briggs and Raye and Ivan wish newly weds Bert and Edith Harkins all the best

phone under any circumstances. Any meeting deemed important we insisted he just concentrate on and we tried to keep him from answering the phone.

Gordon Stobbs (who was Ivan's loyal mechanic from early 1963 until he retired) and Norrie Allan (who Ivan met at his very first meeting at Edinburgh when Norrie was eight years old) would be in the workshop and often Ivan would be out there with them.

They would not allow Ivan near the phone at these times either, as they knew his moods would swing according to his concentration level. Sometimes before a big meeting I even kept the children away from their dad, as he was oblivious to everything else but the job in hand.

I did not like this side of Ivan, but I understood the paranoia of dedication that a true sportsman has. If Ivan wanted to do something, he just did it no matter what or who was in the way.

When the championships were over, he tried to make it up to us all. At the end of the season, we would celebrate with all our friends and our children's friends. Sometimes we would all holiday together in Spain or France.

Ivan had a Mercedes car with a sliding roof and many are the times when our daughter Debbie was in her early teens he would drive her with her friends round the country roads. They would have their heads poking through the roof

HAPPY CHRISTMAS – three kids with Santa Claus

singing and larking around yelling out to people.

My first car was a dirty green ex GPO Mini van back in 1966 when I was really happy to have any car. I was more than delighted when in 1977, Ivan bought me a Mercedes 280SL sports car with special seats in the back for children. Our family loved to drive in it, especially when the roof was off. It was a toss-up as to which car they wanted to ride in.

Julie was always a daddy's girl especially at the tracks when she was little. Whenever Ivan was around she was beside him and there are photos to prove it.

In the Provincial League days Ivan won the Silver Sash at home and away tracks something like 30 times in a row. The first few times there was always a young girl who presented the sash and he would give her a kiss on the lips.

After weeks of this, Julie said to me 'I don't like daddy kissing those girls'. There were snide remarks from people around me, and I thought Julie felt it was not at all funny. I told Ivan how Julie felt and after that, the girls were lucky if they got a kiss on the cheek.

When Julie was at college in Buxton, she would come home at the weekends. She and her friends would ride the bikes in the field at the bottom of our garden for hours.

All our children had their friends over to ride the bikes in the field. It was a great place to rear our children and after living in our house at Woodford for 17 years, we were sad to leave it to go back Down Under.

When our son Kym had a go at speedway as he grew older I was not really happy about it. I had driven him to schoolboy scrambles and worried myself sick when he rode – trying not to let him know how I felt. It was different from when Ivan first started and I was not worried at all. Motherhood makes a difference!

Kym was a reasonable speedway rider and won the New Zealand long track. Everyone says he has a winning personality, always trying to help others, and that he did not have the aggression to race. Maybe this is true, but he was good on a bike just the same.

Debbie was a real tomboy and loved to ride the motocross bikes. Until she was 11 she always wore trousers. I could not get her to wear dresses very often. But she was a daddy's girl too.

Later Debbie became our official photographer when we were travelling, organising the group of riders and positioning them for the shots after which other photographers would move in to take their shots. She had learnt this from watching Alf Weedon, Mike Patrick and Wright Wood who were highly skilled professional photographers.

Ivan showed her where to stand to get the best action shots and quite often, I would see photographers following her around making sure they would get the same shots.

Debbie's photos were in magazines and newspapers around the world, and some of Ivan's books.

Ivan got a new toy of his own in the shape of a video camera when our first granddaughter came along. For some years our grandchildren became his home movie subjects, and it brought him great pleasure to film them.

I recently had the videos put on to DVDs along with old movies we had taken over the years. We have quite a collection so far – 39 DVDs and counting.

CO-AUTHORS –
so Ivan, tell me a story in not more than 150,000 words

Ivan always has been great with the grandchildren. Years ago there were loads of drawings they brought from school which he stuck on the back of a door in his office. They are still there, along with the start of Skye's collection.

I am writing a book for our grandchildren Josie, Sadie, Edward, Zasha and Skye. Ivan and I never knew our grandparents and could not find out much about them.

We felt as though we missed out on something, and that is why I decided to do this for them and hopefully one day our great-grandchildren.

Ivan's father was 29 years older than his mother. We were both the youngest in our respective families. Both our fathers had been married before, their wives had died and both our mothers had worked as housekeepers for them. By the time we came along, our parents were enjoying the freedom of having their children more or less off their hands.

There have been a great many similarities in our lives and I am sure this gave us a better understanding of each other.

Today I feel with Ivan every day brings something new and there is always something to occupy us. We have not mastered, but we have controlled our lives and we both have a sense of achievement.

I plan to give our grandchildren an insight into our lives when the book I am writing for them is finished just as I hope I have given you an insight into Ivan the husband, father and grandfather – the man who has brought many blessings into our life.

Appendix 1

MAUGER CHAMPIONSHIP RESULTS

World champion:
Individual speedway (6) 1968, 1969, 1970, 1972, 1977, 1979
Long track (3) 1971, 1972, 1976
World Team Cup (4) 1968, 1971, 1972, 1979
World Best Pairs (2) 1969, 1970

Silver medallist:
Individual speedway (3) 1971, 1973, 1974
Long track (2) 1974, 1975
World Team Cup (2) 1969, 1970
World Best Pairs (4) 1971, 1972, 1978, 1981

Bronze medallist:
Individual speedway (1) 1967
World Team Cup (1) 1967
World Best Pairs (2) 1974, 1984

Speedway:
European champion (4) 1966, 1970, 1971, 1975
Inter Continental champion (1) 1975
British-Nordic champion (2) 1968, 1971
British champion (4) 1968, 1970, 1971, 1972
Australasian champion (2) 1977, 1981
New Zealand champion (2) 1974, 1981
FIM Internationale (3) 1970, 1971, 1972
British League Riders champion (2) 1971, 1973
Provincial League Riders champion (2) 1963, 1964

League:
Newcastle, Provincial League champions 1964
Belle Vue, British League champions 1970, 1971, 1972
KO Cup winners 1971, 1972
Exeter, British League champions 1974

Appendix II

MAUGER ACHIEVEMENTS

World championship finals: 104
World championship medals: 30
Winner of over 1000 international events in 26 countries
Honorary Sports Ambassador for New Zealand

Awards:
Member of the British Empire 1975
Order of the British Empire 1989
FIM Medaille d'Or 1987
Freedom of the City of Christchurch
Honorary Citizen of City of Gniezno

Voted:
Speedway's Man of the Millennium
Motorcycle News Man of the Decade 1970-80
New Zealand Sportsman of the Year (2) 1977, 1979
New Zealand Motorcycling Sportsman of the Year 1977
Canterbury Sportsman of the Year (3) 1970, 1971, 1972
SWAPA Rider of the Year (2) 1977, 1979
British Sportsman of the Year fourth 1969, third 1970,
    fourth 1971, second 1972, third 1973, third 1979
BBC Sports Personality of the Year runner-up 1970, 1972

Inducted into:
Donington Speedway Hall of Fame 1987
New Zealand Sports Hall of Fame 1990
New Zealand Motorcycling Hall of Fame 2004
New Zealand Speedway Hall of Fame 2005
Sporting Legends of Canterbury 2008
Australian Motorcycling Hall of Fame 2007

**Details of Ivan's results can be found on
www.ivanmauger.com**